STRIKING ROOTS

STRIKING ROOTS

Reflections on Five Decades
of
Jewish Life

by

Aron Horowitz

MOSAIC PRESS
"Publishers for Canadian Communities

Canadian Cataloguing in Publication Data

Horowitz, Aron, 1911-
   Striking roots

ISBN 0-88962-099-7 bd.   ISBN 0-88962-100-4 pa.

1. Jews in Canada - History.   2. Jews in Canada -
Social conditions.   . Canada - History - 1914-
I. Title.

FC106.J5H67   971.004924   C79-094904-0
F1035.J5H67

Published by MOSAIC PRESS, Box 1032, Oakville, Ontario L6J 5E9.
Published with the assistance of the Ontario Arts Council and the
Canada Council.

Printed in Canada.

ISBN 0-88962-099-7 (casebound)
ISBN 0-88962-100-4 (paper)

Cover design by Lynn Naylor and Doug Frank.

Dedicated to my wife Rachel, our sons Gad, Yigal and Asher and to Attarah and Mirit.

Acknowledgements

I would like to thank my son Gad and Professor Howard Aster for their encouragement and valuable suggestions. I am also grateful to the Central Division of the Canadian Jewish Congress and its former Executive Director, Mr. Ben Kafetz, for their sponsorship of my application for a grant from the Multiculturalism Programme.

The writing of this book was made possible with the help of a grant by the Explorations Program of the Canada Council and by the Multiculturalism Programme.

CONTENTS

Chapter 1 From Jerusalem to Winnipeg 7
Chapter 2 Meeting of Two Worlds
Yeshivah Meets College 12
Chapter 3 Prosperity in the Land of Promise 28
Chapter 4 Back to New York 42
Chapter 5 Yerushalayim De'Canada
Jerusalem of Canada 50
Chapter 6 Hebrew Education Emerges from Isolation 63
Chapter 7 A Corner in Our Life 70
Chapter 8 Light and Darkness Serve in Confusion 76
Chapter 9 Vignettes of Zionist-Jewish Realities
in Western Canada 93
Chapter 10 Approaching the End of a Milestone 99
Chapter 11 The Hebrew University Discovers Canada 101
Chapter 12 The Calgary Phenomenon 104
Chapter 13 Zionist Educational Activity
Continues in the West 121
Chapter 14 Some Strange Interludes 132
Chapter 15 The First Years of Keren Hatarbut
Chance is at Work Again 139
Chapter 16 Keren Hatarbut Spreads Its Wings 151
Chapter 17 Preparing to Meet the Messiah 164
Chapter 18 In the Steps of the Messiah 170
Chapter 19 On a Magnificent Mission 180
Chapter 20 On a New Trail 199
Chapter 21 Striking of Roots Accelerates 208
Chapter 22 Keren Hatarbut Becomes
A National Movement 222
Chapter 23 Herzliah Hebrew Teachers
Institute of America 274
Chapter 24 From Stem to Roots 287
Chapter 23 Achievements, Frustration and Debacle 252
Chapter 24 Herzliah Hebrew Teachers
Institute of America 274
Chapter 25 From Stem to Roots 287
Chapter 26 Aliyah, Yeridah and Self-Righteousness 298
Chapter 27 Striking Roots Northern
California Style 306
Chapter 28 How Deep the Roots?
Perspectives and Projections 323
Appendices 370

Foreword

Aron Horowitz has produced a valuable work, and I count it a privilege to write a few words helping to send it on its way. Its journey should be both exciting and significant.

We have had altogether too few persons in Canada possessed of the ability and concern to quarry the historical lode of our past for those Jewish treasures — of events, of persons, and of memory — that enrich our understanding of who we are and whence we came. To chronicle events is a useful thing, but it is not enough. That exercise must be supplemented by the more difficult task of interpretation. How fortunate for us that a person of the caliber of Aron Horowitz has addressed himself that very task, with its challenges, its complexities, and its hopes.

The author expressly declares that this book is not intended to be an autobiography. One may accept that disclaimer but still be thankful that Aron Horowitz emerges throughout the book in a role akin to the ancient Greek chorus — that is to say, as the intelligent spectator, the eye-witness who sees with insight and interprets with understanding.

Aron Horowitz's life has been one of public service. Rabbi, community leader, author, and educator — in all these roles his performance at many, many points has touched the superlative. I rather think that of all the things he has done he would give primacy of place to his work as a teacher. And with good reason. For Aron Horowitz has not been afraid to break new ground. He has been innovative, and his method of approach has won the respect and affection of countless young people whose lives have been enriched in the process.

I can only hope that this book will evoke the response that it deserves. That will be satisfaction enough.

Samuel Freedman
Chief Justice of Manitoba
April, 1979

1

Preface

And furthermore, my son,
Be admonished: Of making many books
There is no end.
  Ecclesiastes 12:12

Why then another book?! For many years I have considered the idea of writing an evaluation of Canadian Jewish life and institutions. During the years of my preoccupation with the flux of events, my urge to write was submerged in the onrush of daily duties, problems and encounters. Writing my book became a near obsession. However, when, in a hospital bed, awaiting the verdict of tests which could indicate that there might be very little time left for me to do anything, I pondered over what I would regret most to leave undone. I was struck with a gnawing pain over my failure to record the events as I had seen them and participated in them during the most fateful times and in the most crucial places in the struggle of our people for survival and national rebirth. Writing my book suddenly appeared to be essential to the meaning and purpose of my life. It was there and then that I realized and decided that write it I must.

As far as I know, little if anything of a primary nature has been recorded by witnesses to and participants in the emergence and maturation of the Canadian Jewish community. Aside from the official records of organizations, and the newspaper reports and articles of the scribes, the future historian will search in vain for the memoirs of those who labored and created in the workshops and laboratories in which organized Canadian Jewish life and institutions have been designed and shaped. It is a pity and a grave loss that persons such as the late Abraham M. Klein, Rabbis Avraham and Baruch Kravetz, Michael Garber, Melech Magid, and Edward Gelber did not leave behind them records of their experiences, observations and views. In fact, Dr. Azriel Eisenberg, an architect of Jewish education in the U.S.A. and a prolific author, told me that when he published his book, *Witnesses to Jewish History in America*, he looked high and wide but was unable to find anything that could be considered primary material by "witnesses to Jewish history in Canada". I therefore do not consider it presumptuous of me to speak, as it were, also for them and others in recording the motivations, the needs, the

3

ideals and aspirations, the problems, the struggles, the failures and triumphs of the many hundreds of people, many of them visionaries and pioneers, who built the Canadian Jewish community.

As one who witnessed the creation of Jewish life in Canada by those whose roots were largely in Eastern Europe, and who was later deeply involved in the evolution of schools, summer camps, youth activities, organizations, institutions and communities, I came in close contact and worked with many of the makers of Canadian Jewry. I witnessed efforts to emerge from the past into a new, free and meaningful existence unfettered by the bonds of ignorance, anti-Semitism and repression. I participated in the struggles against the forces of self-effacement which would submerge our identity in a melting pot they envisioned as a panacea to the ills and frustrations of their forebears. I participated in the painful and rewarding labors that brought forth the renewal of old values, the creation of new forms — the appearance of the first sprouts of synthesis between old and new and between the values of the general Canadian culture and of the emerging Canadian Jewish Community. I thus consider it of some value to contribute through this book to a better understanding of ourselves, of the community we are building, and of our place in the larger Canadian context. I hope, too, that the record of what I witnessed will serve as primary material for the future historian.

Canadian Jewry could not properly be understood without a look into its links with the older and greater Jewish community in the U.S.A., and with Reborn Israel, from which our common roots have sprung, and with whose security, progress and future our own fate as individuals and as a community is closely interwoven. My work, my experiences, my close relationships with leading personalities and institutions both in Israel and the U.S.A. have given me some insights into the influences that these three communities have had one upon the other, the benefits that could be derived from mutual understandings and interaction, the dangers that lurk in the absence of such understanding, and the present trends that should be encouraged or discouraged in our search for purpose and meaning in our lives.

Education has been the focus and work and, at times, the passion of my life. The realities and perspectives of the educational process, crucial as they are to the very existence of our people, thus occupy a central place in my story. In 1946, when the first graduates of the Calgary Hebrew High School made their appearance at the Teachers Institute of the Jewish Theological Seminary of America, the late Dr. Alexander M. Dushkin suggested that I prepare and publish a series of articles on how "the Calgary phenomenon" was accomplished. I told him of my hope that, someday, one of these students would tackle this subject. Though most of them are involved in education, they are apparently too preoccupied with the present to give their attention to the past. I therefore address myself to the Calgary experiment. I also deal at some length with three other types of schools — in Hamilton, Ont., in New York and in Petaluma, Calif., — that were under my direct principalship and where I had almost complete freedom to initiate, innovate and experiment. It is my hope that the stories of these schools will be of some help to similar educational institutions in their search for the ways and means of enhancing the effectiveness of their educational programs.

I should stress that this book is not intended to be an autobiography. Rather, it is the story of an eye-witness who, though an active participant at times, focuses on events and institutions, and on the personalities who brought them into being. The autobiographical elements which predominate especially in the opening chapters, are related to the main themes of the book and are woven into the fabric of the story to give the reader a clue to the organic connection between the author and the events as he saw and interpreted them.

Why the title *Striking Roots*? About twelve years ago, when I discussed the title with the late Moshe Sharett, he was puzzled when I told him of my conviction that the overriding force in the life of Diaspora Jewry, and to a certain extent also that of Israel, was the *lack* of roots. As I have reflected in recent years about the life and fate of Diaspora Jewry, I have increasingly come to the realization that while "Without Roots" and "Scattered Roots" are at the foundation of our life during our long Dispersion, it is the desire to strike roots that will largely determine the future of Jewish communities in the free world as well as in Israel. In a real sense, therefore, the title of this book is the *Triad* — *Without Roots, Scattered Roots, and Striking Roots!*

Aron Horowitz

Chapter 1
From Jerusalem to Winnipeg

My first experience with Jewish life in Canada was to haunt me for many years, up to the time my new outlook on life was crystallized in my new world. My arrival in Halifax in 1926, just before the last days of *Succot*, had been marked by an incident that presaged my future relationships with non-Jews. The captain of the S.S. Metagama, a deeply religious Christian who had taken a special liking to me because of my piety, took my arm with one hand and my suitcase with the other as he walked me down the gangplank with obvious delight. This made a powerful impression on me — a fifteen year old boy who had no contact previously whatsoever with non-Jews other than my usually hostile Arab neighbours and the Gentiles I "met" in the bible. The captain's attitude allayed my concern about life in this strange, non-Jewish world.

Later, however, another incident dampened my cheerfulness somewhat. Since I could not get to my family in Winnipeg before *Shmini Atzeret-Simchat Torah* — when travel would be forbidden, my father had arranged for me to stay at the home of the local *Shochet* (Halifax had no Rabbi at that time) until after the holiday. I was taken aback by the *Shochet's* appearance — his trimmed beard and modern garb. Nor was I pleased by the atmosphere in the synagogue: people were whispering and talking during the services! This was quite different from what I was used to in Jerusalem, where many of the worshippers were Talmudic scholars and the prayers were chanted with reverence and awe. But my real shock came on *Simchat Torah* during the *Hakafot* (the procession with the *Torah* scrolls round the synagogue) when one of those in the procession pointed mockingly at another man during the chant of *Ozer Dalim*, the supplication "Thou who helpest the poor, help us." A brawl ensued: the police had to be summoned to the synagogue. All this was very strange to me. Aside from the irreverent behaviour in a synagogue, I could not understand why a person should be ashamed of being poor. I knew many scholars and other highly respected people who were poor. My own father, formerly Chief Rabbi of Safad and Upper Galilee, and at that time, Chief Rabbi of Winnipeg and Western Canada, was relatively poor. As a matter of fact, even those who were comparatively poor considered it their duty to help those who were even poorer. The mitzvah of *tzedakah*, which — by the way — is mistranslated into "charity" rather than "justice", was such a basic value in our culture, that instead of the poor sulking in their poverty, they were thankful to God for what they had been granted, and shared their meagre bread with their *poorer* neighbors. I remember that before we would sit down to our main meal, my mother would have one of the children (each time a different one, in order to enrich every one of them with *mitzvot*), take some of our food to a poor family. She would ask us to be very careful not to be seen by anybody, for, while people were not ashamed to be poor, they were embarrassed to receive food from their neighbours.

"*Oy, Noch a Yiddishe Heshomeh!*" (Woe, another Jewish soul!) On the long train ride to Winnipeg, I had plenty of time to reflect on the events that had led to my unwilling departure for Canada. I had remained alone in *Eretz Israel* because I did not want to leave the holy land, outside of which I was convinced "Satan prevailed." When my father invoked the Fifth Commandment —"honour thy father and thy mother" — to convince me, a 14 year old boy, to join my family in Winnipeg, I retorted that in cases of conflict between the will of Father in Heaven and the wishes of father on earth, one was obviously bound to obey Father in Heaven. Whereupon my father on earth gave me my first lesson in economics. He promptly discontinued paying for my room and board! To show him that I had studied enough Talmud to "stiffen my neck", I continued to defy him: I used a hard bench in the synagogue as my bed for the next four months. What broke my stubborn will in the end was the *teg* I had to depend upon for my subsistence. *Teg* — receiving one's meals as charitable donations at different homes on different days — was then prevalent in Eastern Europe as a means of enabling poor students to study at *Yeshivot* in cities far from their homes. It had recently been introduced in Jerusalem to accommodate immigrant students, but it was against the grain of native students to engage in this practice. I therefore succumbed to my father's will.

On the train, I recalled the dramatic moment when I took my leave from the *Rosh Yeshivah* in Jerusalem. My teacher, Reb Yechiel Michel Tekochinsky, escorted me to the office of the *Rosh Yeshivah*, Reb Isser Zalman Meltzer, and informed him that Arele (a diminutive of Aron) had come to receive his blessing before departing for "America". Reb Isser Zalman raised his eyebrows toward heaven and cried out: "*Oy, noch a Yiddishe neshomeh!*", which I clearly understood to mean that yet another Jewish soul — my soul — was about to be lost to the world of the profane. Reb Yechiel interjected: "This is not likely to happen to the son of Reb Yeshaye." But the Rosh Yeshivah countered: "In America, I am not even sure about Reb Yeshaye himself."[1]

[1]Though it was clear to all that I was going to Canada, not "America", "America" was the word used throughout this conversation. Then as now, "Canada" refers to the mere hinterland or backyard of the USA.

My *Rosh Yeshivah's* outcry reverberated in my mind during the whole of the trip to Winnipeg, and it was to return to plague me again and again for years to come. I wondered, as I reflected on my Halifax experiences, whether my soul was truly in danger, or whether I would succeed in withstanding the *Yetzer Hara* — the evil inclination — and remaining a pious Jew.

Speaking of the *Yetzer Hara*, his first serious try at me had already been made on board the ship from Haifa to France, whence I was to proceed to Halifax. I shared a cabin with a Parisian Jewish physician who witnessed with more amusement than appreciation my daily schedule of prayers and studies. One day, he requested that I stay away from the cabin in order that he might "enjoy himself with a beautiful *shikse*." Gazing quizzically at me, he said that if I was ready for this type of enjoyment, he could arrange it for me with the same *shikse*. I was shocked and angry. The good doctor tried again when I visited at his home in Paris to seek his medical help for an ailment which I had developed during my long wait for the S.S. Metagame. He called out in French to someone in an adjacent room, and suddenly there appeared a young woman in attire to which my *Chasiddic* eyes were unaccustomed. The doctor laughingly suggested that I might now be ready for the experience I had foolishly rejected on board the ship. I looked away in disdain, and the doctor and his friend burst out into laughter. When I recalled this incident in later years, I was never certain whether the good doctor had been in earnest, or jesting, or perhaps even probing . . . In any case, this incident provided additonal grist for the mill of my concern about my *Yiddishe neshomeh*.

A good antidote to the encounter with the *Yetzer Hara* was my visit at the home of Rabbi Yoel Herzog, then Chief Rabbi of France, grandfather of Israeli Ambassador Yaakov Herzog. The Chief Rabbi's awe inspiring countenance, the atmosphere of his home, the kindly smiling *Rebbitzen* coaxing me to partake of the goodies she set before me, brought me back to my familiar world of Rabbis and *Tzaddikim*. On the occasion of any such visit, there had to be some measure of *reden in lernen*, the discussion of some Talmudic subject. Rabbi Herzog gently tested the extent and depth of my knowledge, while his guest from Poland, another great Rabbi, went at me mercilessly with difficult questions "to see how much or how little a *Yesshiveh Bochur* from Jerusalem really knew". To my delight, Rabbi Herzog put an end to the ordeal with the plea: "Arele is very tired from his travels; let us leave him alone now." This visit left me with the feeling that the *Yiddishe neshomeh* can be safe even in Paris, where the dominion of Satan was reputed to be even more powerful than in Winnipeg and New York.

Winnipeg — "A Jewish City"

Upon my arrival in Winnipeg, I tasted for the first time in my life a real wintry storm. My father guided me out into the backyard to show me the *Succah*, and remarked sadly: "In this part of the world, we cannot always observe the mitzvah of dining, let alone sleeping, in the *Succah*."

A few weeks later, I was caught in a real Winnipeg blizzard, and it was a veritable miracle, as my mother put it (my mother would always interlace statements and wishes with *"a dank zein lieben Nomen"* — thanks to His beloved Name —, or *"im yirtze Hashem"* — Good willing —, or *"unzer fother in himel ken ales machen"* — our Father in Heaven can do everything), that I made it home. The doctor was called and declared that I had frostbite in both my legs. I heard him whispering to my parents that there was a real danger I would never walk again. But it was probably my mother who worked the real miracle of bringing me back to my feet. She was doggedly determined, and so declared in no uncertain terms, that "in partnership with the beloved Father in Heaven", she would make her Arele walk and run again. And I truly believed it was her angelic smiles, her loving care and her relentless urging and coaxing that got me out of bed in about six weeks. To me, whose background was saturated with symbolism, this nearly physically-crippling mishap, which resulted from my ignorance of and unpreparedness for the severe Winnipeg climate, was symbolic of the severe spiritual storm ahead of me. It seemed to be a forewarning of the lurking dangers of my unpreparedness for the near-crippling spiritual storm that was in store for me. And a tough struggle it was indeed — to emerge slowly and painfully from Jerusalem into my new lonely life in my new cold land.

Winnipeg soon proved to be not altogether devoid of *idishkeit*. There was an abundance of synagogues; they were always full of worshippers, many of them bearded devout Jews not very different from those of Jerusalem. Wherever I went I heard Yiddish spoken, as most of the 20,000 Jews were concentrated in the north end of the city and the process of Canadianization was barely under way. Many, my father told me, observed the Sabbath strictly, and when the next holiday came along, I was glad to see that it was celebrated almost as fully and joyously as in "the old country". The Hebrew school — as I was to learn later, when I became acquainted with the state of Jewish education in North America — was full of life and vitality "one of the best on the continent", thanks in large measure to its principal Mr. Levitt, who brought with him from Lithuania the new spirit of the Hebrew Revival. Today, I think it sad that those who came after the early pioneers speak and act as if they had started everything from the beginning. In vain did I search for Mr. Levitt's name in any of the books on Canadian Jewry. Nor did I hear even once his name mentioned during the many years of my contact with Winnipeg's Jewish institutions. Gone and forgotten!

In spite of the fact that the whole city seemed to me to be Jewish, I knew it would be impossible for me to stay there for a long time. For it had no *Yeshivah* or any other institution of higher Jewish learning. As a matter of fact, there was no *Yeshivah* at that time even in Montreal or Toronto. My father and I therefore decided that I would go to New York to continue my studies at the Rabbi Isaac Elchanan Talmudic Academy (later to be known as Yeshivah University). To my consternation, the president of the Yeshivah, Rabbi Dr. Bernard Revel, wrote my father that I was too young for his Yeshivah and that New York held too many dangers for a sixteen year old boy who had but recently emerged "from his sheltered life in Jerusalem". My father was both concerned and pleased when I declared categorically: "To the Yeshivah I will go with or without Dr. Revel's consent!" We started to look for somebody who would be driving to New York, as my father did not have the train fare. After a long search, he learned late on Friday that a Mr. Herman was leaving for New York by car on Sunday. My joy was short lived, because there was no time to obtain a visa before Sunday. To my surprise, it took but a quick call to the U.S. Consul to overcome what seemed like an insurmountable obstacle. After my dilemma was explained to him, he volunteered to postpone his family's trip to the country until Saturday night, when he would be glad to receive me and issue a visa at his home. When I arrived there, I saw his wife and children standing near their suitcases, anxious to leave. Once more I was being given royal treatment by a non-Jewish V.I.P. It was a good opportunity for me to point out to my father that contrary to my prejudices, I had learned how nice *goyim* could be. My father's response was: "These *goyim* are altogether different from those you knew in Eretz Israel. Haven't you yet come across the *Midrashic* statement that the righteous of all nations have a share in the world to come!"

My encounter with Rabbi Revel was short and decisive. A severe stammerer, he stammered out: "Why have you come? I wrote your father you should NOT come." I started crying, and declared loud and clear *"Nafshi chaskkal batorah"*, my soul yearns for Torah!; whereupon Rabbi Revel embraced me, kissed me on the head, and exclaimed: "You will stay, my son!"

Chapter 2
Meeting of Two Worlds
Yeshivah Meets College

Contrary to expectations, I felt almost at home at the Yeshivah. On the surface, it was not much different from the Yeshivot in Jerusalem, except for the "modern" garb of the students (not of the teachers), the very small size —just long enough to conform with the *Din* (the Law) — of the sidecurls of those who did not hide them behind the ears, and the preponderant majority of American-born or Americanized students. As a matter of fact, the natives tended, on the whole, to deviate less from the strict observance of rituals and customs than those of us who came from Europe and from Eretz Israel. We, the newcomers, often discussed this strange phenomenon and attributed it to two possible factors. We were more knowledgeable in the Talmud and the *Shulchan Aruch* (the Code of Laws authored by Rabbi Joseph Karu) and could therefore distinguish between the fundamental and less fundamental rules and regulations. The stronger factor was, however, our very strict orthodox upbringing which caused us to rebel against the "old", the arbitrary "thou shalt and thouh shalt not". This made it necessary for us to reconcile our ultra-traditional way of life with the new culture into which we had suddenly been catapulted well after we had passed our formative years. For me, personally, it was a long and difficult inner struggle to find and shape my new identity (a term never heard in those days), in other words, to be transformed from just a Jew into an American or Canadian Jew.

As one example of the painful and — at times — agonizing struggle I went through on the long road of finding a synthesis between the old and the new, I recall my first *Pesach* as a supervisor at the Borden dairy in upstate New York. A number of advanced students were assigned to stay at all the company's dairies throughout *Pesach*, in order to insure the *kashrut* of the products for the holiday. Since there were no Jews at all in the nearby town, I had to celebrate the *Seder* alone in my room. In the midst of the *Pesach* ritual, I impulsively closed the *Haggadah*, took off my *Kipah* and pushed away the *Seder Plate*. My rebellion triumphed at that moment, but not for long. After pacing the room in a lonely and painful mood I returned to the table and with tears streaking down my cheeks, recited the Haggadah with special devoutness. And I cried myself to sleep that night.

Disappointment in Friendship

Until this day I fail to comprehend how a person reared on high ethical principles could have accused his close friend — without a shred of evidence —of theft. When I was summoned one morning to Rabbi Revel's office, I thought he wanted to compliment me for my hard work on three fronts —Talmudic studies, English studies, and Hebrew teaching. What he had to say struck me as though he had driven daggers into my mind and heart. My closest friend had accused me of stealing the money he had put away in his locker for the duration of the Sabbath. Without saying a word, I cried hysterically. After Dr. Revel succeeded in calming me down, I said nothing more than: "How could a God-fearing person even suspect me of breaking one of the Ten Commandments?" (This naivete was in the spirit of the story of the Chassidic Rabbi who, when told that somebody had stolen something, exlaimed: "Impossible!" "Why is it impossible?" he was asked. "It is impos-sible" he answered, "because it is written *Beferush* (explicitly), *Lo Tignov* —(Thou shalt not steal!)." Dr. Revel patted me on the back as he convincingly declared: "I am absolutely certain you are not capable of such a sin!"

In the spirit of true Judaism, I forgave, and continued my close friendship with my accuser who explained to me that he suspected *Davka* me because I was "the poorest student" he knew. Thus, my very first disappointment in friendship occurred at what I considered my spiritual home. I was convinced at that time — as I still am now — that this could not have occurred in my Yeshivah in Eretz Israel. For, there it was absolutely inconceivable that a *Yeshivah Bochur* would steal even if he were to starve. Was this — the thought that a Yeshivah student was capable of stealing — the first symptom of the erosion of our old values?! Remember? *"Oi, Noch A Yiddishe Neshome!"* Was that to happen eventually?

There was another and much more important difference for me between life in Jerusalem and in New York. In the former, the Bible and — more so —the Talmud constituted my entire spiritual and cultural world. There were no other studies for me, except to learn to write Hebrew, some Hebrew grammar and elemantary arithmetic. In New York, I had a strange new world of learning to confront. To become a rabbi, I was required to complete high school and go on to College. Since I knew very little English and had not studied any "secular" subjects, I had to devote many hours every night to complete my high school program in less than the prescribed four years. I, among many other students, had to teach Hebrew in order to provide for living expenses over and above the bed in the dormitory and the one daily meal supplied at the Yeshivah.

At first, it was very difficult to adjust to the methods of study in high school. The approach and educational methods of the Yeshivah were altogether different and, as I thought then and still think today, much more "progressive" and effective. For the Yeshivah was an unstructured institution of *Torah Lishmah*, of learning for the sake of learning, for the cultivation and sharpening of the mind, for the refinement of the instincts and emotions and for the elevation of the spirit. It was truly *an education for life*, in preparation for an education or training for making a living. There were no bureaucracies, no examinations, no certificates, and no acquisition of knowledge by spoon-feeding. The *Rosh Yeshivah*, the equivalent of the college professor, delivered —usually once a week — a *Shi'ur*, a discourse — not a lecture — but rather "a lesson in the making", and the students were then left to fare for themselves, to think it through, to discuss it with one another, to delve deeply into the *Yam Hatalmud*, the Talmudic Ocean, and to ponder the ways of God and Man. The Rosh Yeshivah would call a student to his office not to examine him but rather *"Tsu reden in lernen"*, to discuss the ideas, maxims and laws under consideration. And, on the whole, the Yeshivah produced fine, ethical human beings, scholars and some intellectual giants such as Achad Haam, Rabbi Dr. Herzog, Zalman Shazar, Bialik and Rabbi Kook — men with great erudition in both Judaica and general knowledge. In sum, we had much of what the bright and constructive rebels of the sixties wanted their universities to offer them. If they had had their way, we should then have seen a sample of progress in the form of *a giant step backward*.

While the calibre of the teachers in the New York Yeshivah was equal, if not superior, in some cases, to that in Jerusalem (for the obvious reason that all of them were European), the levels of the American students were markedly lower. From the very beginning of their formal schooling, their time had to be divided between Jewish and general studies. For all the students, but notably for the "foreigners", the most serious weakness at the Yeshivah was the lack of guidance in the process of achieving some degree of harmony between the old and the new. We were left almost entirely to our own resources. For one thing, the studies were geared to the same type of life we experienced in the old country, without any regard for the fact that in the former there was no conflict among the Yeshivah, the home and the street. Here, in our new world, there were varying degrees of conflict between all of them. There did not even seem to be an awareness, on the part of the administration, of the need to guide young minds into living in a new world that was in apparent conflict with our old world and which could in truth be reconciled one with the other. Nor were the teachers equipped to serve as "guides to the perplexed". While there was an atmosphere of near-complete overt freedom, it was taken for granted that Orthodoxy was to be our mode of living — a situation that bred perforce varying degrees of hypocrisy. Some, therefore, "made it" and have served successfully as Rabbis or leaders in the Modern Orthodox Milieu; others made it half-way; and still others — though a minority, I believe — did not make it at all. As a matter of fact, a cerain number of them found their way to agnosticism, atheism and even Marxist messianism.

As for myself, perhaps because of my previous unbending Orthodoxy, I knew I would not "make it" all the way. When my father got wind of my wavering stand on Orthodoxy, he tried to "save me" by using his influence to have me admitted to the Jewish Theological Seminary, the citadel of Conservative Judaism, though he was most critical of its philosophy. Fortunately or unfortunately, my father's friend — Dr. David deSola Pool —to whom he turned for help, could not convince the Registrar that my superior Talmudic knowledge would compensate for my lack of the B.A. degree, a prerequisite for admission to the Seminary.

My parents' and my own poverty made it impossible for me to go home for a visit until God sent a miracle: I was hit by a truck (the miracle being mainly that I was not killed) right near the Yeshivah. Since this happened not long before Pesach, and I was anxious to go home for the holiday, I urged my lawyer to settle out of court for a mere $150, half of which went to the lawyer (they knew how to charge even in those days). [The general complaints about high professional fees these days have inspired the following story: General Moshe Dayan was asked to explain how the small ill-equipped Israeli army succeeded in defeating the armies of seven Arab countries in their assault on Israel in 1948. "It's very simple", said Dayan, "I put the dentists in the front line, the lawyers in the second line, the accountants in the third, the doctors in the fourth, and I cammanded: 'Charge!' And boy, can they charge!"]

My short visit at home was joyous but somewhat stormy. My father wanted to guage my knowledge and, more so, *Yirat Shomayim* (fear of Heaven). My progress in Talmud and Halachah pleased him, but our theological and philosophical discussions caused him much consternation. Since I never wanted to camouflage my views, my father became aware of my spiritual crisis, for our discussions made it clear to him that I have been "infected" by science and philosophy, and that I had begun to doubt and question such cardinal principles as Revelation, *Torah M'Sinai*, a personal God and the immutability of the Halachah and Tradition. Without regard to the effect it would have on him, I told him about a debate we had had in our German literature class at the university on whether man can be good without the fear of God.

All the students, including myself, took the position, contrary to the professor's view, (the professor was a former Doctor of Divinity) that man could indeed be ethical without religion. To assuage his deep disappointment, I told him that my professor, who knew I was a Rabbinic student, pointed out that if I was really leading a moral life, it was because of my religious and Talmudic background; and that it was precisely that background which led me to think, though erroneously, that man was possessed with a spark of God and could, therefore, rise to moral heights without necessarily fear of God. I further assured my father that I was merely "philosophizing" and that I was still a fully observant Jew. Significantly, my socialist-pacifist convictions received his approval, for "where could we find a greater passion for justice and peace than in Judaism in general and in the Bible in particular". One important subject I avoided completely in my discussions with my parents. (My mother never participated in the excursions into theology and philosophy, but she did take an active part in all our discussions of mundane matters.) I did not disclose to them the serious doubts I already had about my becoming a professional Rabbi. I considered it wiser to defer this subject to a more opportune time, when they might possibly be better prepared for the shock of such an announcement by me.

During the entire six years of my studies at the Yeshiva, I visited my home in Winnipeg only twice. The second opportunity presented itself when my brother Sol asked me to substitute for him as Rabbi of Grand Forks, North Dakota, during the few months of his leave of absence prior to his marriage. This job made it possible for me not only to attend his wedding in Winnipeg, but also to leave the "cloister" of the Yeshiva and have a glimpse into the reality of Jewish life in small communities. In essence, Grand Forks already served for me as a microcosm of the future in most small centres in the U.S.A. and Canada. Already as early as in 1929, there could be a minyan on a week day (a quorum of ten men necessary for public prayer) only when someone had *yahrzeit* (the anniversary of the death of a member of one's family). On the one and only such occasion during my stay in Grand Forks, I was sitting in the synagogue near the shochet's son who was a prominent attorney in the town, I was flabbergasted, to say the least, when he suddenly spat in the middle of the service and remarked: "Phooie to these Jews!" — "What makes you say such a terrible thing?", I asked. He replied: "I was always forced 'to do' or 'not to do' without receiving any reasonable explanation of the whys and wherefores of the 'Thou shalt' and 'thou shalt not'. I was not taught any values, and the facts I was fed were unrelated and mostly meaningless. It was only after I studied Bible at Wellesley College that I realized the profound wisdom of my people's Book of Books and of our people's great contribution to human civilisation."

My Parents Try to Make Me a Shidduch — A Match

My comparatively short stay in Winnipeg was rather eventful, and, in part, even adventurous. My parents quizzed me at length about my economic situation: did I have enough food at the Yeshivah; how did I manage to get two meals a day in addition to the one provided at the school; was my sleeping place at the dormitory adequate, and what about clothing? I sensed they had some proposal they hesitated to mention. They looked at one another as if to say, "you tell him". Finally, my father came out with it: a wealthy businessman had approached him with a wonderful offer. The man was thankful to the Lord for his material success in this wonderful free land, but he was unhappy about his sons' straying from "the tradition". Of what avail were his "worldly" blessings if "the tradition" would not be perpetuated in his family? He, therefore, proposed a *shidduch* (a matrimonial match) for me and his daughter, so that he would have at least one *talmid chacham* (Talmudic scholar) as a son-in-law.

My first reaction was utterly negative, as even many of the traditionalists of my generation looked askance at this old mode of finding a mate. Moreover, it would be sacrilegious even to think of another girl when I had already had serious thoughts about a second cousin of mine (it was common practice to intermarry within the family, especially in Rabbinic circles) in New York who had been my childhood playmate in our city of birth, *Tsfat*. My parents argued that there would be nothing lost by hearing the man's offer. "After all, you will be the one to decide whether to marry her".

My meeting with her father was poignantly dramatic. He held my hand as he said, with tears streaking down his beard, "my life is worth nothing. Of what good are my worldly possessions without the preservation of *yiddishkeit* and Jewish learning in my family? Marry my daughter, and you will be able to devote all your life to Torah. I will build you a home close to your parents, and will provide you with life-time *kest* (kest was the institution whereby a Yeshivah student would be kept by the bride's parents for a specified number of years, so that the groom could continue his Torah studies. In certain cases, life-time kest would be provided to especially talented Talmudic students). I succumbed to his pleadings, and agreed to meet his daughter.

It was pre-arranged that the girl and I would be left alone at her home, so that we could become "properly acquainted". My meeting with her turned out to be quite an ordeal, perhaps for her just as much as for me. She was pretty and seemingly intelligent, but I could find nothing in common with her (something that orthodox parents could never understand in those days). To top our futile evening, she put her hand on my thigh and kept it there until I gently removed it. That was the clincher for the evening!

My parents did not give up so easily. It was particularly my father who continuously pictured to me the easy and lucrative life I would enjoy. He and I could learn Torah together, and his and the family's economic lot would also be improved. My father relented when my mother's understanding heart caused her to blurt out, as she projected her head from the kitchen into my father's study, *"loz im oop"*, (leave him alone); *"Arele is verliebt in Chavele"* (Arele is in love with Eva). And that was that!

A Debate on Capitalism, Socialism and Communism — Which?

During my visit in Winnipeg, I published an article in the Winnipeg Free Press on the then "burning issue" of the German war reparations. I pointed to the dangers inherent in the Allies' insistence on extracting the "pound of flesh" from the Germans and to the dire political consequences of this policy. As a result of this article, I received invitations that opened some windows for me on Canadian affairs. The C.C.F. was then in its heyday in Manitoba. Its leadership was on the alert for the recruitment of active supporters. I was thus approached by Miss Beatrice Brigden, a leading activist of the Socialist Movement, requesting my approval for the republication of my article in the official organ of the C.C.F. Following my acquaintance with Miss Brigden and other C.C.F. leaders, I was asked to represent socialism in a debate on "Capitalism, Socialism and Communism — Which?". The chairman was none other than Mr. James Shaver Woodsworth, founder of the C.C.F. Com-munism was represented by Mr. Joe Zuken, who was quite popular *oif der yiddisher gas* — literally, on the Jewish street — even among non-communists. My main arguments were aimed against intellectual Marxists who were completely blind to the realities of North-American political life and were thus espousing a cause that was, a priori, doomed to failure. Mr. Zuken saw the communist revolution "around the corner", and urged us "to fall in" before it was too late. Although I had little experience as a debator, or perhaps because of it, I used ridicule against Mr. Zuken, and I "brought the house down" with this devastating true tale:

During the thirties, Union Square in New York was alive — among other things — with radicals of every hue and colour. The restaurants, the café's, the streets were seething with groups of people who were discussing, arguing and debating, some earnestly, some passionately, and some even humorously, the issue of the day. I was having a snack at a table where a group of radicals were in the midst of a heated discussion about the state of "the party". One long-haired fellow (some radicals in those days wore long hair naturally, without making it a fetish), whose pockets were bursting with magazines and papers, was the butt of the group. One of the women looked him straight in the eye as she demanded, "why don't you get married?" Another chimed in, "he is entirely dedicated to the party, If he gets married, he will have to share some of his devotion with a wife and children". Interjected another of the group, "on the contrary, if he gets married, the party will be strengthened with the children he will have". Whereupon a character who looked like a real shrew shouted, "what? ! are you implying we should wait with the revolution until he has grown children?" She banged on the table as she screamed: "we want the revolution now! Now we want the revolution!"

I turned to Zuken saying, "you too want the revolution now", and I then shouted into my sleeve: "we want the revolution now! now we want the revolution!"

"Mr. Zuken", I said, "you are shouting into your sleeve. It is for you to join us Socialists and Liberals in our endeavours to change our society without bloody revolution."

Mr. Zuken was not at all a "fire-eating" Communist of the brand I was accustomed to seeing and hearing in New York. His tone and manner were more moderate when he suggested that I had hit him "below the belt". Mr. Woodsworth and Miss Brigden were intent on capturing me for "the movement".

It was revealing to me that none of the Jewish or Zionist groups made any attempt to involve me in their activities. It has now occurred to me that if any such activities took place during my visit, I was unaware of them. . . . As a matter of fact, the Young Poalei Zion (young socialist Zionists) invited me to speak to them only as a result of the publicity in connection with my participation in the debate. The group consisted of a very small number of youths. They were baffled by my statement that it was an error to isolate Zionism from the mainstream of political life in Canada and the U.S.A., that Zionism was not merely a Jewish issue but rather a world issue, and that it was their task to make the Zionist idea and program an integral part of the C.C.F. Program, with which they nominally identified.

I am now convinced more than ever before that the isolation or ghettoization of Zionism from the general political scene was a cardinal sin of the Zionist organization in all countries. We are now paying a high price for this narrowness of vision and perspective. It is interesting that two members of the group, brothers Chaim and Yaakov Lifshiz, were about to go to Palestine at that time. It was a very rare occurrence in those days, and they were probably the first young *Chalutzim* to have emigrated from Canada to *Eretz*, "The Land". Yaakkov eventually rose to a very high rank in the Police Department, first under the British Mandate and later in the reborn State of Israel.

It is noteworthy that when Miss Brigden later learned from one of my sisters about my return to my native land, she expressed her profound sorrow for "the waste of such a talent" in a remote and insignificant place, while I could have been a valuable asset to "the movement in Canada. It would never have occurred to me at that time that I would be back in Winnipeg in less than a decade to serve not those who were interested in me and my future, but rather those who, primarily because of their apathy, had been completely oblivious to my availability, if not to my existence. Little did I know at the time of my impending deep involvement with Jewish life and institutions in Canada.

Rabbinics in Action

Before returning to Rabbinics in theory, I had two lessons in Rabbinics at work:

THE ORTHODOX RABBI'S AUTHORITY

The role of the old time Orthodox Rabbi included not only the functions of teacher and interpreter of The Law. He was also judge, arbiter, social worker, intrepreter of dreams, etc. This time I saw my father in action as arbiter and judge. A middle aged man brought a nineteen-year-old girl from Russia to Winnipeg on condition that she marry him. The morning after the wedding, she came crying to my father. She "could not possibly live with that man". She pleaded with my father to free her from a life that could bring only unhappiness to all concerned. Following a lengthy session, during which my father tried to determine whether this fall-spring union was really kaput, he succeeded in persuading the groom to dissolve the marriage. However, this hurdle surmounted, the bride demanded that provision me made for the man's financial responsibilities in case a child should be born. Whereupon the man claimed *"petach patu'ach matsati"*, meaning literarlly "I found an open door", the Talmudic expression for the loss of virginity. My father suggested that a doctor be the judge. I remember my fascination and amusement at my father's beaming happy face when he heard the doctor's verdict. When the telephone rang, he shut the door to make sure I wouldn't hear the conversation. But how could I have been prevented from hearing it even through the closed door, when his joy was so great that he actually shouted *"azoi, azoi! Es iz geven frish. A dank got zi is a koshere iddishe tochter"*. ("How wonderful! It was fresh! Thank God she is a kosher Jewish daughter".) It was the first time I had an opportunity to actually witness the adroitness and authority a genuinely Orthodox Rabbi could exercise on one of his followers. I could not but admire how such a difficult case was resolved with such finesse without recourse to the courts of law. (At that time, I didn't think of the man's substantial savings in lawyer's and court fees!) This incident armed me with a strong argument against those who criticized the *halachah* pertaining to the right of a man to divorce his wife without her having the same right to divorce him. For I now saw in practice what had been told me by Rabbis: if they were convinced that a marriage was really on the rocks, they would always find a way of prevailing upon a reluctant husband, by friendly or coercive persuasion, to "let his wife go".

RABBINIC RIGIDITY OR INTEGRITY

One Friday afternoon a telephone call was received at our home for my father to deliver a eulogy at a funeral that afternoon. My father was where he always was on Fridays at that hour — at the baths and *mikveh* (a body of water for ritual purification). When I located him and explained the reason for my intrusion, he stared at me for some time in silent anger. Then, he expressed his surprisie that I "who know, or should know, the *din* (the law) would suggest that he deliver a eulogy on Friday afternoon, when it is forbidden to do so (because of the approaching holy Sabbath and because of the danger the funeral might extend to near sundown). I told him I did so at my mother's bidding who asked me to point out the importance of fulfilling the request of the son of the deceased who was the president of one of my father's synagogues. I told him that my mother thought he could "bend a little" in this case — as some other Orthodox Rabbis do — since no basic law was involved and we were dependent for a livelihood on the income from such services. Furthermore my father might lose the support of the president altogether. "Oh, really?" retorted my father: "does it occur to you or your mother for one minute that I would deviate even one iota from the *Shulchan Aruch* (the Code of Law) for even *kol hon de'alma* (an Aramaic expression meaning "all the world's wealth")!

On our way to the synagogue that evening, my father spoke of the great dangers in the new phenomenon that even some Orthodox people, including Rabbis, "rationalize away" some laws and regulations for the sake of convenience and expediency. "The Sulchan Aruch must be followed in its entirety", he said. Once we start whittling down, who is to say where it will end. Rabbinic rigidity? perhaps! But from an Orthodox viewpoint, he was proven right by the gradual erosion of traditional practice in Orthodox circles. As to my father, it was intellectual integrity and a concern for the future of Judaism that sustained him in his strictness. At this point, I should emphasize that, rigid as he was in matters concerning relationships between man and God, he was tolerant of other people, and very liberal and compassionate in the interpretation and application of laws and regulations relating to human health and welfare.

A different approach was represented by Chief Rabbi Israel Kahanovitch. (My father was invited by the Chassidic and more orthodox elements to serve as their Chief Rabbi. He had not known about the then existing rift in the community. There were thus two Chief Rabbis for many years. When the Jewish Community Council was established, my father agreed to be Assistant Chief Rabbi for the sake of unity. After Rabbi Kahanovitch's passing, my father was the undisputed Chief Rabbi until he left for Israel in 1955). Rabbi Kahanovitch was standing outside his home when I passed by one morning. He invited me in to serve as the third member of the Rabbinical Court required for the issuing of a *get* (a divorce). I told him I was not orthodox and was using a razor for shaving, (contrary to orthodox regulations). "Well," he said smilingly, "from tomorrow on you will start using a powder" . . . In spite of my categorical statement that I wouldn't, he insisted on my participation in his Rabbinical Court. Hypocrisy? I don't think so. Rabbi Kahanovitch belonged to the school of orthodox Rabbis who reckoned with the new realities in matters they did not consider fundamental. These two different approaches could be reconciled in line with the spirit of the Talmudic precept, *"Eilu v'eilu divrei Elokim chaim hen"* (These and these are the words of the living God — Euruvin 13). This Talmudic approach is expressed humorously by the story about two litigants who argued their cases before a Rabbi. When the first told his story, the Rabbi said, "you are right". When the second one explained his side of the story, the Rabbi said, "you are right". The Rebbitzin then asked, "How could they both be right?" "You too are right!" answered the Rabbi!

To understand my mother's call for compromise, and to generally understand the Orthodox Rabbi's lot in those days, it should be borne in mind that Orthodox Rabbis did not receive any salary. Their livelihood depended on income from such services as officiating at a wedding, a *Brit*, and a funeral. (The Bar-Mitzvah ploy was not yet in existence, and whoever thought of a Bat-Mitzvah in those days! God forbid!) Surprising as it may sound, some people forgot to pay for such services. There were occasions when my mother didn't have any money for groceries and she would plead with my father to remind them. He, however, would stubbornly insist it would not be right to do so, that perhaps they didn't have any money. It was only in the late forties that the Rabbis in Winnipeg started to get fixed salaries. Those were the years of my parents' affluence, when they were assured of $200 monthly! It is noteworthy that when my father retired in 1955 to spend his remaining years in "the study of Torah and the worship of God in the Holy Land", where he and his forebears were born and lived, the Winnipeg Community Council generously decided to continue to pay him $125 monthly for life. However, when this sum was enough for little more than rent because of spiralling inflation, my father's repeated pleas for an increase were always rejected outright.

Human Cruelty on a Cattle Train

Because of our economic situation, my father and I looked for an opportunity for me to return to New York at the lowest possible cost.

The Great Depression was already at its nadir, and as is often the case, at such times, the "haves" take special advantage of the "have nots". Dealers who transported cattle to the East were required to have an attendant for each fixed number of animals. Since many people could not afford a regular train-fare, many would compete for this "job", and gratefully waive their pay in order to be hired! The dealers could thus get as many attendants as they needed without paying for the job.

A friend therefore suggested that I go by cattle train by way of Montreal. He succeeded in obtaining for me a "contract" that enabled me to travel as a "cattle attendant" on the train. Mine was, of course, a fictitious job, with the full knowledge of the cattle dealer, so that I heard the animals but never saw them. The conditions in the car where I and another few men travelled were intolerable. It was extremely cold and dirty. I had no pillow or blanket, as it never occurred to me or my parents that such essentials would not be supplied to the "attendants". There was never a chance to buy any food at any of the stops the train made along what seemed an interminable *shlep* to Montreal. Fortunately, I took along some kosher food if only for the reason that I would be unable to eat most of the food we might have been provided with. As it was, we received none. It was pitiful to see the hungry eyes that were fixed on me by a few of the men whenever I took out some food, and I, of course, shared much of it with my fellow travellers, in the true spirit of "father Abraham".

My worst experience on the train was as a witness to the cruelty of human beings. From time to time, one or more miserable persons boarded the train "illegally" at various stops. When they "smelled", from a distance, the pending appearance of "guardians of the law", they would scurry like mice off the train or hide under the seats. When one or more of them were caught, they were beaten and kicked mercilessly by the representatives of justice before they were thrown off the train. Only once before had I been witness to human brutality, when, under Turkish rule in Palestine, all the inhabitants of Tsfat — men, woman and children — were summoned to the main city square to watch the hanging of an Arab thief (a despicable inhuman act still practiced in some Arab countries), but at that time I was a long distance from the brutal scene, while here on the train I saw blood flowing from various parts of the bodies of human wrecks.

I thought of the essay I had written only a few months earlier in my English class at the university. It was a naive, romantic vision of man as but "a little lower than God". For the first time, I became aware of the vast difference between reading about and witnessing human violence, and it was the first time I came face to face with humans who were much lower than animals. Here I was in a part of the real world — far away from Talmudic and philosophic discourses — faced with a real moral problem: where and when does a man's responsibility begin and end when he is confronted with brutality and injustice against other people. I was ashamed that I sat all the time, cowered in the fear of being hurt, without uttering one word of protest. I was ashamed I did not raise my voice even though I knew it would be "a cry in the wilderness".

Upon my return to New York, my spiritual crisis deepened. So did my economic crisis. I did not have the financial means to continue my studies at the university. Nor did I know where to turn for guidance and help. I continued to flounder and to waver until the time arrived for a definitive decision as to whether I would become a practicing Rabbi. After long months of agonizing soul-searching, I was determined that, come what may, I would seek my life's work outside of the Rabbinate.

My encounter with Dr. Revel on this issue was brief and straightforward. He wanted to know whether it was true I did not intend to enter the Rabbinate; if so, why, and "wouldn't my father be deeply disappointed and hurt" if I were the one to break the long chain of Rabbis in my family? Though he did not say so expressly, he seemed to understand and reluctantly accept my reasons: I was not Orthodox and was loathesome of hypocrisy; my emotional makeup was not suited to some of the functions of a modern rabbi, such as visiting the sick and consoling the bereaved, and — perhaps of greater importance — it was my strong conviction that educators were destined to make a more valuable contribution to the evolving American Jewish community. My father's reaction to my defection did not at all surprise me: it would be highly immoral for me — a confessed unorthodox rebel — to assume the mantle of a "practising Rabbi" . . . .

The contribution of educators vis-a-vis rabbis will be discussed in later chapters. One thing, however, became increasingly clear to me as I pursued my educational work in Canada and the U.S.A. The "evolving Jewish Community" was much less concerned about Jewish education that I thought it should and would be.

A Traumatic Shock

To find a position in Hebrew education during the Great Depression was well-nigh impossible. The small school in Brooklyn where I had taught closed down, and all my efforts to find work in an established institution were fruitless. It was then that I had my first traumatic shock in the field of Jewish education. It first seemed a God-send when a Chassidic Rebbe's son in the neighbourhood of the closed school proposed that we form a partnership and open a private school in his father's building, which served both as his home and synagogue. The Rebbe's son's main contribution would be the free use of the two available rooms in the basement, and mine would be my reputation as a good teacher, which — we hoped — would attract at least some of my former pupils. The necessity of drawing up a contract completely escaped me. For what transpired later was inconceivable to me. When I appeared at the school on opening-day, the Rebbe's son, fortified by a real tough-looking character, barred my entrance to the building. My protestations were in vain. "What partnership? We don't know you! You have nothing to do here!" My deep shock rendered me utterly speechless. I returned the next day to utter some idle threats: I would sue him, I would bring my case before noted Rabbis, etc. etc. He was laughing and gesturing: "You haven't got a leg to stand on; there is nothing in writing, and there are no witnesses. Your name appeared in the advertisements only as a teacher, and I shall claim that I have since learned that you are not religious enough for a synagogue as Orthodox as my father's." I forced myself into the synagogue where the Mincha Prayers were in progress. I thought that surely his father, "a holy man", would respond to my plea for justice. When I saw the Rebbe with the *Talit* over his head, swaying to and fro in devout worship, it dawned on me that it was impossible that he would be unaware of his son's "coup". Shocked by the apparent hypocrisy, I walked out in disgust. (Years later, I realized that I should have given the Rebbe the benefit of the doubt.) In any event, the thought of further action I might take was put to an end by the unannounced appearance in my room of my "partner" and his tough friend. With hand in his pocket, as if he held a pistol, the tough guy issued a stern warning: "If you bother my friend any more, I'll kill you!" So, this was not only my first traumatic experience, but also the first manifestation of my aversion to being involved in violence —physical or psychological — with "toughies" who, I learned, are to be found in all walks of life . . . .

I continued to drift, and went hungry many times. A few months later my father came to New York to attend a convention of the Union of Orthodox Rabbis. He took me along with him to offer condolences to Rabbi Meir Berlin, then President of the World Mizrachi Organization, on the passing of his mother. In response to his query about my doings, my father told him about my spiritual and economic state. Whereupon Rabbi Berlin fixed upon me what seemed to me his hypnotic eyes and in a pleading voice implored: "Why don't you go home to Eretz Israel? Young men like you, with a good knowledge of Hebrew and English, are needed there, and *that is where you belong!*" It was the very first time it occurred to anybody — including my father and myself — to even suggest this drastic move, which was to change my entire course in life. For although my Zionism was as natural and self-evident to me as "Americanism" to a native American (indeed, Zionism has always been synonymous with Judaism for me), I had envisioned my future life as a socialist-pacifist who would devote his life to building a just society, and, at the same time, bring his ideas and influences to bear on children and youth in the "root-striking" process of American Jewry.

I still wonder at times at the decisive impact of a few words uttered sincerely and forcefully by a great man. For it was there and then that I discovered the answer to the question — "whither?". On the way to my father's hotel, the only problem I posed was: "Where will I ever get the money for a ticket?" My father, who was delighted with this turn of events, assured me he would make every effort to borrow the necessary funds. So, a few weeks later I found myself on a ship going to Eretz Israel (I never used the word "Palestine") with a near empty suitcase and a few dollars in my pocket.

In spite of material hardships and spiritual struggles, New York had its fascinations and compensations. It was wonderful to be there. Merely to walk on Broadway in those days was exhilirating. So enthralling was the flow of artistic and cultural events that many a time I used what little food money I had to take my first love to a play or a concert, and sometimes I would spend the only quarter I had on a copy of "The Thinker" instead of a meal. New York was aglow with intellectual happenings. One week there would be a debate between Bertrand Russell and Will Durant on "Free Love", or between Clarence darrow and a theologian on Immortality. The next week there could be a treat in the form of a symposium on Liberalism, Socialism and Communism, by Bertrand Russell, Norman Thomas and Jay Lovestone, with Scott Nearing as chairman. Events such as these had a profound influence on my thinking, and, to a large extent, shaped the essence of my life work. Many were the times when, during fits of befuddlement and disillusionment, I recalled the illuminating ideas and the inspiring insights of such great teachers as John Dewey and Morris Cohen. I believe that my "love affair" with education was ignited not only by my creative Rebbes in Tsfat and Yerushalayim, but also by men like Russell. In one of his debates on political systems, Russell made the point, in his lucid and pentrating manner, that in our preoccupation with "systems" we tend to lose sight of the fact that political systems are made and unmade by people, and that the focus of our attention should therefore be on education, on changing human beings who, in the final analysis, will change the systems. His brilliant exposition on this theme, which I could not possibly convey as effectively as he did, was not only a flash of light to me in my search for the right and just system, but served also as a guiding light in all my work.

It was therefore not at all easy for me to part with my beloved New York. For a long time after my arrival in my native land, I would cry with nostalgia when I would see a familiar New York sight in a movie, or when I would read about an occurrence there in which, alas, I could not take part.

The voyage was a prelude to the sharp turn my life was to take. I came face to face with the upsurge of Modern Zionism. At the Yeshivah, the age-old yearning for Shivat Zion was taken for granted, and found expression mostly in the study of the past. There was very little about the events that were rapidly shaping into what David Ben Gurion termed *"Hamedinah Baderech"*, (The State in the Making). Nor was there real consideration of what the future might hold for American and World Jewry. It was as if the Rabbis of tomorrow were being prepared for the future largely in the context of the distant past. Suddenly, I faced real Chalutzim, young pioneers from Eastern Europe who were going "to rebuild the land and be rebuilt in it". The singing, the dancing, and the lively discussions of these ardent believers awakened me — a native of "the land" — to the contemporary ideals, aspirations, problems, and needs of my people. It was then that the spectre of Hitler and his evil hordes first appeared to me as a stark reality. It was then, I believe, that began my metamorphosis from a New York cosmopolite whose primary concern was the "world" and "humanity" into a socialist-Zionist who came to realize that Isaiah's prophecy of a united and peaceful world lay far in the unforseeable future, while my people's survival and national revival were at stake in the immediate present. I also realized that my contribution to a better world could best be made through the channels of a reborn, creative Jewish nation.

Chapter 3
Prosperity in the Land of Promise

The early thirties were a period of prosperity and exuberance in Eretz Israel, while the U.S.A. and Canada were still writhing in the throes of the Depression. German Jews, alarmed and bestirred by the acendance of nazism, started to look to the Land of Israel for a haven. They brought with them capital, knowledge, skills and initiative, and made a significant contribution to the economy. There was a general atmosphere of hope, expectation, and a sense of personal participation in a great enterprise. It was not unusual, in those days, to witness traffic stopping for singing and dancing youth at all hours of the day and night. They sang romantic songs about the Revival, about the Return and about the beauty of the beloved Ancestral Land. One thing the country did not need was an American-trained Rabbi, even if he were not to pursue that calling. It therefore took me several months, during which I half-starved by giving private lessons, to be faced with the choice of becoming a translator at His Majesty's Supreme Court or the director of the Labor Movement's Seminary. My decision was made on the advice of Dr. Yitzchak Mirkin, a venerable scholar who authored the very first Hebrew textbook on Psychology. He befriended me because of his association with my father who had been Chief Rabbi of Tsfat and Upper Galillee at the time when Dr. Mirkin was stationed in Tsfat as a reresentative of the *Vaad Hatsirim* (the Representative Committee) of the World Zionist Movement. I therefore had a standing invitation from him to have the Sabbath meal every Shabbat noon with his family. When I told him about my two offers, he solemnly advised me thus: "If you want to be happy in your work, my son, work for goyim and give to Jews. If you work for Jewish organizations, you will have a lot of heartache." This near "anti-semitic" statement puzzled me no end. I knew it was not easy to work for Jewish communities in the Gola, but I was surprised to hear that a similar situation prevailed in the Reborn Homeland. I later understood that Dr. Mirkin's salary was inadequate to support his rather large family and that, being a very honest and naive person, he must have disdained the inevitable politics in every institution. Be that as it may, I followed his advice and chose the position with the Supreme Court.

I am a Suspect in a Murder Case

Several months after my arrival in Israel, and about a month before I started my work at the Supreme Court, I was stopped on the street by a police officer and was informed that I was a suspect in the murder of the noted labor leader Dr. Chaim Arlozorov, whose murder on the Tel-Aviv seashore, had shaken the country and nearly led to civil war between the followers of the Histadrut and the Revisionists, three of whose leading members were arrested as suspects. The officer asked me to follow him to the police station, where I was interrogated at length about my whereabouts on the night of the murder, about my friends and acquaintances, etc. I was allowed to go home, but I noticed a policeman stationed across the street from my room where I could see him from the window. A few days later, after my alibi was established, I was informed that I was completely cleared.

Americans in Eretz Israel

North American Jews, too, many of them young people who could not find employment in their homeland, were drawn to the Land of Promise. I use the word "drawn" advisedly. For, as far as I know, the Zionist "Movement" did not have any plan to *draw* North American Jewish youth to the country. It was always preoccupied with the fund-raising and political fronts, to the almost utter neglect of education and youth. Nor was there any plan to help and guide young people from English speaking countries in their efforts to strike roots in the emerging Yishuv. Some Americans took the initiative in organizing themselves for mutual assistance and for socializing. In Tel-Aviv, where the greater part of the Americans were concentrated, an American lawyer by the name of Nathan Kaplan established the Association of American Immigrants, which sponsored various activities to facilitate the absorption of Americans into the life of the country. In Jerusalem, a group of us organized "The Anglo-American Jewish Association", without any assistance from, or connection with, the Tel-Aviv group. As indicated by the name, we aimed at a broader organizational basis, to include people from all English speaking countries, and we did indeed have members from the U.S.A., Canada, Great Britain and South Africa. We were joined by some Sabras whose main motives were "boy meets girl" and the improvement of their English speech, but who nonetheless contributed to bridge-building between natives and immigrants. Our aims were primarily educational and social. We set out to acquaint ourselves with the life and problems of the country. To this end, we invited as lecturers some of the most outstanding personalities, such as Henrietta Szold, Moshe Shertok (later Sharett), Yitzchak Ben Zwi and Eliahu Epstein (later Eilat). We also held symposia, debates and social evenings, which were open to all young people and which thus brought about not only better understanding, but also "intermarriages". Among some of our most active members were American Rabbinical students who were attending the Hebrew University. Our group was under the auspices of the Histadrut, whose Cultural Secretary was one of the few who understood the importance of our organization and who gave us every assistance, without any attempt to "influence" our political outlook. The Consul General of the U.S.A. was our Honorary Sponsor. As an aside, it is interesting to note that Davka organized Reform Judaism was the first to send some of its Rabbinic students to spend a year at the Hebrew University, the very first one having been Theodore Cook, who was "drafted" by Dr. Judah Magnes, president of the Hebrew University, when he visited Hebrew Union College in 1932. At the same time we set up our group, there were three Reform Rabbis — William Chomsky, Alan Green and Theodore Cook — all of whom were active in our Association. The Conservative Movement had only one representative at the University — Moshe Davis, who was later one of the founders of Hebrew Camp Massad and the Hebrew Youth Organization of the U.S.A. and who is now heading the Institute for Contemporary Jewry at the Hebrew University. As to the Orthodox branch of American Jewry, the time was not yet ripe for them to have even one representative at the "secular" Hebrew University.

My work with the Anglo-American Jewish Association, whose president I was during the first four years of its existence, brought home to me, more strikingly than ever before, the problem of the neglect of American Jewish youth by the Zionist Organization. I published an article in "Davar", the influential daily newspaper of the Histadrut, on "American Jewish Youth and Eretz Israel". The article appeared also in "Ha-Olam", the official organ of the World Zionist Organization, published at that time in London, England.

The appearance of this article (Davar of 21.6.1936) brought me face to face for the first time with Moshe Shertok (an association that added much interest and flavor to my work in later years), who invited me to discuss the contents of the article and the activities we could initiate in this abandoned field. It is significant that Moshe Sharett, at that time the head of the Political Department of the Jewish Agency, who had no official responsibility in education, was the only one who took notice of the article. He also called it to the attention of Berl Locker, representative of the Jewish Agency in Great Britain, and Moshe Kleinman, editor of "Ha-Olam" both of whom were visiting the country at that time. I spent a few hours with them in a comprehensive analysis of these problems, and made some practical suggestions for dealing with them. Unfortunately, my expectations that something would be done were completely frustrated, as absolutely nothing resulted from these meetings. The only justification, or, to be more correct, explanation I could find for their inaction was that all of them were submerged in the turmoil of the Arab disturbances of that period. This explanation may perhaps excuse the inaction of individuals, but it cannot absolve the Zionist movement as a whole.

My work at the Supreme Court became increasingly meaningless to me. I fully realized it was not my purpose to rise in the bureaucracy of His Majesty's Government. When I commenced my work at the Court, Justice Gad Frumkin, the only Jewish member of the Supreme Court, who had read the examination papers of the candidates for the translator's post, expressed his hope that I would succeed in my work, that I would study law and that, someday, I would replace him as the Jewish member of the Supreme Court. Although I had already known that the law could not possibly be my life's work, it was the Arlozorov murder trial that hastened my decision to look for work that would give meaning to my life instead of merely providing a living. Thus, when Judge Frumkin summoned me to his chambers to question the reason and wisdom of my decision to quit, I told him that I could never see myself sending people to their death and that I would rather be a teacher than a judge of human beings. A few months later, I received a renewed offer from the Histadrut to become the director of its "Workers Seminary". At that time, the Labor Movement had only one institution for youth and adult education. Its main purpose was Torah Lishmah, learning for its own sake, for the enhancement of the cultural life of the young and old. My tenure at the Seminary was one of the most happy periods in my life. To me, this particular institution was a modern Yeshivah where the old and the new as well as the Judaic and the general western cultures were blended, and where the love of learning was of paramount importance. A great majority of the teachers were members of the faculty of the Hebrew University and included such outstanding scholars as Prof. Hugo Shmuel Bergman, Prof. Ernst Akiva Simon and Prof. Moshe Weizman (brother of Chaim Weizman), who received no remuneration whatsoever for their services. The program consisted of a large variety of Judaic and general subjects. It was a delight to see hundreds of young and old people flock nightly, many of them straight from their offices and factories and some in their overalls, "to quench their thirst for knowledge". It is noteworthy that even during the disturbances of the Thirties, when the country was plagued with curfews, most novel ways were found to continue the studies at different hours during the day and evening.

Out of their ranks came many of the great of that period in various areas, such as authors Natan Alterman and Asher Barash; scientists Aharon and Ephraim Katzir; artists Nachum Guttman and Rubin; actors Chanah Rovina and Aharon Meskin, and composers Moshe Wilensky and Mordechi Zeira. Berl Katzenelson, the "rebbe" of the movement, and others encouraged budding creative talents. One example is Yehoshua Zeinwirt who later changed his name to Yehoshua Bar-Yosef. I met him for the first time when he was still living in the orthodox Meah-Shearim Quarter. He was still dressed as a "modern" chassid with trimmed beard and miniature sideburns. He came to me to suggest that we form a partnership in his translation bureau that was housed in a small store-front along the road to Meah-Shearim. One day, he pulled out from his pocket several sheets of paper and, blushingly, asked me to read the three literary sketches contained in the sheets. As I finished reading them, I exclaimed enthusiastically, "This is excellent creative writing; have you actually written them?" Quite shyly, he murmured, "Are you mocking me?" It took some effort to persuade him that I was serious. Reluctantly, he agreed that I send them to Berl Katzenelson, editor of "Davar", the most pretigious newspaper of that period, for publication.

It was on Tuesday or Wednesday when I mailed them and on Friday of the same week they appeared on the front page of the literary section of "Davar". This was the beginning of the development of one of the most noted authors of that period, whose best known creation was the trilogy on Safad (Tsfat), the city of his and my birth. Many years later, I read a criticism of Bar-Yosef's works by the noted literary critic Baruch Kurtzweil, in which he was laboring to explain the erotic elements in Bar Yoseph's writings. Being somewhat critical myself of the belabored "digs" of literary critics, I thought, "Wherefore all this pedantic prodding?" It is a very simple matter — Bar Yoseph enjoyed pornography. I recalled that while he was still clothed in his chassidic garb, he once showed me pornographic photos that made me blush up to my ears. Yehoshua Bar Yoseph blushed when he showed me his literary sketches, but he did not blush when he showed me his pornographic pictures! As the Talmud has it (K'tubot 13) *"Ain apotropos la-arayot"*, literally, "there is no guardian for sex", and clearly meaning, in matters of sex no one is reliable.

The Zionist Labor Movement was at that time in one of the brightest periods of its history. It was the spearhead of all the creative and constuctive forces in the country. Its avowed principles were not mere slogans. Socialist Zionism was on the march — Kibbutzim,

Moshavim, Cooperatives, mutual responsibility and help, and — in general — social justice were shining stars on its socialist map and blue-white flag. Its teachers imbued the youth with the ideals of the dignity of labor, (some even spoke of "the religion of labor") of any form of labor, non-exploitation of other human beings, and self-fulfillment through personal effort and achievement. The Labor Zionists were pioneers also in the things of the spirit — in education, culture, literature, journalism and the Arts. The Histadrut leadership were, in the main, inspired and inspiring individuals who lived as they taught others to live — simple, frugal, productive and creative lives. In the institutions and organizations of the Labor Movement itself, the socialist principle of "from everyone according to his ability, to everyone according to his work" was strictly observed. Thus, the married charwoman with children received much higher pay than the general secretary of the Histadrut in Jerusalem who had only his mother and himself to support. I remember my astonishment when I once visited his home on a call of duty, (there was very little socializing in private homes; our social life found expression at educational-cultural "evenings" and at public holiday celebrations) and saw that the two small rooms he and his mother occupied were furnished with the barest items such as *cots*, cheap tables and chairs, and bookcases. In this connection, it is noteworthy that the home of Yitzchak Ben Zwi, then the chairman of the *Vaad Le-umi* (National Council of the Yishuw) and later the second president of Israel, was not much more elaborate. I also recall with nostalgia how deeply hurt I was when Yeduhah Shimony suggested that I should get an increment of two pounds monthly because I "was used to American standards". When he sensed my chagrin, he explained apologetically that he thought I needed the extra money in connection with my duties as Liaison Officer between the Histadrut and the British military authorities in the Jerusalem District.

Shimony was for me a model of modern socialism blended with high ethical Judaic principle and sensitivity. During one of my visits at his home on a Shabbat, his daughter turned on the radio. Shimony became agitated and called out to her, "Arza, Arza, don't you know it's Shabbat today? Please turn off that radio at once". Surprised, I asked, "are you that religious, Yeduhah?" "No", he answered, "but our upstairs neighbors are very religious and will be hurt by what they consider 'chilul Shabbat', (desecration of the Sabbath)." Once, at his office, he had to write something personal for me, and absolutely refused to use paper belonging to the office. I recalled an example of ethical conduct cited to us at the Yeshivah in Jerusalem. A *meshulach* (fund raiser) for the Yeshivah of Rabbi Israel Salanter in Kovno, Lithuania, whose expenses during his travels included cigarettes, would put out his cigarette as soon as the train reached Kovno, and would keep the remainder for his next trip . . .

"Here", I thought, "is a blend of Salant' and 'Borochov' (a Jewish socialist ideologue) in Yehudah Shimony".

Thus came to an end my floundering and wavering that had continued since I had left the Yeshivah in New York, for I found a new Yeshivah, a true modern Yeshivah which embodied the lofty ideals and life-principles of the prophets and sages of old. I finally found (today I would say my identity) myself, my ideal and my lifework. So much so that when the late Yeshayahu Press, an outstanding educator and scholar who was president of the B'nai Brith Lodge in Jerusalem, expressed amazement at my rejection of his offer that I become the general secretary of the National B'nai Brith Grand Lodge at more than twice my Histradut salary, I told him: "I have decided to devote my life to the labor movement". The wise old man smiled wryly and said: "I am very glad we have such dedicated young people, but I sincerely hope you won't regret it some day". So enamoured did I become of the Histradut, of my new Messiah, that money was of very little consequence. What need was there for money on the threshold of the Messianic Millenium!

Be a Tail to lions and Not a Head to Foxes
(Sayings of the Fathers, 5-20)

It was indeed my good fortune to have become "a tail to lions" through my connections with the Seminary and the Histradut, which brought me into contact with such rare individuals as Berl Katznelson, Zalman Rubashov (later Shazar), Zalman Aranowitz (later Aranne) and David Remez. The doors that were thus opened to me, and the opportunities for service in crucial areas, gave me insights into significant events and into the personalities of those who made them. They were a source of inspiration and courage in my work during later years in the Diaspora, especially in moments — and many were the moments — of loneliness, discouragement and frustration because of the surrounding apathy of many people in different spheres of endeavour.

Maimonides Versus Movies

At one of the meetings of the Mercaz Hatarbut (the Central Cultural Committee) under the chairmanship of Berl Katznelson, there was a long discussion about the insufficient interest of youth in the cultural life of the Yishuw. One member bewailed the phenomenon of the popularity of movies. Dr. Yehudah Ibn Shmuel Kaufman, whose book on Maimonides had appeared at about that time, expressed the opinion that this situation was due to our failure in inculcating our youth with the importance of studying our Hebrew sources. As an example, he cited the small circulation of books such as his among the youth. There were some eyebrows raised when I, (a whipper snapper) the youngest in the group, dared tell Dr. Kaufman that it was not books like his that would steer our youth along the right path. What our youth needed, I said, was more comprehensive and deeper study and understanding of our economic and social problems. Dr. Kaufman, my neighbour who had befriended me and given me much encouragement in my work (as a matter of fact, it was to him I owed my position in the Histradut), retorted by merely muttering, "this young fellow will grow up some day". Berl passed on to another subject, but at the end of the meeting he whispered into my ears, "Be not disheartened; both of you are right". In later years, after I "grew up" a little more, I realized that Berl and Dr. Kaufman were right and that my misguided statement had been a vestige of my rebellion against orthodox Judaism.

Ben Gurion and the English Shoe-shine Boy

In one of his reports, at a party meeting, on his negotiations with the British Government in London, Ben Gurion dwelt on the importance of cultivating good relationships not only with British government officials, but also with the British public. In the course of his report, Ben Gurion said that in the presence of Winston Churchill he felt that there was some super-human quality in Churchill's character and spirit. I turned to Moshe Shertok (Sharett), who was sitting near me in the audience (there were no "head-tables" in those days in Eretz-Israel) and told him that I have this same feeling in the presence of Ben Gurion. Shertok's reaction puzzled me — I was not sure whether his smile was one of approval or sarcasm.

Ben Gurion spoke humorously about the "royal" treatment he had given his shoe-shine boy during his latest visit in London, for "some day the shoe-shine boy might become our British High Commissioner". For various reasons, including the lack of a common language, communica-tion between Jews and the British officials and military men was far from satisfactory. Many of my British co-workers in government complained to me about "Jewish standoffishness, bordering on unfriend-liness, towards the British". They could not understand why they were never invited to Jewish homes. Difficult as it was, I had to explain that the main reason was the fear of blossoming love affairs and inter-marriages between Jews and Gentiles, which did happen in fact in some instances where there was communication. Those of us who came from English speaking countries had, in addition to a common language, a better understanding of, and a more liberal approach to this problem. With the help of Rachel Yanait, the wife of Yitzchak Ben Zwi, a number of

American Jewish women organized a committee for the purpose of providing some social activities and amentities for the British soldiers. Because of my interest in this problem, I had the distinction of being the only male member of the committee. And by virtue of my acquaintance with a considerable number of Britons, I was later appointed Liaison Officer between the Histradut and the military authorities in the Jerusalem district.

This was during the Arab "disturbances" of the thirties, when *we* were plagued with curfews, searches, and — at times — even martial law. As Liaison Officer, I was entrusted with the military passes which I was to distribute to individuals who were engaged in essential nightwork, including people who worked in a restaurant that was open all night to the military. It was quite a feat for me to manoeuvre some of these passes also into the hands of Hagganah people without ever arousing the suspicion of the military commander. One of these passes was naturally always in my possession, but on the night my first son was born, *my* pass was expropriated by Hagganah, so that I found myself walking to the hospital with my wife at about 3:00 a.m. at a time when martial law and curfew were in force. I never had qualms about my "duplicity", because the British were busy searching and disarming the attacked rather than the attackers on the principle that they, the British authorities, would defend us, or, that we should not defend ourselves. . . . But Jews had very bitter experiences with their "defenders", and were determined not to rely any more on others to defend them. Secret documents from 1946, published recently after an attempt to delay their disclosure "because of their embarrassing contents", reveal that the Chiefs of Staff of the British Armed Forces, among them Field Marshall Montgomery, recommended the breaking up of the Hagganah as well as the "extremist" Eitsel and Lechi. At a time when Anwar Sadat was in the service of the Nazis, the Grand Mufti of Jerusalem was in Berlin participating in Hitler's "final solution", and Arabs were attacking indiscriminately all Jews —including women and children — throughout the country. His Majesty's forces were engaged in closing all avenues of escape for the tragic remains of Hitler's gas chambers, and were prepared to do away not only with the "extremists" but also with the Hagganah, which was committed to *Havlagah*, restraint, and to *Haggannah*, the use of arms only in self-defense. Thus, I had no scruples whatsoever about my clandestine activities. I was, however, fearful when I played host to British officials in my home, for a few feet from where I sat lay hidden a Haggannah arsenal. Haggannah's fabulous successes when it was transformed into an army of liberation was due, in large measure, to the ingenuity, resourcefulness and experience acquired during the decades preceding the War of Independence. Its leaders' and members' motivation, spirit and discipline were of the highest order. Whoever it was that decided to turn my home into an arsenal did not have to give me prior notice, nor was I consulted about my readiness to face the consequences of losing my life by hanging in case the arsenal was discovered.

It just happened one night, when I saw a line of people headed by Aharon Rabinowitz, the General Secretary of the Histadrut, carrying suitcases and approaching my home. My first thought was that Rabinowitz wanted me to put up those people for the night in the rather spacious house I had rented from an Arab to accomodate myself, my mother and my brothers and sisters whom my father had dispatched to his native land with the intention of following them later. (To his dismay, things did not develop as he had hoped, and my mother with some of the children, returned to Winnipeg.) Rabinowitz quickly scanned the entire house, and without any further ado gave the signal to open the suitcases and store the weapons in an attic above the bathroom. He then informed me that a group of Haggannah members — boys and girls — were stationed in a nearby building and that the weapons were for their use in case of a possible Arab attack in the vicinity. It was a clever scheme to have the arms and the defenders in different buildings, so that in case the arsenal were discovered, only the householder would be implicated, and if there were a search in the other house, there would be no evidence of the existence of an organized defence group. An example of the remarkable discipline of Haggannah members is the case of my brother Asher, who was fourteen years old at that time. One of my friends remarked casually about Asher's courageous work in Haggannah. I was embarrassed to tell him that I did not know about my brother's membership in Haggannah. Since my mother had left him in my care when she returned to Winnipeg, I thought and told him that he should have at least informed me of his dangerous activities. His reaction was, "We were told to speak to nobody about our membership and activities, and 'nobody' includes you". My sister Leah's outstanding and dedicated work in Haggannah was completely unknown to me until we met again in New York in 1939, although she must have known that I too was a member.

Another activity in the area of cultivating better relations with non-Jewish government officials, was my initiative in organizing a club for Arabs, Jewish and British employees of various government depart--ments. The purpose of the club was to discuss subjects and issues on the local and world scenes and to bring about a better understanding of one another's attitudes and views. The Arab members conditioned their participation on the strictest confidentiality of our meetings, as their lives would be "in jeopardy if Arab extremists were to discover their 'disloyalty'." This necessitated the holding of meetings in my home. Since my "socialist" salary did not permit the luxury of serving refreshments at the meetings, I mentioned the problem to Moshe

Shertok (Sharett), who was then the head of the political department of the Jewish Agency. He immediately suggested that his department should cover these expenses because of the importance he attached to this activity. The club disbanded at the height of the "disturbances" in 1937 or 38, but one of its Arab members later rendered valuable services to the Jewish Agency "out of conviction of the justice of the Jewish case". (By the way, he later emigrated to Canada, married a Jewish refugee, and "thanks his lucky stars" for living in a country free of terror and bloodshed.)

My experiences with the Anglo-American Jewish Association, my liaison with the military, and my work with the tri-national club, brought home to me the neglect of the important dimension of public relations, particularly at that juncture in our struggle for the renewal of our national independence. While it is true that, in the end, the outcome might not have been different from what it is today, there might have been fewer obstacles and victims on many of the roads that have brought us hither.

Soviet Russian Anti-Semitism Predicted in Early Thirties

One of my functions as a Histradut activist was to accompany prominent guests on their visits to the country. The three days I spent with Victor Chernov, who had been President of the short lived Russian Consituent Assembly and Minister of Agriculture in the Kerensky Government, was one of the most interesting episodes during that period. Chernov was keenly interested in every phase of the life and problems of the Yishuw, and especially in the philosophy and program of the Labor Movement. He wanted to know what we thought and felt about communist Russia. I ventured to offer him my own opinion, that the nambypamby liberal attitude of sympathy and tolerance towards the "noble Russian experiment", which was nurtured by American Aca-- demia when I was a student at New York University, and which was largely shared by the non-communist intelligentsia in Eretz Israel, was deluded and dangerous.

My personal opinion at that time may have been influenced by my eldest brother's ordeal in Soviet Russia. It was in 1929 when I noticed in one of the daily newspapers in New York (I believe it was in the Sunday Magazine Section of the New York Times) a story about a Rabbi Samuel Horowitz who had been saved from the clutches of the hangman in Soviet Russia through the intervention of the Chief Rabbi of Eretz Israel. as I read the story, it became clear to me that it was my brother who had been condemned to death as a British spy. He languished in prison for about two years before Rabbi Kook succeeded in persuading Maxim Litvinov (by the way, Litvinov had been a Yeshiva student in his early youth), who was then the Russian Ambassador in Great Britain, that this saintly rabbi had nothing to do with politics, let alone with spying. When I later met my brother in Eretz Israel, he seemed to be terrified when I asked him to relate to me the whole bizarre story. He mumbled something to the effect that upon his release he was warned that the KGB's hand would reach him anywhere were he to publicize the macabre details of his torture and agony. I was fascinated by the courage of a young man who, as he told me, relied upon the Holy Book of the Bratzlever Rebbe to get him somehow to the Rebbe's tomb in Uman.* He got hold of a forged passport, and, having very little money, made his long tortuous way to Uman, with what he called the "Rebbe's intercession in Heaven".

As he was praying, one day, together with other Chassidim at the tomb of Reb Nachman, the founder of their movement, some members of the Yevsektzia (Jewish Communist Party in Russia) passed by and ridiculed them. The other chassidim cringed in fear, but my brother, who was accustomed to freedom in Eretz Israel, dared to taunt them. Sensing that there was something strange about this extraordinary daring, the Jewish Bolsheviks asked to see his passport, and it was they who discovered the forgery. From the little my brother did tell me I learned something about the cruelty and inhumanity of the would be builders of the new world. It was this brother of mine who used to enthrall me, in my early childhood, with highly imaginative and engrossing stories about the great and saintly people. He would hammer at me continually that every person can reach the greatest heights in the realm of the spirit. "Arele,' he would repeatedly declare, "If you will it, you could become even like Moshe Rabeinu!"

To return to my conversation with Chernov, I told him that, as to the opinion of the average socialist in Eretz Israel, there was a feeling of satisfaction that anti-semitism had been outlawed in Soviet Russia; there was deep concern about the government's anti Zionist policy, and there was profound bitterness about the Yevsektsie's assault on Jewish religious and national life and institutions. I added, however, that at a time when anti-semitism was on the loose in Germany and in other countries, there was a degree of appreciation that while the "Jewish soul" was under attack in the USSR, the physical existence of the Jewish community was assured. And, "as long as the body was alive, there was always hope that the 'soul' too would come to its own in the future". I was then taken aback by the sudden outburst of this gentle old man. His entire body actually shook as he exclaimed: "How ignorant and naive you people can be about the communist despots! I know them personally to be rabid antisemites. The time will undoubtedly come when it will suit their purposes to assault not only what you call the "Jewish soul" but also the Jewish body. They are ruthless fanatics, and they could be of greater danger to the Jews than are the nazis". (Although this happened when nazism had already reared its ugly and venomous head, nobody could anticipate at that time the extent and intensity of the holocaust.) I dismissed his outburst as the bias of a political adversary. Unfortunately, we know today how tragically right Chernov was. The Jewish people as a whole have paid a high price for the naivety and blindness of those who were duped by the collosal Biro Bidjan fraud and by the illusion that a Jewish national (albeit non or even anti-religious) life could be maintained in the communist "Heaven". Even today there are some Jews who underestimate the danger of soviet communism, not only to the Jews of Russia, but also to the Jewish people and its national aspirations. In order to properly defend ourselves against those who would destroy us, we must become fully aware that Soviet Russia is the spearhead of the evil forces in the world of today.

A Memorable Closed Meeting on Partition

In 1937, following the publication of the Peel Commission Report, which recommended the rapartition of Palestine (the first partition of the Mandate territory having been carried out in 1922, when the Kingdom of Transjordan was arbitrarily established by the British) the Zionist world was divided on the acceptance of the partition plan, which allotted to the Jews only a part of the territory west of the Jordan. There were some very influential leaders, among them Chaim, Weizman, David Ben Gurion and Moshe Shertok, who maintained that it was better to have an independent Jewish State in a part of the Land than to give up this opportunity at a time when many thousands of refugees were knocking at the gates of the Homeland. At that time, Captain Victor Cazalet, a member of the British Parliament, and Miss Blanche Dugdale, a niece of Lord Balfour, were guests in the country. It was my understanding that it was Dr. Weizman who had invited them to address a closed meeting at the Jewish Agency headquarters, in order to endeavour to persuade the opponents of Partition, among them such powerful leaders as Mana--chem Ussishkin and Berl Katznelson, to "accept a half a loaf rather than none at all". Chaim Weizman was chairman of the meeting, which was attended by many leaders from various parts of the country. The long address by Cazalet made a deep and lasting impression on me. I was greatly pained when he pointed out again and again, that the Jewish people had not made the necessary efforts and sacrifices when various opportunities presented themselves to realize the Zionist ideal. The essence of his remarks was that, considering all the factors and circumstances, it would be wise to accept the offer to establish a Jewish state even though it be only in part of Palestine. When he finished, several groups of people stood around discussing among themselves his remarks. I was eager to hear Ussishkin's reaction, which, in brief, was this: A people might be *forced* to surrender temporarily its independence or parts of its land, but if a nation *willingly signs away* even the smallest part of its land, such a people is not worthy of, nor will it achieve liberty and independence. I venture to say that if Ussishkin were alive today, he would — aside from considerations about the security of Israel — continue to stand pat on the principle that a nation should not willingly sign away any part of its land.

Reality Versus Idealism

When I was faced with the reality of supporting a family, I found it necessary to accept a position at the Hebrew University because of the much higher salary it offered. I rationalized my step backwards from pure idealism by convincing myself that I could continue my voluntary activities for the Histadrut even while I worked for a living at the university. In actuality, as I look back on that period, I believe that although there were some strong personal reasons for my decision to go once more to America, I might not have taken this crucial step if I had not left my work at the Seminary. It is true that my work at the Hebrew University was interesting at times, and brought me in contact with great scholars and scientists, but my duties were essentially bureaucratic. And the one thing I was absolutely sure of was that I would not spend my life as a bureaucrat even if this were necessary for making a living. So, in March 1938, I set out (this time willingly!) for the U.S.A., where I intended to continue my studies and "make a contribution in a sorely neglected area — the education of our youth in the spirit of our National Renaissance". As to making a living, I armed myself with four letters of recommendation I naively thought would surely help me get a good position: from Prof. Shmuel (Hugo) Bergman, then Rector of the Hebrew University, to Prof. Israel Davidson of the Jewish Theological Seminary of America; from Moshe Shertok (Sharett) to Louis Lipsky, then President of the Z.O.A.; from Dr. Alexander M. Dushkin to Dr. Israel Chipkin, a leading American educator, and from Supreme Court Justice Gad Frumkin "to whom it may concern".

Chapter 4
Back to New York

If my return to *Chutz La'aretz* (outside of "The Land") was free from thoughts of Satan and the *Yetzer Harah*, my *Yetzer Hatov* (the good inclination) had to muster all the strength he could to weather a new round of re-orientation and adjustment. When I arrived in Eretz Israel from N.Y. in 1933, my hardships had been entirely my own, as they had been in New York for several years prior to my return Home. But upon my return to the Land of Opportunity, it was not with an easy conscience that I saw my wife and our first born, who was but a year old at the time, as full partners in privation, for it took about half a year before I found employment. The U.S. was still in the grip of the great depression, and jobs, particularly in the field of Hebrew education, were scarce. At times, it seemed that on top of the loans I had received from the Hebrew university and my parents-in-law to enable me to go to America, I would now have to search hard for another loan to go back in the other direction. I quickly learned, much to my surprise, that even the personal letters from some of the Great of Eretz Israel to their counterparts in New York were of no avail in the stark realities of the depressed financial situation in Jewish educational institutions and organizations in the U.S.A. The letter from Prof. Tur-Sinai, head of the Bible Department at the Hebrew University, to Prof. Israel Davidson, one of the most distinguished scholars at the Jewish Theological Seminary, did no more than open to me the Davidson home. Upon reading Tur-Sinai's letter, Prof. Davidson exclaimed cheerfully: 'One who was a *Ben Bay'it* (a person who is always welcome) at the Tur-Sinai Home will be welcome as a Ben Bay'it in my home. However, his and his wife's frantic telephone calls to individuals and institutions brought no results at all. There were simply no openings! Nonetheless, the genuine warmth and friendliness of both the professor and his lovely and sympathetic wife encouraged me to "carry on" . . . with my letter of recommendation from Prof. Bergman to the Registrar of the Jewish Theological Seminary. Here, the response was a matter of fact and categorical "nothing available"! A few weeks later a ray of hope appeared. Dr. Davidson informed me that the Toronto Hebrew Free School (now, Associated Hebrew Schools of Toronto) were searching for a principal and that Dr. Israel Chipkin, director of the Jewish Education Association in New York, to whom I had a letter of introduction from Prof. Alexander M. Dushkin, could clinch it for me.

My hopes ran high at the prospects of my return to live and work in Canada, where my family lived and which was reputed to be, as indeed it was, more Jewish than the U.S.A. But alas, it was a "matter of principle" for Dr. chipkin to recommend only persons whom he had personally seen at work as teachers and/or administrators. Years later, when I met Dr. Chipkin at conferences, I had the satisfaction of his telling me that perhaps he should have made an effort to become acquainted with me, which might have resulted in accomplishing on a much larger scale in Toronto what was achieved in Calgary. I let the compliment stand, though I had more than serious doubts as to whether the Toronto school would have allowed me to introduce the revolutionary changes I had instituted (though with some initial resistance by the community leaders) in Calgary. There remained but one more avenue of hope: Mr. Louis Lipsky, the then president of the Zionist Organization of America, to whom I had a letter from Moshe Shertok-Sharett. I had pusposely left the politician to the end. I preferred to work in an Hebrew Afternoon School, so that I could possibly devote at least part of the day to further my education.

My meeting with Mr. Lipsky was the key to my rethinking, or perhaps it would be more correct to say, to my thinking at all on the *meaning* of Zionism. In my childhood and early youth, I never heard the word Zionism. What I did hear incessantly was the word *Mashi'ach*, Messaiah. In speaking about bad times, people would say: "well, let us hope the Messiah will appear soon". In greeting one another the best blessing was: "You should live to welcome the Messiah". To us, "Zionism" — when this word came into use some years following the Balfour Declaration — was very simple. It did not need definition or interpretation; it was in no sense a dubious or controversial concept. The idependence of our people had come to a forced end at the hands of the brutal Roman Empire. Since that time, and throughout the ages, the Jewish people continued to remember, to wish, to pray, to yearn, to hope for "The Return" and to vow *"Im Eshkachech Yerushaly'im"*, "If I forget thee O Jerusalem, may my right hand forget its cunning, may my tongue cleave to the roof of my mouth if I do not remember thee, if i do not put Jerusalem above my chiefest joy". I would often recall the tears welling up in our eyes in the Cheder when our Rebbe would reiterate to us dramatically that, according to *Yulkut Shinonry* (on Psalms), the Babylonian Exiles bit off the tops of their fingers when their captors tried to force them to "sing and play of the songs of Zion". I would often remember the moaning of my father and older brothers, as they sat down after midnight, ashes sprinkled on their heads, to weep over the destruction of the Holy Temple. With what youthful excitement I joined them in this ritual of *Chatzot* when I reached the ripe age of twelve! How could I forget the unplastered part of the west-wall in our living room "in memory of the *Churban*, the Destruction"! Even people who were too modern to mar their living room wall, displayed a picture or painting of the *Kotel Ma-Aravi* (the Western Wall) with the inscription *"Im eshkachech Yerushalay'im"*. *We did not need the Balfour Declaration, or any other human declaration. We had the promise, the Vow of the Ribbono Shel Olam*, the Master of the Universe. When the Balfour Declaration did come, it was obviously the Hand of God, to fulfill His Promise of "the return". Those who did not believe in the "Return" — and they were very few indeed — were not "good Jews" (the word "assimilationists" also came into use much later). They were not anti-Zionists or non-Zionists, they simply did not care any more about the continuity or revival of the Jewish nation.

Mr. Lipsky awakened me with a shock. I had not realized there were any in-between multitudes who did not have my background, whose national senses were dulled by the long *Galut*, but who at the same time were not ideological assimilationists. It dawned upon me gradually that these people were cut off from their roots to the extent that though many called themselves "Zionists", they did not comprehend the true and full meaning of Zionism. (It is interesting to note that the word "Zionism" is really a new "modern" term which was first used or coined by Batahn Birnbaum (in his "Self-Emancipation", published in 1886) who turned from assimilationist to nationalist). In other words, the term was not needed by those who "never left home"; it was given unto us by those who came back home to us from without . . .

Likspy read Shertock's letter, looked up and declared: "Shertok writes that you could help us in educating our youth — who needs Palestinians to educate our youth?" (He disregarded completely the fact that I had lived in the U.S.A. and Canada for many years and had received my secondary and higher education in N.Y.) "For this we have Rabbis! Shertok could do a real service for Zionism in America if he were to send over fifty strong young men to display their muscles at Madison Square Garden". I was so flabbergasted that I took the letter out of his hand, sprang to me feet and said, "Good-bye Mr. Lipsky". There was, however, some real value in this meeting. It set me thinking in depth about the Zionist condition in general and in America in particular.

I was about to direct my attention to my second "Return" to Eretz Israel when I saw in the paper that a principal-executive director of a Hebrew school and Centre was required for a congregation in th Bronx. I applied for this position without any real hope. My appearance before the Board of Directors for an interview was quite an experience for me. It gave me a vivid view and a strong taste of the condition of Hebrew education; it took me back a while to my experience with the Rebbe's son in Williamsburg, prior to my first "Return" . . . The large, well furnished board room was filled with smoke and with what seemed to be a large number of "Alrightnikes" (individuals who by virtue of their affluence or aggressiveness assume the air of bosses). The chairman (who, I was told, was the biggest building contractor in the Bronx) proceeded "mich zu nemen offen zimbel", a Yiddish expression equivalent to "the third degree". The bombardment of his questions which had no relevance to my qualifications ended with, "we'll let you know if we need you". Great was the astonishment of the chairman and his cigar-munching colleagues at my audacious response: "I believe it is my turn to ask you some questions now". The chairman was so startled that I thought the chair would give way under him. He then chuckled as he turned to his audience with "the young man wants to know whether he likes us!" Turning to me, he muttered, "what would you like to know young man?" I was surprised at myself that, desperately though I needed the job, I dared ask, among other questions, "Did the previous principal leave of his own accord or was he forced to resign, and if so, why?" "Aha!" roared the chairman, "this smacks of unionism; we are not exactly in favour of unions here. Of what concern is it to you why we fired him!? Well, young man (by that time I was thoroughly convinced of my youth . . .), we shall let you know if we need you!" At this moment, a gentle voice, or should I say the voice of a gentleman, addressed the chairman: "Just a minute, Jack, I would like to ask him some questions". This man proceeded to query me on my educational views, on the program and methods I would introduce, and concluded with the most welcome question as to what I considered the most important area of a conservative congregation's work. I said, in essence, that the school is and should be treated as the foundation and heart of the community, and that we should concern ourselves largely with the adolescents and young adults. Sensing that the questioner, education chairman Smuckler, was respected by the Board, I was emboldened to speak freely about the neglect of our youth, of the failure to understand them, and the over-emphasis on the ritualistic aspect of Judaism. (It is noteworthy that the Rabbi was not present at this important meeting!). Whereupon Mr. Smuckler announced, there and then, "I like this fellow and want to work with him". I was asked to leave the room for a while, and upon my return it was Mr. Smuckler who was in charge of the proceedings. It was agreed that I would be given the opportunity to find a place in the school for the previous principal and that I would be independent — of the Rabbi too — in the formulation and implementation of the educational program. Interestingly enough, the previous principal continued to work there for many years, and long after that short episode in my life escaped my mind.

Mr. Smuckler was the ideal education chairman. Mindful of the unwritten law that the chairman must always be consulted, whether or not he is capable of giving advice, or whether or not advice was at all needed, I would turn to him, initially, for his opinion on various matters. It did not take long for him to make it very clear to me that, as he put it, "what do you know about my business, Aron? That is as much as I know about yours. You are in charge, you have my full confidence, and you are free to make all decisions in educational matters". If all the Hebrew schools in America were blessed with this type of education chairmen, one of the main obstacles to the smooth and effective operation of Hebrew schools — education committees and particularly their chairmen — would be eliminated.

I later learned that Mr. Smuckler was a novice in the congregational business. He told me he had been alienated from the synagogue precisely because it did not function in accordance with the principles I had outlined at the meeting. He was now among the heaviest financial supporters of the congregation because his father — on of the founders of the synagogue — made him promise on his death bed that he would do so. He added that he felt duty-bound to fulfill his father's wishes, also because of the grief he had caused him by marrying out of the Jewish faith. This intermarriage, a much rarer and more disturbing occurrence at that time, was the very first I was aware of directly.

If the situation at the Concourse Centre of Israel was typical of the general condition in Jewish education at that time — as I think it was at least in many schools — then we have at least one clue to the ineffectiveness — to say the least — of the Jewish Education System. It provides at least one answer to the question "why were so many of that generation lost to Judaism?" The congregation was in a middle class neighbourhood in the West Bronx. Its members were, in the main, professional and business people. What was referred to as "the sanctuary" (to me, it is highly pretentious to call these places of prayer "the sanctuary") was quite spacious, with beautiful decor and stained glass windows. Some of the officers told me with pride that they had recently spent a large amount of money on fixing the massive artistic door. However, *the school*, which in Jewish tradition takes precedence over the place of worship, was in the basement, as in many other synagogues at that time. There were no real classrooms, but rather sliding doors which were hastily shifted into classrooms in the afternoon and slid back at night to serve as a hall for various affairs. There were no educational facilities, nor was there a children's library. The "curriculum", the archaic text books and teaching methods were most certainly not designed to educate knowledgeable and conscious Jews. If I had any illusions about changing the situation, they were soon dispelled, mainly because of the attitude of the president, an active member of the Democratic Club (Tammany Hall). He was always around, while the chairman of the Board of Education lived in the outskirts of N. Y. and was much too busy to make his presence felt in the congregation or the school. The president, whose understanding and interest in education were nil, nevertheless constantly interfered with my daily routine. I once heard him shout "our executive director hobnobs with the teenagers and actually joins them in their games and dances". How undignified! When he appeared one day in my office with a little dog in one of his coat pockets and a bottle of liquor in the other, a good portion of which he had obviously imbibed, I first tried to cajole him to go home and sleep it off. As he became abusive in the presence of some parents and pupils, I had no alternative but to "help" him out of my office. I knew we could not dwell together in that place. . . .

Unbelievably, Mr. Smuckler, when I told him about the incident, insisted that he would under no circumstances accept my resignation. He would see to it, president or no president, that I should not be interfered with by any officer or board member. I was, of course, delighted by this turn of events, and was awaiting eagerly the crucial meeting where the president would be "put in his proper place in a tasteful and peaceful manner". However, I never did have the satisfaction of witnessing Mr. Smuckler perform this "historic" operation, for, in the time intervening between the incident and the meeting, I received a call from Mr. Mendel N. Fisher, National Executive Director of the Jewish National Fund of America, who offered me the position of national director of the organization's Youth Department. I then called personally on Mr. Smuckler to plead for my release from my commitment to the congregation. Gentleman that he was, he "very reluctantly" condeded that I should avail myself of this coincidental God-send. Much as I would have preferred to work in a school, I convinced myself and Mr. Smuckler that the atmosphere at the Centre would not be conducive to harmonious and effective work. The 60% higher salary of the J.N.F. was of no consequence at all, nor did my wife mention this advantage at any time as we weighed the pros and cons of the new offer. . . .

There was one aspect of J.N.F. activities that particularly appealed to me most. Its leaders valued education as an integral part of the organization's general program. The J.N.F., though it was created for the express purpose of redeeming the Land of Israel for the People of Israel, was the only world Zionist body to have had, at that time, an education and youth department, which developed plans, projects and materials for the education of children and youth *Beru'ach Hamoledet*, in the spirit of The Homeland. I, therefore, rejoiced in the thought that I might now be able to put to the test the ideas and plans I had discussed two years previously with Sharett, Locker and Kleinman, following the publication of my article on this very theme.

The genuine interest in the work of the department that was evidenced by the president, Dr. Israel Goldstein, and the Executive Director, Mr. Mendel Fisher, was most heartening. These two men had built the J.N.F. into a thriving and prestigious organization, and they seemed to be determined to make the Youth and Education Department equally successful. I, therefore, proceeded to design, with confidence and enthusiasm, an elaborate program that would encompass all the schools and youth organizations in the U.S.A. The emphasis was not to be on fund raising but rather on imbuing the young generation with the ideals and aspirations of our National Renaissance. Fund raising would result naturally from this type of program.

That, however, was not to be! My U.S. visa was about to expire, and Dr. Goldstein and Mr. Fisher wanted me to apply for permanent residence. Since an application for immigrant status has to be made while the applicant was out of the country, it was decided that I undertake a tour of several major cities along the route to Winnipeg, where I would apply for entry into the U.S.A. as a permanent resident.

My visits to Detroit, Chicago, St. Paul and Minneapolis gave me the opportunity to acquaint myself with the situation, the needs and the possibilities in the schools and youth organizations. There existed in each city a J.N.F. Council, representative of all the Zionist parties and groupings. Whoever was the father of this idea made an important contribution to the unification of all sections of the community at least under one of the banners of the Zionist Program. What I learned about the workings of these councils gave me the idea later on of extending this type of united effort to all areas of Zionism in Western Canada. I was also impressed and encouraged by what I found in the Hebrew schools, especially those in Detroit and Minneapolis. Although they were far from being in tune with modern educational theory and practice, they were a very far cry from the realities at the Concourse Centre of Israel. In Detroit, I met with a body of teachers who seemed to be united in purpose. They did not rely entirely on the then available mediocre text books. They created their own educational materials; they experimented with different methods of teaching, and sought to learn from each other's experience. In Minneapolis, it was delightful to see that the foundations built by the late Dr. George I. Gordon, were still healthy and firm. I recalled my first visit to that school ten years earlier, when I was practically glued to my seat with wonderment at the simple and natural atmosphere in the classes I visited. At that time Dr. Gordon was still the living and moving spirit in the Institution, which gained a reputation as the very best one in America. I believe that my work later in the field of Hebrew Education in Canada was, to some extent, influenced by the inspiration I had received during my first visit at that Talmud Torah! Detroit and Minneapolis were living witnesses to me of what could be accomplished by men of faith and vision, such as Gordon in Minneapolis and Bernard Isaacs in Detorit. It should be noted that in both these schools *Ivrith Be'ivrith*, the natural and living method of teaching Hebrew, without resorting to artificial translation, had already been firmly established. I was disappointed, though, that the Sephardic pronunciation had not yer been introduced even in those vital schools.

While I was waiting in Winnipeg for my visa, I was offered the newly created position of Western Executive Director of the Z.O.C. Perhaps it was the challenge of being a pioneer in virgin fields which beckoned to me and caused me to forego the much wider field of activity in N.Y. My father warned me that I would regret it if I stayed in Winnipeg. He tried very hard to convince me that I could not and would not achieve much with the limited horizons and the mediocre leadership of that remote region, while the J.N.F. offered a golden opportunity of working with outstanding people in the centre of Jewish life in the Diaspora. It would perhaps have required an extraordinary psychologist to fathom the reasons for a decision that was and still is inexplicable to me.

Dr. Goldstein and Mr. Fisher were somewhat restrained in expressing their obvious anger. Mr. Fisher tried to dissuade me from this "foolish" act and was sure I would regret it. As will be seen later, Mr. Fisher, an outwardly brusque fellow with a non-nonsense manner, but with a very warm heart and a deep sense of fairness and true friendship, had several occasions to refer in later years to my "original" foolishness . . As a matter of fact he made several unsuccessful attempts to "bring me back to New York".

And so started a fresh chapter in my life which, for better or for worse, was to be written almost entirely in Canada.

Chapter 5
Yerushalayim De'Canada
Jerusalem of Canada

Whether or not other Jewish communities concede this imposing and challenging title to the Winnipeg Jewish Community, few people would question its outstanding role in Jewish education. Its schools, especially the United Talmud Torahs, have won the plaudits of educators, scholars and leaders from various countries. The Winnipeg Talmud Torah was a pioneer in the Day School movement as well as in other cultural fields. The general atmosphere of *Yidishkeit* was, however, markedly different when I arrived there in March 1939 from what it had been in 1926. There was already a growing generation of native Canadians who had shed many of the manners of life and customs of their East-European forebears — the Canadianization process was taking firm hold! Many had already started to penetrate the professions, the schools and the political arena; and the Jewish peddler and corner grocery were beginning to give way gradually but surely to large business establishments. The synagogues were not as fully packed as they had been in 1926, and many of the young were giving expression in various forms to a revolt against the old traditions. The "old" was giving way to the "new" to such an extent that none of my younger brothers entertained the idea of continuing the wtelve-generation-old Yeshivah and Rabbinic tradition of our family. As a matter of fact, I was surprised to find that my younger brother, among many other bright students, was an ardent member of the London (England) based Left Book Club. He and his friends confronted me me with many questions about the meaning, validity and justice of Zionism.

They Made Me Keeper of the Vineyards,
Mine Own Vineyard Have I Not Kept
((Song of Songs, 1:6)

Zionist educational and cultural activity was at such a low ebb at that time that there could be little wonder about the many students, even from religious homes, who were attracted by radical organizations. While there were undoubtedly some knowledgeable Zionist leaders, there existed no organized group whose express function was to guide and assist young and old in the study and understanding of Modern Zionism. Zionist activity was limited almost entirely to fund-raising, and even that was done in a haphazard manner. In Winnipeg, the centre of the region, both the administrative and secretarial work was done by a single part-time employee; in the medium-sized and small centres, the secretarial work was done by volunteers. The fund-raising drives in the small centres were conducted annually by the Western National Vice-President who lived in Saskatoon. In Winnipeg and in the middle-sized cities, the campaigns were conducted by "guest speakers" who were engaged for this purpose by Head Office in Montreal and who were almost always imported from the U.S.A. The appeals for contributions were largely senitmental and tear-jerking in form and content. The emphasis was on "helping our poor brethren in Palestine", on the poverty and misery of East European Jewry who were in dire need of a haven. There was hardly any mention of national rebirth, or cultural revival, on the rebuilding of the land and people of Israel. Hadassah (whose exemplary fund-raising achievements were due entirely to dedicated volunteers) professed education as an integral part of their program, but "education" to them, as to all other Zionist groups, usually meant "educating the public for generous giving". My protests that we were denigrating a great Renaissance Movement by turning it into a mere charitable organization, were countered by officials and speakers alike in terms such as these: by appealing for money we do educational work, for in order to succeed we must tell our listeners about the situation, the problems and needs of our people in Europe and in Palestine. The definition of a Zionist, attributed to the King of Bulgaria, as "a person who approaches a second person for a donation in order to send a third person to Palestine" would thus have to be paraphrased, as applied to Canada and the U.S.A., as "a Canadian Zionist is a person who obtains a donation from a second person to send a non-Canadian or non-American Jew to Palestine".

Naturally, those most neglected by this approach were the schools and the youth who had little money to contribute. It was not only the West that had no Young Judaen Director; there was not even a national youth director at that time. As to the schools, "what does Zionism or the Zionist Organization have to do with or in the schools?", except of course to raise whatever little money is possible for the Jewish National Fund, in order "to educate our children to give when they grow up". Small wonder then that many young Jews in Canada (and elsewhere) were cultivating all kinds of vineyards, except their own.

No Jewish Background Necessary

Jewish knowledge or Zionist orientation were not necessary qualifications for those who served as leaders or employees of the Zionist Organization. The person in charge of the Zionist office thus had very little Jewish background, and could not offer any guidance to students who were more informed than he. Unbelievable as it may sound, an active Young Judaen member who later became a paid official actually asked me whether Jerusalem was in Palestine. It is a telling commentary on the Zionist leadership that they considered the home-base of the First National Western Vice President, a small community with about 125 Jewish families, to be the natural centre for the Executive Director and his office, rather than Winnipeg with its vital Jewish community of about 25,000. As a matter of fact, the law office of the Vice President was to serve also as the executive director's office. It is quite indicative of the prevailing attitude in Jewish life that the person who happens to be the chairman of an organization or school is considered better qualified to direct their activities than the trained and experienced professional executive director. After all, the chairman is a volunteer, while the expert "is merely a paid official". As a matter of fact, when I dared, on a number of occasions, to disagree with the opinions of leading officers, I was reminded that I was a paid employee. So, without any thought about the merit of the case and without asking the paid official about his view, I was dispatched with my family to Saskatoon.

My stay in Saskatoon was short lived not because of the leadership's sudden awareness that a small community was not an appropriate centre for an intensive and extensive Zionist program. It was rather brought about by the impolitic act of a chairman in a small town, who showed me the letter he had received from the vice president about my visit. In essence, he introduced me thus: "we have engaged a young, inexperienced fellow as our executive director for a trial period. Please observe him carefully and let me know as soon as possible whether he is suitable for the position". This was my introduction in an organization where the artificial "build-up" was considered the most effective means of insuring the success of their "guest" campaigners! I immediately dispatched a wire to head office in Montreal and to the national vice president in Winnipeg demanding that my head office be moved to Winnipeg or I would move myself forthwith out of the picture. Fortunately, the campaigns I had already conducted in some of the small towns had been so successful that the national office acted promptly to accede to my demand. Recalling my father's advice against my accepting the position in Western Canada, I could not help but reflect: "I have come all the way from Jerusalem and New York to be judged as to my fitness to conduct campaigns in two-bit towns". Apropos this feeling of mine, when I explained my sudden reappearance in Winnipeg to my colleague Yehoshuah Giladi Geldfarb, a hale and hearty Hebrew scholar and wit, he related to me a story which expressed his and my father's feelings about the level of Jewish scholarship in Winnipeg. Mr. Giladi once met my father walking alone late at night. Giladi confronted him with the Talmudic injunction *"a talmid Chacham* (a scholar) ought not to go out alone at night for fear of the *mazikim* (evil spirits)"*, (Brachot 43). My father responded: "I have two answers for you, Mr. Giladi: First, the Winnipeg mazikim are incapable of distinguishing between a talmid chacham and an *am-haaretz* (an illiterate); second, the Winnipeg mazikim do not consider me a talmid chacham." As to the meaning of this Talmudic statement, I understood, at that time, the word mazikim to mean literally "evil spirits", but as I think of it now I believe it to mean such dangers as those presented by "ladies of the night". . . .

The response of the national office emboldened me to take a giant step forward (skipping so to speak from kindergarten to post graduate work in the political sphere. . .) in proceeding to map out courageously and clearly what I considered to be the appropriate domain and scope of Zionist work. However, notwithstanding the support from the two-thousand-mile-distant national office, I would not have been able to get off the ground without the tacit approval of Reub Kimmel, the Winnipeg National Vice President, who later defended and supported me in my revolutionary endeavours. He once explained to me that it was not really difficult for him to stand by me, because these endeavours did not in the least affect my success in fund-raising; "as a matter of fact, they seem to be a factor in your success".

The Zionist office was contained in one small room in the Israelite Press Building, which was situated on an out-of-the-way street. In considering the proper location for the Executive Director's office, the vice president and others thought the downtown business section to be the most suitable because of its accessibility to business and professional people. Knowing there was a very large room available in the Talmud Torah building, I maintained that it should be the natural home of Zionist activity. To strengthen my case, I argued that the rent would be considerably less. Furthermore, I reasoned, an office in the business section would come to a standstill at the end of the business day, while the Talmud Torah building with its large hall and meeting rooms could and should be the centre of Zionist educational and cultural life. Logical as these reasons were in and by themselves, my secret motive was — to be close to what I considered the foundation and heart of Zionism: the Talmud Torah, its hundreds of pupils, its teachers and its leaders. Many months later, when it became abundantly clear to all concerned where my heart lay, one of the very top Hadassah leaders reacted thus to this strange phenomenon:

Feigning a foreign accent, she exclaimed: "Our Executive Director spends much of his time with Hi brew tichers!" Indeed, woe would have been to the "paid official" if he had spent any of his "fundraising time" for this unimportant pastime. as it was, nobody dared fault me for giving much of my time and effort to education and youth, because it was never at the expense of any "legitimate" Zionist activity. My preoccupation with education, however, came under blistering criticism when I declared at a Hadassah Convention that the first and most sacred duty of Jewish mothers was to ensure that their children receive an adequate Jewish education both at home and in school. I even had the chutzpah to emphasize that if there be a conflict between Hadassah work and looking after the children's education, the latter must come first. While the public criticism of my sacreligious declaration was subdued and gentlewomanly, the leaders let loose their fury in private. I was surprised they did not ask for my resignation. I was consoled, however, by the compliments of Mr. Max Freedman, the noted foreign correspondent and brother of Chief Justice Mr. Samuel Freedman. Max was also a guest speaker at the convention, and he congratulated me publicly and personally for my vision and courage.

How Do We Know You Too Are Not a Crook?

The first U.P.A. (United Palestine Appeal) drive I conducted could have been amusing were it not for its serious overtones. The town's thirty Jewish families — men, women, and children — gathered in the synagogue. Wihtout knowing the reason, I sensed that the atmosphere was highly charged. The audience listened intently to my description of the situation in Europe, the struggle of the Aliyah Bet Movement (what the British Authorities considered illegal immigration) to save as many Jews as possible from what was soon to become the nazi inferno, and the determined efforts to continue with the revival and rebuilding of the people and land of Israel. As I sat down with the feeling of satisfaction about the apparent good effect of my speech, the chairman sprang to his feet and nearly knocked me out of my senses with his question, "How do we know that you too are not a crook?" When I came too, I could hardly hear my voice murmuring, "what is the meaning of this?!" The chairman held forth about his community's distrust of organizations and their fund-raisers. On one occasion, he said, an individual sold them sh'kalim, but none of them ever received shekel (the shekel was a means by which the purchaser declared himself to be a member of the World Zionist Organization and was thereby qualified to vote for delegates to the World Zionist Congress). On another occasion, they had been sold "nachshon" shares (Nachson was an organization in maritime development, created by the Histradut after the ports in Eretz Israel had been closed down by Arab stevedores), but none of them ever saw their shares. Furthermore, he continued, their complaints to the organizazations were never answered. Difficult as it was for me to give credence to such serious accusations, I decided not to question them. Instead, I pointed out that I was not a representative of any of these organizations, nor was it fair to question my integrity because of other persons' dishonesty. Following a somewhat lengthy discussion of the attitudes of national organizations to small communities, the meeting decided unanimously to proceed with my campaign. As further evidence of their trust in me, "especially since I was the son of Chief Rabbi Horowitz", they handed me the cash proceeds of the meeting.

This experience left me in a state of shock and bewilderment. Coming as I did from a place in which the head of the education and culture department of Histradut in Jerusalem would not use a sheet of the organization's paper for personal purposes, I could not lightly dismiss this incident. Without waiting for my return to Winnipeg, I immediately despatched a report to the national office and sent copies to the Western vice presidents. To my amazement, I received no reactions at all from any of them throughout the three or four weeks of my tour. When I confided this story to some leading Zionists, I was advised not to concern myself with this matter, "as it has nothing to do with our organization". Months later, I repeated the story at a meeting in one of the larger cities, and I questioned the justification and the wisdom of such cover-ups. The consensus was: As it is, we have a very difficult task in raising sufficient funds. Should such matters become public knowledge, it could seriously affect our campaigns. I disagreed, but was too preoccupied with my work to give the matter any further consideration.

The State of Jewish Education in the West

Because I considered education the very foundation of Zionist philosophy and achievement ("Zionism" being defined as the national and cultural renaissance of the Jewish people in its ancestral land), I devoted much time to the study of the state of Jewish Education in every community I visited. The general situation as I saw it is described in the appendix "Jewish Education in Canada — Suggestions for Reform". Here I shall relate a few events, incidents and anecdotes that will contribute to an understanding of the state of Jewish education in Western Canada during the thirties and forties.

A School is Like a Grocery Store

The first school I visited was, on the surface, much like other schools I had known. A teacher with an East-European background was waiting with little relish for his pupils to trickle in from their full day of studies in the public schools. Bristling with pent-up physical energy, they were obviously too tired mentally to absorb a "foreign language"; to wade through the difficult Biblical text, "simplified" and truncated though it was in their so-called modern books, and to try "to find their hands and feet" in the maze of historic (at times I could become hysteric while watching young children "give back" the historic facts), dates and boring data. The teaching methods were largely archaic — learning by rote, by the medium of translation and, of course, in the tedious ashkenazic pronunciation. When I was invited by the teacher to test his pupils, it was clear to me that even if a student translated correctly the meaning of a total sentence (which was not a frequent occurrence), he would often fail to understand the meaning of individual words. The whole atmosphere in the classroom was so stultifying that I had to struggle against dozing off right there and then. After the children were "dismissed" (a more suitable term would be "liberated"), I attempted to discuss with the teacher-principal questions of purpose, content and method. He dismissed me with the assertion: "I see my task as that of a grocer. I give my customers what they want. If it is *tsibeles* (onions) they desire, *tsibeles* they get. Those who ask for Hebrew, I give Hebrew, and those who like Yiddish, get Yiddish". Fortunately for both the children and the teacher, he moved at the end of the school year to the East where he became a truck driver. The teacher-principal who followed him, Rabbi Sol Horowitz, was their first modern spiritual leader (until then, the *shochet* had served also in that capacity, a common phenomenon at that time even in the larger cities). Though using more or less the same content and text-books, he infused some life into the school with his vitality and sense of humour, and by linking closely what the children studied in the school with the life of the synagogue. The Regina Junior Congregation became a model to teachers in the area, who came to observe and to emulate. . .

"Halechem Haklokel" — The Miserable Bread

It was my friend Yechiel Walker, a Hebrew teacher from Lithuania, where the Jewish teacher was highly regarded, who characterized the meagre livelihood of the Hebrew teacher in Canada as *halechem haklokel*, the miserable bread (in the sense the Israelites complained to Moses "and our soul loatheth this light bread", Numbers 25,5), which was of course a direct result of his status in the community. It was a striking indication of the decline of the Judaic tradition that the people who were the first in history[1] to introduce compulsory education for the children of all the people, now relegated the teacher to the lowly position of a "melamed" (a term which literally means teacher but which carries the connotation of an impractical, ineffectual person who is incapable of making a living in a productive or really useful manner). True, the effects of the Great Depression were still very visible in 1939, but Jewish communities were not so poor that they had to deny a "decent living" to the teachers of their children. Furthermore, leaders and parents alike failed to realize that the low status of the Hebrew teachers prevented them from having any impact on the children; teachers were seldom, if at all, invited as guests to their parents' homes or to social affairs. Generally speaking, the Jewish teacher was isolated in "his" community. No wonder therefore that no Canadian Jewish boy or girl (and much less their foreign-born parents) would deign to even consider donning the mantle of a *melamed*. That "job" was definitely not for a Jewish boy or girl!

In one of the first cities I visited I encountered the *lechem haklokel* situation in its extreme form. The quivering voice on the phone was that of a distraught person. Would I kindly give him some of my time. He had heard of my deep interest in education and wanted to discuss with me his distressed situation. He entered haltingly my hotel room, with hat in hand, veritably as an *ani bapetach*, as a "beggar at the door". I put him at ease and made him feel he was speaking to a fellow *melamed*. Fully familiar though I was with the general situation, I was shaken by his story. He had appealed to the chairman of the board of education for an increase in his scanty salary to enable him literally to "keep body and soul together". The chairman was adamant in his rejection, pleading the community's budgetary difficulties. To stress his dire economic condition, the teacher raised his shoe to show him the torn sole of his shoe. The reaction of the chairman? He remonstrated with the teacher for endangering his health by wearing torn shoes in the winter! "I am sure", declared the chairman, "That Mr. Y. (owner of a large general store) would let you have a pair of shoes on the instalment plan, or he might even present you with a pair as a gift." Disgusted though he was, the teacher further dramatized his condition by stating that many a time he did not have a stamp to send a letter to his son. "Shame on you, Mr. D. I am really surprised at you. Don't you realize I would gladly give you some stamps once in a while!" Unbelievable? Yes, I thought so too, until the story was verified in my discussion with the chairman, who — by the way — was a very fine and friendly successful business man and devoted communal leader.

The plight of the Hebrew teacher of that period is illustrated by the

[1]H.G. Wells writes in his History of the World: "The Jewish religion, because it was a literature-sustained religion, led to the first efforts to provide elementary instruction for all the children of the community". And the Talmud records (in Tractate Baba Batra 21) that Yehoshu'ah Ben Gamala, who lived in the first century B.C.E., enacted the law that there be a teacher in every province and in every city. And in Tractate Sanhedrin page 50, we read: "It is forbidden to live in any city where there is no teacher."

following story. A committee was considering the qualifications of an applicant for a teaching post. His curriculum vitae as well as his recommendations were highly satisfactory. The chairman concluded the discussion, stating, "then we are agreed, gentlemen, on the appointment of this candidate". At this, one of the members banged on the table and said, "just a minute, gentlemen, I am strongly opposed to this person". Asked to explain, he expressed his surprise that they had ignored the all important fact of the number of the years of his experience. To the chairman's query as to whether twenty years were insufficient, the objector declared, "on the contrary! With as many as twenty years' experience, he either didn't work hard enough to teach his pupils anything, or, if he did, he most certainly must have a *tchichotke* (tuberculosis) by now!" (In those days, some people thought that tuberculosis was caused by hard work!)

What then caused such an attitude to the teacher of one's children? Could it have been that the exhortation "thou shalt teach them diligently unto thy children" (Deuteronomy 6:4-9), which Jews are enjoined to recite daily, had been turned into a mechanical recitation by people who did not even comprehend its meaning! Could it have been caused by the complete unawareness of the existence of a *yehoshu'ah Ben Gamala* and of the primary role of education from the very beginnings of Jewish history?

Though I encountered only one more such pitiful case in my extensive travels in the West, and though these were extreme manifestations of the beginnings of the deterioration process of basic Judaic values, Jewish education looked much like the economic and social status of the teacher in those communities. It would, however, be entirely misleading to suggest that the principal-"grocer"-truck-driver was in the least representative of those who carried the burden of Jewish education at that time. While the situation described here may have been symptomatic of the incipient erosion in the primacy of Jewish education, most teachers in the West were knowledgeable in Judaics; they were genuinely concerned about and with the preservation of *yiddishkeit* as they understood it, and were dedicated to their tasks in spite of their economic and social hardships. No matter how critical one could be of the way they envisioned, or failed to envision altogether, the changing nature of Judaism in the emerging Jewish community; no matter how much one may have questioned their educational methods, or lack of educational methods, the teachers of that period knew at least what they were teaching, believed — on the whole — in what they were doing, and worked hard to transmit some of their knowledge to their charges. If they had little success in educating a generation of Jews with an adequate knowledge and — more important — with the proper orientation and direction about their future as Canadian Jews, this was chiefly because they, their programs and their methods were transplanted from a Jewish milieu vastly different from the new Canadian Jewish society in its formative stages. Thus, bearing in mind the European background of both the teachers and the lay leaders, they established and conducted what could be considered, in the main, good schools, especially in Winnipeg, Calgary and Edmonton. Furthermore, the more learned and effective educators did leave their imprint on many of their students, some of whom are to be found in the forefront of many Jewish endeavours in Canada, the U.S.A. and Israel.

Everything Depends on Chance, Even the Torah Scrolls In the Holy Ark
(Habent sua fata libelli)
Zohar, Naso 134

Surprising as it may be, the first Hebrew Day School was established neither in gigantic New York nor in big Montreal, but in remote Edmonton, a small Jewish community of about 135 Jewish families. When I first saw this wonder with my own eyes, I thought of the statement in the *Zohar* that "everything depends on chance, even the Torah Scrolls in the Holy Ark". A small group of people, spearheaded by Jacob Baltzan, its founder and first president, and by a Hebrew educator, the late Arie (Leo) Pekarsky from Poland, had the vision and spunk to pioneer, earlier than Montreal and New York, in an area that was to contribute enormously to the vitality of Hebrew education and the preservation of Jewish life in Canada and the U.S.A. Pekarsky became its first principal, and when he took up the practice of law he continued to give to the school much of his time and devotion. He was followed by three competent and dedicated educators, Messrs. Leibel Tussman, Ephrayim Malamuth and Moshe Goelman, who each contributed to the development and success of this remarkable institution. When I first visited it in 1939, I was impressed with its comparatively high scholastic level and with its natural atmosphere. Edmonton was also unique in that it had (and still has, I believe) only one school which is supported by almost the entire Jewish community. The clamour of some people at different times for a separate Yiddish school or Sunday school was always successfully withstood by the united community's intelligent, resourceful and strong leadership.

A Good Afternoon School in Calgary

Although the day school was to be established in Calgary much later than in Edmonton, the Calgary Hebrew School was one of the best afternoon schools I had seen anywhere. Its founders included some learned individuals, such as H. Cooper, J. Diamond, J. Dubisky, H.L. Epstein, Henry Goldberg, Shaye Jaffe and J. Joffe. Their orientation was national-religious, and they always made every effort to obtain the best possible teachers. To a certain extent, the element of chance played its part also there. For its first highly qualified principals and teachers came by chance rather than by design. When I first visited this school, its principal was David Eisenberg, an experienced and devoted teacher from Bialiystok, but people were still speaking with reverence about Moshe Levine, a Hebrew scholar from Poland who had laid the foundation of its modern curriculum. It was equally by mere chance that Ella Katzin (Stoffer), an experienced Kindergarten teacher from Poland, had settled in Calgary, which made it possible to establish a Kindergarten. The curriculum was ambitious and elaborate, especially during Mr. Levine's tenure, when it included the study of Chumash and Rashi in the original texts as well as some Talmud. The first crop of graduates included highly informed and dedicated young men who became the vanguard of organized Jewish life and activity in the city. Some of them achieved distinction as scholars and leaders, notably Dr. Willaim Epstein, a lawyer-scholar who later became the Chief of the Disarmament Commission of the United Nations Secretariat and is serving at present as Special UNITAR Fellow at the U.N. and as Visiting Professor at Carlton University in Ottawa and at the University of Victoria in British Columbia; Dr. Joseph Cooper, a brilliant chemist; Nathan Safran who served as Vice Principal of the Alberta School of Art and Technology; Dr. Carl Safran, a psychologist who rose to the position of Chief Superintendent of Schools in Calgary; and Ben Sherwood, a chemical engineer who later became the manager of Imperial Oil Co. Of equal importance to me and my story was that they, more than any other group of young people, formed the nucleus of a revitalized Zionist Movement in Western Canada.

Apropos the element of chance in determining the types of schools that came into being in that formative period, the question comes to mind as to whether a day school would have been established in Calgary had Mr. Pekarsky made his home there instead of in Edmonton. While the right individual is essential for such events, the elemtns of the proper social context plays an equal if not more decisive role in such developments. The Jews of Edmonton were a much more cohesive community than those of Calgary, for the majority in the former city were of a similar "ethnic" origin, namely from Russia and Lithuania, while the Jewish population in Calgary was more heterogenous and included a large proportion of Polish Jews, many of whom happened to be yiddishists and bundists whose orientation was socialist rather than Zionist, and non-religious (some even anti-religious) rather than traditional. These elements therefore established their own school, the

J.L. Peretz Shule, so that the forces and resources of the community were sharply divided.

In Winnipeg too the elements of chance and Jewish population-composition played their role in the emergence of their educational institutions. Winnpeg had several distinguished Orthodox Rabbis, a significant number of learned European teachers, many traditional Jews, a very capable and dynamic principal by the name of Levit, and some generous philanthropists, notably Joseph Wolinsky, David Secter and J. Weidman: all contributed to laying the foundation of one of the most successful Hebrew schools in North America. I recall how deeply moved I was when I first visited this Talmud Torah during Chanukah of 1926. Hundreds of children, boys and girls, participated in a lively program: they recited, acted, danced and sang, all in Hebrew. The school was given the enthusiastic support of the Orthodox Rabbis though it was co-educational (the orthodox Rabbis of Winnipeg were undoubtedly as pious as the present orthodox Rabbis and leaders in Montreal and Toronto, who do not sanction co-educational schools), and included in its curriculum such "secular" subjects as Modern Hebrew Literature. On the professional side, it was the principal-superintendent Rabbi Sol Horowitz who gave it his entire devotion, his resourcefulness in initiating various novel fund-raising schemes, and his ever alertness to the implanting of new ideas and competent instructors.

As in Calgary, Winnipeg had a large proportion of Polish Jews, a great many of whom brought along with them the socialist-yiddishist-bundist ideology. They too established a *Peretz Shule*, whose aggressive leaders such as Alter Cherniak, Velvel Keller, Feivel Simkin, and the Selchen brothers, gave much of themselves to maintain a very effective school which enjoyed an enviable reputation throughout North America. When I arrived on the scene in 1939, its principal was Mr. Avraham Golomb, one of the most noted yiddishist ideologues. Although we never met face to face, and had no occasion to discuss our divergent views, I felt very strongly his antagonism to much that I represented.

However, not all the yiddishists in Winnipeg were non-Zionists. Many of them were socialist-Zionists and supported the labor movement in Eretz Israel. There thus arose another educational institution, the Folk Shule, which used Yiddish as the language of instruction, but included the study of some Hebrew, beginning from Grade Four. It too gained a distinguished reputation.

Although I stayed in Winnipeg for only a short time after my first arrival in 1926, and my visits from the Yeshivah were infrequent and short, I made an attempt to compare — with the help of my father, my brother Sol and others — 1939 with 1926. In summary, my conclusion was that signs of decline were already visible in people's dedication to the

Jewish education of their children. Some of these were: 1) There were no more individuals like those in such small towns as Brandon, Manitoba, where a single family, Mr. and Mrs. Reuben Shechter, went to such lengths as to plead with my father — in 1927 — to send my 17-year old brother Sol to join them in Brandon for the sole purpose of teaching their children *yiddishkeit*, for which he received board and room and spending money. The salary he was paid for teaching the children of the other 30 families went to my parents and contributed substantially to my father's meagre income; 2) During my extensive travels in the West in 1939, I heard the wondrous tales of single families in small places who maintained *"a gantsen melamed"* (a full-time teacher) to teach their children, but those were tales of times gone by; 3) Educators of the calibre of Melech Magid, poet Dr. Shimon Ginzberg, scholar Moshe Levine, Leo Pekarsky and Israel Baruch were not to be found any longer in Regina, Saskatoon, Calgary, Edmonton and Vancouver — respectively. Magid was needed in big Montreal, Ginzberg went to Eretz Israel where he became the editor of the Do-ar Hayom, and Baruch tired of and retired from Hebrew education. (Note the Hebrew names of these educators as compared with the anglicized names of present day Hebrew function-aries whose European accents are heavier than those of their predeces-sors.) 4) There was already a Sunday School in Winnipeg (unthinkable in the twenties), and new voices, albeit relatively few, were already heard in the land in clamor for sunday schools in some of the larger cities West of Winnipeg.

Chapter 6
Hebrew Education
Emerges from Isolation

Isolation, caused in part by geographic factors and mostly by the absence of a regional or national coordinating body, was perhaps one of the main obstacles to progress in Jewish education. The great distances between cities and the long severe winters tended to isolate Jewish organizations, especially Hebrew schools, in each community. There was practically no communication whatsoever between school administrations and staffs of different centres, and each institution was an island unto itself. This situation contributed much to the helpless feeling of "aloneness" not only of Hebrew teachers and pupils but also of school committees who were always at a loss for lack of some "address" where they could turn for guidance and help. I therefore set out to establish a central body for the purpose of bringing together all the schools in areas where joint planning and action were desirable and feasible. To me, it was natural that the Zionist Movement should be the father of such an organization, but it took some insistent persuasion to obtain the official approval of the Zionist leadership in Winnipeg to what seemed a revolutionary idea. In no small measure was this achieved by the previous preparation of the ground in all centres, large and small, in Western Canada; this in turn was facilitated by the fact that, unlike Winnipeg, many communal leaders were active on both Zionist and school boards, which in itself may have been an indication of the organic relationship between Zionism and education.

The first step was to call a Western Educational Conference, which was held in September 1939, about four months after I took office. All the major cities, (except Vancouver, which was then really "an extension of Seattle Washington") and many of the smaller centres were represented by both professional and lay people. The three-day sessions dealt with the philosophy and content of Hebrew education, with the realities and possibilities for improvement, and with the ways and means of forming a permanent central authority for the whole region. The public meeting (in those days such gatherings were referred to as "mass meetings"), which attracted many hundreds of people into the large hall and balconies of the Winnipeg Talmud Torah, gave its attention to the status of the school in the community and to the youth problem. (It was not necessary at all to speak in Winnipeg on the importance of Jewish education. That was taken for granted!) It is significant — both in a positive and negative sense — that nobody brought up the problem of the economic situation of the teacher. That was in harmony with "the tradition". The teacher's raison d'être was to devote himself to the education of the young! If any participants had any thoughts about their material needs, perhaps they realized intuitively that any change in that direction was dependent on the emergence of the school as the focus of the community.

To insure the effectiveness and continuity of a coordinated educational program for the West, a Hebrew Educators Council was elected, with educator Yehoshua Giladi-Helbfarb as president. The Executive and Council included professionals and officials of all the major centres — including Vancouver — as well as a goodly representation of the small communities. Some of the important decision were: a) general guidelines for a uniform curriculum should be submitted for study at the next conference; b) the study of Zionism and Eretz Israel should be an integral part of the educational program; c) new staff members should be engaged with the knowledge, guidance and assistance of the executive; d) a conference should be held annually, each time in a different city. Although I realized that I and my office would have to give much time to make the Council and its work a reality, it did not occur to me that I would be called upon, by unanimous voice, to act as the official consultant-supervisor of all the Hebrew schools in the region. I thus found myself holding what amounted to two full-time positions with the one salary of $100 a month. It didn't occur to me or to anybody else that I should receive even a nominal remuneration for the additional position. As a matter of fact, when Mr. David Secter, honorary president of the Zionist Organization and of the newly created Educators Council, suggested to me, on the occasion of the birth of my second son, that I receive a $25 increase in my monthly salary, I stated categorically that I was working for "a poor people" with tremendous needs and that, furthermore, if twenty pounds monthly were adequate for Moshe Shertok, then head of the political department of the Jewish Agency, my equivalent of $100 should be sufficient for me and my family! As I write this I cannot help thinking about the hierarchy and budget that present day bureaucrats would require to do the work I did then in an area that extended from the twin cities of Fort William-Port Arthur to Victoria B.C.

Yiddishists vs. Hebraists

The repercussions of the conference were not entirely positive. The ideological Yiddishists, who have always constituted an aggressive and powerful group in Western Canada and especially in Winnipeg, were aroused by the success of the Hebraist-Zionists. There was keen competition *"oif der Yiddisher gas"* (literally, "on the Jewish street"), in Winnipeg for the souls of Jewish children, and it is to the credit of the Yiddishist-Leftists that they were more highly motivated, better organized and more dedicated than "the other side". That was why their influence in the community, particularly in the Canadian Jewish Congress, was by far out of proportion to their numbers. A campaign was started against the "usurpation" by the Zionists of a function that rightly belonged to the Canadian Jewish Congress. They disregarded the fact that there had been a vacuum in this area. It is true that there had been a regional educational convention, under the aegis of the C.J.C., in 1925(!) in Saskatoon, but there had been no continuing program of activities, whatsoever. Mr. Meir Averbach, Secretary of the C.J.C., would offer some guidance to small communities (the larger ones did not consider him an authority in Hebrew education), but his approach to educational content and methods was precisely one of the reasons that prompted us to include those small centres in our program.

Their arrows were aimed largely at me personally for the obvious reason that it would be easier to discredit an individual than to take on the Zionist Organization. My frequent travels outside the city left the Winnipeg arena free for agitation against me. The bugaboo of "disunity" was raised against "those who would *machen shabbes far sich"*, (literally, "making Sabbath for themselves", denoting the segmentation of action), in the educational field. But, here too, another reality was completely disregarded. For the "segmentation" was a stubborn fact of life, brought about by the fundamental disagreement between the Talmud Torah and Peretz Shule about the philosophy and content of Jewish education. One of the reasons why the time was not ripe for working together in such areas as education was the Yiddishists' negative and, in some cases, hostile attitude to the revival of Hebrew as a spoken language. I personally never had the opportunity to come in contact with the extremist Yiddishist-bundist elements. Even so, I was astonished when I was told by Baruch Zuckerman, a very popular world Labor Zionist Leader, whose attitude to Yiddish was certainly most positive, that he had heard Mr. Keller, a top Yiddishist and C.J.C. leader in Winnipeg, refer to Hebrew as "a *neveile"* (a corpse), and "a *gepeigerte shprach"* (a dead language). (The connotation of these two expressions in Yiddish is much more offensive than their English counterpart). I do not remember whether Mr. Zuckerman was treated to these offensive remarks in a private discussion or at a public meeting.

The Yiddishsts' negative attitude to Hebrew as a spoken language was probably motivated by their fear that the revival of Hebrew, already widely used by a renascent and vibrant Jewish community in Eretz Israel, would pose a serious threat to the preservation of Yiddish as "the language of communication among the Jewish masses". There was then, as there still is today (though in very limited circles), a heroic devotion to keeping alive the cultural values of the Yiddish language and literature for future generations.

Speaking Yiddish at all times and preserving the "purity" of the language thus became a sacred task even more than Hebrew among Hebraists. Some Yiddishist devotees would go so far as to render into Yiddish some untranslatable English expressions no matter how ludicrous they may have sounded. Thus, in referring to the soft drink 7Up, they would say *"ziben aroif"*. The story is told about Mr. A. Golomb, then principal of the Peretz Shule, who was walking with a young woman, a teacher at the Shule, along Portage Avenue in Winnipeg. When they passed by Child's Restaurant, he decided to invite her in for a snack. Intent on using "pure" Yiddish, he asked her *"wilt hier gehn mit mir tzu kind?"* *Kind* is the Yiddish for child, and *"gehn tsu kind"* means to give birth to a child, so that the question whether she wanted to go with him to Child's Restaurant could be taken to mean "do you want to have a child with me?" The young lady quickly retorted: *"a dank, nisht mit eich"*, ("thank you, but no, not with you!")

Furthermore, it would have been impossible to work together with them at that time on such subjects as Jewish educational ideology and content because of the violently anti-religious and anti-Zionist attitudes of the bundists and of a goodly number of the ideological Yiddishists. It is a fact that some of these people were *apikorsim lehachis* (atheists for spite). Some of them would deliberately congregate, in those years, in front of synagogues on Yom Kippur to eat and smoke in public. *"Gei mach Shabbes met azeleche"* — try to make sabbath with such . . . (it is ironic that the sacred word Sabbath was used by these anti-religionists to express the idea of separate action).

The argument of "disunity" brought forth a controversy as to the functions of the Zionist Organization of Canada vis-a-vis the Canadian Jewish Congress in the field of Jewish education, which will be dealt with later. I was, however, distracted, to some degree, from my many obligations and tasks. Even my president Giladi-Gelbfarb would waste much of our time on rumours and gossip. I was amused one morning when he barged into my office and, clasping his huge hands, exclaimed, *"Aren, du veist wose die shtot zogt?"* (Do you know what the city is saying?"). He then proceeded to tell me "what the city was saying" (the equivalent of "they say"). When these morning visitations turned into a regular ritual, I cut him short once and demanded, "tell me Gelfarb, how is old Mr. Cooper this morning?" For what happened was, that on his way to the Talmud Torah, Mr. Gelbfarb would never fail to first have a chat with the old proprietor of a tiny candy store just across the street from my office, and it was from this omniscient Mr. Cooper that Mr. Gelbfarb would learn "what the city was saying". That finally put an end to the sessions on *"wose die shtot zogt"*.

I thus had to counteract false accusations that I was anti-Yiddish, anti-C.J.C. and, of all things, anti-Histradut, of which I happened to be an ardent follower. One fellow even tried to intimidate me. This person was a member of both the Jewish National Fund and the C.J.C. executives. One morning he entered my office unannounced and told me solemnly that he came with some friendly advice. "Aron", he said, "you have set against you some very powerful forces. They could break much stronger people than you. My advice to you as a friend is to desist". I was flabbergasted! I pointed out to him that to be for Hebrew does not mean to be against Yiddish, to be for Zionism does not mean to be against the C.J.C., and to work for the Z.O.C. does not mean to be against the Histradut. I challenged him to prove to me that I ever uttered even one word, orally or in writing, against Yiddish, the C.J.C., or the Histradut. I made it clear to him that an education system that focuses on the national Hebrew revival is the prerogative and responsibility of the Zionist movement, that people who represent other philosophies are entirely free to cultivate their own gardens, that all our activities are "for" and not "against", and that nothing would deter us from our course to strengthen Hebrew education. He smiled knowingly, saying "watch out Aron, they'll get you!" Amused more than angry, I assured him he need not worry about me. It was unlikely, I said, that I could be forced out of my job by intrigue, but that if such intrigue would make it impossible for me to do my work effectively, there was no need to be concerned about my future, for I had decided a long time ago that the whole Jewish world was my home. I never knew, nor did I inquire as to whether he brought me his own "message", or whether it was "inspired" by others.

"Jealousy Among Scribes Increases Wisdom":
(Baba Batra 21)

The positive result of this controversy was, to paraphrase a Talmudic saying, that the jealousy of scribes increases action. Both sides sharpened their alertness and enhanced their activities. On my part, I spent many hours in the schools of all the communities I visited, I studied their realities and potentialities, I attended school-board meetings, I focused on ecudation and culture in all my speeches and lectures, and I made every effort to help in the improvement of the economic and social status of the Hebrew teacher.

The second annual conference took place in Calgary, which — always alert and attuned to the needs of Jewish education — almost insisted on hosting it. The curriculum, prepared by the president, Giladi Gelbfarb, and my syllabus on Zionism and Eretz Israel, had been submitted to all the schools well in advance of the conference, so that we were in a position to exchange views and incorporate the ideas of other educators. While the program was adopted by all the participating institutions, it was agreed that complete uniformity was not desirable and that the curriculum was to serve only as a basis, allowing and even encouraging variations in accordance with the particular circumstances and needs of each community.

The meeting of minds and hearts of teachers and laymen engendered a feeling of satisfaction, and all noted the progress that had been made in the space of one short year. There was a realization that the individual schools were no longer alone and that we were well on the road to securing a continuing central body that would concern itself with the needs and problems of all the Hebrew schools in the region.

It Is Forbidden to Live in a City Where There Is No Teacher (Sanhedrin, 17)

It is natural for a society that prohibits taking away children from their studies "even for the building of the Holy Temple" (Shabbat, 104) to place the highest value on those who are to teach the children. We thus find in Tractate Shabbat 119 that a community whose children do not attend school is destined to destruction. And obviously, there cannot be any children attending school without teachers.

The surest measure of the maturity of a society is therefore in its efforts to train teachers for its children. By this criterion, the Canadian Jewish community was yet in its diapers at that juncture in its history. All the teachers came from the outside, mostly from Europe and a mere trickle from Eretz Israel, and there was not even an awareness of the need to think of the future. When the outside sources were closed with the outbreak of the Second World War, there were simply not enough teachers to go around. Not even then could I detect any thinking about the necessity of establishing a teachers training school to alleviate the acute shortage and eventually to free us of our total dependence on others.

The small communities were again the greatest sufferers, for what chance was there for any instructors to go to such places as Moose Jaw and Medicine Hat? Our Educators Council therefore made what seemed a most unrealistic attempt to prepare teachers specifically for those towns. The ubiquitous realists scoffed at us with the question, "where will you Don Quixotians find young people who will agree to go to Melville or Lethbridge?" To our own amazement, we succeeded in rounding up about twenty Young Judaen and Habodim activists, who — unlike their elders — understood the critical nature of this problem, and who — fired with a sense of mission — volunteered to be trained for a year of service in such remote places as Leader and Kamsack.

What happened to that grandiose scheme? It existed for a little over a year thanks to the educators who volunteered their services: Yehoshua Giladi-Gelbfarb, Garfinkel, Klein, Kushner and Aron Horowitz. They believed that "the community" would surely rejoice in the seminar's success and would agree somehow to find the small amount that was required for its continued existence. Alas, the project came to an end when it became clear that no organization (not even my Zionist movement) or group of individuals were ready to finance it when "all the available money was needed for our poor brethren in Europe and Palestine". For all that, this project did produce some fruit: All the students benefitted from a year's study of Bible, Hebrew literature, Talmud, History of Zionism and Eretz Israel, and Child Psychology; a few of the students did indeed go to teach in some of the smaller communities, and some of them later became Hebrew teachers and principals in Canadian and American cities. (This subject is also treated in the Appendix "Hebrew Education In Canada — Suggestions for Reform".)

Chapter 7
A Corner in Our Life

The debate was raging in Winnipeg: Should the United Palestine Appeal be amalgamated with the Welfare Fund Campaign, or should it continue to be conducted separately? As in other matters, Canada followed the lead of the U.S.A., where the welfare fund movement was already firmly established. Toronto led the way in Canada, where a welfare fund was inaugurated in 1937. In Winnipeg, the wealthier Jews, those of the "right side of the tracks" were envious of the progressive Torontonians and were determined to emulate them. The main arguments for amalgamation were: it would bring order out of the chaos of multiple campaigns and thereby save much time, effort and money, and it would ensure a more rational distribution of the available funds. The opposition, of which I was a staunch supporter, argued that raising money for the rebuilding of Eretz Israel should not be combined, and thereby identified, with campaigns for *charitable* organizations; that the special message of Zionism would be lost in the welter of claims to be stressed by the campaigners; and that those who head welfare funds are not usually the most ardent Zionists, so that there was a real danger of "diminishing returns" for Eretz Israel. To strengthen our case, we invited the revered National President of the Zionist Organization, Mr. A.J. Frieman, to visit in Winnipeg and to bring his influence to bear on wavering individuals as well as on the general public.

It was my first meeting with Mr. Frieman. Because of his heart condition, he had to rest periodically from the tiring meetings and exhausting discussions. He asked me to meet him in his hotel room to chat about various Zionist matters. When the question of amalgamation came up, he held his hand to his heart, as he was lying in bed, and said with deep emotion, "I have been pleading with them to let us alone to conduct our U.P.A. Drive separately; I tell them 'take everything, but give us *this corner in our life*'," Although I well understood what he meant by "this corner of our life", I was eager to hear how he would explain it. A man of profound sensitivity and genuine compassion, he spoke with deep feeling of the enormous financial resources required for saving as many of our people as possible, for transporting them to Palestine and for rebuilding the country. To raise such vast sums of money, we must be independent in our efforts to reach the maximum number of people for the highest possible financial results specifically for Palestine. So the lesson I got on the meaning of Zionism was the same I had heard many times before. It was clear that fund raising was the aplha and the omega of the Zionist purpose in Canada. I suppose it required some courage for me, a mere regional employee, to gainsay the Chief's exposition. I proceeded to explain that Zionism was not a mere corner in our life, that it encompassed all aspects of Jewish life, that — to me — it was synonymous with Judaism. Therefore, I said, not only the U.P.A., but also Jewish education must be kept out of the welfare fund orbit. I was surprised and pleased by his reaction (I had feared a response similar to that of Louis Lipsky): He looked at me intently and said, "I want you to speak on this subject at our next national convention". He also asked me to send him a memorandum on the subject "Zionism and Jewish Education in Canada".

Jewish Education "A First" at a National Zionist Convention

I did, indeed, speak on "The Mission of Zionism" at the Z.O.C. National Convention in Montreal on January 19, 1941. It was my first address to a huge audience, which filled to over capacity the large hall of the Sheraton Hotel. I felt veritably as an extremely pious *Shaliach tsibur* (a spokesman of the congregation) feels on Yom Kippur, as I spoke with awe and great expectations about a subject which I was deeply convinced would determine the future of Zionism and thus of Judaism in the Diaspora. I feared as a *shatz* would fear that he might falter in his prayer and fail his "senders". I cannot vouch for the accuracy of the dramatic statement made to me by Mr. Israel Medres, who covered the convention for the newspaper the Canadian Jewish Eagle of Montreal. He rushed over to me and warmly clasped my hands, as he declared, "this is a historic day, this is the very first time a Zionist convention deals with Jewish education". I was naive enough to hope that the prominent headlines and Mr. Medres' enthusiastic remarks in his newspaper were the harbinger of a revolution in Zionist thought and activity in Canada. In truth, the Zionist eminences who adorned the stage had congratulated me, and Mr. Frieman had assured me there and then that "something would be done".

I later sent Mr. Frieman the memorandum he requested on Zionism and Jewish Education (see Appendix), to which he responded promptly and enthusiastically: "I want to thank you for your memorandum on Zionism and Jewish Education as well as a copy of the address on the same subject which was delivered at the Zionist convention on January 19 of this year. I was very much impressed and I held it in abeyance until I could present it to my colleagues of the National Council, which I did last Monday. We referred same to a committee of which Rabbi Charles Bender is Chairman, and the Committee is to report to us within two weeks. You will no doubt hear from us again." In June I received a copy of the minutes of the National Council meeting of May 26, in which I read: "Reporting for the Committee on Education which has been designated at the last meeting of the National Council to study a memorandum prepared by Mr. Aron Horowitz, the Western Executive Director, Rabbi Charles Bender, convenor, stated that the Committee recommended as a first step the summoning of a preliminary conference of the principals and teachers of the Talmud Torahs, Folk Shule and congregational schools in the city of Montreal. The Committee felt that before making any decisions with respect to a Dominion Conference of Jewish Educators, it was desirable first to probe in a limited field what specific assistance the Zionist Organization can give, within the limits of its other functions, to strengthen such Jewish education as will produce a youth that will be devoted to the Zionist cause. Mr. Horowitz, the Western Director, is to be invited to attend the Conference."

That was the last I heard about it, and that is where the matter rested. When I moved to Montreal at the end of 1946, I found myself in a blind alley as I tried to discover the whys and wherefores of the collapse of this project even before it was born.

In retrospect, I think of one or more of these possibilities: The Montreal educators wanted to be left alone ... perhaps they thought the time was not ripe for bringing together different educational ideologies. It is worth noting that the Peretz Shule was not even included among the schools to have been invited to the Conference. Perhaps some Canadian Jewish Congress leaders did not look with favour upon leaving the educational field to the Z.O.C. Maybe the chairman of the Committee and others were preoccupied — as usual — with more important matters or — as Rabbi Jesse Schwartz, the National Director of the Z.O.C., wrote to me in one of his letters in later years, "the Zionist Organization cannot become the Surrogate for Jewish education".

For my part, I published the address in several Anglo-Jewish newspapers, including The Jewish Spectator of New York (the South-African Zionist Times copied it from the Spectator), and sent copies to all active Zionists in Western Canada. I was heartened by the reactions, especially that of Mr. William Epstein, who later became the acting chief of the Middle East Department at the United Nations. He wrote me that he used my address as his credo and Bible, and in subsequent conversation he compared its impact on him to that of Dr. Theodore Herzl's Judenstadt on those who welcomed it when it was first published. It was also republished in the Canadian Jewish Eagle nineteen years later, on October 5, 1960, with this note by the editor: "The National Convention of the Zionist Organization of Canada, which will be held in Montreal at the end of this month, will deal with many important problems, including the role which Zionists must now play vis-avis

Israel. Pertinent to this problem is the address delivered by Rabbi A. Horowitz, of Montreal, National Director of Keren Hatarbut, at the National Convention of the Z.O.C. held in January 1941. Although delivered almost twenty years ago, the problems discussed by Rabbi Horowitz are still relevant today in any appraisal of the future of Zionism."

The purpose of mentioning all this is to emphasize my conviction that Zionism failed to fire the imagination and capture the hearts and minds of our youth in the Diaspora because of its presentation as a fund-raising organization at one extreme, and as a sacred obligation for personal *Aliyah* at the other extreme. It is for this reason that I am including here this article as an Appendix. For it is clear to me that the Zionist "movement" and Israel's leaders have not yet found the effective road to a creative and meaningful Zionist Philosophy for thinking people who do not intend to make their physical home in the Land of Israel.

A Zionist Benedict Arnold

To increase the prospects for a successful *separate* U.P.A. Drive, Head Office sent us Dr. Nachum Goldman to speak at the Campaign Dinner. At that time, Dr. Goldman was the most popular world Jewish leader in Canada. I was both irritated and amused to see the local celebrities swarm around him in awe and admiration. Generally speaking, the orator had it made in those days. So, in considering whom to invite as "guest speaker", the most important if not the only necessary quality was his oratorical prowess, and it was always funny to hear the *machers*, (the big shots) doing a post-mortem on the oration rather than on its contents. At times, I wondered whether some of the *machers* understood or even listened to the substance of the discourse of Dr. Goldman or any other speaker. It seemed to me that they were rather enthralled by his reputation, his unique German accent, his mannerisms and gesticulations. At first, I attributed this inflated hero-worship to the provincialism of the remote or small community, but I later witnessed the same scenes around Dr. Goldman and other famous orators also in Toronto and Montreal. I believe that this adulation — a la Elvis Presley — contributed more than a little to Dr. Goldman's highly exaggerated self-esteem and chutzpah. Seeing the tremendous influence he wielded on his audiences, I sought to win his ear for my pet "obsession". It took some maneuvering to corner him away from his bevy of fans, especially the ladies. I presented to him my case about the Zionist Movement's neglect of eduction, about its abandonment of our youth and the university campus.I concluded with the dramatic statement that if we did not undertake great deeds on those three fronts, we would surely lose the rising generation. To this day, I am not certain about what he really thought of me — a *shlumiel* executive director? (which a bureaucrat dare not be!), a *melamed*? or — at best — a dreamer. He did not react at all to what I said. He had a bored look about him, and suggested that I send him a memorandum on the subject; I did so, but never received even an acknowledgement. I suppose I was more than naive to have thought that this great world leader would find time for such subjects as education and youth.

In this connection, I could never understand or forgive outstanding leaders who could not find time to visit Hebrew schools during their visits in various Canadian cities. I once pleaded in vain with the hebrew poet Leib Yaffe, head of the Keren Hayesod, to spend a few hours at the Talmud Torah during one of his extended visits in Winnipeg, in order to lend some much needed encouragement to the teachers, pupils and board members. As far as I can remember, the only exceptions during all my years in Western Canada were Baruch Zuckerman; Rabbi Ze'ev Gold, the President of the World Mizrachi Organization; M. Meriminsky-Merom, treasurer of the Histadrut, and Eddy Gelber.

I had a strong sense of distrust of Dr. Goldman the very first time I met him. It was not only his charming theatrics and egocentricity that repelled me, but more so, his see-sawing acrobatics in analyzing the conflicting interests in the Middle East. I once caught myself saying to a close friend, "should circumstances produce a Jewish Benedict Arnold, Dr. Goldman would be It!" In later years, when Dr. Goldman assumed the mantle of self-appointed representative par excellence of the Jewish people and had the chutzpah to act as if he alone knew what was best for them, I had occasion to mention to Jewish leaders my long-standing suspicion of his motives and my apprehension of his partisan activities, I was invariably told I was a bit prejudiced against him. In 1963, when Dr. Goldman made his infamous overtures to Nasser, I was meeting with Moshe Sharett, in his capacity as Chairman of the Jewish Agency, on matters concerning the Hebrew Movement in Canada. When the name of Dr. Goldman came up apropos his *dabbling in Jewish education* matters, I referred to him as "the Jewish Benedict Arnold". Sharett's reaction was *"lo ad kdei kach"*, not so far as that. I reminded Sharett of Goldman's intensive activity in support of the U.S. State Department in its efforts to thwart the establishment of the Jewish State following the U.N. decision on the partition of "Palestine". I added that Goldman has been and will continue to be consistent in his "Munich" mentality. True, other leaders were ready to knuckle under the pressure of the State Department, but they did not assist the adversary in its machinations. Now, as I write this, I have read that, according to the "New York Magazine" of April 24, 1978, Dr. Goldman allegedly advised Secretary of State Cyrus Vance and Zbigniew Brzesinski as long ago as November 1977, to "break the Jewish influence in America", and declared that the Jewish Presidents Conference is an obstacle to peace. According to the Yiddish language paper Algemeiner Journal of New York, dated April 21, 1978, "some Jewish leaders characterized as betrayal Dr. Goldman's advice to the Carter Administration on how to combat American Jewry's influence". In these leaders' opinion, "this veteran Zionist must be completely senile". I completely disagree. I think Goldman's betrayal goes far back and is not now entirely due to senility.

Apropos my discussion with Mr. Sharett on educational matters, he asked me what I thought of Goldman's plans for a World Conference on Jewish Education and for the establishment of a World Bureau of Jewish Education. My reaction was *"od mamzer nefel shel Goldman"*, (another of Goldman's abortive bastards). When I was later invited by Dr. Samuel Lewin of the Canadian Jewish Congress to attend the Conference as a delegate of the Congress, I declined. It is true that my official reason for declining was the Congress' objection to my going as a delegate of the Keren Hatarbut, but had I thought the Conference would accomplish anything worthwhile, I would have sought some compromise with the Congress.

When I learned that my friend Dr. Azriel Eisenberg had been offered the position of Executive Vice President of the World Bureau, I advised him strongly "against falling into a politicians' den". I do not know the specific reasons for his resignation following a relatively short period of intensive efforts, but I do know he left the bureau with a deep sense of disillusionment and frustration. The best that can be said about this grandiose scheme is that a huge mountain gave birth to a little squeaky mouse. It is too bad that Jewish roots are so scattered that there is nobody to demand an accounting for the vast sums of money that were squandered on this and other such "abortions".

Chapter 8
Light and Darkness Serve in Confusion

(Rashi, Genesis 1)

When I started to make my rounds in Western Canada, Hitler's onslaught was in full force. Although the war was very remote from our doorsteps, people were troubled and bewildered. There was hardly a Jewish family that did not have some relatives in the Nazi hell. Though not fully aware of the enormity of the tragedy in Europe, people sensed that horrible things were happening to their loved ones for the mere reason of their Jewish origin. It was thus all the more difficult to plow for Zionism-Judaism in a near-doom atmosphere. At the same time, precisely because of the general gloom, it was essential to bring some message of faith and hope to the people, and to encourage communities and institutions to carry on with even greater ardor. Since we were practically cut off from the source of Jewish faith and inspiration, from Zion, it was very difficult for me to find within myself the inner strength that was necessary to overcome the prevailing passimism and near-hopelessness. But as I made my way from community to community and from individual to individual, I was heartened by the response of the people. Though there were very dark moments in this odyssey of mine, there was by far more light than darkness.

The Leaders and the People

Since my high school days, when I was assigned an essay on whether the great leader or the common people is the determining factor in historic events, I have attempted to relate this problem — as a witness to and participant in the flux of events — to the realm of Jewish life in Canada, the U.S.A. and Israel. My own experience has been, on the whole, that while the leaders in Israel were ahead of the people, or at least did not lag behind them, in the U.S.A. and especially in Canada the people would have responded to a much higher degree, if the leaders had had the vision and the courage to present them with greater challenges. Canadian Jewry has suffered from a shortage of leaders of high stature, with sufficient knowledge and intellectual capacity to comprehend the rapidly changing Jewish scene, to understand the needs and the potentialities of their communities, and to translate opportunities into realities. This may explain, at least in part, the discrepancies in the general educational and cultural climate among communities of more or less equal resources. I believe this general picture will emerge from my unfolding story.

A quotation is in place here from an article by Elchanan, (the pen name of Mr. E. Hanson), on "Zionism and Education in Edmonton", in the Israelite Press of November 18, 1941: "For nearly the last two decades we did not have in Edmonton a Zionist organization worthy of the name. We had only an executive. When a general meeting was called for the election of officers, people didn't show up, even though admission, 'with refreshments', was free. Thus the executive had to elect itself 'by acclamation'. The reasons were simple: Either leadership was entirely absent or it was very weak. There was a lack of adequate intelligence and especially of idealism for an understanding of the Zionist cause and its objectives. The leadership knew only one thing — to raise more and more money. To educate the general public for Zionism, to bring up the young generation in the spirit of the Land of Israel — this was apparently considered superfluous. So, as the saying goes: 'Sow the wind and reap the whirlwind'. The situation became so bad that there were hardly any people with whom to conduct a campaign.

Elchanan, whom I later came to know as one of the few who had high expectations, may have exaggerated a bit about the gloomy situation in Edmonton, but in the main, he was accurate about the dearth of intellectual leadership and the absence of activity outside campaign times: this was more or less true of the entire West.

Long Odyssey Begins

The primary objective of my first tour was, of course, connected with fund raising. I set out to survey the situation with regard to the annual U.P.A. campaigns, to strengthen the existing committees, and to acquaint myself with the Zionist "presence" in the homes, in the schools and in the communities at large.

A Near Calamity

Regina was the first large city I visited. I purposely did not inform the committee of the time and means of my arrival, in order not to trouble anyone to meet my train very early on a Sunday morning. As I walked out of the station, I saw two hotels, one to my right and one to my left. I decided on the one to my left, because it was smaller and would therefore be less expensive. At a "decent" hour, I phoned the chairman, Martin A. Rose, an agreeable fellow with a non-nonsense manner. When I told him the name of my hotel, he gasped and chided me in an agitated voice: "Don't you dare tell anybody where you are. I'll come at once and get you out of there". Even though the daily rate was only two dollars, I was puzzled by what seemed to me his undue alarm. Mr. Rose arrived in no time, paid the clerk for one day and explained apologetically, "The Rabbi was not aware of the arrangements we had made for him". As we emerged from the hotel, Mr. Rose murmured that we were lucky the street was still empty of people. He then proceeded to lecture me softly and respectfully, about "the importance of the status and prestige of our executive director". I argued that we were a poor people and that Zionist officials should spend as little as possible and thus demonstrate dramatically the urgent need for more and more funds to save lives and to build Eretz Israel. He was going to take me to the Saskatchewan Hotel, the most expensive of course, but we settled for the Drake which charged about half the rate of the Saskatchewan. I told him I did not see any connection between successful Zionist endeavour and high expenditures. "On the contrary" — I told him — "people will have greater confidence in, and will respond more readily to, officials who are careful with public funds". I quoted from the Talmud (Yoma 39): "the Torah commands us to be sparing with the public's money". While I did not repeat the same blunder in other communities, I made it clear I would not stay in expensive hotels. So I settled for the Corona instead of the Macdonald in Edmonton, the York instead of the Palliser in Calgary, the York instead of the Bessborough in Saskatoon, and the York instead of the Hotel Vancouver in Vancouver. In retrospect, there is no doubt in my mind that if I succeeded in my work, it was due, in part, to my frugality.

In Regina, I found an enthusiastic committee composed mainly of business men, simple people whose emotions were highly charged as they prepared for their U.P.A. Drive. The spirit was near Chassidic when I met with the small group consisting of Martin A. Rose, A.D. Samuels, Sam Portigal, the brothers Sam and Lou Promislaw, and — last but not least — Joe Shwartzfeld who was dubbed *der bloozer* (the blower) because when the campaign time came around he bubbled ceaselessly about the ways and means of obtaining the greatest amounts from the greatest number. The group in Regina was the most cohesive and harmonious I found anywhere — no pretences, no jealousies, and no complications. Though there were equally dedicated individuals in all the other large cities, they all presented problems because their Jewish populations were much more heterogenous than in Regina.

Zionist Partisianship in the Diaspora

It is significant that Canadian Zionists united and coordinated their efforts under the banner of the Jewish National Fund. There existed at that time Jewish National Fund councils consisting of representatives of various Zionist political parties, as all Zionists were in agreement on the importance of this Fund for the redemption and reclamation of the land. That is where Zionist unity began and ended. There existed a Manitoba Zionist Council, but it included representatives only of General Zionist groups. To me it seemed obvious that Zionists should unite and coordinate their efforts also in such areas as political action, public relations, and some aspects of Jewish education. During one of his visits in Winnipeg, Baruch Zuckerman asked me why I, an ardent member of the labour movement in Eretz Israel, kept away completely from the movement in Canada. I told him that in my opinion there was no room for Zionist parties in the Diaspora, where all Zionists should work for the common goals of our national renaissance. I could see the need for raising funds for Histradut or Mizrachi by those who are sympathetic to those organizations, but I could not see the need for Zionist parties parallel to those in Eretz Israel. Zuckerman disagreed with me, but commended our efforts for coordinating activities of common interest to all Zionist factions.

Zionists Unite for Action

After the reorganization of the Manitoba Zionist Council to encompass all parties and groups, with Roy Calof as its chairman, I set out to establish such councils in every major center. I encountered many difficulties not only because of local conditions, including shortage of leaders, reluctance of capable people to assume responsibility, personal jealousies and even feuds, but also because of general apathy. Nonetheless, we succeeded in developing effective councils in Calgary, Edmonton, Regina, Saskatoon and Vancouver. Their functions were to coordinate and intensify fund-raising activities, undertake educational activities, give guidance and cooperation to the youth groups, and raise the prestige and increase the influence of the Zionist Organization within the life of the community.

Feuding Clans in Edmonton

Of special interest is the story of how the Zionist Council came into being in Edmonton. I was told it would be practically impossible to bring together under one roof two feuding prominent families. If one were in, the other would be out. This brought to my mind my new version of the old story about the only two Jews in a small town, who had two synagogues, because each individual "would never set foot in *that* place", in the other fellow's synagogue. My version was that they proceeded to build a third one. When asked "why a third one? Doesn't each one of you already have a separate place of worship?!", the answer was "We need a neutral place"!

Because of this situation it was difficult to find a prominent person to head the council. It took a lot of background-maneuvering and friendly persuasion by people who had influence on both families to enlist their cooperation, on condition that Dr. E. Wershof, a noted physician who was respected by the entire community, would serve as chairman of the council. Dr. Wershof agreed, on condition that he would not attend the founding meeting and that he would be elected unanimously to the position of chairman. We were jubilant at our success, and a date was set for the historic meeting to take place at the most prestigious hotel. I returned on that date to make sure that the birth of the council would not be aborted. There was a *yomtov shtimmung*, (a holiday mood), as we sat around the long table to commence the proceedings. By some quirk of fate, the refreshments were served at the beginning rather than at the end of the meeting. The head of one of the feuding families took a look at the sandwiches, shouted *"traif!"* and walked out of the hall in a huff. I thought there and then of the historic occasion when the first class of Hebrew Union College in Cincinanati was graduated in 1883. The Rabbinical ordination banquet was the highlight of the convention of the Union of American Hebrew Congregations. Two Rabbis rose from their seats and rushed from the room when shrimp (a forbidden food) was served as the opening course of the feast. (See American Judaism by Nathan Glazer, chapter 4, page 56). However, while in the U.S.A. that was the end of the plan that Hebrew Union College might serve all American Jewry, in Edmonton it required only a bit more friendly persuasion and an additional meeting to bring the parts together again.

Under the leadership of Dr. Wershof, the council proved to be one of the most successful in the West. Elchanan wrote, in the Israelite press: "If other Zionist councils function as ours under the leadership of Dr. Wershof, we may hope that Zionism will be resurrected. There are already hopeful signs. The council meets regularly, and every group reports fully on its past activities and its future plans, so that the various activities are coordinated. As far as fund-raising is concerned, the U.P.A. has raised this year about 5000 dollars compared with 3500 last year, and the results of the Yom-Kippur Land Fund Campaign more than trebbled, from 250 dollars last year to 800 dollars this year. The educational committee of the council under the chairmanship of Louis Rudolph does good work, and the cultural evenings it has sponsored have been very successful."

"Mechayil El Chayil" — From Strength to Strength
(Psalms 84, 8)

Once the Zionist councils were firmly established, I thought the next step should be the organization of men's Zionist clubs, which would serve as a platform for study and discussion of Judaic subjects. I, myself, could never see the separation between male and female in cultural and social activities. Perhaps it was or still is because of the traditional separation between men and women in the House of Worship. Apropos the attempt to separate the inseparable, my brother Sol related to me the following as a true story: My father once asked him what kind of a rabbi he was. "Well', he answered "you know father, these days one has to be modern." "What exactly do you mean by modern, do men and women, for instance, sit together during Services?" "Well, father, is it really such a great sin for men and women to pray together?" "Tell me, son", asked my father, "are you a good speaker?" "Yes, I'm considered quite a good speaker." "Are you so good that nobody ever dozes off during your Services?" "Well, I guess it could happen sometimes". "Ah, ah!", exlaimed my father with a gleam in his eyes, "it may not be a sin to pray together, but it is definitely a sin to sleep together!"

I did make endeavours to bring men and women together in the quest for knowledge, but to no avail. So, it was strictly men's Zionist clubs that I set out to bring into being.

Why was I a suspect? A series of incidents provided sufficient circumstantial evidence to arouse suspicion: The chief suspect, Avraham Stavsky, a member of the Revisionist Party, which was accused by the Histadrut leadership of masterminding the murder, had been a passenger on the same ship that had taken me from Marseilles to Eretz Israel, a fact, by the way, of which I had been completely oblivious. I had been seen with him at the same table at the Cooperative Restaurant, where I had my meals regularly, and where people would often sit at the same tables without knowing each other or even without speaking with one another. One of my cousins was married to a Revisionist leader, and I thus became acquainted with some of its leading members. Revisionist youth would march, often eight abreast, in the streets, which thundered with their songs *"Zabotinsky chai, chai chai vekayam"* (Zabotinsky lives; he is alive and everlasting), and *"Shtei Gedot Layarden, Zu Shelanu, Zu Gam Ken"* (the Jordan has two banks, each is ours as much as the other). My cousin's husband, whom I accompanied on several occasions as an onlooker at those marches, dared me once to join in the march. I did so in a spirit of fun, without realizing that one day soon I would be implicated (guilt by association, which was not unusual in "Palestine" at that time) as a rabid Revisionist. I should add that the tense political atmosphere did not allow for close friendships among political rivals, which seemed a rather strange phenomenon to a liberal socialist from New York. On the day Arlozorov was murdered I was not seen at all at the Cooperative Restaurant. For, on that very same day I had gone to Tel-Aviv at the behest of the lawyer for whom I was working temporarily as a substitute for my revisionist relative. Since I had a letter to Arlozorov from one of his friends in Canada, I tried unsuccessfully to see him at the hotel where he resided! Had I not been the victim of a second degree sunburn that afternoon at the beach, as a result of which I had been confined to bed for about a week, I would probably have found myself in court as a fourth defendant. All this was explained to me later by the police officer in charge of the investigation, when — ironically — I translated much of the material in this trial, in my capacity as translator of the Supreme Court.

The Arlozorov murder trial became a cause celebre. The entire Yishuv was divided into two hostile camps. The Histadrut and its sympathizers were certain that the Revisionist leadership had engineered and executed the murder, while the Revisionists and their followers accused the Histadrut leaders of deliberate and despicable libel. Aba Achimeir, a prominent Revisionist ideologue, was cleared in the preliminary investigation in the lower court, and Stavsky and Zwi Rosenblatt stood trial in the Criminal Court, where the latter was cleared and Stavsky was found guilty of first degree murder and sentenced to death by hanging. The verdict shook the country and nearly led to civil war. Sides for and against the verdict were now taken also by judicial experts and by such prominent leaders as Berl Katznelson, the most revered ideologue of the Labor Movement, who welcomed the verdict and condemned the entire Revisionist movement, and — on the Nay side — by Chief Rabbi Yitzchak Hacohen Kook, who was highly respected by all elements of the Yishuv, and who considered the accusations against the Revisionists as a blot on the entire Yishuv. Although I was a follower of the Histadrut and an admirer of its leadership, I was convinced that the evidence, which I had translated into English almost in toto, was far from sufficient for a guilty verdict. As it turned out later, the Supreme Court quashed the judgement of the Criminal Court and Stavsky was set free but exiled from the country. I well remember the dramatic and highly charged atmosphere at the time of the Supreme Court decision. Thousands of people thronged the streets, the rooftops and the trees around the court. Each side tried to drown out the other with their partisan songs, and here and there fist-fights had to be quelled by British and Arab as well as Jewish policemen. I was standing in the Judges' Chambers near Chief Justice Sir Michael McDonald, as he looked out at the throngs and remarked: "In England, I would have confirmed the Criminal Court's Judgement on the basis of the evidence of the single witness in the case. Here, the law provides that no judgement shall be given in a criminal case on the evidence of a single witness unless such evidence is admitted by the accused, or is corroborated by some other material." As for myself, I thought: "Thank God for this provision of the Palestine Criminal Law, as I am convinced both in mind and heart of Stavsky's innocence".

The aftermath of this trial continued to fester in the country for many years and exacerbated the bitterness between the Histadrut and the Revisionists. This whole episode provided me with a striking example of how rational, decent people could be blinded by partisanship to condemn a priori political opponents because of prejudice and enmity. I personally had a bitter taste of it when my friend Yehudah Shimoni, general secretary of the Histadrut Cultural Committee in Jerusalem, became furious with me for "siding with the opposition". Said he, "Who are you to gainsay the conviction of our great leader Berl?!" Even such a wonderful and rational person as Shimoni, whom I truly revered for his exemplary life, did not care to hear my opinion, based on the materials I had studied, nor did he suggest that we examine the evidence. Sufficient unto him, too, it was to follow the great leader!

The Arlozorov Affair is still shrouded in mystery, and to this day it has not been established who was responsible for the murder. There have been several theories. One is that the British Colonial Office wanted to get rid of a most capable and dynamic statesman who, more than any other Zionist leader, understood already at that time, the overriding importance of active communication and rapprochement with the Arabs. Others maintained it was a conspiracy by Arabs who were opposed to any accomodation with the Zionist Movement. Revisionists stooped to the malicious accusation that it was Sima, Arlozorov's wife, who was responsible for the murder because of an illicit love affair, and vicious songs to that effect were heard throughout the land. On June 6, 1956, 23 years after the murder, Mr. Menachem Begin, head of the Cherut, which superceded the Revisionist Party, made the following statement in the Knesset (according to Mr. Begin's article in Maariv of February 25, 1977): "On the 18th of June 1933, two persons met for the first time in their lives. One was a police officer, and the other a handcuffed prisoner. Said the former: 'murderer, why did you do it?' The prisoner replied: 'I am innocent!' Twenty-two years later, the same police officer, Mr. Arzi — a Hagganah veteran — declared publicly on the basis of documents he had in his possession, and on the basis of facts known to him: 'Avraham Stavsky was completely innocent!'" Continued Mr. Begin, "In view of this disclosure, can we go on as if nothing has happened?" Mr. Begin pleaded for the establishment of a judicial commission "to investigate the circumstances and accusations in connection with the murder of Dr. Arlozorov". His pleas fell on deaf ears. It is interesting that as late as 1949, a member of the Mapai Central Committee told me cheerfully: "Stavsky met his punishment when he died on the Altalena (the ship that tried to unload armaments acquired by the Revisionists at the time of the War of Liberation, which was blown up at the command of David Ben Gurion on the ground that its Commander refused to surrender it to the established authority), on the very seashore where he was alleged to have murdered Arlozorov!" As I was writing on this matter, I came across Mr. Begin's statement (in Maariv of June 9, 1977) to the effect that several years ago one of the chief spokesmen of the Labor Party had told Mr. Begin, "We investigated the Altelena affair and arrived at the conclusion that Ben Gurion was misled in this matter." Mr. Begin asked who had misled Ben Gurion, how he had been misled, and how the misleaders could have brought themselves to this bloodshed, but the man stubbornly refused to answer, saying, "I cannot add anything to what I have told you, nor will I say more in the future."

Even the most active Zionists cautioned me that the time was inauspicious for such organizations. France had fallen, and Rommel was storming the gates of the Middle East; "Whose head is open now to academic discussions!" Nor did I get any encouragement from Head Office. To quote just one sentence from a letter by Rabbi Jesse Schwartz: "We are faced with the question of what happens to these groups that are organized, after we leave the community?" Nonetheless, I felt that this very situation called for "daring" and persistent action. My first target was Calgary, where there was a comparatively large group of young intellectuals. As it was a Sabbath, and I had not as yet decided to request friends to drive me on Shabbat, which I did in later years, I walked from house to house and from office to office until I had blisters on my feet. I did not "let go" of any individual until he promised to attend the first meeting.

The Sharon Zionist Club of Calgary, under the chairmanship of Dave Chertkow, became a source of strength to the Zionist Organization and a model to other communities. The leadership was assumed by a group of knowledgeable, energetic first-generation Canadians. The nucleus of the club consisted of Dr. William Epstein, a brilliant attorney who later became the Acting Chief of the Middle East Department of the United Nations; the late Nathan Safran, who was vice principal of the Alberta School of Art and Technology and a person possessed of extraordinary verve and drive; Max Katzin — a rare human being who gave his heart and soul to Zionism and the community; Ben Sherwoud — an engineer with Imperial Oil and Sol Stamer — the sole immigrant in the group, who with his Hebraic background served as a sort of catalyst of the club. Their effectiveness was enhanced by the dedicated "elders" — Charles Waterman, Morris Wolochow, Shaye Jaffe, Sam Datner and Norman Gould — who worked in unusual harmony with the younger set.

In Edmonton too the initiative was taken by a group of capable young men, consisting of Dr. Max Dolgoy (chairman), Louis Rudolph, Wolf Margulis, Leo Pekarsky, and with veteran Zionist Saul Loeb, as a link betwen the new "B'nai-Zion Club" and the demised B'nai Zion organization that had looked after the annual U.P.A. campaign.

"Al Tehi Tsadik Harbe" — Be Not Overmuch Righteous (Ecclesiastes 7, 16)

I arrived in Regina at night on the last lap of my tour, and found a telegram, informing me that my wife was scheduled for an emergency operation the following morning. My tours would take me away from my home for months in succession, and I never allowed myself the luxury of a long-distance telephone call to my wife, who was alone with a six months old baby and a four year old boy. I was faced with quite a dilemma. The Regina club was to be organized at a luncheon meeting the next day. I had already visited Regina a few times to prepare the ground. If I left that night, my friends told me that the success of the meeting would be jeopardized. If I were to leave the following night by train, I would arrive after the surgery. The solution was therefore to go by plane after the meeting. That was the very first time I allowed myself to fly. I did not think at that time that it was extraordinary for me to cover the difference between the train and plane fares out of my own pocket.

The club in Regina was spearheaded by practically the same people who were active in the Zionist Council, except for its chairman Dr. S. Kraminsky who was the only person in the group who knew modern Hebrew. In Regina then, the club served de facto as the educational arm of the council.

The treasurer of the Western Division, a very quiet man who was very sensitive about expenses, was always impressed with my small expense accounts. When he noticed that I paid out of my own pocket the difference between train and plane fare, he muttered approvingly, "Hm, hm!" I didn't even tell him that the difference I paid was between my clergy fare, which was fifty per cent of the regular fare, and the full plane fare. When another colleague learned that I was using a clergy certificate, he expressed his amazement that I did not charge the organization the full fare, since it was not they who obtained the clergy certificate for me. As I think of this now, I am bothered by Ecclesiastes admonition "be not righteous overmuch". I fully realize now that overcommitment is, in most cases, as wrong as no commitment, and that I was very unfair to my family in involving them in my overcommitment.

In Winnipeg, the Sharon Zionist Club had been in existence since 1935. However, some people felt that a city of the size of Winnipeg needed more than one men's Zionist group. Furthermore, they saw the need for a club that would not restrict its discussions to political subjects, but would deal also with philosophic and cultural themes. They thus organized the Weizman Club in 1940. Both groups made a significant contribution to the cultural life of the community.

Of an Editor's Problems

Winnipeg had three Jewish newspapers, a Yiddish-language daily — *The Israelite Press*, and two English-language weeklies, *The Jewish Post* and *The Western Jewish News*. Since Zionism, to me, was the core of Jewish life, I expected the Jewish newspapers to give full and adequate coverage to Zionist events, including the activities of the Zionist Organization in Western Canada. On the whole, the English weeklies mirrored satisfactorily Zionist activities in the region, but I felt that the Israelite Press did not treat the Zionist Organization as the major, or at least one of the major, organizations in Jewish life. Since the owners — the brothers Abe and Feivel Simkin — as well as the editor, Mark Selchen, were Yiddishists, I suspected a deliberate bias against our movement. Although the Zionist office was at that time in the Israelite Press building, my first face to face meeting with the editor took place when I walked down to his office to protest against his attitude to our organization. He was a short man, with a sensitive and kindly face. When I looked at him, my first thought was, "this person is the picture of calm". When I finished telling him about the purpose of my visit, he was shaking all over; he rose from his seat and, with quivering lips, went into a fury about an editor's independence and freedom to do with his paper as he damn-well pleases. Our conversation was short and stormy. What surprised me about this man, for whom I later developed a genuine respect, was his official complaint about me to the Western Vice President, who seized upon this incident to proclaim his superiority and to exert his authority. He wrote Mr. Selchen that I was a young man (which indeed I was), that I had started to work "on the wrong foot" and that he would be coming to Winnipeg to straighten out matters. I promptly informed him that I was not in need of his help and would fight my own battles, and mend my own fences. I realized that Mr. Selchen had mistakenly thought that I meant to infringe on his independence, and that I had been remiss in explaining myself properly to him. I went down to his office to apologize and to clarify. This time we had a long and friendly conversation and agreed to disagree sometimes on various issues. To give me an idea of his problems as an editor, he related to me some amusing stories, including one about a *loiz committet* ("Louse" Committee). One morning he saw through his office window a group of old women trudging their way towards the building. Sensing that he would be a target of criticism (appreciation was never expressed in person by groups), he started to go over in his mind recent stories in his newspaper. He couldn't think of anything that could call for criticism. Soon he was faced with a furious delegation. They all fumed incoherently. When he succeeded in calming them down, they said in unison *"Loiz Commitet!* Indeed!" It turned out that in an item published about their "society", the letter *Lamed* (the L sound), was substituted for the letter *Hey* (the H sound), so that instead of reading Mrs. so and so, chairman of the *Hoiz Committet* (House Committee), it read *Loiz Commitet* (louse committee). It took all of Mr. Selchen's powers of persuasion to put the ladies at ease by explaining that it was an unfortunate mistake of the *"Habocher Hazetzer"*, (the typesetter).

Interestingly enough, during all the ten years of my work in Western Canada, I received from Mr. Selchen more understanding, appreciation, and encouragement than from Zionist officialdom. For Mr. Selchen was genuinely interested in education and culture, and was respectful of other people's opinions.

British Colonial Office on Guard

Another sorely neglected field was what is known as "public relations" and what I prefer to call public education. When I addressed service clubs, such as the Elks and the Kiwanis, I was surprised to find how much the audience knew about the Arab case, and how little they knew about the Zionist cause. As far as I knew, there was no organized Arab propaganda at that time in the West. It therefore occurred to me that the British Colonial Office, always intent on annulling the Balfour Declaration, must be doing the Arabs' work for them. They didn't have to expend any efforts and resources then, just as the oil interests and international capital attend now to the Arabs' nefarious designs throughout what is called "Western civilization". My suspicions were substantiated several years later when the Colonial Office went to the trouble of sending Freya Stark, a top colonial intelligence officer, to "inform" those who form public opinion in Canada. (This story will be related in a later chapter.) I therefore tried to speak to as many service clubs as possible, to meet with influential individuals, such as Richard Needham who was working at that time at the Calgary Albertan, and gave interviews to the press in all the larger cities. I also tried to awaken the head-office of the Zionist Organization to the need for a Pro Palestine committee. Such a body was later established in the early forties with Herbert Mowat as its national director. When I met Mowat on his travels, I was not impressed with his knowledge of Zionism, but he seemed eager to learn.

An Encounter with Peretz Hirschbein

The Calgary Yiddishists were very proud of their adopted son, Peretz Hirschbein, a noted Yiddish author-playwright. He married a local girl, Esther Shumiatcher, daughter of a prominent family and an author in her own right. Hirschbein was in Calgary during one of my visits there. Our "boys" thought it would be a nice gesture for me to attend a reception in his honour at the home of Abe Busheiken, one of the Yiddish stalwarts. "It might be of help to the U.P.A. Campaign among these "elements". Aside from this consideration, I was very much interested in meeting and hearing Peretz Hirshbein. The Yiddishists manifested high regard for their teachers, scholars and intellectuals. They treated their authors with adoration, almost like Chassidim stand in awe before their Rebbe.

Hirshbein was sitting on an imposing chair in the center of the room and looked like a king on his throne before his admiring entourage. He was speaking slowly, weighing carefully each word as if he were stringing pearls. Somebody mentioned "Palestine". It seemed to me that Hirshbein was glad of the opportunity to tackle this subject. To quote him, "I asked Bialik: How is Palestine going to solve the Jewish problem? At the most, there could be there about a million Jews in about twenty years. If and when this maximum number is reached, there will probably be by then about twenty million Jews in the rest of the world (this was said while Hitler was in the midst of *his* "final solution" of the Jewish problem). How could one million Jews influence twenty million?!" I was dumbfounded! How could intelligent, well-meaning people go to such lengths as to become insensitive and illogical in seeking to justify their ideology!! So as not to be discourteous where I was a mere outsider-guest, I tried to refrain from reacting, but I could not contain myself completely, and blurted out, "Have you heard of the Bible and its influence on humanity!? How many people authored it, and how many people did it influence!?" There ensued complete silence, and Hirshbein stared straight away from me without giving me a tumble.

Everybody Must Help Extinguish a Fire
A Tribute to a Gentle Soul

When I returned once from one of my extended tours, I learned about my brother Asher's intention to go to Eretz Israel to join the Hagganah. He was a student at the Teahcers' Institute of the jewish Theological Seminary of America, and was a rare Jewel of a human being. His teachers foresaw a great future for him as a scholar. Some spoke of him as an Ilui (genius), but to me what was most remarkable about him was his gentle and pure soul. He was home for the summer, but spent his vacation preparing leaders for the Habonim Youth Movement. Quietly, almost anonymously, he went about selecting a core of outstanding boys and girls who would form the nucleus of a Habonim movement in Western Canada. This young boy understood what Zionist officialdom could not see — that the first step in building an effective youth movement is to cultivate knowledgeable and dedicated leaders. And succeed he did — Winnipeg became a stronghold of Habonim. At first I thought I would appeal to the girl he loved to dissuade him from what seemed to me an almost suicidal act, but I realized that she might have done so of her own accord and that he would be hurt by this type of intervention. To be sure that my parents would not learn accidentally about his intentions, I walked around with him on the streets for hours. We traversed ancient and recent Jewish history, the great ideals and aspirations of our people, our hopes for the restoration of Zion, the realities of the great Jewish tragedy, and the cruel apathy of world leaders. I used all my inner powers to try to convince him that he was wrong to endanger his life, when he was barely seventeen years old and not even eligible for military service. His calm and determined response was: "When there is a fire, everyone must help to extinguish it". He volunteered in the U.S. Merchant Marine with the intention of getting to Eretz Israel where he would join the Hagganah. The ship he was on was sunk in the Pacific Ocean.

Everybody Loves Youth . . .

Everybody speaks about the importance of youth for the future of the nation and the world. Everybody professes a love for youth, and everybody complains about the neglect of this all-important "resource". But, as a French poet said about certain people who profess to love but do not know how to love, we seldom know or care to know what to do about the youth we love so much. We usually treat them as children but expect them to behave better than adults should behave.

As a result of the revitalization of the Zionist Organization in Western Canada, a group of young people became enamored of our national renaissance and were ready and eager to build a vital and inspired youth movement. The Zionist Organization could have had in them a potent and creative force for all its endeavours, but the youth leaders were hampered in every way possible. When they suggested to the Zionist Council to organize a public march, especially of youth, on Chanukah, and turn it into a protest against the British Government's inhuman policy regarding those who tried to save themselves from the Nazi hell by escaping to their promised land, ("illegal immigration", the British called it!) their seniors told them that it would create antisemitism. Then, Sid Buckwold (now professor of soil chemistry at State College in New Britain, Conn.), Hymie Molotsky (now Dr. Molotsky, Patent Liaison and Technical Coordinator at Moffest Technical Centre in Argo, Ill.), Max Yan (now Manager of Central Research Dept. of Abitibi and Adjunct Professor at the University of Toronto), my brother Isaac Horowitz (now Professor of Applied Mathematics and Electrical Engineering at the Weizman Institute and at the University of Colorado) went ahead and organized a very successful and impressive march. They defied the prohibition of the Zionist director (I was already working in Calgary at that time) to carry a sign in *English* with the inscription: "If I forget thee O Jerusalem, may my right hand forget its cunning". He did permit them, though, to carry such a sign in *Hebrew*!

When they called for *Aliyah* (that long ago!), they were called "militants". When they participated in raising funds for the Histradut, they were dubbed socialists "who had no place in the General Zionist Organization". In short, they could now tell (if they were asked) those in Israel and in the Zionist Movement who are bemoaning the alienation of our youth, they could tell them where to look for the causes.

A Jewish Background is the Only Thing He Lacks

During my tenure as an employee of the Zionist Organization, I made a nuisance of myself on three fronts — education, youth and a pro-Palestine Committee. I would return to these subjects time and time again. It is interesting that the most fundamental of these areas, education, elicited the least response from the Zionist leadership. To this day I am baffled by the lack of understanding that without education there is no youth, that without a foundation there is no structure. In his letter of November 16, 1941. Rabbi Schwartz wrote me:

"You raise the question again of a department of education. Where are we to get the funds? We are pledged to engage a field organizer for Young Judaea. They have clamored for one for years. Obviously, neither I nor the regional directors are in a position to give detailed attention to the problem of Young Judaea. All this expenditure comes out of the U.P.A. funds. I cannot see our Organization engaging a special man at this time to run a department of education. You might say: Let the Young Judaea director, when we engage one, do it. But he will be in the field most of the time, according to the view of the Young Judaea National President."

Early in 1942, Chaim Weizman visited Montreal. Zionist leaders and officials were summoned from all parts of the country to meet him. When I arrived in Montreal, Rabbi Schwartz apologized for having reserved a room for me at the Queen's Hotel, because there were not sufficient rooms at the Mount Royal. Later that day he paid me a visit in my hotel room. When he discovered that there was no washroom in my room — I told him I had asked for these accomodations — he stated authoritatively, "We appreciate your saving us money, but we do not expect you to go to such lengths." "Yes," I said, "*you* don't expect it of me, but I expect it of myself." I knew that Weizman had come to dramatize the dire need for funds, and here I was being told not to deny myself what I considered a luxury. I did realize that my savings would make no great difference, but I thought that if all "Zionist travellers and spenders" would be "sparing with the public money", an education department could perhaps be maintained with the savings.

Before returning to Winnipeg, I visited the Zionist office to chat with Rabbi Schwartz on various subjects. As I sat down, he told me triumphantly: "I have good news for you Rabbi Horowitz. We have finally succeeded in engaging a national Executive Director for Young Judaea." "Who is he and what is his background?" I asked. "His name is Manny Batshaw; he has a degree in social work from McGill and he has had experience in working with handicapped children". "Rabbi Schwartz" said I, "what is his Jewish background?" Rabbi Schwartz leaned back in his chair as he declared: "That is the only thing he lacks!" He asked me to meet with Mr. Batshaw and to offer him some guidance. I found that he had heard of Dr. Herzl, but not of such Zionist classics as *Auto-emancipation* and the *Judenstal*. He was truly lacking in a Jewish and Zionist background. He was, however, very eager to learn, to explore the Young Judaean situation and to succeed.

Leaders Deliver the Jewish Vote

A sad aspect of my work was the knowledge that Zionist and other Jewish causes were used by some individuals for the advancement of their personal interests. Political parties had the erroneous idea that a president of an organization was in a position to "deliver" the Jewish vote. Some leaders thus received patronage from the party in power. "The King's Carter" was a glaring case. A leader was awarded for his help to the party by giving him the concession for carting goods from the border to the Customs House. It was explained to me that the concessionaire had only to engage a few trucks for this service, and he was thus able to devote much of his time to public service, or have a job or a business on the side. Since the concessionaire did give much of his time for the benefit of the Zionist organization, I was not too upset by this phenomenon. I was, however, annoyed by the request that I participate actively in an election campaign. I refused categorically on the ground that the interests of Zionism might suffer by such political alignments. I suspect that my refusal weakened my position in the organization.

When it was suggested to me that certain professional men were seeking offices on committees or boards of directors in order to obtain and/or increase their clientele, I dismissed it as malicious gossip. In the course of time, however, I learned that a certain doctor or lawyer would withdraw from active service in the organization because he became "too busy" in his profession. I realized that organizations and institutions were being used by some individuals. Especially shocking to me was the case of a broker who spoke incessantly about the sales he was going to make at the forthcoming Zionist convention. He spoke with gusto about the suite he had reserved and the liquour he had ordered for this purpose. To my remark, "the way you talk your main purpose in going to the convention is apparently to make a lot of sales", his reaction was, "what did you think I was going to the convention for?"

Pants vs. Skirts

This attitude was also manifested by convention delegates whose primary purpose — so said the cynics — was to sell or buy their wares. We were discussing the most suitable time and place for a convention. Some suggested Vancouver in the Spring because businessmen from the East go there at that time to buy skirts. Others thought that the best place would be Montreal in the Fall when people go there to buy pants. I summed up the discussion by saying: "Then, Ladies and Gentleman, it's a case of skirts vs. pants". Some seemed to look at me angrily, but some laughed! In pondering this human foible, I thought of Reb Levi Yitzchak of Berditchev who would always see the positive side of human action. When he saw a coachman oiling his wagonwheels while praying, he exclaimed, "Master of the Universe, see how wonderful your children are, they pray even when they oil their wagon-wheels". To paraphrase this saintly Rabbi, "How wonderful are Zionist leaders; they work for Zionism even when they buy pants or skirts". In truth, the Talmudic statement (Jerusalem Talmud, Chagigah 1) "from doing something not for its own sake, you will eventually come to do it for its own sake" is applicable here. Most of these people, even if they started out with an ulterior motive, became engrossed in and dedicated to the organization they served.

Chapter 9
Vignettes of Zionist-Jewish Realities in Western Canada
Small Communities Go Constitutional

The trend to do away with separate fund-raising campaigns started in small centers whose Jewish communities numbered betwen twenty and forty families. They served as an easy target for hordes of representatives and Meshulachim (solicitors for *yeshivot* and other orthodox institutions), who would go from house to house and from store to store to solicit contributions, and each one would describe his "cause" as most important.

People were escpeically annoyed by Meshulachim who, as the rumors had it, received fifty percent of the "take", in addition to their expenses. In self defence, these communities organized "budgets" from which allocations would be made to various organizations. They fortified their position by adopting constitutions with the provision that no separate solicitation for funds should be permitted. While this was a reasonable solution to a chaotic situation, the leaders of some of these communities did not distinguish between a *yeshivah* or a charitable organization and the United Palestine Appeal. Some allocated funds from their budget to charitable organizations, but insisted that the J.D.C. and the U.P.A. should conduct a united drive. These leaders were encouraged by the J.D.C., which competed strongly with the U.P.A. The J.D.C. preferred to be partners with the U.P.A. in communities where their prospects were not favourable, while they conducted separate drives in cities where their position was stronger. In Daupin, Manitoba, I had made arrangements for a separate U.P.A. Campaign, with Mr. A.M. Shinbane, one of the most prominent attorneys and Zionist leaders in Winnipeg, as the guest speaker. Mr. Louis Rosenberg, then Western Executive Director of the Canadian Jewish Congress, proposed that a joint drive should be held with the J.D.C. On September 8, 1940, I wrote Mr. Rosenberg, "We are bound by a resolution of the last National Convention of the Zionist Organization of Canada, under which we have no authority to permit joint campaigns." Mr. Shinbane informed me that if the leaders in Dauphin insisted on a joint campaign, he would have no alternative but to comply. As far as I remember, we went ahead with our own campaign, but I do not recall whether Mr. Shinbane was the guest speaker.

I am Nearly Thrown Out of a Home

Medicine Hat, Alberta, was one of the communities that had a budget. Its allocation for the U.P.A. in 1940 was 150 dollars. Upon my arrival in Medicine Hat, the president of the community told me I could not expect to raise even one cent more. My policy was to disregard such statements and to put my case before the U.P.A. meeting. I made a strong appeal, and raised there and then in cash 211 dollars over and above the 150 allocation. I was invited to speak the next day to a Hadassah meeting at the home of Mrs. Harry Veiner, whose husband was then the mayor of the city. In a conversation I had had with him earlier, he made clear to me his anti-Zionist stand and his opposition to my raising funds in his community. He was a huge fellow who could intimidate anyone by his mere size. It was said that he had knocked out all the teeth of a fellow who had made a snide remark about Jews. When, in the middle of the meeting, giant Veiner suddenly barged into the room, I knew there would be trouble. He snarled at me with his bellicose voice: "What are *you* doing here? If you don't get out, I'll throw you out!" Were it not for his embarrassed wife, who positioned herself between him and me, I believe he would have been ready to throw me out bodily. He walked away angrily when his wife insisted she would not allow any abuse of her "honoured guest". Many years later I was both amused and pleased to see in the newspaper a picture of Mr. Veiner in his ten-gallon-hat standing and smiling beside Mr. David Ben-Gurion. Mr. Veiner had become an enthusiastic supporter of Israel.

"I Don't Invest in Lost Causes"

In one of the larger cities, I was told that a leading businessman had refused to make a contribution to the U.P.A. Somebody suggested that if I would accompany him on a visit to this person, he would probably be induced to "come across". After listening to our story, he stated categorically that Rommel would "soon enter Palestine and *that* would be the death knell of the Zionist dream". "I am a practical business man", he said, "and I do not invest in lost causes." We did not let go, and the practical businessman risked an investment of 25 dollars. Some years later, he became one of the leading national Zionist leaders. In 1949, when I was about to return with my family to Israel, and Mr. Edward Gelber proposed a resolution, at a meeting of the National Executive of the Zionist Organization, expressing gratitude for my outstanding contribution to Zionism and Hebrew Education in Canada, this practical businessman was opposed on the ground that "Rabbi Horowtiz educated our young people to be Israelis rather than Canadians". I regret that he is no longer among the living and can't see the numerous Canadian Zionist-Hebraists I helped educate, many of whom are to be found serving Canada in the universities, in the professions, in education, and in Government. True, a sizable number are serving in the same fields in Israel, but they also contribute to forging cultural links between Canada and Israel. He and others had the erroneous idea that a person's Canadianism was diminished to the degree that his Zionism-Judaism was enhanced.

"Our Constitution Precludes Our Receiving You"

Trail, British Columbia, had not been on the Zionist map for who knows how long. All I know is that after I broke through the "Trail Wall" against fund raisers, Rabbi Jesse Schwartz wrote me in his letter of November 17, 1940, "To be guilty of a poor pun, you opened up a new trail". Little did he know that it took quite some chutzpah to do it.

In reply to the notice of my arrival on a certain date to conduct the U.P.A. Campaign, I was told in no uncertain terms that I would not be welcome. Trail had a constitution and a budget and would make an allocation to the U.P.A. I explained to them in a long letter the tragic situation of our people, the need for understanding and for a sense of unity of our people everywhere, in order to bring about an end to our homelessness and to reconstitute our nationhood in our land. They were adamant in their refusal, and informed me by wire that nobody would receive me. I replied by wire that I was coming and that I wanted to see whether they would really not receive me. When I arrived, I phoned from the train station to the home of the leader with whom I had been in contact and was told that a meeting was in progress to decide whether to give me a hearing. I should wait at the station until they inform me of their decision. I remember my feelings of dejection. I could not comprehend why a group of Jewish people anywhere would deny a hearing to a representative of the Zionist Movement. They could have said, I thought, "we'll be glad to hear your message, but will adhere to our decision to make an allocation from our budget." After all, they were isolated from the Jewish world, and could have at least had a desire to hear a Jewish speaker once in so many years. It gave me a taste, a very bitter taste, of the bleak future that faced outlying communities. After waiting for what seemed to be an endless time, I was informed of the good news; they would hear me! The large room where all the members of the community were congregated was full of cigarette and cigar smoke. The tension must have been very high, for after all they had just had to make a world-shaking decision. I started my message by waving their wire at them. I said in a genuinely impassioned voice, "The grand mufti of Jerusalem, who is now in Berlin scheming with the Nazis on their "final solution" of the Jewish-Zionist problem, would gladly pay for this wire a much larger amount than your possible total contribution could be tonight". My compensation for the anguish and exhaustion I suffered came right after I sat down. One of the fellows exclaimed, "I know all about our constitution, but after hearing this here guy, I say 'you can shove your contitution up your ass', and I am the first one to give one hundred dollars!" Mr. Leo Levy, now Judge Levy of Vancouver who (I was to learn later) had been working tirelessly in the background to break the Trail wall, must have felt as triumphant as I at the results. (When I told the story later to Max Waterman, tears were flowing down our cheeks.)

Whether You Like It or Not, You Now Have a Jew

After I had set out on my way to the two Northernmost Jewish communities, Le Pas and Flin Flon, I learned that there was no train to bring me to Flin Flon on time for the meeting I was to address. I tried to make my way by hitch-hiking, although I was told of the law against picking up hitch-hikers on that route. Two salesmen finally took pity on "the gentleman with the large suitcase in his hand", and drove me up to a town the name of which I have forgotten. When I entered the lobby of the only hotel, it was full of men smoking, chewing tobacco and spitting from various directions into cuspidors. I approached the desk and inquired as to whether there were any Jews in town. The fellow looked up at me in amazement and shouted, "You hear what this fellow is asking? Is there a Jew in Town?" He answered his own question, "No, we don't have and we don't need any Jew in town". All eyes turned on me when I exclaimed loud and clear: "Well, you now have one!" The same fellow went out of his way to get somebody to drive me to Flin Flon. In thanking him, I queried, "what is stronger, your desire to help me, or to get rid of the only Jew in town?" Hearty laughter followed.

Flin Flon was the newest town in the north. Mines of zinc and copper were discovered there, and Jews are of course always among the first settlers. The whole atmosphere reminded me of a town in its beginnings in Israel. Here, too, I was faced with a constitution, but here too we succeeded, with the help of A. Ostry and Moshe Fox, in being unconstitutional. It was, I believe, Mr. Fox who set an example to others by declaring that he could not make a sizable cash contribution, but the U.P.A. would henceforth be a monthly item on his budget, just like water and electricity.

Many of these contributors everywhere in Western Canada were hard-working people who felt they had to make sacrifices for the Zionist cause. That was especially true of the small number of Jewish families in Leader Saskatchewan. In Leader, more than any other place, I saw the signs of the Depression and the drought. It was the first and only time I saw children running around barefoot on the streets anywhere in Canada. The leader of the Jewish community, attorney S.W. Kesten, in whose home my meeting was held, told me he had seen very little cash in recent years. How did he make a living? His clients paid him with chickens, dairy products, etc. Davkah here, there was no sign of reluctance to participate in an open campaign, and contributions were willingly made by everyone.

A Jewish Mayor in a Town with a Handful of Jews

When I got to Le Pas, I was surprised to learn that Mr. Dembinsky, in whose home my meeting took place, was the very popular mayor of the town. Obviously, it was in small remote places that Jews first struck deep roots. It is sad that, in many cases, their Jewish roots were entirely submerged in the process. I could not help but wonder why these Jews were satisfied to live in such a remote place where there could hardly be even a semblance of organized Jewish life. Is it possible that they could not find *parnasah* (a livelihood) in a place with a Jewish community!

On the other hand, I met parents who made heroic efforts to bring up their children with Jewish knowledge and spirit by teaching them themselves, by telling them stories of Jewish life in the "old country", and by surrounding them with materials and books of Jewish content. An excellent example was the Harry Olyan family of Vegreville Alta., where there were only a few Jewish families. When I came into their home, I became aware at once of the atmosphere of genuine warm hospitality bequeathed to us by "Father Abraham and Mother Sarah". The Olyan home was always open to guests, and they never denied help to anybody. Mrs. Olyan not only taught her own children, but volunteered to give of herself and her knowledge to the other Jewish children in town.

A Lithuanian Jew in the Middle of Nowhere

The larger of the smaller towns, such as Yorkton and Kamsack, Saskatchewan, did not present us with "constitution" or "budget" problems. Not only did they hold regularly their annual U.P.A. drive, but they always endeavoured to bring to their meetings Jews from isolated places within a radius of about a hundred miles. I was told of one mysterious fellow who never came to the meetings. One of the leaders of Yorkton offered to drive me to his place. When we arrived in that remote corner, dusk had already settled on the area. All I could see were little dancing lights from distant farms that seemed to beckon the lone store that provided them with their manufactured and industrial goods. And who was the owner of this general store, who but a Lithuanian Jew who lived there in loneliness and isolation. At first, he looked at me as if I had descended from the moon. It took some time before he gave up his reticence and led us into a very small room that was curtained off from the store. Imagine my astonishment when I saw many shelves laden with the sixty-three volumes of the Talmud and with such Hebrew classics as Mendele, Peretz, Achad-Haam, Bialik and Tchernichovsky. Who knows what motivations, what traumas had brought this scholarly Lithuanian Jew to that remote outpost? I was tempted to try to penetrate into his soul, but — right or wrong — I sensed that I might bestir some painful memories.

Baron De Hirsch vs. Theodore Herzl

For some time, I had known of the existence of Baron De Hirsch colonies in Western Canada. I had learned and taught in Zionist History courses about the French Jewish baron who rejected the call of Dr. Harzl to help rebuild Eretz Israel, and chose rather to invest huge sums in establishing Jewish agricultural settlements in Argentina and Canada. I wanted to see and compare such a Hirsch colony with the agricultural settlements in Eretz Israel. I was forewarned that the Yiddishist-Bundists of Dysart Sask. would not look forward with enthusiasm to a visit by a Zionist leader. "Well', I thought, "this will not be the first place about which I heard such stories". What I saw in the Dysart colony filled me with sadness and sympathy — old people with lack-luster expressions, whose entire bearing showed little satisfaction with the present or hope for the future. It was clear to me that what I saw was the end rather than the beginning of a project. Their children would obviously not continue their work!

The room where the meeting was held was so overcrowded that there was no space between me and my audience. I was somewhat ill-at-ease when I described the joy of the farmers in the kibbutzim and Moshavim in their work for the rebuilding of their own land. I felt as if I were a *"Lo'eg La'rash"* (literally, a mockery of the poor); for according to Proverbs 16, 5, "Whoso mocketh the poor blasphemeth his Maker". Nonetheless, I overcame that feeling and spoke about Zionism with even greater enthusiasm than before other audiences. The people listened attentively, but right in front of me sat a bulky woman with her arms folded on her big bosom, murmuring: "Hah, Kibbutzim . . . Hah, Moshavim . . . Hah, Palestine . . . H'm, Zionism . . ." When I finished speaking, I was surrounded by many people who were anxious to know more and more details about the Promised Land. I did get an argument, however, from the bosomy lady.

Chapter 10
Approaching the End
Of a Milestone

Politics Reared its Head

The first chapter of my service was about to come to an end quite unexpectedly. I had great satisfaction in my work, and my expectations for the future were high, even euphorious at times. In 1939, at the beginning of that chapter, the Zionist office was contained in one small room, and the staff consisted of a part-time executive secretary, who looked after all the work, including typing for Hadassah. Three years later, there were an executive director, a full-time executive secretary, and two full-time typists. The office was in charge of all Zionist activities — fund raising, education, youth, etc. in an area extending from Fort William-Port Arthur, Ontario, to Victoria, British Columbia. The income from all sources grew very substantially from year to year, and Zionism became the most potent force in Jewish life. Unfortunately, prosperity brings along with it the game of jockeying for power and position; in a word — *Politics*. And, right or wrong, I run from politics as from a plague.

While I was away from the city on one of my long tours, the national vice president for Winnipeg, and the executive secretary, (who served also as the editor of the *Jewish Post*), put their heads together and decided that the Winnipeg office should be separated from the regional office. I could not see rhyme or reason for such separation. Winnipeg was the largest and the most active center. To separate it from the other communities seemed to me to be tantamount, as it were, to cutting the head from the body. This scheme, I thought, could only have been concocted by individuals who did not consider the realities and the best interests of the region, but were motivated by personal reasons. What riled me most was that this plan was conceived and executed during my absence and without consultation with me and other communities. To put it simply, I was convinced that the editor was being rewarded for his political support.

When the Judaean leaders were thinking aloud, so to speak, about their inability to pay a director, I told them I would contribute my three weeks' vacation (the period set for the duration of the camp) to the project. Since I *took* no vacation during the three years of my work with the Zionist Organization, I was given three wekks' vacation with pay, a week for each year, which made it possible for me to volunteer my services to the camp. (In fairness to the Zionist Organization, I should point out that I do not remember whether I asked or they offered three weeks for three years). Much could be learned from this episode about the "head offices" attitude to their peripheries. While the youngsters in Winnipeg could not get any subsidy or any other substantive help from their parent organization, Camp Hagshamah was coming into being at about the same time in the East. It was organized by the Young Judaean Exective Director, and received all the necessary assistance from the head offices of both the parent and youth organizations. I therefore referred to the camp in Winnipeg as the "first in Canada", because of its *chalutzic* nature and because of the circumstances under which it was born. It is doubtful whether Hagshamah would have materialized that year without the time, effort and substance afforded to it by the energetic Judaean Executive Director.

The activities consisted mostly of *Sichot* (discussions). At the urging of the leaders (they had to stay at their jobs in the city, but joined us on weekends), I devoted as many as six hours daily to *sichot*. When it rained for the first time, a vote was taken whether to play some indoor games or to have an additional *sichah*. All but the youngest one voted for a *sichah*. When I had discussed an alternate program for rainy days with the leaders in the city, they had strongly urged me not to leave the decision to the kids. A few days after I arrived in camp, I received a letter from Sid Buckwold urging me "to stuff them with more and more Zionist ideas and facts", since I would shortly depart from Winnipeg.

It is interesting but not unusual that one of the very top Zionist leaders, whose children were active in Young Judaea, was skeptical about the kids' ability to conduct a camp properly. The parents therefore did not allow their children to join the camp until they themselves made a long trip to Winnipeg "to see with their own eyes". When they witnessed the enthusiasm and high spirits of the campers, the decided to entrust their children to us. I was not sure, however, that the leader's "satisfaction" was not in the nature of *Vayichad Yitro* — and Jethro rejoiced. In Exodus 18-9, we read, "and Jethro rejoiced for all the goodness which the Lord had done to Israel". Rashi interprets *Vayichad* (he rejoiced) to mean "his body broke out in goosepimples" (free translation), as *Vayichad* also means — he had pain or anxiety.

Chapter 11
The Hebrew University Discovers Canada

When I left for America in 1938, I was requested by the Hebrew University in Jerusalem "to work on its behalf in Canada and to disseminate information regarding the significance, structure and aims of the university", and I was given "full authority to represent" it. During the year I spent in New York, all I could do was to address a few groups on the importance of the Hebrew University. In Canada, working for the Hebrew University blended naturally into the cultural activities of our total Zionist program; for I conceived of the Hebrew University not merely as another house of learning where the sciences and humanities are studied and furthered, but as an organic part of our National Renaissance. To me, its main mission was to serve as a directive force in the shaping of our reborn Hebrew civilization in the land that had given to the world, to all humanity, some of its greatest spiritual values.

Our cultural program therefore included the annual celebration of the founding of the Hebrew University. The first such celebration happened to fall on the 15th anniversary of the institution.

I had been told that a brilliant young lawyer by the name of Samuel Freedman (now Chief Justice of the province of Manitoba) had evinced a keen interest in the Hebrew University. I invited him to be the main speaker at the celebration, and he in turn suggested that we have among the speakers Rev. Dr. E. Guthrey Perry, professor of Hebrew at the University of Manitoba, who had represented Canada at the opening ceremonies of the Hebrew University in Jerusalem.

The event made an indelible impression on the overflowing audience that filled the large hall and balconies of the Talmud Torah.

Mr. Freedman spoke in glowing terms about the significance of the Hebrew University. Professor Perry related his experiences on his journey to the university, and drew a vivid picture of the imposing opening-event in the presence of some of the greatest world scientists and leaders. He amused the audience with anecdotes, the only one of which I remember is that when he sat down to "break bread" with a group of shipmates, which included Dr. Shmaryahu Levine and other Hebraists, they were impressed when he offered to lead in the recitation of *Hamotzi*. Professor Perry then proceeded to recite to us the *Hamotzi*, and his Winnipeg audience gave him one of the greatest ovations I ever witnessed. I was more puzzled than amused by the enthusiasm of a Jewish audience over the fact that a "goy" could recite a Brachah in Hebrew . . . I mused: would this audience be equally enthusiastic about the fact that I, who didn't know the English alphabet up to my arrival in Canada at age 16, could speak English far better than Prof. Perry could speak Hebrew!

My activities on behalf of the Hebrew University, limited as they were, brought me in contact with Mr. Samuel B. Finkel, then the director of the American Friends of the Hebrew University. In 1941 he invited me to visit him in his New York office to consult with me on the ways and means of establishing a society of Canadian Friends similar to the one in the U.S.A.[1] I suggested that all efforts be made to recruit Mr. Allan Bronfman[2] as chairman of such a society. Later, when I decided to leave the Zionist Organization, I informed Mr. Finkel of my readiness to organize the society in Canada and to serve as its national director. Mr. Finkel immediately contacted Salmann Shocken, then chairman of the executive council of the Hebrew University, and obtained his approval of my appointment to this position. I had already started to formulate plans for this large undertaking, when I received an urgent request from Mr. Shaye Jaffe. president of the Calgary Hebrew School, that I find a replacement for Mr. David Eisenberg who had suddenly resigned his position as principal. Had this letter arrived a few weeks later, I certainly would have been the one to lay the foundations of the Canadian Friends of the Hebrew University. When the letter arrived, my wife, who was unhappy at the prospect that I would continue to wander throughout Canada, seized this opportunity to point out to me that I could now meet the challenge of proving the validity of my ideas about revolutionizing Hebrew Education in Western Canada. When I would return home from

[1] Recently, I asked the office of the Canadian Friends of the Hebrew University to send me material on the history of the Canadian Friends. Not at all surprising, the memorandum I received starts with the year 1944 when the organization was officially inaugurated. I therefore interviewed Chief Justice Samuel Freedman during my recent tour of Western Canada, about *T'kufat B'reshit* (literally the period of "In the beginning"), on the events preceding 1944. In fairness to "history", the summary of this interview is included here as an appendix.
[2] About two years later, Mr. Finkel informed me that "Dr. Walter Ficshel was successful in having Allan Bronfman assume the presidency of the Canadian Friends of the Hebrew University". A full time Canadian national director was not engaged until 1949.

my frequent visits to the Hebrew schools in the larger communities, I would tell her that the teachers, and especially the principals, were always telling me that my ideas were sound in theory but impractical in reality. "Well", she said, "you are now faced with the challenge of proving to yourself whether your ideas are practical and if they are, you can then make a significant contribution to Hebrew education in the *Galut*". My wife's attitude and logic made it easier for me to renege on a commitment for the second time (the only two times) in my life. This time I rationalized that my agreement with the University was only in principle, since we had not come to an understanding on the terms and conditions of my position. Mr. Shocken and Mr. Finkel were very understanding and gracious . . .

It was thus that Calgary became the laboratory for my experiments in Hebrew Education.

Chapter 12
The Calgary Phenomenon

The Calgary Hebrew School was one of the best in Western Canada, and therefore in the whole of the Dominion. It was a good school in the sense that it succeeded in meeting the requirements of the community as understood and interpreted by its lay leaders. Their requirements, however, were not based on a conscious philosophy embodying a clear definition of the aims of Hebrew education, the ways and means of attaining them and the testing of their efficacy with a view to ensuring the continuing progress and evolvement of the educational process. The "requirements" consisted rather in an automatic transfer of the contents and methods of the East European Cheder, which was largely in harmony with Jewish life in the *shtetel*, to a new environment, which was progressively in conflict with the old way of life.

Not only to Jewish parents, but also to lay leaders and teachers, Jewish education meant:

Teaching children to read Hebrew, so that they would be able to *daven* (pray):

Giving them some knowledge of Yiddish, in order that they would be able to communicate with their grandparents;

Imparting to them some knowledge of Hebrew language and grammar, so that they could "study the holy Torah" (even though their knowledge of Hebrew was never sufficient to really understand, much less appreciate, Torah);

Teaching them some "History", which very rarely went past the *Churban*, the destruction of the Holy Temple in Jerusalem. And the one conscious goal was to insure somehow that they remain and marry Yidden.

The national and cultural aspects of Judaism were almost entirely ignored. The emphasis was thus on the cognitive and ritual, so that "Jewish education" was largely a technological and mechanical rather than an educative process.

It was therefore natural that, with the weakening of religious faith and practice, and in the absence of a strong national feeling, the emphasis began to shift gradually from the goal of remaining Yidden to the increasingly overriding goal of striving to strike roots in Canada. This process began to develop at a time when there was no philosophy or spirit of multiculturalism, but rather when immigrants of various ethnic cultures were intent on shedding their "green horn" mantles and becoming submerged in a general "melting pot". There were no scholars or intellectual leaders to evolve a conscious philosophy and program that would serve as a design for new immigrants to become an integral part of an emerging Canadian Nation while simultaneously preserving and developing the languages and cultural values of their native cultures. To be a "true-blue" Canadian meant to escape from one's history and traditional modes of life. Even the Rabbis lacked the intellectual capacity to develop such a design. Almost all of the modern Rabbis were imports from the U.S.A., where the melting pot was the ideal and norm. Their near fatal mistake, *at that juncture*, was to believe and preach that the synagogue and its lifeless rituals would be capable of stemming the tides of assimilation, or, as I prefer to call it, the disintegration of one's original cultural values. Judaism was thus relegated to the status of a creed. As Chaim Nachman Bialik put it, "a nation of three thousand years' existence suddenly made the self-calumniating announcement that it had no culture of its own and had to go to learn from others. The nation that was the first to create a school for the children of the people became a child at the schools of strangers. The culture of Israel, of four thousand years' duration, was declared worthless".

Thus, most of the modern Rabbis, who were trained as functionaries of ritual and social acrobatics, fashioned their programs in imitation of Christian denominations. Hence, one could hear not only lay teachers but also Rabbis refer to Jews as Americans or Canadians of Jewish persuasion. Thus, people started to think of Judaism as merely another religious denomination, and thus started the emergence in Canada, and the poliferation in the U.S.A., of Sunday Schools (or as I used to refer to them unequivocally, *Shande*, shameful, schools), which were and are one of the chief causes of the disintegration of Jewish life in America.

Fortunately, there was no modern Rabbi at that time in Calgary. There was an orthodox *shochet-cantor*, Rabbi D. Barenholtz. He attended also to ceremonials such as weddings, and I represented the Jewish to the general community. The school was therefore unfettered by rabbinic interference.

My first meeting with the leadership of the school was somewhat dramatic. I started my presentation with a quote from one of my own lectures: "Education is much more an art than a science. It is a sacred, magnificient and inspiring art. It is the greatest of all the arts. For the educator-artist must find also within himself the fine-sensitive tools with which to mould, shape and unfold the most complex, the most mysterious and the most fascinating of God's creations — the human mind and soul." I then defined our educational philosophy as three dimensional: preparation for Jewish living (paraphrasing Herbert Spencer); the passing on of our culture to the new generation (paraphrasing John Stuart Mill); and the achievement of a synthesis between the values of our Hebrew civilization and the culture of the country wherein we live.

To attain these aims, I said, we would have to transform the technical-mechanical approach, (which John Dewey termed "the art of taking advantage of the helplessness of the young"), into a living and creative *educational* institution. Our ultimate goal, I said, should be, to provide suitable conditions and facilities for the cultivation of a Jewish personality that will draw its cultural and spiritual sustenance from the rich heritage of Israel, a personality that will be rooted in both Hebrew and Canadian culture, a personality that will be a part of a living Jewish and general community and will participate in all phases of its life.

We shall have to discard the old methods of teaching by rote — by recitation, memorization and regurgitation of words and facts, without any relation to or interaction between what is learned and life situations and between the past and the child's present life experiences. We shall not limit ourselves to book learning, and we shall not count the pages to be learned. We shall endeavour to educate not only by *"limud Hameivi lidei Maaseh"*, by learning that leads to doing, but also by learning through living.

For this purpose, we shall introduce the Sephardic, the living pronunciation that is used by those who are reviving our Hebrew language in Eretz Israel. We shall endeavour to turn the school into a place where children will think, learn, question, discuss, play, sing, dance, create and live. The students will be given the freedom and the opportunity to express their views, to plan, to prepare and to carry out educational and social activities. In a word, they will be given the opportunity and encouragement for self-expression and for development as individuals and as part of a vital community.

When I finished my presentation, there was dead silence for a few moments. The audience seemed to be deep in thought, when Mr. A.I. Schumiatcher, K.C., one of the first teachers of the school, interrupted their thoughts with a bang. "Who are we, a small community with about four hundred Jewish families to revolutionize Jewish education? Have our neighbours in Edmonton introduced the Sephardic pronunciation, and if it is to be preferred, why haven't the largest communities in Canada, Montreal and Toronto, introduced it?" Another member chimed in: "Won't this change make for confusion in the Synagogue, where the Ashkenazic pronunciation predominates?" I thought it remarkable that very few participated in the discussion. When it ended, I addressed myself only to the argument about the Synagogue. I pointed out that our pupils will have their own Junior Congregation, and it was my hope that by the time they were ready to participate actively in the Synagogue, the trend will be for the adoption of the Sephardic accent.

Mr. Schumiatcher then moved that no changes should be made in any area until the opinion of such educators as mr. Magid of Montreal and mr. Moshe Goelman of Edmonton were canvassed.

I rose from my seat and stated calmly: education is much more complex than medicine, and a physician would not agree to be directed by laymen in his healing methods. Nor would he agree to be guided by other physicians. (I wondered how the physicians in the audience felt when I compared *melamdut* to their honourable profession). It is a very simple matter," I said. "If you want me to be your doctor, you will have to give me the confidence and freedom to follow my own philosophy and methods. If you disagree, we shall remain good friends. I will make to financial claims on the school; I will help you to get another doctor and will move out as soon as one is obtained." Mr. Jaffe pulled me by my sleeve and eclared loud and clear: "Sit down, Rabbi Horowitz; you have our full confidence, and you will have all the freedom you need and want". I looked around the hall and asked, "Is that clearly understood and agreed upon?" I took the silence to mean approval, and the meeting moved on to other matters. In retrospect, I wonder whether there would have been even one other school in Canada that would have tolerated such *chutzpah* from a *melamed*. The leadership of the Calgary Hebrew School *was* indeed unique!

(When Mr. Goelman learned about my "revolution", he expressed the same sentiments as Mr. Schumiatcher. I was in no position to know what Mr. Magid's reaction might have been, as there was no communication between us at that time. When I moved to Montreal at the end of 1946, he seemed to have appreciated my "courage" as the first to introduce the Sephardic pronunciation on the American continent, and he was among the very first to institute it in his school after the establishment of the State of Israel.)

Who were some of these people, with whom I worked most closely, and who had the insight and the courage to go along with us in our experiments?

Shaya Jaffe, the most knowledgeable of the group in Hebrew sources, son of a Lithuanian Rabbi, a book lover whose seeming greatest delight was when he heard children study Torah and speak Hebrew;

Charles Waterman, a wise man, who gave much of his heart and substance to every constructive endeavour, who, though possessed of power, used his authority only in crucial situations; .

Joe Joffe, an extraordinary human being whose seeming greatest satisfaction was to bring cheer to other human beings;

Morris Wolochow, a sagacious man, who gave practically his entire time to the community;

Henry Goldberg, a knowledgeable and wise gentleman par excellence;

Sam Datner, who fought hard for his convictions, but went along with the group, and gave of himself to a variety of organizations;

I. Engle, who preferred to be in the background, but who quietly used his influence for the good;

Max Katzin, an unassuming selfless person, who quietly, almost anonymously, contributed much to Zionism and Hebrew education, and one of those people who enable you to maintain your faith in human beings;

Nathan Safran, the youngest of the group, a dynamo for Hebrew education and Zionism, one of the most outstanding products of the school he served with singular dedication.

Now It Can Be Told

I was puzzled that our "revolution" was going so smoothly. I had expected strong opposition, and steeled myself to ignore any rumblings that might occur among leaders and parents. I had a feeling that some people were displeased, if not up in arms, about the radical changes that were taking place in the school, but I was too immersed in the work and pre-occupied with the children to pay any attention. About half a year later, Mr. Jaffe disclosed to me that the school leadership had deliberately shielded me from the wrath of some of the parents. He and others would get phone calls demanding why time was wasted on such things as dancing and playing (disregarding the fact that all such activities took place outside of classroom time). "These activities", they said "belong in Young Judaea, not in school". Eventually, some of the students revealed to me that, "in the beginning" there were heated debates in their homes about me and my methods.

That was the easiest hurdle, which had to be followed by the painstaking process of gradually translating lofty ideas into reality. We began the new pronunciation in the kindergarten and in the first and eighth grades, and then proceeded quickly from the seventh grade down until the change was completed within two years. The Israeli accent did much to enliven the studies and activities of the school.

The Proverbial "Dumb-Class"

Among other problems we had to tackle was that of the so-called "dumb class". An easy solution had been found for the slow learners. They had all been dumped into one class, where they were fed with a special low-study diet, given primarily in the Yiddish language, because they were "too dumb" to learn Hebrew. And who was assigned as their teacher? The one who had the most trouble maintaining discipline. We gradually phased out this class by individual coaching and by instilling the students with self-confidence. The stigmatised teacher too was given a new lease on teaching in the changed general atmosphere of the institution.

It is not my purpose to describe step by step the developments, the progress, the problems, the frustrations, the failures and the achievements. That would require a separate book. Here I shall merely outline briefly what it was that gave birth to the "Calgary Phenomenon".

The First Hebrew-Speaking Youth Movement in Canada

We brought into being a "student council" that was truly active and self-governing and that transformed itself two years later into a Hebrew Speaking Youth Movement in which all pupils from grade three and up were involved. This organization was created at a Youth Conference that lasted for five days during Chanukah 1944. The senior students planned and executed the entire program; they were the speakers and debaters; they framed the rules and resolutions; they made all the organizational and technical arrangements; they did the cooking and the baking; they set the tables, and served the meals; and they washed the dishes and cleaned the kitchen. They had gained the ability to do these things during the preceding two years, from the monthly Oneg Shabbat which was open to the public and which featured a Shabbat meal and program. At each Oneg Shabbat, all the three Hebrew-speaking *Chugim* (clubs) presented programs that were designed by their members. We were blessed with some very talented students, notably David Sidorsky, Dvorah Smolensky-Yehoshua and Esther Wise, who wrote (all in Hebrew) skits, dramatizations and poems. One of those poems was created in a rather strange setting. A number of students were visiting with us one evening (our home and library were always open to them). We were chatting (all in Hebrew) about this and that, when I noticed "Davey" Sidorsky scribbling on a sheet of paper. He crumpled the paper and threw it at the wastebasket. (He missed the mark!) I picked it up and was astonished to read a beautiful poem, "The Chain of Sparks", conveying in capsule form different voices, the Voice of Rachel in Ramah (Jeremiah 31:15), the voice in the Ghetto, the Voice in America, and the Echo from the Mountains of Judea. Prof. Hugo Shmuel Bergman, philosopher and first Rector of the Hebrew University in Jerusalem, later wrote me that this poem made a great impression on him, especially the part that speaks of the situation in America. It was nothing new to me that David could write beautifully in English; a year earlier, he had written a magnificent poem in English, *Yizkor*, about the Holocaust! But I did not think he could compose a poem in such meticulous and beautiful Hebrew while he was still a student in our Hebrew High School. When his Hebrew poem was recited (with an English translation) for the first time by his eleven-year old sister Ninah, many people in the audience had tears in their eyes. I have been using both these poems throughout the years on various occasions.

The Calgary Hebrew Youth Movement affiliated with the *Noar-Ivri* (Hebrew Youth) in New York, which had been organized a few years earlier by a group of young American-born Hebrew idealists, led by Shlomo Schulsinger, the indefatigable pioneer of Hebrew camping in America; Yaakov Kabakov, now Hebrew literary critic and professor of Hebrew at Hunter College, and Moshe Davis. We had to affiliate with our American counterpart, because there was no such organization in Canada at that time.

Speaking Hebrew in Calgary

We were faced with the problem of how to create a Hebrew speaking atmosphere in a place where nobody spoke Hebrew. It was no easy task. We knew that the path of reward and punishment would be ineffective. We set about to gradually create a natural Hebrew speaking atmosphere in and around the school. The *Ivrit B'Ivrit* method (teaching without translation) had already been well established in the better schools in the U.S.A. and Canada, but even this method did not bring forth Hebrew speaking kids. The texts, almost always above the language-comprehension levels of the students, were explained in simpler Hebrew, but it was a far cry from natural-flowing speech. At times, I would have to restrain myself from laughing when I heard teachers explain texts in Hebrew. Here is one example (for those who know Hebrew): *Va-Adonoy — ve-Hashem; hitzliach — heivi lehatzlocho; darki — haderech sheli; (osso she'zliach); shalchuni — shalchu ossi; ve'elcha la'adoni — ve'ani eilech la'adoni — ve'ani eilech la'adon sheli* (Genesis 24:56). We therefore made every endeavour to use easier texts, to explain in spoken Hebrew, and to stimulate speaking by the question and answer method. In the beginning, I personally did a lot of speaking, much more than pedagogically sound.', until my students became used to the sound and flow of spoken Hebrew.

We, the students and the teachers, decided that only Hebrew would be spoken within the classrooms and the confines of the school. We, the teachers and the senior students, were careful not to admonish anyone for not speaking Hebrew and not to coax anyone to speak Hebrew. If anyone would turn to us in English, we would simply repeat the question in Hebrew and proceed to answer it in Hebrew.

Hebrew Speaking Clubs

We realized that Hebrew would not become a spoken language if used only within the school. We therefore organized three Hebrew speaking groups that purposely met, weekly, in private homes, in an informal, tension-free atmosphere. The conversations, discussions and educational games were always followed by singing and, sometimes, dancing. As mentioned before, all the three *chugim* met together once monthly, so that the kids met four times a month in a Hebrew speaking environment.

Hebrew Library

We encouraged reading for enjoyment outside of the school. For that purpose, the student council built up, with their meager means, a library that in 1945 already contained 120 books, and 300 booklets for younger children. Many of the kids really read books. In her report on the library, Sarah Srolowitz, chief librarian, reported that the most popular books were: "Pinochio in Eretz Israel" by Avigdor Hame'iri, and "The Dwarfs in Tel-Aviv".

Hebrew Synagogue

Our synagogue, which was attended also by the teachers, was not called junior congregation, but Bait Ha-knesset, and was conducted by the pupils entirely in Hebrew. Every Shabbat, a different pupil spoke in Hebrew on the portion of the week, and only Hebrew was heard during the social period that followed the Services.

Niru Lachem Nir — Break up for you a Fallow Ground

Even before the Hebrew Youth Movement was established, the student council started to publish (in actual print) an annual Hebrew newspaper as a vehicle of expression for the students. It included compositions, stories, poems and detailed reports of their activities. They called it *Nir* (literally, a ploughed field), to indicate their ploughing in the fields of Hebrew culture. This name was inspired by Jeremiah's exhortation "Break for you a fallow ground, and sow not among thorns" (Jeremiah 4:3).

One year, "Nir" was published in the Israelite Press, to make it available to all the Hebrew schools in the West. This edition inspired the editor, Mark Seltchen, to devote not only an editorial but also his daily column to an enthusiastic appraisal of the Calgary Hebrew Hebrew School and its Hebrew Youth Movement.

A Part of the Jewish Community

Since all our activities were conducted in Hebrew, there was a danger of our isolating ourselves from the community. To be a part of the community and not apart from it, we were careful to make as many contacts with it as possible. Not only parents of our pupils but the entire community was invited to our *Ongei-Shabbat* and to all our holiday celebrations. The audience participated in the singing at the *Ongei-Shabbat*, and the holiday programs were explained briefly in English by the students. Every year, January was Hebrew Month. During the month, leaders of the Hebrew Youth Movement spoke at the meetings and gatherings of many community organizations about the importance of the Hebrew language and about our efforts to revive it and use it in our lives. Other pupils, young and old, were involved in selling raffles and tickets for the final event of the month. The pupils were prepared not only to sell the tickets but to explain to the buyers the importance of the Hebrew language. The program of the first such event took the form of a public trial, in English, in which the Hebrew youth accused those who neglected Hebrew education and culture. The program also included a Hebrew dramatization of the life of Eliezer Ben-Yehudah[1], the father of modern spoken Hebrew. The play was written and presented by the pupils of grade three. The income from the affair was divided equally between the Histradut Ivrit of America and the Hebrew Youth Movement in Calgary.

A Part of the General Community

We used every opportunity to identify ourselves with the total community. I, as representative of the Jewish community, participated in various public affairs, such as brotherhood Week and Education Week. I joined the Ministerial Association only a few years after my arrival in Calgary because I had not known that a Rabbi could be a member of this Christian religious fellowship. My first contact with it was accidental. Rabbi Harry Stern of Montreal was the guest speaker at one of the meetings and I was invited to introduce him. At the conclusion of the meeting, the president asked me why I was not a member. I told him I did not know that a Rabbi could join a Ministerial Association. His reaction was: We would not want Catholic priests as members, but a Rabbi would be most welcome.

When the Canadian Youth Commission was inaugurated in 1945, our Hebrew Youth Movement was represented by its secretary, Esther Wise. When a coordinating Youth Committee was formed "to implement the findings and proposals of the Commission", I was invited to serve on its Advisory Committee.

We Go On Radio

We also instituted an annual Radio Program to reach not only the Jewish but also the general public of Alberta. Radio Stations C.J.C.J, C.C.C.N. and C.F.A.C. put at our disposal, completely gratis, 30 to 60 minutes. The

[1]My son Gad was one of the authors of the dramatization. On this occasion, I pointed out to him the similarity between him, my first born son, and the first-born son of Eliezer Ben Yehuda. Gady was delighted when I told him he was the first Hebrew-speaking child in Canada, and indeed he was and is fully bilingual, in Hebrew and in English, though he was only about a year old when he first came to America.

programs were on such subjects as "The Struggle of the Jewish People for Freedom Throughout the Ages", and "The World and the Jew". They were presented in the form of dramatic skits consisting of commentary, recitation and singing, and were received enthusiastically by the people in the entire area. We received more telephone calls of congratulations and appreciation from non-Jews than from Jews.

Why Did the Jews Kill Jesus?

One day, my son Gady came home from school crying bitterly. When his mother and I succeeded in calming him down he asked, still sobbing, "Why did the Jews kill Jesus Christ?" He was six years old at the time and a very sensitive child. Though he was unusually intelligent, it was no mean task to explain to him the background of this tragic fable. We finally convinced him that it was the Romans, the enemies of the Jews, the destroyers of our country, who had murdered Jesus, among many other Jews, and later shifted the blame on the Jews themselves. A few days later, I attended a meeting of the above-mentioned Advisory Committee. There I told this sad story of the infliction of emotional violence on a young child by a public school teacher. I expressed my astonishment that something like this could happen in our day and age in a country like Canada. The chairman, the minister of a church, was not at all troubled. He declared: "obviously, the solution is that you people should have your own schools". He was then "gracious" enough to listen silently to the elementary lesson I gave him in the meaning of religious tolerance and of public education in a democratic country. The other participants took no sides. This incident, though an isolated personal experience in my many years of work with non-Jews, left an indelible mark on me. I cannot recollect what action, if any, was taken as a result of my protest to the principal of the school.

Solving the Problem of Continuity

The Calgary Hebrew School was not different from other institutions, where education came to an end with the completion of grade seven. It was no accident that this coincided with the age of Bar-Mitzvah (no one thought of Bat-Mitzvah in those days!). Instead of establishing a high school immediately, we extended the elementary program to eight grades. At the same time, we laid the foundations of a high school. David Sidorsky, Dov Chetner and Sylvia Baren, who had graduated several years previously, expressed their desire to continue their Hebrew studies, so that they became the nucleus of the future high school. When it was established a year later, with the first graduation of an eighth grade, David and Dov unhesitantly joined the fresh graduates in what became the first year of the high school. The formal curriculum included an intensive study of Bible, Hebrew literature, History (from the Spanish expulsion up to contemporary times), Aggada and an introduction to Mishnah and Talmud. The high school students were among the leaders of the Hebrew Youth Movement and of Young Judaea. (A student of the University of Toronto, Allan Livingston, made a research-study of the High School from 1942 to 1946. A copy is available among the "Horowitz papares"(call number MG 31 H 103,) at the Public Archives of Canada, Ottawa, Ontario.)

Special Classes

Our "educated" estimate in the early forties was that about eighty five percent of school-age children attended the Hebrew school or the Peretz school. In 1944, our enrollment reached a total of 174 (124 in the elementary division, twenty-five in the high school, and twenty-five in the two special classes), and the Peretz school had a total of about a hundred. I always resisted the organization of a Sunday school for some of the fifteen percent who received no Jewish education at all. But I did give in to the pressure to open two special classes for teenagers who had been deprived of a Jewish education, so that, as some of the parents put it, their children "should know something about Judaism". These classes also included former Peretz School pupils who wanted to study Hebrew. They met three times weekly. Two days were devoted to the study of Hebrew, and Sundays to Judaic subjects in English.

Educational Activities for Adults

In addition to the regular lectures and discussions of the Sharon Zionist Club, a weekly adult class was held for the purpose of studying and discussing Jewish history, Bible and contemporary Jewish life and problems. It is noteworthy that this group included also highly educated individuals, as well as some communal leaders.

Shortage of Teachers

We were faced with the difficult problem of the lack of sufficient teaching staff. There were altogether four teachers, two who had been there before, Mr. Yechiel Walker and Mr. M. Freidman; my wife Rachel, and myself (I taught full time, from 4:30 to 9:00 p.m. daily). The source from which the Canadian Jewish community had drawn its teachers was completely closed by the war. As was stated before — (see chapter 6, page 8) — Canadian Jewry was too preoccupied with its multiple organizations and fund raising to give its attention to the training of teachers, so that there was no national organization to which to turn for help. As our elementary and high school grew we were understaffed and had to resort to improvisations. To make things worse, one of our teachers went into the grocery business, but chance came to our rescue. My sister Dvorah wanted to live as near as possible to Lethbridge Alta., where her husband, Mr. Ephrayim Malamuth was stationed in the Canadian army. Our school thus benefitted from Edmonton's loss.

"You People" Again

(My sister and her husband were teaching at that time in Edmonton, when he was drafted into the army. The Edmonton school was thus in a difficult position, and I was asked by its board to appear before the Draft Commission, in my capacity as chairman of the hebrew Educators Council of Western Canada, to appeal for his release. In rejecting my appeal, the commission's chairman, the chief justice of Alberta, said in effect: where will *"you* people" be if Hitler wins the war?! Let the parents give their children a religious education! After I left the meeting room, I regretted that I had not reacted to his "you people". To this day, I'm not certain whether Mr. Malamuth's service in the Hebrew school in Edmonton would not have been more beneficial to Canada than his serving as a guard at an army prison camp.

My brother Yaakov, (who had been a student of the short-lived teachers course mentioned in chapter 6,) was at that time on the staff of the Winnipeg Talmud Torah. When my parents learned about my predicament, they made every effort to have him realesed from the Winnipeg school, but it was unthinkable to them that he would go to Calgary without finding a replacement for Winnipeg. The story as it was told to me by my brother is dramatically illustrative of the dire situation that prevailed then. He was walking on the street when he saw a former classmate of his making bread deliveries. He signaled to him to stop his wagon, and asked him how much he was earning on his job. "What would you say if you would be offered twice your salary to teach in The Winnipeg Talmud Torah?", inquired Yaakov. "I would be delighted", answered the bread-man. And so the Canadian Jewish Community was enriched with another "teacher" from nowhere . . . and my brother was added to our staff.

With all this effort, our problem was not yet solved, and during the next few years we had to recruit four of our senior students (Yehoshua Maerov, Dvorah and Ziporah Smolensky and Esther Wise) as part-time teachers.

The First Hebrew-Speaking Camp in Canada

It is difficult to describe the joy with which the Hebrew Youth Movement set about (in 1944, the first year of its existence) to create the first Hebrew-speaking camp in Canada. (Their joy was somewhat marred, however, by the lack of cooperation of some of the community's leaders. I deliberately refrained from intervening because I considered this part of the process of education by experience. It was painful for me, as it was for the youngsters, when I saw them coming out crying from the meeting. The committee had absolutely refused to lend them the dishes of the community centre! The problem was resolved by Mr. and Mrs Dave Smolensky who lent them some dishes from their store. In the end, they were able to buy the dishes with the surplus of the income from the camp, so that the Hebrew Youth Movement now had its own dishes.)

They rented a ramshackle camp from a church. The cabins had no beds or other furniture. We slept on sacks filled with straw. There were no inside toilets or running water, and it took much resourcefulness to turn the surrounding grounds into sports fields.

They were inspired by what they had learned about Kibbutz life in Eretz Israel to model their camp after it. The name *T'chiyah*, revival, was chosen as a symbol of their participation in the rebirth of the Hebrew culture. Everybody shared equally in the expenses and in the work, and nobody received any pay. They were adamant in their refusal to accept my share of the expenses. On my part, I refused somebody's offer to fill my sack with starw for me, and I insisted on participating in all the chores. One task, however, was denied to me. The youth in charge of cleaning the latrines absolutely refused to allow me "to engage in this type of activity."

Although the duration of the camp was only two weeks, it contributed much to the strenthening of the movement. The campers spoke only Hebrew throughout this time; some of the seniors conducted the *sichot* (discussions) of the juniors; some wrote and directed Hebrew skits and programs, and some acted as specialty counselors. The treasurer, Yaakov Chetner, who planned the budget, made the purchases, etc., was a mere boy of fifteen. Their spirit and sense of achievement were high, and they continued to speak for years about their camp experiences.

Mechayil El Chayil — From Strength to Strength

Our efforts brought forth fruit. The school and the Hebrew Youth Movement struck roots in the educational-cultural life of the community. Children spoke Hebrew not only in school and at meetings but anywhere and everywhere. In 1944, one could hear Hebrew spoken on the street and on streetcars! We even started to organize bowling games in Hebrew. One of our friends used to open his bowling alleys especially for us on Sundays, so we could spend a few hours bowling in a Hebrew atmosphere. On their own initiative, two students composed a Hebrew school song. Esther Wise wrote the words and Naomi Wolochow the music. It was sung at the opening of all activities, and in some classes at the beginning and end of studies.

Parents took pride in the enthusiasm and achievements of their children. On occasion, a mother would phone to entreat me that I influence her child not to go with a fever to Hebrew school.

In Tune With the Community

The school actually became the center of Jewish life in Calgary, not only because of its vitality and achievements, but also because of its leaders' identification with all other phases of Jewish life. They considered the school the foundation, but did not neglect the superstructure. They were involved in the leadership of every major organization, and supported all local and national endeavours. As soon as the Canadian Friends of the Hebrew University was inaugurated, a local chapter was organized. As its first chairman, I aimed not to confine its work to fund-raising, but also to bring to the fore the university's national significance and special mission. Already in its first year, the Friends succeeded in enrolling about seventy members who contributed about a thousand dollars, a significant sum in a year when the community was burdened with the largest number of campaigns in its history. When I left Calgary in 1946, Mr. Sam Datner became the chairman, and he developed the chapter into one of the most active in the country. The Sharon Zionist Club was also spear-headed by Talmud Torah people. It continued to build on the foundation that had been laid by Dave Chertkow, William Epstein, Nate Safran and Ben Sherwood. It developed into the cultural voice of the community. In the mid-forties, the high school students and graduates started to become involved in its activities, so that there was communication between the adults and the youth.

A Hundred-Page Yearbook

The popularity of the movement spurred its leaders to undertake what appeared to be an impossible project for a group of kids. They were going to publish a yearbook that would mirror not only the creativity of the school, but also the history of the Jewish community. With great enthusiasm and effort, they put out, in 1945, a one-hundred page paperback yearbook; fifty-four printed pages contained Hebrew compositions, essays, poems and reports by students ranging from the highest grade in the high school to grade three in the elementary school. The other forty-six pages were in English, and consisted of short histories of every Jewish organization in the city. The history of the J.L. Peretz Shule appeared in Yiddish. This venture entailed an expenditure of over a thousand dollars (a huge sum in those days), which was covered by a twenty-five dollar levy on each organization and by contributions from friends and admirers. The book was reviewed favorably in various periodicals, among them: *Shvielei Hachinuch* (pedagogical publication from Eretz Israel); "Most of the articles, stories and poems are written in beautiful style on various Hebrew subjects, testifying to the high calibre of the school". The Hebrew Section in the Canadian Zionist, by Y. Weingarten: "this entire interesting publication reflects — faith, enthusiasm and progress. Fortunate is the Jewish community in Calgary that it has such an excellent school. This publication is an innovation in the annals of Hebrew education in Canada". Prof. H. Bergman, Rector of the Hebrew University, wrote: "I read it with great interest and admiration". Historian A.L. Sachar, commented "I was interested in the history of Jewish life in Calgary, since it adds useful source-material for a definitive study of the early history and development of the Canadian communities."

Calgary Hebrew School "Invades" Teacher Institute in N.Y.

In our studies of North American Jewish life, the absence of native Canadians in the field of Jewish Education (the few who were engaged in Hebrew schools at that time were untrained) was often discussed. I was careful never to challenge any of my students to pursue any specific career. I would speak generally about the essential need for Hebrew educators to insure the continuity of Jewish life in the Diaspora. I was gratified, however, when David Sidorsky told me upon his graduation from high school, that he would like to continue his studies at the Teachers Institute of the Jewish Theological Seminary in New York. I realized that this could be made possible only if we would establish a scholarship for this purpose. The difficulty I encountered in the realization of this goal is a sad commentary on the state of Jewish life at that time. In rejecting my request for a one hundred dollar allocation by the Zionist Organization, Rabbi Schwartz used his favorite phrase, "we cannot become a 'surrogate' for Jewish education". I alienated my good friend, the chairman of the Jewish National Fund Committee in Calgary, because I fought hard to overcome his strong objection to "diverting to other causes money intended for Eretz Israel". We eventually succeeded in creating an annual three-hundred-dollar scholarship, contributed in equal amounts by the "Mothers Club" of the Talmud Torah, the Jewish National Fund and Hadassah. A year later, two students of the first graduating class, Dvorah Smolensky and Zehava Hanen, joined David at the seminary. Within a few years, the Calgary group, eleven in number, formed the largest contingent from any other single community, including New York itself, at the seminary. All of them were admitted to the second year of studies. One of them told me later how astonished Prof. Abraham Halkin was when she told him she had studied *Achad Ha'am* in the original and without vowels. The Calgary group became famous for its high motivation, substantial knowledge, and extraordinary fluency in speaking Hebrew. They were appreciated fully by the administration in spite of their occasional rebellious actions, as for example, their demand to have the notices on the bulletin board in Hebrew and to have *Hatikvah* sung on all occasions. I listened with pleasure to the story (told me by Yaakov Chetner) of how it was prearranged with a neighbouring church to ring out the Hatikvah (which was not sung them at the Seminary) on their caroline precisely at the conclusion of the Commencement Exercises at the seminary. It was through these students that I gained a reputation as a good educator, and it was they who put the Calgary Hebrew School on the "map" of Jewish education.

These eleven students and another nine, who did not continue their Hebrew education at college level, served as Hebrew teachers in the following ten communities: Vancouver, Edmonton, Calgary, Toronto, Los Angeles, New York, Boston, Seattle Washington, Elizabeth, N.J., and Kingston N.C.

It is interesting that only three of these eleven pioneers who were the first Western Canadians (if not the first Canadians) to venture into the realm of Jewish education, still continue to serve in this field. Dvorah Heckleman (Smolensky) is an instructor in Hebrew language and literature at Union College in Albany N.Y.; Esther Dubin (Wise) teaches in Hebrew educational institutions in Los Angeles; and Naomi Taplar (Wolochow) serves as a Hebrew teacher in Philadelphia. Four, Yaakov Chetner, Zwi Sherman, Yocheved Gelmon (Fishman) and Ziporah Swartz (Smolensky) withdrew from the field for various reasons after many years of service in Canada. David Sidorsky has made his mark as a teacher of philosophy, lecturer, author and leader in the U.S.A. Following a year of teaching in a Hebrew school, Yitzchak Jacobson transferred to the public school system "because of its clear definition of duties and prerogatives, and stability". Zehavah Hanen and Avraham Baber taught Hebrew only during their student-years and turned to other careers.

The Other Side — The Peretz-Shule Community

Calgary's Yiddish school was perhaps more leftist than its counterpart in Winnipeg. Hebrew was out, religion and Zionism were taboo, photographs of Marx, Lenin, Stalin, etc., adorned the classrooms, and the Yiddish language and literature were the Alpha and Omega of Jewish life. Its followers were not a monolithic group. Some were just Yiddishists; some were Bundists; a few were Communists; and some even supported the Labour Zionist Movement in Eretz Israel. What united them was their love for the Yiddish language and literature and their determination to preserve it. We thus had two Jewish communities, and there was a gulf separating them. The *Baruch Habba* they gave me was hostile. Soon after my arrival in Calgary, I was told that the principal of the school (in Yiddishist schools the pricnipal was a sort of Rabbi and rebbe rolled together) had attacked me, my ideology and my methods, at a public meeting. My informers tried to instigate me to retaliate. I made it clear, however, that I would not engage in any "duels". "Let us" I said "devote our efforts to constructive work, and let us hope that they too will direct their activities in productive channels".

"Horowitz is a Fascist"

The complete separation between me and their leaders continued until Mr. Israel Meriminsky, who was then the treasurer of the Histadrut in Eretz-Israel, came to Calgary as the guest speaker at the annual Histadrut campaign. When he arrived at the railway station, he asked the reception committee (all of them Yiddishists), "where is my *chaver* Horowitz? Isn't he on the reception committee?" "That fascist", was the rejoinder, "that *shwartz-mayinic*" (equivalent to "a member of the black guard"), that hater of Yiddish is your *chaver*?!" Meriminsky told me it was not easy for him to put across the idea that a Hebraist is not necessarily an opponent of the Histadrut or a hater of Yiddish and that many of the most devoted workers for the Histadrut in America were Hebraists. In any event, he insisted that I introduce him at the campaign meeting. That gave my detractors the opportunity to hear my views of socialism in general and the Histadrut in particular (I was still a socialist in those days). As a result, a line of communication was opened between me and the more liberal elements among the Peretzists. Those who worked for the Histradut lost no time in inviting my assistance, and I subsequently became publicity chairman of the Histadrut Drive.

Chapter 13
Zionist Educational Activity Continues in the West

During the years I was director of the Zionist Organization in the West, people came to identify Zionism not only with fund-raising but also with all other aspects of Jewish life. The real test for the Zionist Organization came soon after I left its employ. People began to confront me with the question whether it was really the philosophy of the Zionist Organization I had been espousing when I used to speak on its behalf, or whether official Zionist activity in the spheres of Hebrew education and culture departed to gether with me from the organization. The work of the Hebrew Educators Council did continue and there were also some new things happening in Young Judea, but these were the activities of communities and individuals rather than of the Zionist Organization.

Educators Council's Work Continues

At this time, the Regional Zionist Office was not in a position to continue the work of the Educators Council. As a result, I was requested by the schools of the larger centers to continue my visits to them in order to maintain our regional setup. The Council's president, Mr. Giladi Gelbfarb, had moved to Vancouver to head its Hebrew school, and I was asked to serve also as the regional chairman. Several years after the inauguration of our Council, the Keren Hatarbut was organized in Montreal for the purpose of "spreading the Hebrew language and culture in Canada". At the same time, there existed a separate organization, *Igud*, (Association of Hebrew schools), whose purpose was to serve as a coordinating body for the Hebrew schools. The work of both these organizations was perforce narrow in scope because of their meager funds, and their activities were confined mostly to Montreal. At the end of 1944, Yerachmiel Weingarten, director of the Keren Hatarbut, visited Western Canada on behalf of his organization and the Igud. At his request, we agreed to affiliate with the Keren Hatarbut "on condition that it unite with the Igud into one national organization for the common purpose of revitalizing Hebrew education and furthering the Hebrew language and culture throughout the country". We could not understand why there was a need for two organizations, especially when both of them were *kabtzanim* (paupers). Weingarten explained some of the political difficulties, and promised to try to head towards union. This was not to be until the late fifties. We did establish, however, some communication with both of them. (I do not remember to what extent, if at all, they contributed towards defraying my travelling expenses in the region.) Be that as it may, the schools in Winnipeg, Regina, Saskatoon, Calgary, Edmonton and Vancouver continued to maintain some of the work originated by the Educators Council.

Teacher Snatching

The shortage of teachers became increasingly acute during the war years. The one source that was not cut off by the war, the teacher seminaries in the U.S.A., could not meet even American needs. It was, therefore, not uncommon for one community to try to snatch teachers from other communities by offering them better conditions. A case in point is the attempt to lure me to the Vancouver Hebrew School. Previously, I referred to the fact that Vancouver was considered an "extension of Seattle Washington" because of the greater inroads assimilation had made in the community. During the forties, there was a migration of Jews from the Canadian Mid-west to Vancouver, among them such leading Zionists as Max Waterman and Moshe Chertkow of Saskatoon and Morris Wolochow of Calgary. They added their strength and leadership to such Zionists as Sam and Abe Rothstein, Akiva Katzenelson, Dave Nemetz, Harold Freeman, and Meyer Freedman. Zionism and Jewish education in particular benefited from this influx. Moshe Chertkow directed his efforts mainly towards the improvement of education and the eventual establishment of a Day School. Though an orthodox person, he did not flinch from his trying to snatch me from Calgary. He appeared in Calgary one day in June for the specific purpose of enticing me to Vancouver. He offered me a much higher salary and other attractive conditions. I told him that even if he would have come much earlier than June, under no circumstances would I consider leaving Calgary in the lurch. Convinced that he could not move me, he left, saying "I think you owe it to yourself and your family to think of your own welfare, but I am glad we have such ethical and dedicated people as you". A few weeks later, I ran into Abe Rothstein in Banff, and he greeted me with, "Well, I'm happy I shall be seeing you soon in Vancouver". He was surprised when I told him I would not be leaving Calgary. He asked what Chertkow had offered me. When I told him, he said angrily, "we authorized him to tell you the sky is the limit". He looked completely baffled as he realized that even that would not have helped. I wondered whether it was really their great concern for Hebrew education that prompted honorable men to overlook the ethics of the case. And so, schools struggled in their search for teachers and principals.

Striking Roots By Name Changing

While in Banff, I witnessed an amusing incident, which throws some light on the strong desire to strike roots. I went with a friend to rent cabins for our summer vacation. The proprietress wrote down my name, etc. When she finished with me, she turned to my friend, who was looking very Jewish (if there is such a thing as looking Jewish) and spoke with a very heavy East European accent: "What is your name, sir?", she asked. "Artur Vells," was the answer. "Come again?" said she. This time he tried hard to pronounce his name to sound more like Arthur Wells. At this, she raised her head from the form she was filling out, looked him straight in the eye, threw her pencil on the counter, and exclaimed loud and clear "Is that so!" My friend's reaction, as we were leaving, is even more illustraive of the desire to blend into the whole. "I am sorry," he said in Hebrew, "I didn't have the presence of mind to ask her why the goyim have the right to use our names — David, Joseph, Sarah etc. — and nevertheless want to deny us the right to use theirs. I said to him jokingly that one of the tasks the Lord assigned to the goyim was to make it difficult for us to lose our Jewishness.

We read in Vayikra Rabba, 32: "Israel was redeemed from Egypt for three things: they did not change their names, they did not change their language, they observed the Sabbath".

If these three elements are important in the preservation of our people's culture, the propsects for American Jewry are not very good. All three are rather shaky in the entire Diaspora. Historians and sociologists points to the fact that assimilation (disintegration) begins with the changing of names. One historian observed that if a person changes his name, he consciously or subconsciously wants to forget his past. It is especially puzzling and irritating when people who are paid guardians of Jewish cultural and spiritual continuity, Rabbis and educators included, jettison their Biblical names for Wasp names, (it is noteworthy that Yiddish educators do hold on to their Yiddish names). Does one really have to change one's name to strike roots in Canada?

The Educators Council and the Canadian Jewish Congress Education Committee

Taking advantage of the vacuum that ensued in the Winnipeg Zionist office in the field of Hebrew Education, the education committee of the Canadian Jewish Congress, dominated by the Peretz and Folk-Shules, made several unsuccessful efforts to organize a regional committee representing all the schools in the West. A controversy developed about what national organization should have the prerogatives in the field of Jewish education. Reference was made time and again to the resolutions on education that had been adopted at regional and national conventions of the Congress. The fact of the matter was that, in spite of all the resolutions, Congress had no national education department. Ontario was the only region where there was some coordinating set-up, initiated as a result of a memorandum by Mr. Yeshaye Rabinowitz, literary critic, who was then the principal of the Folk-Shule in Toronto.

(For an account of the history and activities of the Ontario Education Committee, see the comprehensive Hebrew article on the education situation in Canada in Shvielei-Hachinuch (issue of Adar-Nissan-Iyar, 5700, pages 80-95) by M.2. Reichenstein-Frank, published in New York. In that article, he discusses fully the attitude of the Canadian Jewish Congress to Jewish education. He also makes a short reference to the Educators Council in the West, "As far as I know, there is a central organization of the Jewish schools in Western Canada, whose Jewish communities were always more alert to such matters, and there the initiative was not of the Congress but of the director of the Western division of the Zionist Organization.")

In 1945, I published an article in the CanadianZionist (issue of November 8) on "The Forgotten Cause", in which I discussed fully the functions of the Canadian Jewish Congress and the Zionist Organization of Canada in the sphere of education. (See appendix on this subject.) This article aroused the ire of Mr. H.M. Ceiserman, national secretary of the Congress. He sent me a copy of a "Rebuttal" which he was dissuaded from publishing by his colleagues. There was, therefore, no further communication or public discussion of the issue, and matters stood where they were. It should be mentioned that the Keren Hatarbut received no financial support whatsoever from the Congress, and the Igud received a mere pittance.

Young Judaea Surges Forth

In spite of difficulties and little help from the parent organization, Western Young Judaea, especially in Winnipeg, was at its zenith in the forties, thanks to the idealism and steadfastness of its leaders. They maintained strong links between the center and the periphery, and served as a catalyst for Zionist educational activity. Lacking funds, one of their leaders, Isaac Horowitz, visited the various branches by hitch-hiking from city to city, and by sleeping and having meals at friends' homes, and, sometimes, at a community center. Their success was due in large measure to the assistance of such individuals as Nathan Safran, the regional president; Sid Buckwold, now Senator Buckwold; and Dave Nemetz.

For Out of the West Shall Go Forth Leadership

The same small group of Judaean leaders in Winnipeg were the ones who took the initiative to establish the first Young Judaean Leadership Camp in Canada, which was held in Watrous Sask., in 1943. Teenagers from various parts of the West and also a few from the East devoted three weeks to study and discussion of basic Jewish-Zionist subjects. I remember how pleased and somewhat amused I was when some of the future leaders were concerned about a very important ethical problem: Was it morally right to take out a girl for the sole purpose of bringing her within the fold of Young Judaea, although you were not at all interested in her as a girl? It was heart-warming to hear these youngsters discussing seriously this and other moral questions.

It would be interesting to know where all these people are today and in what they are engaged. I do remember the impression Allan Gottlieb made on me. This was the first and only time I had anything to do with him, although he was the son of Hadassah president Sally Gottlieb. His parents, like other famous Zionist leaders, would not send him to a Hebrew school, but rather engaged a private teacher for him and his sister. I was very pleased to see him among us. He evidenced unusual curiosity and a very keen mind. It was good to have somebody who had not been intellectually "brainwashed" and who challenged various ideas that were accepted as truisms by the others, who, by the way, were also gifted intellectually and highly mature for their ages.

Young Judaea and the Hebrew Youth Movement in Calgary

Because Zionism and activities were absent from the schools, Young Judaea presumed to fill this gap. Even if Young Judaea had had a national program with leaders able to supplement formal education, its desire-ability would have been debatable. The main question would be, whether learning and acting can be separated into different domains. As it was, however, Young Judaea had no such program or leadership. As in other areas, it depended very much on the local realities. By and large, young children, often as young as six, and older children would be organized into clubs that were led by somewhat older children with insufficient educational background and experience. They would sing, and dance the Hora. In places where there were knowledgeable adolescents, they would conduct sichot. In some cases, Young Judaean clubs served as a haven for those who did not give their children a Jewish education. The slogan was, "as long as our children meet with other Jewish children." Since some of our best students were Young Judaean leaders in Calgary, a "clash" of interests was inevitable, in the beginning, between the Hebrew Youth Movement and Young Judaea. When we came across Zionist ideas in literature, my approach would be challenged, even in my classroom, especially by one of my best students, Yehoshua Maerov. (An occasion presented itself recently for me and Maerov to recall these discussions. We pointed out that a comparatively large number of the Calgary students became Hebrew teachers without my having called upon them to do so, and that those who preached Aliya did not necessarily practice it.)

He pointed out out that I never called upon him or others to prepare for personal *Aliyah* (immigration to Israel). My reaction was that it is not the function of the educator to preach or to propagandize, but rather to stimulate thinking, to help, to analyze, to clarify, and to guide. The *educator* should not call upon anybody to do anything. I, therefore, never called on anybody to become Hebrew teachers although I am convinced that Jewish education in Canada will be in a bad state if Canadians will not enter this field. I used the analogy of explaining and trying to understand all the elements in a painting or a picture. Similarly, the educator should deal with all the needs, realities and possibilities. But it is for every individual to find his own place in the total picture.

Our discussions led to a harmonious solution. We came to an agreement that the Hebrew Movement would concentrate its efforts in the Hebrew school, and Young Judaea would devote itself to the youth found outside the schools. It was also agreed that both movements would work in cooperation and harmony. And so they did!

Judaean Summer Camps

The Western Judaean leadership spared no efforts to ensure the continuation of the summer camps. The second camp was held in Watrous, following the leadership camp, and was directed by Rabbi Sol Horowitz; during the third season, in 1944, it was moved to Alberta, where the organization was at the peak of its success, and Biela Lepkin directed the camp. The fourth camp season, under my direction, saw a new development. The progress that had been achieved in Hebrew studies made it possible to conduct the sichot of the senior group entirely in Hebrew.

Freya Stark Comes to Town

In 1945, the Jewish world was seething with indignation at the socialist government in Great Britain for shutting its gates on the only possible haven to the remnants of the Holocaust, and for its betrayal of Zionism. I received a call from Mr. Sam Helman, K.C., to inform me that Freya Stark, authoress and one of the most able intelligence officers of the Colonial Office, was to address the Overseas Club on the situation in the Middle East. Mr. Helman, the only Jewish member of this closed club, had the privilege of inviting a guest. He cautioned me that the rules of the club would preclude me from entering into polemics with her. I could, however, formulate my questions in a way that would refute any incorrect statements she might make. With painful control I listened quietly to the tirade against Zionism by an agent who was delegated by the Colonial Office to "inform the makers of public opinion in Canada of the true situation in Palestine." Among the many gems that issued from her mouth, the one that infuriated me most was the statement that the Jewish natives of Palestine were against the Zionists, "who were mostly socialist and communist elements from Russia." Upon the completion of her remarks, the chairman said, "We are fortunate in having among us as a guest a native of Palestine, who might want to ask some questions of the speaker." Freya's eyes started to rove from one end of the room to the other to spot this Palestinian native who might support or try to shake her "house of cards." In her address, she had made frequent reference to "Winnie" (Winston Churchill); Winnie said so, and Winnie said this. I formulated my remarks in the form of questions and proceeded to quote Winnie and other British statesmen refuting entirely her "facts". I started my statements by asking "Isn't it true", or "isn't it a fact that...." She was very agitated, but kept her colonialist cool, when I asked where she got the strange idea that the native Palestinians were against Zionism. "Aren't you aware Mrs. Stark," I asked, "that the native Palestinian Jews were the forerunners of the modern Zionists, who by their teeth held on to their ancient promised — by God and by Britain — land?" Refraining from answering any of my questions, she looked at me and said coldly, "I hope now that the war is over you will make your way back to Palestine in a peaceful manner".

What agitated *me* was the apparent unawareness of the Zionist Organization of Freya's mission, and the possibility or probability that she "was getting away with it" in other cities where there were no Mr. Helmans to alert informed Zionists.

In the forties, the press was unbiased in its attitude to Israel, unlike many of the media today. On his own initiative, the editor of the Albertan told me he would give me an opportunity to refute Miss Stark's statements, because the press report on Miss Stark's address would not include my remarks. We met for lunch the next day, and my refutation appeared in the Albertan a few days later. During our luncheon meeting, the editor brought up a subject that was unrelated to the Stark affair. Following is a part of our more or less accurate conversation. "Tell me, Rabbi, do Jews still respect Rabbis and scholars as they did in the past?"

"Yes, on the whole, I believe they do."

"Can you honestly tell me that you have as much influence in Jewish community affairs as Mr. (here he mentioned the name of a rich uneducated businessman)?"

"Yes, I believe I have more influence that he and others put together."

"Tell me then, why don't you or the community expel Mr. so and so (here he mentioned the name of a person who was known for his shenanigans in business matters) from the Jewish community?"

"Why don't the Scots, the Italians, etc. expel their rascals from their midst?"

"Well, Rabbi, the Jews are more vulnerable because of anti-semitism."

"Then I think it is our duty to eradicate this double standard from our life. It is high time," I said, "to balance the equation."

I believe our conversation contributed to a much better under-standing between two Canadians of different backgrounds. This and other such experiences strengthened my conviction that much more communication and dialogue among people of different religious and ethnic background are essential for the evental development of the Canadian nation as an orchestra playing a harmonious symphony with its variety of instruments.

"Judge Every Man By The Scale of Merit" (or "Judge All Men Meritoriously) (Pirkei-Avot 1:6)

The exhortation in Saying Of The Fathers, "Judge *every man* by the scale of merit" reads in Hebrew *"Hevei dan et kol ha'adam."* The literal meaning in Hebrew of *"kol ha'adam"* is, the *Whole Person*, rather than *every* person (*"kol Adam"*). My interpretation of this saying is, therefore, "judge the *whole person*," instead of only certain aspects of his personality, or some of his isolated actions. If we consider the whole person; his background, his situation, and his total actions, we shall be inclined to judge him by the "scale of merit".

This interpretation is by way of an introduction to the anecdote that follows:

Max Katzin and Shaye Shlafmitz did not confine their Mitzvah-doing to Calgary. Occasionally, they would venture out into the surrounding area to "collect" for various causes. The story goes that they once visited a wealthy businessman (who was known for his flair at "pulling people's legs") somewhere in Alberta, to collect his pledge for the U.P.A. The following conversation took place.

"Hello, what can I do for you?"

"We have come to collect your pledge."

"What pledge, vus pledge?"

"Your pledge to the U.P.A."

"I pledged money? Do you think I am crazy to give away money?"

"But Mr. K., several hundred people heard you make your pledge at the fund raising dinner."

"Alright, alright. If you say I pledged, I pledged. How much did I pledge?"

"Three thousand dollars."

At this, Mr. K. jumped to the ceiling, and exclaimed: "What? Do you really think I'm that foolish, to give so much money?!"

"But Mr. K., the same people heard *the amount* of your pledge."

"Alright, if you say I promised three thousand dollars, then I promised three thousand dollars. But tell me, how much did Mr. Charlie Waterman give?"

"He gave five thousand dollars."

"Charlie gave only five thousand?! If he gave five thousand, I give three hundred!"

"But Mr. K., you're much wealthier than Mr. Waterman. If he gave five thousand, you should have pledged at least ten thousand."

"Now, I ask you, gentlemen, a few questions. What does Mr. Waterman do when he gets up in the morning?"

"He goes to the synagogue to pray."

"What does he do after prayers?"

"He goes home for breakfast, and pays a short visit to his office."

"What does he do after that?"

"He spends practically all day collecting."

"What does he do evenings?"

"Following evening Services and dinner, he attends meetings practically every week-night."

"Now, I ask you, why does Mr. Charlie Waterman need money? I need plenty of money, because I have *nakaives* (women) in many places. On Monday I can be here, on Tuesday in Honolulu, and on another day in Paris, etc. I need money for all these *nakaives*, but what for does Charlie need money? Let Charlie give his money for Mitzves!"

It took me many years to discover how people are sometimes hoodwinked by politicians. The recent publication of Mr. King's diary has revealed, among many other interesting revelations, that his "careful consideration" was being given in the opposite direction. I have become increasingly convinced that *our* Jewish politicians concentrate too much of their efforts on the politicians, while sorely neglecting the grass roots.

I recall that I sent, in 1943 to Liberty Magazine (the most widely read weekly in Canada at that time) a copy of my address on "An appeal to the conscience of Britain". The publisher, Mr. Joseph Lister Rutledge, responded very warmly. He wrote me, inter alia, "I was very greatly interested and much impressed by the force of your appeal. At the moment, I do not quite know how I can use it, but I will try to make some use of it." About fifteen years later, Mr. Edward Gelber disclosed to me that one of those Jewish "low-key" leaders, who serve as advisors to the "goyim", was at least responsible in part for the fact that it was not "made use of".

Having had his fun, Mr. K. piped down and paid up. People who know Mr. K. say about him that, shrewd as he is in business and unethical as he may be at times in his dealings, he is a "soft-touch" for all kind of mitzves himself. I once bumped into him and asked him: "How do you do Mr. K.?" "How do I do?" he chuckled, "I always do fine. *I* sleep nights, because nobody owes me money; I owe others lots of money."

Could my interpretation of *kol ha'adam*, to judge the *whole* person, be applied to Mr. K.?

To "Judge the Whole Person" In Reverse

During this century, Jews have been looking to new political and social movements for salvation from anti-semitism, persecution and oppression. How could socialists be anti-semites, if they are so compassionate about the poor and down-trodden?! Surely communists, who heralded a workers' paradise for all mankind, could never be anti-semites. Many Jews have prayed, dreamt, and hoped for centuries for justice and peace, embraced all types of progressive movements, socialist and communist included. Labour Zionists thus looked forward with great expectation to a political victory of the Labour Movement in Great Britain, when justice would be done also to their Zionist cause. How shocking and traumatic it was for them, as for all Zionists, when they woke up one day to hear the victorious socialists in Britain rant and act against those who had turned a desert into a garden in the Promised Land, promised not only by God and the Bible, but also by the English, the Americans, the French, etc. Who would have dreamt that a Labour foreign minister, Ernest Bevin, would bark — along with his enforcer General Barker in Palestine — as a good old "dyed in the wool" anti-semite!

The principle of judging the *whole man*, or the whole movement for that matter, thus applies also in reverse. It might thus be found that they should be judged by the scale of demerit. Socialists or communists, or what have you, could be concerned about certain injustices, especially when their interests are affected, and at the same time they can be completely insensitive about others.

The Zionist Organization of Canada called upon its constituents to organize protest meetings throughout Canada. Again, I had an opportunity to learn how uninformed many Jews and non-Jews, including those who form public opinion, were about Zionism and Palestine. It took much effort to enlist the help of some Ministers and community leaders for our objectives. In the end, our protest meeting were attended by hundreds of people, including representatives of non-Jewish service clubs, civic organizations, and churches. A strongly-worded resolution was adopted, "vehemently protesting against His Majesty's Government White-Paper policy with regard to the Holy Land." When I, as chairman, read the resolution and called upon the over-capacity audience to rise and sing Hatikvah as an indication of their approval of the resolution, three Jewish members of the audience remained seated (I'm not mentioning their names because they would be ashamed to do so today), while the hall reverberated with the determined voices of the Hatikvah singers.

The meeting decided to send the protest resolution to Prime Minister Mackenzie King. In my letter, I added some strong words to the resolution, including, in my reference to Bevin, the quotation from Proverbs 30:21, "For three things the earth doth shake", one of them being "for a servant when he reigneth". The reply from the Under Secretary of State for External Affairs stated, "I have been asked to acknowledge your letter of January 2nd, addressed to the Prime Minister. The resolution concerning Jewish immigration into Palestine, adopted at a mass meeting in Calgary on December 30th, has been noted and careful consideration is being given to the issues to which it refers."

Chapter 14
Some Strange Interludes

In 1945, one of our children took ill with rheumatic fever. Our pediatrician advised us that if at all possible, we should move to a warm climate. (It was in Calgary that we learned that physicians treated the clergy either gratis or at a discount, and it was *davka* a non-Jew, Dr. H. Price, who absolutely refused any payment from us. When we told him we did not feel right about this and that he should at least charge us something, he mumbled quite convincingly, "you will then have to get another doctor". Seldom did we experience such concern and devoted care as we received from Dr. Price.)

Since the war had not yet ended, we could not return to Eretz-Israel. We were, therefore, considering a proposal to go to California for a few years, where I was offered the directorship of the Labour Zionist office. The alarm of the community leadership in Calgary at the possibility of our departure was another indication of their unusual devotion to Hebrew education. Mr. Henry Goldberg was delegated to make every effort to prevent our leaving. He was so determined and persuasive that I could not reject his pleas. In later years, when I was actively involved with the leadership of many institutions, it became clear to me that their strength could be measured by, and was largely due to, their leaders' persistence in obtaining and keeping capable personnel.

Hebrew Schools Versus Canadian Jewish Congress

In the meantime, things were happening in Montreal. The acute shortage of teachers brought to the fore the need for a teacher-training institute in Canada. While the Canadian Jewish Congress decided to found one institution that would serve all types of schools, leaders of the Hebrew schools were opposed to this plan for the same reasons we in the West could not find a common language with Yiddishist and leftist schools. The leadership of the Talmud-Torahs suggested "the establishment of two seminaries that would meet the different needs of the two major streams in Jewish education, the national-religious and the national-radical" (quoted from resolutions presented by Mr. Melech Magid, principal of the United Talmud-Torahs of Montreal, at the National Educational Conference of the Canadian Jewish Congress).

Our sentiments in the West were best expressed in a letter from Mr. S. Jaffe to Mr. Saul Hayes, Executive Director of the Canadian Jewish Congress: "With regard to the proposed Seminary, the arguments we have advanced against the engagement of a director for the different types of schools apply with equal force against the establishment of a seminary which would serve the different educational systems. We wish to emphasize that the decisions made by the recent meeting of the so-called National Educational Committee is the strongest proof of our arguments. These decisions have only strengthened our opposition to the whole committee. The fact that this committee is composed of a majority of Yiddishists, in spite of the fact that a majority of the schools in Canada are Hebrew institutions, and the fact that this majority reaches decisions with complete disregard to the views of the Hebrew educators, only prove the justice and logic of our contention that the Congress should engage only in such activities about which there is unanimity. We reiterate that we shall not recognize or participate in any projects that will be decided upon arbitrarily by a fictitious "majority". In a letter to Mr. Sam Bronfman, it was made clear that "no organization will be able to implement a national program 'from above', and that no one has been authorized to speak in the name of the West at the National Education Committee Conference". An example of how truly we were represented was the statement by Mr. M. Averbach that the principal of the Winnipeg Talmud-Torah had authorized him to speak in his name, when a "protesting telegram" arrived from the president of the Talmud Torah in Winnipeg.

The upshot of this controversy was that the Canadian Jewish Congress resolved to proceed with its plans for a Yiddish seminary, and the Hebrew Schools, with the cooperation of the Igud, decided to establish a Hebrew teachers seminary.

The Challenge of Pioneering the Hebrew Seminary

While the above debate was going on, the war had come to an end. I was seriously considering returning to Eretz-Israel, when I received an invitation to be a pioneer in the formation of the seminary and to direct it. I could not resist this challenge, and was fired with enthusiasm to achieve something I considered of crucial importance to the future of Jewish life in Canada. I accepted without hesitation, although Melech Magid and Mr. Mordecai Mendelson emphasized in their invitation the uncertainty about the sources of student-candidates for the institution.

An Interlude on the Way to Montreal

A few days before my departure for Montreal to conclude the agreement, I received a call from Mr. Edward Gelber of Toronto that he wished to speak to me about an important matter. I told him I could not absent myself from Calgary longer than I had planned, and suggested that he meet me at the Toronto airport on my way to Montreal. He and the principal of the Associated Schools in Toronto, informed me of the decision to establish a Bureau of Jewish Education in Toronto. They tried to persuade me that I was the most suitable candidate for this position because I could represent ably the teaching profession to the community and its leaders, including those who were fully canadianized. I tried to convince them that such a bureau was entirely superfluous, that it would eventually develop into an enormous bureaucracy and would "eat-up" much of the meager educational budget. I argued that whatever coordination was necessary could be undertaken by a representative committee of the various schools, with the principals rotating as chairmen and with the engagement of a capable secretary.

(I recalled an American Rabbi's statement that Canadian Jewry was a century behind American Jewry. What an exaggeration! At the rate we are going, we will catch up much sooner. I pondered the imported values and influences from the U.S.A. Some American Rabbis brought us the Sunday-School, and hastened to "Americanize" us before becoming acquainted with our realities and potentitalities. Now, American bureaucrats will bring us the bureaus. It can now be stated as a matter of record that our bureau directors have all been Americans.

Eleven years later, I had a long session with Mr. Gelber at his home in Toronto, (at that time he was already shuttling between his homes in Toronto and in Israel). We discussed the whole educational panorama in Canada, and he agreed with me that I was right in the opinion I had expressed at the airport in 1946. What would he have said now that the administrative budget of the Board of Jewish Education has jumped this year (in 1978-79) to three hundred and twenty six thousand dollars! Recently, Mr. David Newman, Q.C., one of the educational pillars of the Jewish community, expressed his doubts about the priority of such an "Establishment". Granting that a Board of Jewish Education is now essential, I venture to say (based on my 32-years of experience in the U.S.A. and Canada in teaching at all levels, in administration, supervision, camping, youth leadership and teacher-training) that an independent truly-expert-study would find that its real needs and performance do not warrant an *administrative* expenditure of $326,000, particularly when many educational institutions are struggling for existence. Much of this money could be put to better use by applying it to the development of a teachers institute worthy of its name.

An Encounter with a Boss

My meeting with the large, august seminary committee at the Mount Royal Hotel was impresive and enthusiastic. There seemed to be a general feeling that we were on the threshold of a great development that augured well for the future of Jewish education in Canada. The formalities over, I excused myself and went out to make a telephone call. I noticed the chairman, Mr. Ben Beutel, trailing behind me. My telephone call completed, he asked me to sit down with him in the lobby. Without much ado, he proceeded to tell me how the institution would be run; he covered almost everything, from the students' prayers in the morning (at the *seminary*) to the number of years of study. When he finished his presentation, I told him I was pleased we had had this one-sided conversation, because it will avoid a lot of trouble for both of us. "Mr. Beutel," I said, "you have my resignation even before the birth of the seminary!" "Why, why, what is the matter?" I asked him what his profession was, and he told me he was a clothes manufacturer. "Would you seek my knowledge and expertise for your factory? Here we are, with an institution that is not yet a fact, with very few students in sight, and you, a clothing manufacturer, have not lost any time in 'laying down the law to me'." Alarmed, he asked me to reconsider and, at least, to refrain from informing the committee of my decision there and then. I assured him I would not cause any problems, and upon my return home would inform the committee that I changed my mind, without even referring to our tete-a-tete. I kept my promise, and said nothing even to my colleagues who were very anxious for me to assume this task.

The reaction to my resignation was followed by a flurry of letters from Rabbi Charles Bender, chairman of the educational committee, Messrs. Magid, Mendelson, Weingarten and others, who all urged me to rescind my resignation. I then decided that if the committee would approve all my essential terms, I would chance it. Our negotiations finally collapsed primarily because of a clause in the contract proposed by the committee, stipulating that "*in all matters*, the activities of the director shall be subject to the *directions* and *prior approval* of the educational committee". Since there were already sharp difference of opinion between me and the committee (for example, my insistence on a three-year program of studies as against a two-year program already decided upon by the committee), I sent my counter-proposals to Rabbi Bender. I made it clear that I would withdraw unless these terms were met. His response was, "I personally feel that a modus operandi could be effected if we were all to remember that the creation of so spiritual an undertaking as an institution of higher Jewish learning, requires a certain amount of mutual confidence and trust." My reaction was "I agree with you that the creation of so spiritual an undertaking as an institution of higher Jewish learning requires a certain amount of mutual confidence and trust! Why then discourage the director at the outset by the inclusion of a clause stipulating that 'in all matters, the activities of the director shall be subject to the directions and prior approval of the educational committee.'"?

My final negative decision was made when I received a letter from Mr. Beutel, following Rabbi Bender's letter by about six weeks, stating: "With regard to the other matters referred to in your letter of the 14th instant, the Board wishes to advise you that we do not feel that any change can be made in the terms of the contract as drafted, it being naturally understood that the Educational Director will generally sit in at meetings of the Educational Committee, and so his opinion will in most cases form part of the considerations on which the decisions will be taken". Mr. Beutel and the committee were condescending and generous enough to allow the director to "*generally* sit in at meetings, and his opinion will in *most* cases form *part* of the considerations." And so my great dream went with the wind!

The two teacher institutes that came into being that year had a total of about twenty-two students, the Yiddish one outnumbering the Hebrew more than two to one. Ironically, the latter could not even provide enough students for the Minyan the president thought should start the day at the seminary. Of the five graduates of the Calgary high school who were to join me in Montreal, one withdrew completely and the others preferred to study at a well established institution with a four year joint program that awarded a teachers diploma and B.A. degree from Columbia University and the teachers institute.

Following years of struggle and vicissitudes, the two institutes amalgamated in the late forties. After thirty two years of existence, it now has a total of about thirty students, half in the day class and half in the evening class. The program of the former is based on a two-year study-program with twenty seven hours of study per week, and the latter on a three year program of fifteen hours study weekly. As one who headed a recognized teachers institute with a four year program, and as a former member of the Committee of Hebrew Teachers Colleges in the U.S.A., I can say categorically that the teacher institute of Montreal is a far cry from a true teacher-training institute. It is interesting that the present program includes only three hours of Yiddish studies weekly, and that the director is a graduate of a Lubavitcher teacher-training yeshivah in Israel.

The Strangest Interlude

As if the *Hashgachah Elyonah* (Providence) was synchronizing these events, my plans to return home were interrupted again. Mr. Isaac Hamlin, director of the Gewerkschaften Campaign in America, appealed to me to help with the organization of that year's drive. The Histadrut was not in a position to spare capable individuals for the campaign in America because of the Yishuv's struggle with its Arab and British adversaries at that time. I was stationed with my family in Baltimore, Maryland, where

I had for the first time a taste of devoting myself entirely to campaigning for funds. Devotee of the Histadrut though I was, I knew I could not take it for more than one season, and turned my eyes again homeward, to Eretz Israel.

My stay in Baltimore for about six months gave me an opportunity to have a close look at the state of Jewish education in one of the larger American centers. My wife took on a class at one of the Hebrew schools, and we both became aware for the very first time of the abnormal situation of having in the same class pupils ranging in age from six to eleven! A short time later, I received an invitation to deliver a lecture to the students of the local teachers institute. When I said as a matter of course that my lecture would be in Hebrew, the dean countered with, "If you want the students to understand you, you better speak in English." I recall my conversation with Dr. Louis L. Kaplan, Exec. Director of the Jewish Education Bureau in Baltimore, on our way to the synagogue on *Tish'ah B'av*. We were debating whether students could be taught to speak Hebrew. His reaction to my statement that "It has already been done" was, "*You* have proven that it *cannot* be done". I was jolted, because I thought he was questioning what had become known in educational circles, that the Calgarians at the teachers institute in N.Y. were actually speaking Hebrew fluently. Noticing my blush, he added, "because you are the only one who has succeeded in doing it." I countered by pointing out that "quite a few others have done it", and thought to myself, "to what lengths some people will go to prove that what they don't believe in *cannot* be done!"

My wife and I were in the midst of our plans to return to Eretz-Israel, when I received a few attractive offers. Dr. Alexander M. Dushkin wanted me as supervisor-consultant of Hebrew schools in N.Y. Mr. Bernard Isaacs was planning to establish a teachers institute in Detroit, and I was asked whether I would agree to head it. There was also an offer of a principalship of a Hebrew high school in Miami, Florida. In the meantime, I went to N.Y. to see Dr. Moshe Ben-David, the adminitrative secretary of the Hebrew University in Jerusalem, who was then on a visit to N.Y. and was later among the victims on the bus that was ambushed and burned on its way to the Hebrew University on Mount Scopus. I had very high regard for this man of integrity and humanity, whose assistant I had been at the secretariat of the university. I wanted to consult him about returning to Eretz-Israel. He told me, "I strongly advise you not to return unless you have a big *shissel* filled with gold." By-and-by, I received an invitation to become the director of the Keren Hatarbut in Canada. My wife was strongly of the opinion that any of the positions offered me in the U.S. would hold much better prospects of achievement and satisfaction than the Keren Hatarbut. I, however, was enthused as I put it, "about the opportunity to do for the whole of Canada what I had done for Western Canada in general and Calgary in particular." I truly had great faith in the potentialities of a Hebrew Renaissance Movement in Canada. And so I became the national director of Keren Hatarbut in Canada at the end of 1946.

Chapter 15
The First Years of
Keren Hatarbut
Chance Is At Work Again

In the late thirties, there existed a "United Committee" (*Hava'ad Hame'uchad*), whose function was to coordinate the limited Hebrew-language activities of some schools and organizations. In the early forties, Yerachmiel Weingarten, one of those who succeeded in escaping from Poland — via China — before the Holocaust, settled in Montreal. He became active in Hava'ad Hame'uchad and was later instrumental in establishing the Keren Hatarbut Ha'ivrit, literally, The Hebrew Culture Fund. This name was chosen as a sort of footnote to the unsuccessful clamor by such culturists as Achad Ha'am and Bialik for a national culture fund to supplement the Keren Kayemet (the Jewish National Fund) and the Keren Hayesod (the Foundation Fund). It is now a matter of history that the Zionist movement has been paying a very high price for its failure to establish such a fund, with which to plough and sow in the fields of education and culture. Mr. Weingarten and some of his Hebraist colleagues therefore had the gradiose idea of establishing such a Fund in Canada. However, this name was a misnomer for Canada because of the association with raising funds which it brought to mind rather than the emphasis on educational-cultural activities. Of course, it never became anything resembling a "culture fund" alongside the two other funds.

The work of the organization was perforce limited by its scanty finances. When I took over the directorship of the organization, its activities were confined primarily to Montreal, and consisted of Hebrew language classes for adults, an annual series of Hebrew lectures, a few children's Hebrew speaking clubs, a Hebrew Writers Week, devoted to publicizing the life and work of a prominent Hebrew author, and the promotion of the sale of Hebrew books and periodicals. The office was located in a small rented room of the Jewish Folk Shule's building, where the Board meetings were usually held. Sometime after my arrival, the school needed this extra room. Because of the acute-housing shortage and our limited funds, the organization remained without a home. I was surprised that my wife didn't object to my suggestion that we move the

Keren Hatarbut office into our livingroom, where it stayed for about half a year until a small room became vacant in the same building where we lived. My wife came to the rescue again when our part-time secretary (the whole office-staff) resigned when she became a mother, and it was impossible to find a Hebrew typist in those days. We did have one candidate, a young girl from Eretz Israel, who claimed she was proficient in all types of office work, including Hebrew and English typing. Since there were no other candidates, I asked her to come to work the next day. When I witnessed in amazement her struggles to insert a paper in the typewriter, I asked her why she had misinformed me about something that would surely be discovered right away. Her astonishing reply was, "When I left for America, I was told that I was going to a 'land of bluff' and I would succeed only by bluffing my way." Unbelievable? It really did happen!

The Great Challenge Cometh

The greatest challenge and achievement up to that time was undoubtedly the decision to establish Hebrew Camp Massad, "in accordance with the principles of the Hebrew camp that had been established in New York" in the early forties. Mr. Isaac Gold, an effervescent Hebraist-philanthropist, had forced the issue by investing three thousand dollars of his own funds as a deposit for a camp-site near Lac Quennuilles in the Laurentians. He was bubbling with enthusiasm as he drove me to the place. His whole demeanor was as if we were going to lay the foundation for a Holy Temple. When we arrived on the spot, he turned to me in Biblical Hebrew, "Lift your eyes and gaze upon this beauty, these charming hills, this expansive lake". There and then he dubbed the lake *Agam Kana-ee* (sounding like Lac Quennuilles and meaning the "zealots' lake") as a symbol of the zealousness that is required to make the Hebrew camp idea a reality.

The High Cost of Inexperienced Enthusiasm

A beautiful site it was indeed! But to use an understatement, it was unsuitable for a children's camp. There was hardly any level ground for a sport field; there was only one hall to be used both for dining and for all activities; there was no pier, and there were only a few showers. Much as I disliked to dampen Mr. Gold's enthusiasm, I told him that to lose the three thousand dollar deposit would entail the least financial loss. He became agitated and insisted that even if I were right, it was too late to start looking for another site. It took years and many thousands of dollars to level some hills and build proper sports fields. Mr. Gold gave the three thousand dollars deposit as a gift to the camp, and lent the camp additional sums of tens of thousands of dollars without interest. Looking back to those days, I have no doubt that were it not for this stubborn man's zeal and generosity, there would never have been a Camp Massad, or its establishment would have been deferred for many years.

This matter settled, we had to turn our attention to the recruitment of campers and staff. Few people believed that parents and children who had become accustomed to luxurious summer-camps would agree to become guinea-pigs even for such a "sacred task" as a Hebrew speaking camp. I rejected the suggestion that I visit families for the purpose of persuading them to be Massad pioneers. I always maintained that solicitation of pupils or campers would jeopardize the independence of institutions in such matters as educational content and method. Instead, I met with groups of parents and pupils in the schools and explained the purposes and programs of Massad. It was part of the miracle that about eighty children were entrusted to us for a camp whose materialization was doubted by many.

Whence a Hebrew Speaking Staff

There were in Montreal some youths who could speak Hebrew, but none of them had experience either as campers or as counsellors. Fortunately, a group of Hebrew speaking Calgarians who had been trained at the Leadership Camp in Watrous and who had had experience at Hebrew camp T'chiyah as well as at Young Judaean camps, answered the call to serve at Massad. They, Dov Eisen (now Robert Eisen, Q.C.) of Toronto who had been a junior counsellor at Massad in N.Y., a small group of capable Montrealers and a sprinkle of experienced New-Yorkers, formed the pioneering core of the camp. As an interesting aside, it is noteworthy that we could not recruit even one counsellor through the good offices of Massad in N.Y. When I informed its director that I had succeeded in persuading David Sidorsky to be our head counsellor, he chuckled in amazement, saying, "David Sidorsky is an outstanding intellectual, but he would be useless as a head-counsellor in a camp." I smiled with satisfaction, because I knew for certain he would be a tremendous asset in all areas of camp life. And indeed he was, in spite of the fact that he had to jump around on one foot because he had broken his leg early in the camp season.

The organization of the camp was the most difficult task we, my wife and I, had ever undertaken. In Winnipeg and Calgary, there were youth organizations which did most of the technical work. In Montreal, my wife and I had to work feverishly day and night to make sure that everything would be ready for camp opening. The camp manager, *kibbutznick* Mordechai Garfinkel, was looking after purchasing and the physical preparation of the camp, but there was nobody to help in the registration, in the preparation of the programs, in all the paperwork, etc. In addition, I had to give much of my attention to meeting with the inexperienced Montreal staff members, (the experienced ones from Calgary and N.Y. came just before the opening of the camp season) to discuss the workings of the camp that was to compete with well-established and prestigious camps in the area. That too was part of the miracle — that we succeeded in winning our race against time.

To Serve "K'Lal Yisrael"

The underlying principle of Massad, as of its parent organization the Keren Hatarbut, was to serve "K'lal Yisrael", the total Jewish community. We were going to cater to people of all religious and political ideologies, and we did, indeed, have Modern-Orthodox, Conservative, (we had no Reform only because their pupils' knowledge of Hebrew was inadequate), Rightists and Leftists, and even some students from the Lubavitcher and other yeshivot. Aspiring to become a truly national movement, we established partial scholarships to make possible the participation of campers and counselors-in-training from Toronto, Ottawa, Winnipeg, Calgary, Edmonton and Vancouver. Our common denominator was Zionism in its broadest meaning and the revival of Hebrew as the spoken language of the people. The program was planned in such a way that every camper and staff member should feel completely at home, that while traditions would be fully observed, no one group would force its views or practices upon the others. For example, there were the three regular daily Services, but no one was forced to attend. Interestingly enough, all the older boys and girls, even those who didn't go in the city, attended daily. As for the young ones, our flag raising ceremony included the recitation of "Shma-Yisrael", "Al Naharot Bavel" (to remember daily the loss of our national independence) B'shuv Hashem, (to express daily our faith in the Restoration of Zion), an appropriate thought or saying from the Bible or from another Hebrew source, and Hatikvah, to emphasize our participation in the rebuilding of Eretz-Israel. O'Canada and God Save the King were sung at the lowering of the flag ceremony.

A Hebrew Speaking Island in the Laurentians

It was easy, of course, to decide that evrything in camp would be conducted in Hebrew, but the implementation of this decision was not at all simple. Although a majority of the campers came from the best day and afternoon schools, they had never used Hebrew as a spoken language in their daily lives and activities. Furthermore, they had not been used to the sephardic pronunciation that we introduced in the camp at the very beginning.

It was one of our guests who, upon spending with us a day at the end of the season, exclaimed "this is a veritable Hebrew speaking island in the Laurentians". Everything was in Hebrew — the names of the bunks, the paths, the hall, the groups, etc. The names were decided upon by the campers at sessions where the general theme of the season — *"Hachut Hameshulash Le'olam Lo Yinatek"* (the three-fold cord will never break) —was explained ("the three-fold cord" representing Torah, Land and People) and discussed. The campers were guided to select names that had historical or contemporary bearing on the general theme. These names and their significance were then dramatized by the respective groups. All the activities were in Hebrew, and the natural methods described in the chapter on Calgary were used in getting the children into the habit of expressing themselves in Hebrew. In general, efforts were made to have the campers initiate and carry out programs. For example, every morning a different group was assigned the task of preparing and conducting the flag-raising ceremony; every group was assigned to take charge of programs at *Medurot* (campfire sessions), to conduct services, and to lead in *Birkat-Hamazon (grace after meals), etc.*

He Who Pays the Piper Calls the Tune

I referred previously to a phenomenon that bedevilled and continues to bedevil Jewish institutions, namely, the assumption that the big contributor has the privilege to "call the tune", irrespective of its resulting quality. It was thus presumed by Mr. Gold that he would stay with us in camp all the time. I had serious misgivings about this but was willing to give it a try, especially because he was really helpful in many ways. It would be nothing for him, for example, to leap into his car and drive to the city to fetch something that was missed. But when he assumed the role of supra-educator, *"menaheil al menaheil"*, as he expressed it in an *ashkenazic* accent, he compounded my difficulties in running the camp. From supra-director he turned to supra-director. He insisted, for example, on complete silence during meals, and persisted in instructing me to tell the counselors this and tell the counselors that. Because of my high regard for him, it was with reluctance I eventually told him that there could be only one director, he or I. And if I was to be the director, he would have to agree to visit the camp only on special occasions. He dashed into his car, drove to the city and complained to the Keren Hatarbut president, "Horowitz threw me out of the camp!" But I was steadfast in my resolve, and Mr. Gold gracefully accepted the verdict and never mentioned the matter again, nor did he harbour any ill feelings toward me.

Come My Beloved, Come — Let Us Welcome the Queen

Kabbalat Shabbat, welcoming the sabbath, was one of the most beautiful and meaningful scenes. It was held out of doors in a breath-taking setting. At the sound of the *shofar,* Massadnicks, all dressed in white, streamed from all sides towards the circle where the *T'filot* (prayers) took place. The beauty of the site was a perfect frame for the happy faces of childhood and youth.

The prayers started with a Keren-Kayemet ceremony. Representatives of the various cabins, starting with the six year olds, came forward to deposit in the large box — the handiwork of campers — their weekly contributions to the Jewish National Fund. Each week, a different camper represented his or her group, and each one made an appropriate declaration in its name. The childish singing voices of the campers echoed from the surrounding hills. Some of the older ones told me that the whole scene was a real transcendental experience for them. This brought back my memories of the charm of Tzfat, the city of my birth, where Lechah-Dodi, one of the finest religious poems in Hebrew literature, was composed by Kabbalist Shlomo Halevi Alkavetz in the 16th century. Even in my most intense chassidic years in Yerushalym, I had not experienced such rapture and fervor.

At our first Kabbalat Shabbat we had as our guests some of the camp committee members. Moshe Surchin, National President of Keren-Haratbut, turned to a beaming Yitzchak Gold with, "Look at this beauty, the charming hills, the shining lake, and the setting sun." Mr. Gold in turn, apparently thinking of my earlier pronouncement about the unsuitability of the site, looked at me with head held high and with triumph on his countenance, as if to say, "you see how wrong you were!" David Finestone, Secretary of Keren-Hatarbut and Massad, a young fellow and the only one of the Keren-Hatarbut-Massad *machers* who was brought up in Montreal and understood the unquestionable value of sports, looked at me smilingly and knowingly, as if to say, "what do these fuddy-duddys understand about camping."

The prayers completed, the campers, starting with the youngest group, walked out of the circle in a chain and entered the hall as they were singing marching songs. The atmosphere in the hall; the happy voices; the Zmirot Shabbat; the Birkat-Hamazon, conducted in unison each time by a different camper; the oneg-Shabbat following the meal; the dancing and singing, all exerted a profound and enduring spiritual influence on the whole camp community.

A Time to Laugh, A Time to Weep
(Ecclesiastes 3:4)

Tish'ah Be'av, the fast-day marking the destruction of the Temple, is observed in America by comparatively few people. The children whose parents do not mark this fast-day are almost oblivious to this important historic date, because it falls in the summer when there is no Hebrew school. As this day approached, we planned a program that would endure in the memory of our campers. All of us sat in circles on the floor, with a lit candle inserted in a potato in front of each one of us. The readings from *Eicha* (Lamentations); the recitations from other literary sources; the old and new sad songs bemoaning the destructive forces in our history; the allusions to the Holocaust and to the Chlautzim who fell for the restoration of Zion, and the melancholy voices, all left an indelible impression on our minds and hearts. Nature too assisted us in our dramatic presentation, with the rain pounding on the roof, with the sound of thunder, and with the flashing of lightning. Tears streamed from children's and adults' eyes as we made our way silently out of the hall into the clear night (the storm had ended by then) and straight to our cabins. The counselors marvelled for some time at the complete silence of the campers throughout the night. It was difficult to dissuade younger children from fasting the whole day, and the educational effect of *Tishah-Be'av* was more profound than we had anticipated.

The end of the fast was marked with a festive meal and with dancing and singing until the late hours of the night, to impress upon the young minds our undaunted faith in and indomitable will for national Survival and Revival.

"Mamavdil Bein Kodesh Lechol"
Distinguishing Between the Holy and the Ordinary

In the Havdalah ceremony, we thank God for "making a distinction between the holy and the ordinary". In Massad, too, all was not holy. Some of the "ordinary" things were fraught with obstacles, with difficulties and even with danger. To begin with, we suddenly discovered that the water-supply, which might have been adequate for a small resort place, was insufficient for the population of over a hundred people. At one time, the water supply was so low that for three days we had to bring in water from the outside for the most essential needs. During this period and for some short periods thereafter, we could not flush the toilets; we could not take showers, and we had to use water for washups most sparingly. This resulted in an outbreak of diarrhea.

Children who had been accustomed to proper sportsfields had to use makeshift patches of ground for their limited games. Trying to use Hebrew terms while playing games was frustrating. There was thus the danger of creating tensions that would nullify the unique values of Massad. Somewhat aggravating this situation was the attitude of Hebraists who never laboured in a "language laboratory" and expected *all the campers* to speak Hebrew *all the time*. So unrealistic were they that even Moshe Surchin, who had been an effective teacher of Hebrew in Quebec City, rushed over to me one day and shouted with great disappointment, "Aharon, Aharon, I have just heard two campers speak English!"

Not by Might, Nor by Power But by My Spirit (Zechariah 4:6)

The power of the spirit, however, was so great that even young children ignored inconveniences and hardships and became part of the general atmosphere of expectation and cheer, expressed through the singing and dancing that pervaded our little community. Mr. J. Rabinovitch, editor of the Canadian Jewish Eagle, described this spirit in his daily column (Volume 42, No. 129, August 1947), "I spent Shabbat Nachamu at Massad . . . I felt like a tourist in "Galut" who finds himself in a Kvutza somewhere in the valley of Jezreal. I tasted both of them and can therefore guarantee the similarity . . . The atmosphere is throughout like in Eretz-Israel. The singing and dancing I witnessed on Friday night reached depths of Chassidic fervor . . . The Havdalah at the end of Shabbat was unusually impressive."

A Dedicated Staff

If we succeeded in coping with the difficulties, it was in large measure due to the understanding and dedication of the staff. Notwithstanding the difficult work all of them did during the long days, they readily met with me every night to review the events of the day, to discuss problems, and to search for ways and means of improving all phases of camplife. These sessions were a veritable workshop for exchanging experiences and views and for evolving new methods and programs. At the first of these meetings, for example, a counselor referred to the fact that attendance at Services was not obligatory, while every camper was expected to participate in all other activities. I pointed out that one of our fundamental principles was to refrain from using coercive methods in *any* of the activities. Since many of the counselors had been accustomed to the arbitrary rules and regulations of schools and clubs, a lively debate ensued as to whether this principle of freedom would work. It was finally decided to experiment in this field and to work hard at devising educational means of persuasion rather than follow the shortcut of "you must do this, and you must not do that". On the whole, our experiments worked quite well.

While in other camps, counselors received one day off weekly, ours were content with one day monthly. A few even followed my example, and refused to leave the camp during the whole two months of its duration.

I did leave the camp for about 2 hours daily, six times weekly, to deliver and pick up the mail at the "general store" at Lac Carrè. I assumed this chore in order to make close personal contact with the older campers. Every day I took a camper along with me, and we conversed in Hebrew all the way, mainly about his or her life at camp. This gave me an opportunity to gain some insight into the makeup of about fifty boys and girls, with a view to continuing communication with them through the Hebrew Youth Movement we were about to create,

"Ain Tzadick Ba'aretz...."
There is No Compeletly Righteous Person
(Ecclestiastes 7:20)

I have had occasion many a time to say humorously, "even I am wrong sometimes". And so, all was not righteousness and harmony in our midst. There were deviations from the norm and infractions of the rules we had arrived at by consensus. As a matter of fact, some of the counselors told me years later, "Ahron, you think you knew everything that was going on in camp. You would be surprised about how much you didn't know." "Well", I said, "you would be surprised how much I knew that you thought I didn't know". However, the violations were not of the kind that would shock anyone, especially not these days.

One night I heard voices from the direction of the lake. As they became louder and louder, I decided to investigate. Lo and behold, I saw from a distance some of our most trusted counselors swimming at about two a.m. Withought their noticing me, I sat down in a spot they were bound to pass on their way back to their cabins. As they approached, I turned on my flashlight, said "Laylah tov" (good night) and turned my back on them. In the morning, one of my Calgary protoges came into my office and said angrily, "Your punishment was too severe!" The others kept mum.

Kids on Strike

We established the position of waiter for some good students, who could not afford the camp fee, to enable them to come to camp. Except for the few hours a day of waiting on tables, they were like other campers in all respects. Because of the shortage of kitchen-help, the camp manager required our waiters to set and clear the tables, which they claimed to be contrary to their agreement. One bright Sunday morning, "Strike, Strike" reverberated in the dining-hall. Our waiters, led by my youngest brother, decided to strike. I refused to negotiate with them, because they had decided to strike without prior notice. They threatened to leave the camp and proceeded to order a taxi. Our usual Sunday guests pleaded with me to give in to the strikers. "Imagine," they said, "what impression this will make in the city at a time when the success of our project is still in doubt." My reaction was that responsibility and self-discipline were essential for our success, and that allowing ourselves to be intimidated by anyone would be more detrimental in the long run. The taxi arrived; the strikers entered it and drove away. A few minutes later, they reappeared and stated that they realized their act "would hurt our common cause". Our negotiations brought forth an amicable compromise whereby they would set but not clear tables. It was encouraging to hear these fourteen-fifteen year old kids say: "We took into consideration the fact that our camp is not a business venture."

Foundation for Leadership Training

Aware of the need for trained counselors and youth leaders, we laid the foundation of a leadership training institution by involving all the senior campers ("counselors in training") in a special program that included the general subject of "how to", how to organize a children's club, how to conduct a meeting, how to teach singing, etc. They also attended discussions on such subjects as the History of Zionism, and were required to read at least two Hebrew books during the season in addition to the regular Shabbat reading-hour. The counselors too organized their own discussion group.

They That Sow in Tears Shall Reap in Joy (Psalm 126)

We did not get the whole-hearted support of the educational institutions in the city. The Adath-Israel school, under the principalship of Mordechai Mendelson, where Mr. Gold was highly influential, gave us the utmost cooperation. Melech Magid and other educators were supportive as individuals. At the end of the season, a parent told me she had consulted Mr. Magid about entrusting her children to Massad. His response was, "Officially I cannot endorse or recommend it, but I do know that if this fellow Horowitz undertook it, he will kill himself, if need be, to make it a success."

There were, however, the inevitable sceptics and prophets of doom who were eagerly waiting, I was told, for the news of our failure. When the word of our unusual success went out, we received the following official accolade from the Board of Education of the United Talmud Torahs, which had witheld from us their official endorsement: "At a Board of Education meeting of the United Talmud Torahs in Montreal, held on August 20, several members who had visited Massad during the summer, shared with us their impressions on what was happening at the camp. We all heard the report with full satisfaction and with enthusiasm for a great new idea that is being realized in the field of Hebrew education in Canada. The meeting decided unanimously to convey to you, director of Massad; to the Keren-Hatarbut committee that initiated this project, and especially to Yitzchak Gold, president of the camp, our warm congratulations and profound recognition for your wonderful efforts in face of all the terrible obstacles you experienced in your untrodden path. May your hands be strengthened. B.M. Weiner, Chairman, on behalf of the Board of Education." Mr. Gold was jubilant, and the other *machers* were beaming. I had tears in my eyes when I saw many children crying as they reluctantly boarded the buses that took them home.

In evaluating the educational and social benefits of the camp, I stated publicly that if I were faced with a choice of sending my children for ten months even to a very good day school or for two months to camp Massad, I would unhesitatingly prefer Massad.

National Hebrew Youth Movement Comes into Being

The two months in camp provided us with the opportunity to lay the groundwork for a national Hebrew Youth Movement. As soon as the younger children returned home, the camp became the scene of a three day conference attended by the entire staff as well as the older campers. The high level of the discussions and resolutions provided us, the leaders of Keren Hatarbut, with additional evidence of the effectiveness of our new educational venture. We were encouraged by the seriousness with which these young people, — ranging in age from thirteen to twenty — discussed Zionism and the state of Jewish life in Canada. They decided to establish a Hebrew speaking youth movement wherever there was a good Hebrew school that could be a source of members for such an organization. And they proceeded to implement their resolutions.

With very little financial help from the parent organization, they organized in Montreal four active clubs, a choir and a dramatic group. Already in the first year of the movement's existence, they published a Hebrew magazine, *"Hagesher"* (The Bridge). In his introduction, the editor Yitzchak Moshe Kaplansky, wrote about its three-fold purpose: to create for our members a platform for thought and expression on events in the Jewish world; to serve as a bridge between our youth and the people of Israel, and to link together the various branches of the movement. It contained serious essays on literary subjects, even on such a theme as Hebrew in the field of science, compositions by younger members, and reports on the activities of all the branches. To strengthen the work of the branches and the links among them, the president, Meshulam Pearl, now professor of gynecology at Albany, N.Y. visited the Ottawa and Toronto branches, and the secretary, Israel Silverman, now Rabbi of Beth Jacob congregation in Hamilton, made a tour of Winnipeg, Calgary and Edmonton. In all, the movement numbered a few hundred graduates and students of the best Hebrew schools in six cities. It was this movement that provided leadership for Massad and other Zionist camps. Because of the lack of experienced Hebrew-speaking camp directors, Meshulam Pearl, Israel Silverman and Yechiel Glustein practically organized and ran the camp in 1949 when I left for Israel. When Massad Bet was opened in Toronto in 1952, under the directorship of David Taub, it was Meshulam Pearl and Gina Petrushka who assisted him and provided the experience they had gained in Massad Alef and in the Hebrew Youth Movement. Esther Wise and Yaakov Chetner brought their experience to assist Ephrayim and Dvorah Malamuth in directing camp T'chiyah in Calgary, which served then also other schools, notably Edmonton, and continued to exist up to 1947.

Chapter 16
Keren Hatarbut
Spreads Its Wings

1947 was a year of dramatic events. The agonies following the full disclosure of the Nazi nightmare, the poignant tragedy of the closed avenues of escape to the survivors of Hitler's infernos, and the struggles in "The Promised Land" against British betrayal, aroused Jews throughout the world to the realization that the time had come to take their destiny in their own hands and renew their national independence. Many people, though by far not enough, perceived the close relationship between physical and spiritual redemption, and were more receptive to the work of the incipient Hebrew movement. An increasing number of people, though by far insufficient, started to study Hebrew. Our classes were augmented to include such subjects as Bible, Hebrew Literature and History of Zionism. Some of our students were so advanced that when the World Union for Hebrew Education established, in 1948, the Hebrew Matriculation Examinations for students of Hebrew throughout the Jewish world, three students of our Hebrew courses, E. Pugach, David Finestone and Israel Silverman, were among the first to pass them.

A symptom of the reawakening was the case of one, E. Pugach, who caught my eye during the first meeting of my class in Hebrew Literature. He was a man of about sixty who radiated enthusiasm when he or others hit upon a literary gem or a beautiful expression. He would impose freely upon my time for the mere opportunity to *speak* Hebrew. He would phone me often to invite me to a cafe for coffee or a drink for the sheer purpose of *speaking* Hebrew. With our growing friendship he told me his story. He had received no Hebrew education and had been inspired by Marx and Lenin and enamored of the myth of Stalin's millenium. He was a hard working man who saved pennies for years to enable him to gain entry, though for only a short time, into the communist paradise. He entered as an intoxicated believer and emerged a sober heretic. He then returned to his people and its culture. As a sure cure for the starry-eyed Bolsheviks in Canada, he recommended a short visit to the communist heaven.

We Look to the Zionist Organization

It was clear to us that if our organization was really to "spread its wings", it would have to obtain much greater moral and financial support from the Zionist organization. The relationship between "us" and "them" was tenuous. Keren Hatarbut had no official status within the Zionist organization. Whatever we achieved was by dint of the efforts of influential individuals of the Zionist Organization and of the Keren Hatarbut. With the approach of the 29th national convention of the Z.O.C., which featured the slogan "The Year of Redemption", our influential members lobbied influential leaders of the Z.O.C. to give greater prominence to Keren Hatarbut at the convention. To rally Hebraists behind the Keren Hatarbut, I wrote in our Hebrew weekly section in the Canadian Jewish Eagle and in our monthly Hebrew page of the Canadian Zionist: "The very fact that we have two separate conventions, one for Zionism and one for Hebrew Culture, is an indication of the gap between the body of Zionism — its political and financial instruments — and its soul — Hebrew culture, which gives Zionism purpose and meaning. The fact that the Hebrew gathering is dependent entirely on the Zionist organization is additional evidence that the wide public is still very far from understanding the value of Hebrew culture for the redemption of the people of Israel in its land and for the preservation of Judaism in the Golah. We confess and are ashamed that the Hebraists — the few who believe and know that without the spirit of Israel there is no meaning to, nor even justification for, the existence of Israel as a state —would be unable to rally, on behalf and with the strength of Hebrew Culture, hundreds of people from all parts of the country for the purpose of considering and discussing matters of concern to the soul of Zionism. The Hebraists therefore ride on the coat-tails of the Z.O.C., and hold a few meetings in the 'twilight' of the Zionist convention." I called upon Hebraists "to emerge from their isolation and turn the Keren Hatarbut into a mass movement".

I had attended previously two national conventions as a delegate from the West. The one in Jan. 1941 took place in Montreal before the Keren Hatarbut was established. The night before it opened, the *Va-ad Ha'me'uchad* sponsored a *Melaveh-Malkah* in the small Z.O.C. hall on Sherbrooke St. (The convention itself was held of course at the Mount Royal Hotel.) Rev. J.K. Goldbloom of London England, who was at that time the national director of the J.N.F., spoke on Eliezer Ben-Yehudah, and I on the need for a national movement for Hebrew education and culture. An indication of the Hebraists' self-imposed isolation was the fact that the invitation as well as the proceedings were entirely in Hebrew, precluding thereby people who did not know Hebrew, but who understood its importance. I felt strongly, as did Rev. Goldbloom and others, that the time had come for Hebraists to emerge from basking in their cocoon with *Loshon Kodesh*, and bring the message of the Hebrew Renaissance, in English if need be, to all the people.

The second convention took place in Toronto in Jan. 1946. The Keren Hatarbut was already in existence, and I participated in its one meeting as the representative of the Educators Council in the west. This time there was an Oneg-Shabbat where the program was again conducted entirely in Hebrew. Yerachmiel Weingarten engaged me in button-holing influential Zionists to plead for their cooperation with Keren Hatarbut. I had the unpleasant feeling of acting like the proverbial *shtadlan*, an intercessor. The Hebrew word *shtadlan* has the connotation of a poor helpless fellow appealing for understanding. I recalled Moshe Sharett's description of how he had felt when he had to buttonhole statesmen and politicians in the portals of international conferences prior to the re-establishment of the Jewish State. As an official delegate to the Zionist convention, I did have an opportunity to speak at a plenary session. It may have been then that some Easterners, with whom I had not come in contact, formed an image of me as an extremist. I felt very strongly about the continued inaction of the Z.O.C. in the field of Jewish education during the five years that had elapsed since the National Council's decision to establish a national education committee following my address on this subject at the 1941 convention. Some of the leaders on the platform cringed as I shook my finger vehemently at them and the audience and warned that "we are bound to lose another generation if we continue to neglect education". One friend told me smilingly, "Notice the high tension in the hall. It is so hot you could light a match!"

The convention in Jan. 1948 marked a turning point in our relationship with the Z.O.C. Our lobbying efforts bore some fruit, thanks in large measure to Eddy Gelber's special empathy with our movement. For the first time in its history, the Z.O.C. included on its convention program a lecture and discussion on Hebrew. Mr. Edward Gelber chaired the session, and I spoke on "The Hebrew Language and Culture and the Jewish State". The work of the Hebrew movement was thus brought to the attention of the entire convention plenum. The convention took place in Ottawa, where we had already a Keren Hatarbut chapter and a Hebrew speaking youth group. The success of Massad and the Hebrew Youth Movement had already made its impression in Ottawa as well as in other centers. Our national officers were encouraged when they saw for the first time a large representation from near and far. The Z.O.C. agenda included also the agenda of the Keren Hatarbut, though it was still listed as "under the auspices of the Keren Hatarbut." We had three sessions: an Oneg-Shabbat where English was also made use of to inform the general public of our objectives, an informal luncheon after the Services on Shabbat at which delegates from various cities reported on their problems and activities, and a business session in the form of a Melave-Malkah. We emerged from this convention with a sense of confidence in the future of the Keren Hatarbut.

The Blight of Fear

The intensified conflict between the British administration and the Yishuv resulted sometimes in violent confrontations between Hagganah and the British armed forces. The sight of homeless refugees on the high seas, the thousands of concentration-camp survivors crammed into new camps to prevent them from reaching their only possible haven, the increasing hostility of the British government, and the open support and arming of the Arabs by the British administration in Eretz-Israel, necessitated what the British termed illegal acts. As long as armed conflict had been confined to the Stern Gang and the *Irgun Tzva'i Le'umi*, Jews in Canada consoled themselves with the explanation that the Revisionist renegades acted against the will of the organized Yishuv. Now that Hagganah was forced to change its policy of *Havlagah* (self-restraint), some Jews in Canada started to become fearful lest British and Arab propaganda identify them with the "trouble makers" in a domain of the mother country. That attitude was natural for people with a long history of persecution and fear. I was greatly shocked, however, when a manifestation of this fear seemed to seize also Zionist leadership. It was at a meeting of the National Zionist Council in Montreal that the chairman, Mr. Michael Garber, made a statement to the effect that we might soon have to come out publicly against the Hagganah. I looked around for the reaction of the members. There was none! I instinctively sprang to my feet and demanded, "Are we to be that frightened, are we so helpless as to scurry like mice into the holes so soon after the Holocaust and at a time when our people are fighting for their very survival?!" I was shaking all over when I sat down and waited for any reaction. There was none! The chairman proceeded with the other items on the agenda. I later approached two persons who I thought should have protested! Mr. David Chertock, representative of the Jewish National Fund to Canada, told me he did not consider it appropriate for an "outsider" to intervene but was glad that I, a Canadian, spoke up. Mr. Edward Gelber, one of the most knowledgeable and dedicated Zionist leaders, shrugged and remarked, "You saw for yourself that it was of no use to protest"!

In contrast to the timidity manifested at times by the Zionist leadership in the East, the Winnipeg Zionists under the leadership of Mr. Sam Drache, then Vice-President of the Zionist Organization of Canada, took a fearless stand on the Palestine issue and pulled no punches in criticising the British Government's policy and actions in Palestine. Their courageous political actions were all the more remarkable because the predominant power structure in the West was of British origin and pro-British, while in Quebec the French Canadians were anti-British on principle, particularly during that period.

Another purely Western manifestation of bravery was the political activity of a young couple, Isaac and Channah (Shankiyan) Horowitz. At a time when they were barely making a living, they purchased an old printing press and published (in their home) a periodical, "Let The Truth Be Told", which they mailed, all at their own expense, to parliamentarians, editors, clergymen of various denominations, etc., in Canada and the U.S.A.

Paper Bridges

There is a Talmudic saying that after the Messiah comes the righteous will cross to Israel on "paper bridges". This saying undoubtedly means that those in the Galut who will desire to identify with the people of Israel will do so through the paper bridges represented by language, literature, art and music, and by cultural, social and religious values. To these must be added, of course, "bridges" represented by people, trains, ships and planes, to convey the *contents* of the "paper bridges". They must also be two-way bridges to ensure their effectiveness and permanence.

While our movement was not in a position to invite authors, scholars and artists from afar, we did take advantage of those who came on fund-raising missions. We thus did not have to rely solely on such lecturers from the U.S.A. as literateur Hillel Bavli, historia Avraham and poet Shimon Halkin, poet Zalman Schneur and author Daniel Persky. We could also hear such renowned personalities as Vitzchak Ben-Zwi, who later became the second president of Israel, and Israeli authors of the calibre of Yehudah Yaari and Yeacov Kahn. Their Hebrew lectures attracted hundreds of people. Ben Zwi came in the interests of the Histadrut campaign. When he appeared on the "Duchan Ivri", literally "the Hebrew Platform", the seats in the Folk-Shule hall could not contain the throngs of about seven hundred people, many of whom crowded the platform, the aisles and the corridors.

Yiddishist Appreciates Hebraist

Yehudah Yaari came to campaign for the Keren Hayesod (now the U.I.A. Drive). At his lecture on "Windows to Modern Hebrew Literature", Yechiel Shtern, the former principal of the Calgary Peretz-School (who later became a religious "Ba'al-Tshuvah") had his first opportunity to meet with me face to face. He was one of those Calgarians in whose eyes I was "a fascist hater of Yiddish". During the question and answer period, Mr. Shtern requested permission to speak in Yiddish. The Keren Hatarbut officers who occupied the front row motioned to me with their heads that I should not allow it. I ignored them and did permit it. Instead of asking a question, Mr. Shtern proceeded to discuss some of the speaker's observations. My Keren Hatarbut "bosses" signalled to me to stop him. I did not comply! When it seemed that Mr. Shtern intended to speak at length, one of them stood up and demanded that I cut the questioner short. "Isn't it enough" said he, "that you originally allowed Mr. Shtern to ask a question in Yiddish?! We are not here to listen to Mr. Shtern, and the chairman should stop him forthwith". My reaction was, "Although this is a Hebrew meeting, there is nothing wrong in asking a question in another language, especially Yiddish. As to Mr. Shtern's prolonged remarks, I am certain he is aware that his views could be aired on some other occasion and that the audience is anxious to hear from the guest speaker as much as possible". Mr. Shtern then wrapped up his remarks quickly.

At the end of the lecture, Mr. Shtern approached me saying, "I'm very grateful for your understanding and tolerance. And I thought you were an opponent of Yiddish"! "Well," I said, "I am not an opponent of any language, let alone of my mother-tongue". Our differences, I said, are mainly pedagogical, as I am convinced that we cannot possibly impart to our children both Hebrew and Yiddish under the dire circumstances of Galut. In view of the revival of Hebrew as the spoken language in Eretz Israel, it is through Hebrew that we will be able to preserve and develop some kind of Jewish life in the diaspora. Mr. Shtern did not say whether he had come around to my opinion on this question, but he did agree with me that we should not judge people on the basis of mere hearsay.

Links with the U.S.A.

One of our first steps was to form strong links with national institutions in the U.S.A. There were certain projects we could not possibly undertake on our own. We therefore combined our efforts with those organizations. Joint sponsorship helped them as well, because they too suffered from a lack of sufficient funds. Both sides realized that partnership and cooperation would benefit both countries. When the National Council for Jewish Education and the Jewish Education Committee in New York inaugurated a program for the publication of Hebrew literature for children, I was invited to serve on the committee. The Keren Hatarbut became joint sponsors of the project, and one of the earliest books was published entirely at our expense. We also acted as the representatives in Canada of the Hebrew Arts Foundation of America for distribution of their Hebrew films. Our national office ordered all the films for circulation among the various branches that could not afford to subscribe to them. We became a full partner with the Histadrut Ivrit of America in sponsoring Hebrew Month, initiated by them some years earlier. The purpose of the Month was to focus interest throughout the country on the importance of Hebrew education and culture. Our Hebrew Writers Week was later integrated into Hebrew Month. Emphasis during Hebrew Week was on the life and works of a single outstanding Hebrew author. In connection with this project, a booklet containing some of the celebrant's writings was published and distributed, together with other materials in Hebrew and in English, in all Jewish schools.

A Great Israeli Poet Comes to Canada

Our links with the U.S.A. enabled us to learn in advance about the forthcoming visits of distinguished people in America. It gave us the opportunity to contact some of these eminences in time for the inclusion of Canada in their itinerary. We thus had the privilege of welcoming to Montreal and Toronto Yaacov Kahn, one of the most outstanding poets-dramatists. On this occasion, we decided to honor him by dedicating Hebrew Writers Week to his life and work. Instead of issuing the usual booklet, we bore half of the expense of a special edition of the "MUsaf Lakore Hatza'ir", a biweekly "Supplement for the Young Reader" of the New York Hebrew weekly "Hadoar". One of our purposes was to bring to the attention of a much wider public, especially youth, the poet's declaration of, "No More Shedding of Jewish Blood in Vain", and his call for "an end to degradation, an end to humiliation, an end to the galut and an end to wanderings". His visit coincided with the time of the Declaration of Independence of the Reborn State of Israel, and people were receptive to Kahn's call in some of his poems for the renewal of our independence and national dignity. In Canada alone we distributed an extra thousand copies of the MUSAF to pupils who did not subscribe to it and we thereby brought its existence to the attention of many schools throughout the country. Kahn did not just deliver his lecture and run. He stayed with us for several days, took an interest in our work and problems, and inspired us to greater achievements.

Not By Lectures Alone

As soon as we learned of Shoshannah Damari's presence in N.Y., we contacted the Zionist Order Habonim in Montreal and we jointly invited her for an all-Hebrew-song-concert at the Monument National Theatre. She was at that time the most popular singer in Israel. The audience of many hundreds of people were fired by her beautiful national songs and were charmed by her beauty and grace. The music critic J. Rabinovich wrote, "When Shoshannah sang excerpts from the Song of Songs, I was transplanted to ancient Israel and saw before my eyes the Shulamit of the Biblical love song". The pianist was one of the most outstanding Hebrew composers, Moshe Vilensky, and the Israeli actor Joseph Golan amused the audience with sketches of life in Isreal. The Keren Hatarbut leadership was jubilant at the success of the first such daring venture, which could have resulted, if unsuccessful, in a serious dent in our picayune budget. It was interesting to witness Hebraist-culturists basking in the presence of the famous artists, and trying, each in his own way, to impress beautiful Damari. It was also the first time somebody thought of taking pictures, and it was amusing to see the maneouvers to be positined as near as possible to the celebrities.

"Yesh Me'ayin" - Creating Something from Nothing

I Hebrew circles, we would often use the phrase "Yesh Me'ayin", to "create something from nothing". We had a very ambitious program, but our financial resources consisted of a seven thousand five hundred dollar annual allocation from the Zionist Organization of Canada, sufficient to pay the staff's salaries, and a few thousand dollars income from a limited membership drive in Montreal. To raise even this small amount, it took great efforts on the part of a small number of people. Our national treasurer, Menachem Mendel Grover, a no-nonsense fellow with a nack for humorous stories, would tell me of his tactics to extract contributions from business associates who had little understanding of and cared even less for Hebrew culture. Since only the Creator produces Yesh Me'ayin, one of my purposes when I undertook my first tour was to obtain financial commitments from the branches I was to organize.

Montreal — Toronto Rivalry

As far back as I can remember, there was always rivalry between the Jewish communities of Montreal and Toronto. In the forties, Montreal had a Jewish population of about ninety thousand and Toronto about eighty thousand. All the national offices were located in Montreal, and - as I heard often from Torontonians - Montreal had a larger nuber of affluent Jews. I am not sure whether this rivalry or jealousy increased wisdom, as it should have according to the Talmudic saying (Babba Batra 21), but it did produce some resentment and, sometimes, even hostility.

In Toronto, the founders of Keren Hatarbut were even more of the old-world "Maskilin" type than in Montreal. They did receive sympathy and some cooperation from Canadianized Hebraists like Eddy Gelber and David Newman, but it was my impression that the president B.Z. Hyman, the part-time director, M. Wittemberg (a Hebrew teacher who could devote only a little of his time to Keren Hatarbut) and the other few active members of the committee, could not find a common language, even in Hebrew, with the more Canadianized elements. For the Toronto Hebraists, the struggle for Hebrew was therefore much harder.

Their financial poverty struck me when I met the president in his store, at that time the only Hebrew bookstore in Toronto. It was a small crowded place where there was not even room for a chair to sit down. The Toronto Hebraists did not even have what we had in Montreal as an "excuse" for an office. Our conversation was interrupted each time a customer came in. It was devoted almost entirely to his complaints about "you fellows in Montreal tale all the money". I conceded that communities where national offices are located are the prime beneficiaries because their national directors tend also to the local activities. I told him our national officers wondered why the Torontonians didn't organize a membership to take care of their local needs. The real problem as I saw it was that, aside from the occasional contributions by a few people like L. Lunsky, M. Kohl and A. Matlow, the committee never succeeded in attracting some businessmen of means to do for Toronto what Isaac Gold did for Massad and Solomon Gordon for Keren Hatarbut in Montreal.

What the Torontonians did accomplish was therefore due to dedication and hard work. In 1948, they had reached a significant number of about a hundred and fifty students in their Hebrew courses, and managed to hold a monthly Hebrew lecture with local speakers. Recognizing their difficult circumstances, we agreed that whenever a guest speaker was invited to Montreal, he would also visit Toronto at the expense of the national office. In addition, I visited Toronto often: sometimes to lecture, sometimes to help in the solution of local problems, especially in the organization and maintenance of the youth group, which was almost always an "on again off again" affair.

One of my visits in Toronto happened to fall on the day of the U.N. decision on the partition of Palestine into a Jewish and Arab State. I was in my hotel room preparing for the lecture I was to deliver that night on "Canadian Jewish Life — Realities and Prospects", when I heard on the radio the news of the U.N.'s decision. My eyes were welling with tears of joy, when Eddy Gelber phoned me to suggest that the meeting be turned into a celebration of this historic event. Although the hour was too late to phone people who would not ordinarily be expected to attend a Hebrew lecture, the small hall was overfilled. Yehuda Yaari, who was in the audience, suggested that I touch on the question of what would happen to Zionism with the establishment of the Jewish state. I expressed the idea that we were in a crisis situation, in the sense of the Chinese definition of the word. The character for "crisis" in Chinese is formed by a combination of the ideographs for "danger" and "opportunity". The danger lay in the possibility that people will relax their efforts for Eretz Israel, and since Zionism is centered around fundraising, Jewish National life in general might be affected by a weakening of Zionist activity. On the other hand, there would be great opportunities for a resurgence of Jewish values through strong educational-cultural links with the emerging independent Jewish state. I shortened my speech to allow time for singing, and to give Gelber, Yaari and some others a chance to speak about the U.N. decision. The jubilation of the audience was rather restrained. People seemed to be fully aware of the dangers that the fledgling Jewish state was facing.

This dispute brought about the formation of two opposing sides, and I and others were diverted from our work. The National Head Office was supportive of my position, but they could not or would not "direct" the region from Montreal. I therefore submitted my resignation. The leading officers in the East tried hard to dissuade me from this step. They sought to define the separation in a way that would enable the Executive Director to continue to initiate, innovate and direct the work in Winnipeg as well as in the periphery. The National Vice President, Mr. Samuel Schweisberg, one of the most knowledgeable and sincere Zionist leaders, and one of the very few who knew or read Hebrew, was particularly concerned about the situation and personally appealed to me to desist from my decision. I, however, smelled and felt the poisoned atmosphere in the office, and was convinced that my work would be seriously hampered. I was adamant in my decision to make a detour in my work for Zionism. I did get a nice letter from the National President, Mr. A.J. Frieman, who wrote me on July 3, 1942:

"I have learned with deep regret of your resignation, I might state that there is not a man in our organization whom I thought of more highly than of yourself. You always impressed me as being a most sincere, able and energetic Zionist, and your services were appreciated not only by myself but also by my colleagues". I was astonished — to say the least — by the National Executive Director's "compliment" for my continued hard work and devotion during the remaining months prior to my departure, even though I was about to leave my office.

Youth Acts — The First Zionist Summer Camp is Born

While I was embroiled with the politics of the day, the group of Judaean leaders referred to earlier were hard at work establishing the first Judaean camp in Canada. Aside from my frequent writing and speaking about the importance of such an educational institution, they had no help from anybody. At their own initiative and with their own untiring efforts, they rented a bare site at Winnipeg Beach. There was only one small structure, which contained a kitchen, s small dining room, and a tiny room in which one bed was placed for the director, his wife and their two small children. Tents for all the campers were rented and pitched by the kids themselves. It is difficult to convey the kids' excitement about their *chalutzic* (pioneering) enterprise. I wonder whether there was greater elation when the Jews built their *Mishkan* (Tabernacle) in the desert on their way to the Promised Land. The camp was modelled on the Israeli *Kvutzah*. Nobody received any pay; everybody worked. The total cost was shared equally by the campers. The director was exempted from paying his share, because he received no remuneration for his work.

A Plea for Unity

Later the same year I was invited to speak at the Igud convention in Toronto on "The State of Jewish Education in Canada". (See Appendix) It was the largest Igud convention ever held, with popular Prof. Zwi Scharfstein of N.Y. as guest speaker. All the delegates were from Montreal, Toronto and some small centers in Ontario. There was no representation at all from the West or from east of Montreal. The large audience that attended the public sessions consisted of Hebrew teachers and people who were interested or involved in Jewish education. I ended my address with a strong plea for the unification of Keren Hatarbut and Igud. My lecture (see appendix) was published in Shvilei Hachinuch, but I omitted from the published version my offer to resign from Keren Hatarbut in order to stress that my proposal for unity was not motivated by a desire to enlarge Keren Hatarbut's sphere of influence, but rather to combine all our forces for the achievement of our goals. Regrettably, my plea fell on deaf ears. There were some attempts to negotiate a merger. On the part of Keren Hatarbut, there was a decision to amalgamate. A committee consisting of the president, the director, Messrs. M.M. Grover, S.S. Gordon, M. Magid and L.J. Shine, was appointed "to discuss with the Igud the possibility of amalgamating" the two organizations. A few months later I left with my family for Israel, and upon our return in 1955 I failed in my attempts to ascertain why the merger had not been accomplished.

The Lack of Dynamics in Jewish Education

In spite of the division of functions between Igud and Keren Hatarbut, there was close cooperation between them. Just as I represented also Igud when I visited distant places, the director and other officials of Igud were often asked to attend to Keren Hatarbut matters when they visited centers in the East. Every summer the Igud sponsored a *Yom Iyun*, a one-day seminar for teachers, with guest lecturers from New York. In 1948, Melech Magid suggested that we dispense with guest-lecturers and that the whole day be devoted to the subject on "The Lack of Dynamics in Jewish Education", with me as the speaker. I made the general point that our educational system lacked dynamics because its program was still very much like the curriculum and methods of the old Cheder and was not in tune with the needs and developments of our times. Without mentioning Calgary at all, I presented for consideration the program described in the chapter on Calgary. As I expected, there were sharp differences of opinion on such subjects as whether Rashi and Talmud should be taught in elementary schools, something I opposed, and whether the school is the place for activities "that rightly belong to a youth organization". On the question of introducing the Israeli accent (the State of Israel had already been founded), the consensus seemed to be in favor. There was, however, one loud dissenting voice, that of Shloime Wiseman, a founder and principal of the Jewish People's Folk Schools in Montreal; pointing to the palm of his hand, he declared in Yiddish, "When hair will grow in this palm of my hand, will I introduce the Israeli pronunciation!" When I returned to Montreal in 1955, Mr. and Mrs. Magid tendered a reception at their home for me and my wife. Mr. B.M. Weiner approached me and suggested, in his unique Ashkenazic accent, that I ask Mr. Wiseman to show me the hair on the palm of his hand, for by that time the Israeli accent had been well established in all the Montreal schools, including the Folk-Shule.

Some Not-So-Strange Diversions

The high tension of constant involvement in the struggles for Zionism and Hebrew education was eased at times, though not often enough, by amusing incidents.

"I Have Succeeded in Assimilating"

On one of my trips to New York, the person who was sitting opposite me at the table in the diner interrupted my deep thoughts by introducing himself and inquiring about my name and profession. When he heard the word Rabbi, he leaned forward to declare in a whisper, "I was once one of you, but I have succeeded in assimilating completely". I leaned towards him and whispered back, "I don't think you have succeeded completely" (with the emphasis on completely). Baffled and blushing, he blurted out, "Why, what do you mean?" I leaned forward even closer and whispered even lower, "because you are whispering!" Although I was very tired, we spent a few hours in discussing anti-semitism, escapism, identity and self-dignity.

One of Those Fellows

I was invited to speak at a fund-raising meeting for Hagganah at a private home in a N.Y. suburb. I was cautioned that the audience would consist of third and fourth generation American Jews who were far down the road of assimilation. The smoke-and-noise filled basement was full of men holding a cocktail in one hand and a cigar or cigarette in the other. There was a sudden hush when I entered. Before I had a chance to sit down, I heard a giant of a fellow ask his neighbor in a reverential tone, "is he one of those fellows?!" Curious about what type of fellow I might be, I asked the giant what sort of fellow he wanted me to be. "Why of course, you must be one of those *Hagane* fellows who beat the daylights out of those *Airabs* and British who attack Jews!" It gave me an opening for an explanation of the humane and ethical principles of Hagganah and the reasons that prompted its deviation at times, from its strict course of resorting to violence only in direct self-defence. I was struck by the deep-seated desire of these assimilated individuals to hit back hard at those who abuse Jews. I pondered whether it was motivated in part by the fact that they knew more about the persecution of Jews than about their creativity and contributions to civilization.

A Glimpse into Sleuthing

During the period that the U.N. debated the Palestine partition-plan, my brother David lived in New York. There was something mysterious about his whereabouts when I tried to reach him at his home. There was never any reply when I phoned, even very late at night, and he evaded my queries about his absence from home every night. He finally confirmed that he was doing some sleuthing for the Jewish Agency. He was stationed in a hotel-room centrally adjacent to the cluster of rooms occupied by Arab delegations to the U.N. With the cooperation of a hotel employee, he used a device for recording their conversations. He would insert it after the occupants thought they had ascertained the absence of such a device. He was very frustrated that he could understand only a little of what was said because the conversations were mostly in Arabic. However, he was compensated somewhat by hearing and understanding all that went on with the comings and goings of high class whores for the enjoyment of high-class Arabs. He would deliver the recordings to the only two persons who knew about it, Moshe Sharett and Abba Eban. My brother swore me to secrecy, but he and I enjoyed these goings on whenever I visited New York. I learned from him at that time about my brother Yaakov's involvement in the purchase and running of arms to the beleagured Yishuv.

At Last — A Home for Keren Hatarbut

By the end of 1948, our activities had increased to such an extent that it was absolutely impossible to carry on in the small room we occupied on Park Ave. It was so cramped that Mr. Gold had to keep Massad documents in his business office. The youth movement was going strong, but always had to beg for the privilege of meeting in other public institutions. Massad enjoyed unusual popularity. We did not have to search for campers any more. Our problem was rather the lack of accommodations for those we had to turn away. Enrollment in our Hebrew courses had reached a total of about two hundred. But there seemed to be no solution to our housing problem, until Mr. Solomon Gordon offered to enable us to purchase a small building on Jeanne-Mance St. by giving Keren Hatarbut a loan, interest-free. By the time we were ready to move I was about to leave for Israel.

Chapter 17
Preparing to Meet
The Messiah

When I assumed the position of director of Keren Hatarbut in 1946, I made clear my intention to return to Eretz-Israel in a few years. My wife and I had reached this decision long before anybody dreamt that a Jewish state was on the way. After its establishment, I was consumed with desire to "return home" and help in the "building of bridges" between Israel and North America. Although we wanted to return soon after the end of the camp season, in September or October 1948, we finally set March 1949 as the time of our departure, in order to consolidate the projects that had been initiated and to transfer my duties smoothly to a new director.

Strengthening the Ties Between the Z.O.C.
and the Keren Hatarbut

I was convinced that the work of Keren Hatarbut would be effective and enduring only if it would receive the wholehearted cooperation of the Z.O.C. I envisioned an independent Hebrew movement (with the emphasis on movement rather than organization) that would serve as the educational-cultural arm of the Z.O.C. At the end of 1948, I made a special trip to Toronto to discuss this vision with Samuel J. Zacks, President of the Z.O.C. It is a measure of the gap that existed between Hebraists and Zionist officialdom that before I left on this mission, a leading officer of Keren Hatarbut told me with an air of confidence that "since Mr. Zacks is now married to a Hebrew speaking Israeli, he will probably be more amenable to our objectives and needs." Whether or not Ayalah Zacks, a connoisseur of art and culture, had anything to do with it, Mr. Zacks was receptive and responsive. (On that occasion, Mr. Zacks told me he had personally heard from Major Burns that the Israelis would be vanquished by the Arabs within two weeks.) This was the first time a president of the Z.O.C. invited me to "break bread" with him at his home. He suggested that I send a detailed memorandum and a copy of our budget to the Zionist Executive, and promised to invite me to a meeting of the Executive in order to present the case of the Keren Hatarbut for a substantially increased allocation.

In the beginning of 1949, a Keren Hatarbut delegation consisting of M.M. Grover, S.S. Gordon and myself, appeared before the National Board. I outlined our plans for 1949 and asked for a subsidy of $17,775 to cover the expected deficit of that year. The Board decided to allocate us $10,000, an increase of 25% over the previous year. The letter informing us of this increase contained also the following resolution.

"Mr. Edward E. Gelber then presented the following resolution in tribute to Rabbi Horowitz:

The Zionist Organization of Canada, in Executive Committee assembled, wishes to record its expression of gratitude to Rabbi Aaron Horowitz, on the occasion of his departure to resettle in Israel, for his distinguished services to Canadian Jewry during the years of his residence in this country.

His direction of Zionist affairs in Western Canada gave new life and a sense of national ferment to the many communities in that vast region. His organizing talents were much in evidence in this work and many new Zionist societies were established there owing to his efforts.

To the discharge of his duties he brought a sense of dedication in constantly striving to infuse into the people he was serving a sense of personal participation in a magnificent undertaking.

His contributions to the renaissance of Hebrew in our country are of first line importance, both from the viewpoint of the technical excellence of the organization he fostered through the Keren Hatarbut, Massad Hebrew Camp and the whole gamut of activities contained therein, and the spirit of life he breathed into them."

Brought Up Israelis, Not Canadians

Some years later, Eddy Gelber told me that when he had finished reading his proposed resolution, the chairman said, "the resolution is adopted unanimously". Mr. John Dower raised his dissenting voice, saying, "I disagree!" Asked whether any part of the resolution was contrary to fact, he replied, "no, but I object because Rabbi Horowtiz brought up Israelis, not Canadians." I failed to inquire from Mr. Gelber whether Mr. Dower agreed in the end to make the resolution unanimous, or whether he prevented history from recording a unanimous tribute to me. How far a person's logic can be distorted because of his "nervous" desire to "strike roots".

Meeting the Poet Laureate of Canada

Moshe Surchin told me he was looking for somebody "special" as the main speaker at our farewell affair. He had asked Eliyahu Epstein (later, Eilat), with whom I had had a close relationship in Eretz Israel, but he couldn't leave his post at that time because he was busy setting up his office as the first Israeli ambassador in Washington. Surchin finally approached A.M. Klein, who told him that although he had not been making any public appearances for some years, "for Horowitz I'll do it without any fee". I had enjoyed some of Klein's writings and made use of some of his translations of Bialik from Hebrew into English, but I had never seen him or spoken with him before. His statement was therefore puzzling to me until I heard him speak at the affair. Our great affinity in matters of the spirit became clear to me that evening. He spoke about the Anglo-Jewish newspapers he had perused in his capacity of editor of the Canadian Jewish Chronicle. They had been full of the usual "stuff" — fund-raising meetings, head-table lists, people who were honored, etc. Suddenly, there had been a complete transformation: They carried articles by Aaron Horowitz on Achad Ha-am, Bialik, education, culture; they reported on efforts to enhance Jewish life, to encourage creativity, and to cultivate the young. He spoke with deep feeling about things of the spirit that will ultimately determine our future and the quality of our life both in Israel and in the Diaspora. I felt profound regret that Klein and I had not been brought together during all the ten years of my work in Canada.

At that time, I knew nothing about Klein's life. Intuitively, I felt that "Bamistarim Bachtah Nafsho". This is a paraphrase of a Hebrew saying "My soul weeps in secrecy". When I returned to Montreal in the fifties I learned much from my friend Medresh, a Yiddish journalist-author, about Klein's suffering in a society and world where he did not really belong. It is a tragic commentary on a period in Canadian life — Jewish and general — that a man of his sensitivity and creativity had to depend for his livelihood on individuals and circumstances he must have abhorred at times. I was therefore taken aback when I viewed recently David Kaufman's film on A.M. Klein. In it there was only a slight and subtle reference to what was at least one of the causes of Klein's tortured soul. There was no reference at all to Klein's affinity with the Hebrew Renaissance and no mention at all of his excellent translation of Bialik.

A Gentleman and a Batlan

I read recently about the late Lord Edwin Samuel's quip on the meaning of the words "gentleman" and "batlan". His father, Viscount Herbert Samuel, the first British High Commissioner to Palestine, had once tried unsuccessfully to explain to Menachem Ussishkin the meaning of the concept "gentleman". Years later, Ussishkin's son tried unsuccessfully to explain to Edwin Samuel the meaning of the concept "batlan'. Now, said Edwin Samuel, when people asked him why he, who should be fully aware of the economic advantages of owning rather than renting in Jerusalem, had not acquired a house or an apartment of his own, he fully understands the meaning of "batlan". (It is difficult to explain in English the full meaning of that concept, but the long and short of it is, "an unworldly person", or one who does not know how to get out of the cold.)

A Melamed and a Batlan

On my travels, teachers would sometimes harp on their sorry lot. I would do everything possible to raise their spirits by emphasizing the high value of teachers in conversations with community leaders and especially in my speeches and lectures. People did not, of course, look upon me primarily as a teacher but rather as a leader and lecturer. I would therefore identify with teachers by declaring on various occasions that I am a *melamed*. I never thought of myself as a *batlan*, but after reading Edwin Samuel's reason for considering himself a *batlan*, I have come to the conclusion that I was both a *melamed* and a *batlan*. When Massad's second season came around, Mr. Gold told me he thought it was unfair that my wife and I should not receive any remuneration for our work in camp. He suggested an honorarium of $700 for me and $300 for my wife. I protested! I said the camp could not afford more than $500 for me and $100 for my wife. Several months before we left for Israel, Rabbi Jesse Schwartz phoned to tell me that he had something important to discuss with me. When I arrived at his office, he told me a Hagganah representative was seeking funds through unofficial channels, "for obvious reasons". He asked whether I would be willing to give the Hagganah representative the dollars I was to take to Israel in exchange for Israeli pounds which I would receive upon my arrival there. He emphasized that all I would get upon handing over the money to him would be an unsigned note to the Anglo-Palestine Bank to pay me a certain amount of pounds at the official rate of exchange at the time, $3.15 to the I£; the exchange rate on the unofficial market was just the reverse, #I£ 3.15 to the dollar. On the ship to Israel, Poet Yaakov Kahn, Dr. Simcha Petrushka (a renowned scholar who translated the Mishna into Yiddish and compiled a Yiddish encyclopedic dictionary) and I talked about how much money was required to purchase an apartment and other essentials in Israel. When I told them about the exchange rate at which I had sold my dollars (without mentioning the Hagganah), they both expressed their profound sympathy and called me more picturesque names than *melamed* and *batlan*. They pointed out to me that the reverse actual-value rate of exchange was used by *everybody*, that my loss of two thirds of my savings would therefore not make an iota of a difference for the country, and that my family's successful absorption in Israel was at stake because of the small amount at our disposal.

Eretz Israel is one Big "Beis-Medresh"

In the late forties, my father started to plan for his retirement in the Holy Land, where he would devote his last years to study and worship. He visited there in 1948, in the midst of the Arab attack against Israel. Without informing me, ("I know you have a lot of work, and didn't want to take you away from it", he said), he stopped off in Montreal on his way to Winnipeg. Suddenly one day, there was a knock on the door and my father entered. Before I had a chance to say anything, he raised his hands towards heaven and exclaimed, *"Aren, Eretz Yisroel is ein groisser Beis-Midresh"*; Aron, Eretz Israel is one big house of study (The connotation of Bet-Midrash is much wider than the literal translation "House of Study"; it includes house of worship and house of cultural-spiritual living). "Come, come father," I said, "whom are you kidding? You know very well that many people there don't attend synagogue, eat·traifa (non kosher meat) and do forbidden things on the Sabbath!" With a wide benevolent smile, my father said, "Yes, but they are saving the lives of many refugees, they are building and defending the country, and they are reviving the Hebrew language!" He related to me that one Sabbath eve in Israel he was walking from the synagogue in the company of some of his Chassidim, when they saw through the thick fog some young people smoking. "Here Rebbe, see whom you are defending; they are smoking on the holy Sabbath!" "Let them be", said my father, "cigarettes are probably as essential to them as bread when they are fighting for the life of our people". He also told me that when he was riding on the bus from Haifa to Tel-Aviv he felt somebody pulling his scarf out of his pocket. To save the would be thief from an *Averah* (transgression), my father said silently, "I am giving it to him as a gift!"

Looking for a Successor

A new director had to be found for Keren Hatarbut, and once again we were faced with the reality of the shortage of capable and experienced Hebrewspeaking personnel. We looked high and wide for a replacement and came up with only one possible candidate from New York. He came to Montreal, listened to us, took a look at us, and said, "No!" Consequently, a delegation pleaded with me that I should postpone my return to Israel for another few years. They were deeply concerned "what would happen to all our achievements at a time when they were not yet firmly rooted". They were ready to pay all the expenses of renting an apartment (pay "key money", if need be), make up the loss involved in buying new furniture, dismantling the "lift", etc. Much as I wanted the movement to grow, I could not resist my stronger yearning to meet the "Messiah". In the end, Mr. Leon Kronitz, then principal of Herzliah Junior High School, was appointed as the national director of the organization.

On a Rocking Tub to Israel

The only "excuse for a ship" that went at that time from New York to Israel was the Marine Carpe. It was over-crowded; it was shabby inside and out, and the facilities and food were poor. To accommodate all the passengers in the berthcongested "large" cabins, husbands and wives were assigned to separate cabins. I shared one with Yaakov Kahn, Simcha Petrushka and a six-footer of a missionary. His knowledge of Hebrew and Hebrew sources was astounding. Even more surprising was the fact that never during the month-long voyage did he try to convert us. Our relationships were more than cordial, but they were somewhat marred by the furious outburst of his wife who roomed with my wife. One day I went to her cabin to speak with her. Since there was nobody there, we exchanged a few kisses. Lo and behold, in walked Mrs. Missionary and vented her fury, "how shameful, how disgraceful!"

They Shall Come with Singing Unto Zion (Isaiah 35:10)

With song we truly came. Our joy was indescribable. After centuries of longing, praying and struggle, *we* finally were coming to our own independent Jewish state! Our hopes and expectations were high. My wife and I put in a separate bag all the gifts we had purchased and displayed them with thrilling pleasure before the customs officer. With tears of joy, I told him how happy I was to pay duty in Hebrew in the independent land of the Hebrews.

Chapter 18
In the Steps of the Messiah

According to the Talmud, the coming of the Messiah will be followed by a period of turmoil and strife: "In the steps of the Messiah, *chutzpah* (impudence) will rise, youth will insult elders, elders will stand before youth, a daughter will confront her mother and a daughter-in-law her mother-in-law, one's own household will be his enemy. And on whom can we depend? On our Father in heaven!" (Sanhedrin 97). The concluding words of this statement, tantamount to "there will be no salvation other than from Heaven", express forcibly the state of affairs that could be expected in the aftermath of a long struggle for liberation. In the mind of the suffering masses, the appearance of the Messiah would usher in bliss and tranquility; the Talmudic insight into the realities of such an aftermath was probably intended as a caution against the euphoria of Messianism.

We arrived in Israel when people were still in a euphoric state. There was Spring in the air and elation in the heart at the victory of the few defenders over the many attackers. There was the wishful thinking, or perhaps feeling, that that was that!! The Arabs had tried to nip the State in the bud and were taught a lesson that would prevent them from trying again. It did not take long, however, to awaken to the realities of the aftermath: the shortage of everything, including food, and the abundance of refugees who of necessity filled the *Maabarot* (the transitory dwellings consisting of shacks and hovels) and with whom the scant resources and means had to be shared. *Tzena* (austerity) beclouded the Spring in the air, and anxiety mingled with the elation of the heart.

Our "Chevlei Mashiach"

We felt the *chevlei-Mashiach* (the Messiah pangs) soon after our welcoming him. It became clear that our three thousand I£ would not even purchase a small one bedroom apartment. The shock of "non recognition" was even more painful — all the years of "recognition" of my devotion and work for "the movement" could not of course serve as collateral, nor could it even get me a guarantor from among my Histadrut colleagues for a loan at "Bank Hapo'alim" (the *Histadrut* bank) to supplement the amount we had for the purchase of the apartment. For some reason I had thought my nearest relatives would not be acceptable as guarantors, but it was they who finally saved the day for us. Upon the arrival of the cherished day of registering the sale, I was again taken by surprise. In addition to the disproportionately high registration fee, a representative of the Jewish National Fund (for which I had worked and contributed for many years) demanded another high fee for the Fund. Thinking for a moment that the registration could be completed without payment of this extra fee, I said that much as I valued the Keren Kayemet, I could not afford such a large contribution at that time. "Well", said the official, "no contribution, no registration!"

Simultaneously with the search for an apartment, there was the hunt for a position. I naturally turned to *my* "movement". There was no vacancy in any of its institutions. My second natural try was the Zionist movement. This time there was greater "recognition". I was received by none other than Berl Locker, the chairman of the Jewish Agency. I told him of my great interest in helping to "build bridges" between Israel and the English-speaking Diaspora. He referred me to Dr. S. Ben-Shalom who, as General Director of the Youth and Chalutz Dept., was interested only in one-way bridges, from the Diaspora to the Homeland! He sent me a wire to Tel-Aviv, where my wife and I stayed in a small furnished room (our two boys were stashed away with their maternal grandparents in Tzfat), to come to Jerusalem for an interview on a certain date. As usual, I arrived ahead of time. Each time I approached the secretary's desk to inquire when my long wait would end, she said, "I can't tell you because I am *afraid* to interrupt him." After I had waited for a few hours, I insisted that she dare ask him when he would see me. When I got the verdict that he couldn't possibly see me that day, that I should go back to Tel-Aviv and he would inform me by wire when I should come again, I told her to tell her boss for me, "I do not care to work with such an inconsiderate person". Years later it occurred to me that my article on "The Mission of Zionism" possibly influenced Dr. Ben-Shalom's attitude to me. During my interview with Mr. Locker, he had asked me whether my writing ability in English was as good as in Hebrew. As evidence that it was, I gave him a copy of my booklet *Zionism — A Way of Life*. I referred him especially to the article on "The Mission of Zionism". In my naivete, I believed he would be impressed by my thesis that "Israel and the Diaspora are like the siamese twins" (see appendix). I should have known that to him and especially to Dr. Ben-Shalom this was the antithesis to Zionism. I know for a fact that Ben-Shalom read this article, which he may have done after he had invited me for an interview.

In logical sequence, I then turned to my third "love", the Hebrew University. Since my interest was in "building bridges", I applied to its Organization Department, which was in communication with all English speaking countries. Surprising as it may sound, there was a repeat performance of l'affaire Ben-Shalom. After having waited for Mr.

Cherrick for hours in his Jerusalem office, his secretary announced that he would not be able to see me that day! I repeated my performance by telling her I was not interested in working with him. In his case, there were certainly no ideological reasons.

A few weeks later, my friend Yehuda Yaari told me I would be invited for an interview by the mayor of Haifa, Aba Chushi, whom he had told about my abilities. I responded with a feeling of great expectation to the popular mayor's invitation for a meeting with him. Unbelievable as it may ring, there was the exact same repetition in Haifa!

My Chance to Build Bridges Finally Arrives

One day in June, I was summoned to a meeting with Zalman Aranne, the Secretary of Mapai, the ruling Labour Party. The proposition he made enchanted me. Prof. Abraham Katch, director of New York University's Hebrew Culture Department, was to arrive in Israel with about sixty-five undergraduate and graduate students from 20 U.S. universities for a workshop in "Life and Culture in Modern Israel". The workshop would be held at Bet-Berl, the Katznelson institute for Higher Learning. The party, as well as Ben-Gurion and Shazar, he said, attached great importance to the success of this project. It would be attended not only by Jewish and non-Jewish students but also by noted academics and by Dr. Carl Hemann Voss, well-known theologian and chairman of the American Friends of Israel. Aranne asked me to direct the workshop, adding: "If the project will succeed, the position of director of Bet-Berl will be yours." Although there were only several weeks left to organize it under the difficult conditions prevailing at that time in the country, I accepted with great enthusiasm. I learned later that the programs suggested by a number of Israeli candidates for this position had been considered totally unsuitable by the party's American "specialists" and that the party had become seriously concerned about the possible failure of the project.

The party secretary then turned me over to Mr. Chanoch Soroka, an affable party functionary whom I later dubbed "the party commissar". There started a relationship between us both agreeable and disagreeable, harmonious and disharmonious, though, on the whole, comradely. The disharmony was caused by seeming trivia at a time when I had to work frantically to ready a host of arrangements in a short period. Much time was wasted in arguments about the installation of Mezuzot at the Institute and the conversion of its kitchen to comply with the dietary laws. "Berl would turn in his grave", pronounced my commissar," at the sight of Mezuzot in the Institute that bears his name!" "You would not say so, if you really knew Berl", I retorted. This party-man was obviously in complete ignorance about Berl's positive attitude to tradition. According to Baruch Zuckerman, Berl himself told him he never ate shocked by the absence of Mezuzot in an Israeli institution of learning. This controversy was finally resolved by Shazar. And so it came about that *Mezuzot* were installed and the kitchen was made kosher at the Katznelson Institute. Berl would have been delighted!

The organization of the workshop was no simple matter. Communications were very erratic. It took hours and sometimes days to reach by phone people who were in the thick of the hustle and bustle of *treifa*, nor did Soroka know that there were *Mezuzot* in Berl's home. I tried to explain to Mr. Soroka that some of the students and instructors were bound to be observant Jews and that all the Jewish students would be the dynamic new-born state. Our American guests wanted to see and hear practically every celebrity, including the President and Prime-Minister. Although all the doors of the great were generally open to an institution whose executive chairman was David Ben-Gurion, it took much resourcefulness, maneuvering, effort and travelling. (It was sometimes faster to travel from Tel-Aviv to Haifa to speak to somebody than to reach him by phone) to round them all up for some kind of involvement in the project at a time when the country was making extraordinary demands on their time and energies. Mr. Soroka, who was very much impressed with my ambitious plans, remarked that he would be highly pleased if only fifty percent of the plans were implemented.

The opening ceremonies were very impressive. The large hall of the institute was filled with much of Israel's "pnei", the elite of all walks of life. Shazar, then Minister of Education and Culture, delivered one of his fiery orations on "The Forces that Contributed to the Realization of the Zionist Dream". Various notables, including the President of the Writers Association, Asher Barash, and representatives of the foreign office and the U.S. embassy, addressed themselves to the relationships between Israel and the world. Outstanding Israeli artists enchanted especially the Americans with vibrant music and songs of revival and joy.

The program encompassed the various aspects of the life and culture of modern Israel: Geography, types of agricultural settlements, the Economy and Industry, foreign policy, education and culture, political parties, and Israel and the Diaspora. Students were also given the opportunity to attend classes in Hebrew language and literature. Evenings were devoted to music, drama and dance. The faculty included some of the most outstanding scholars, scientists, educators, authors, artists and political leaders. The six-week-course carried six and eight university credits for undergraduate and graduate students respectively.

The lectures were accompanied by extensive field trips from Dan to Beer-Sheba. A contributing factor to the project's extraordinary success was the rational division between study and travel periods. The only other seminar for American students that year was initiated by the Jewish Agency in cooperation with the Hebrew University. That group was subjected to much inconvenience and fatigue due to the lengthy tours following the long stretches of lectures. Our group apportioned several days weekly to visiting places that related as much as possible to the subjects covered on that week's lectures. The students were thus not exposed to over-long periods of lectures or of travels, and both were more interesting because they supplemented each other.

Another contributing factor to the success of this pioneering venture was the Student Council that worked in close cooperation and harmony with the administration and the faculty. The Council was also responsible for the duties devolving upon the student-body, such as regular attendance at lectures, social activities, and assignment of table service.

The Serious, the Humorous, and Some Faux-Pas

During the few days prior to the opening of the sessions, the students were briefed on the history of Bet Berl, its objectives, and its programs. They were given an earful about the greatness and achievements of Berl Katznelson, the most revered ideologue and beloved leader of the Labor Movement. Learning that his wife was still alive and that she would be present at the official opening of the Workshop, the students expressed the desire to see and hear her. Aware of her modesty and simplicity, I said all I could do was to introduce her and hope she would agree to make some brief remarks. She was sitting somewhere in the back of the hall, and I had completely forgotten my promise. When a student came over to remind me, I announced that she was present and asked whether she would say a few words about Berl and the Institute. The admiring audience sat in silent expectation as my eyes scanned the hall for Leah Katznelson. There was no sight or sound of her. She had slipped quietly out of the hall. Whereupon Shazar whispered to me in a somewhat scolding voice, "You are so much an American that you forgot that people with Leah's background and life-style look with disfavor on such gestures." Embarrassed, I proceeded with the program. In the succeeding days, I had to explain to the Americans why people like Mrs. Katznelson shy away from *kibbudim* (honors) and do not understand why a program should be trimmed, ala-America, with hors d'oeuvres and icing.

Only in America?

A few moments later, I had an opportunity to prove to Shazar that America has no monopoly on *kibbudim*-seekers. Somebody rushed over to inform me that Yoseph Shprintsak, Speaker of the Knesset, was waiting outside the hall to be introduced. Shprintsak was a short man with a huge moustache and a flair for the dramatic. Up to that moment, I had not been sure of his participation. When I had phoned him to inquire whether he would attend, he replied, "How do you expect me to be there if you didn't invite me?" Perplexed, I reminded him that I had sent him an official invitation. He reacted somewhat angrily, "so you think an invitation to the speaker of the Knesset should be like an invitation to *kol hane'arim* (a Hebrew expression meaning "all the ordinary boys"). So, I now had a chance to atone. In loud and measured tones, I announced: "Ladies and gentlemen, the speaker of the Knesset, Mr. Yoseph Shprintsak; please rise!" He paused for a while at the entrance, scanned the audience, smiled ecstatically and strolled up to his place at the head-table to the sound of strong applause. Turning to Shazar, I said, "Did Shprintsak also live in America?" Shazar chuckled.

Tears of Disillusionment

The ceremonies over, some Israeli friends I had not seen since 1938 came over to greet me. One was the wife of a deceased colleague I had worked with in the Histadrut. I didn't know her because they married after my departure for America. With tears in her eyes, she told me, "N. spoke about you often, and I feel as if I have known you for many years. It is to you therefore I have gathered the courage to reveal that I'm sometimes glad N. is not alive any more, because he would have been heart broken to witness the decline of some of our values and dreams." Her words were especially painful and disturbing to me. I had been cautioned by Soroka and others not to give heed to critics, because they consider themselves *mekupachim*, unjustly overlooked in appointments to positions of importance; for Mrs. N. did successfully hold a very high position!

Not Like in America

The planned program included a symposium on political parties in Israel, to be presented by the chief spokesman of the major parties. I could not envision any objection to something that was natural in the American liberal tradition. Our American students looked forward with keen interest to a political wrestling-match. Soroka, however, considered me politically naive indeed. "Do you really think we shall allow you to invite our political antagonists to *Bet Berl*?!" As usual in such cases, we went to Shazar, the recognized spiritual Rebbe of the Institute, to resolve the issue. Once again I was impressed with his adeptness in diplomacy. I had made clear that under no circumstances would I agree to have a representative of mapai speak on the other parties. Shazar then suggested professor A. Dinaburg as the sole lecturer on all the parties. Though he was officially a member of Mapai, Dinaburg was highly respected in all circles as a scholar and historian.

The lecturer on Israeli Contemporary Literature was Dr. Baruch Kurtzweil, a staunch opponent of socialism and Mapai. I was therefore surprised there was no objection from Soroka. Perhaps *he* was naive about the relevance of literature to politics. When I visited Dr. Kurtzweil at his home to invite him, he remarked sarcastically, "Are you sure you are in the right place? Is it possible Mapai would consent to me as a lecturer at Bet-Berl!" My reaction was, "perhaps both sides exaggerate the degree of animosity between them."

Two Nations Divided by a Common Language

One of the lecturers on foreign policy was Dr. Walter Eytan, a former Oxford don, and Director General of the Foreign Office who had to his credit the organization and direction of the Diplomats Training School. He was abrupt in his replies to students' questions. In one instance, he snarled, "Why do you Americans ask such stupid questions?!" Whether because of timidity or politeness, they were not riled by his attitude. I, however, was looking for a way to react to the abrasive "diplomat". In thanking him, I said, "Some of you may think Dr. Eytan was uncomplimentary to Americans. Perish the thought! As pointed out by George Bernard Shaw, 'America and England are two nations divided by a common language'. Some of the terms Dr. Eytan used therefore have different connotations to him and to us". Dr. Eytan did not join in the laughter.

Amends Made by Sharett and MacDonald

Moshe Sharett, the Foreign Minister, and the U.S. Ambassador James G. MacDonald were to speak at the closing exercises. Since they were busy that evening, they agreed to lecture at the regular sessions. It was good that their appearance followed l'Affaire Eytan. They both fascinated the students with their interesting lectures and charismatic personalities. Sharett, who in my opinion epitomised a synthesis between Western and Hebrew culture, unfurled a lucid and comprehensive panorama of Israeli foreign policy. His replies to questions were incisive, concise and witty. MacDonald soared in prophetic terms on the blessings to flow from the communication between American and Israeli creativity.

Must Everybody be Received by the President?

I do not know to what degree people from other countries suffer from the malady I call *Kelberne hispaylus*. (A Yiddish expression literally meaning excited calf-like admiration, the connotation being the exaggerated awe before dignitaries). While this malady brings with it large, sometimes very large, contributions by people who are seated near a consul general, an ambassador, or a general, (not to speak of a cabinet member or a prime minister!), it is a reflection on the mentality of *machers* and "big givers". The other side of the coin are the quarrels and occasional defections of those who are not properly seated. In our case, it wasn't really the students but rather some of the Workshop's officials who clamoured so much to be received by Chaim Weizman, the first President of Israel. He had originally refused to give them an audience, but I was greatly pressured to persuade him to rescind his decision. When I was received by him in his office, he looked very sombre (his vision had already been severely impaired) as he asked, "must everybody be received by the President!" Although I agreed with him in this matter, I spoke about the contribution such a meeting would make to strengthening the relationships between the U.S.A. and Israel. He finally consented, but stipulated that he would greet them briefly and there would be no questions and no clicking of cameras. I'm not sure whether this intrusion upon the president contributed anything to American-Israeli relationships but it did enhance the status of the publicity seekers.

Israeli Versus American

There was no lack of humour and fun at Bet Berl. Soroka was fond of using his few English words to pull the Americans' legs and make comparisons between Israeli and American ways of life. One such subject was Israeli versus American morals. There were no separate dormitories for males and females at the Institute. Some American students kibbitzed Soroka about this "immorality" and about some Israeli girls wearing short-short pants. Sneered Soroka, "What about American girls' low-low decooeltes?" There was a lot of palaver about the miraculous Israeli victories over their Arab attackers. Chimed in Carl Hermann Voss: "What is so new about these miracles? The Lord God has always wrought miracles for his chosen people!" The true miracle, said Voss, "was that this time it was not the Lord God but the Israelis themselves who did it!" Our twelve-year-old Gad contributed to the American-Israeli fun by relating to us some of his experiences at Haddasim, a children's village near Bet Berl, where we had placed him and his younger brother Yigal for the duration of the Workshop. The children at the village taunted them about the affluence of the "spoiled Americans". "How many cars does your father have? Do you cross the street by car? How many black slaves does your father own?" Our youngest really did it by asking in a serious childish tone, "Mr. Soroka, is Israel a civilized country?"

Communication Leads to Understanding

The presence of Israeli students at the Institute made for better understanding between them and the Americans, as reported by the New York University Jewish Culture Foundation:
  "During the course of the Workshop, a seminar for twenty-five Israeli students was held nearby and the students had an excellent

opportunity to exchange experiences and problems. This group had vacated the dormitories for the American students, but continued to share the common hall. When the first strain of newness wore off, these young people no longer ate at their own tables in the dining hall but shared tables with the American students. By the end of the season there was almost a complete integration of social living — so much so, that, before the termination of their course, the Israelis gave a party in which the Workshop students were guests. The very next night the Americans tendered a party to the Israeli students. The group also shared singing and dancing programs. One of the members of the Israeli seminar was the regular Monday evening dance instructor, and another taught songs."

Ben-Gurion Charms the Americans

In addition to a lecture at the final session, Ben-Gurion was the main speaker at the closing celebration. He delighted everybody with his informality and friendly manner. He mingled with the students and inquired about their studies and interests. He saw from a distance our two boys, walked over to them, and carried on a conversation with them. Ben-Gurion's presence and remarks served as an impressive and inspiring climax to a remarkable educational project that contributed to an American-Israeli meeting of minds and hearts.

The Morning After

As I was accompnaying Ben-Gurion on his way out, he put his arm on my shoulder and complimented me for my "ability, resourcefulness and devotion, evidenced by the outstanding success of the Workshop." My thoughts therefore turned to the promise that I would be appointed as director of Bet-Berl. The next morning brought with it one of my most shocking disappointments. Soroka proposed that I go with my family to the U.S.A. in the interests of the Institute. I told him this was unthinkable. "We have not even had the opportunity to move into our apartment, let alone to rest from the stresses and strains of the past months, and you are already suggesting that we take up the wandering staff again! What about the promise that I would head Bet-Berl?" I was dazed when I heard him say, "That is impossible because of the objection of certain elements, especially of the kibbutz people, to a person who had been absent from the country for ten years and whose socialistic loyalties have not been sufficiently tested."

Another reason surfaced later. A leader of Habonim, the Mapai youth movement in America, had arrived in Israel, and his placement at Bet-Berl had been pressed by Habonim. Although he was not a candidate for director of the Institute, they wanted "one of their own" to influence

American youth. At that moment I recalled the flare of bewilderment that seized kibbutzniks and leftists at the sight of a large crate, addressed to "Rabbi Aron Horowitz", right smack on the Institute grounds. (Our "lift" was stationed there, because our apartment had not yet been ready for occupation). It took some time for remarks such as "how does a cleric come to Bet-Berl?" to subside. (By now, many readers may know already of the dichotomy in Israel, especially during the early period, between the "religious" and the "secular". One is either orthodox or "irreligious" — with no "in-betweens".) I then realized "my goose had been cooked" by my Rabbinic and American background long before the closing of the Workshop.

I could not contain my anger, and declared there and then to the commissar that I would have nothing to do anymore with Bet-Berl. He allowed us no more than a week's stay at the Institute, irrespective of whether or not our apartment would be ready by then, "because all the space would be needed for a new batch of students from Israeli settlements." Fortunately, our apartment was ready, and we moved out of Bet-Berl with the absolute thought that we had kissed it goodby forever.

Chief Rabbi Isaiah Horowitz reads a prayer at a mass meeting at the Forum, in Winnipeg in 1945, to protest against British Policy in Palestine.

Rabbi Horowitz speaks at Dedication Ceremonies of Camp Massad, Galil Unit, in the Laurentians, in 1958. Front row from left: C. Maizel; Mrs. M. Simon; Dr. Michael Simon, Consul General of Israel; S.S. Gordon; Mrs. Gordon; Mrs. J. Margulis; Mr. J. Margulis; Mrs. E. Shuchat; Mr. E. Shuchat. Back row: Mrs. L.J. Shine; Mr. L.J. Shine; Mrs. J. Rosenblatt; Mr. J. Rosenblatt; Mrs. M. Yagod; Mr. and Mrs. Nathan Roskies (partially hidden).

Rabbi Horowitz addresses National Zionist Convention in Toronto in January 1946.

Rabbi Horowitz addresses Annual Dinner of Herzliah Hebrew Teachers Institute in 1965 at the Pierce Hotel in New York. From left: Mrs. Jacob Goodman; Jacob Goodman, Treasurer of the Institute; Jacques Torczyner, President, Z.O.A.; Rabbi Arthur Hertzburg; Mendel Haber, President of the Institute.

First Shabbat Service at Massad Alef in the Laurentians in 1947.

Poet Abraham M. Klein addresses Farewell Gathering in honor of Rabbi Horowitz in 1949. From left: Rabbi Horowitz; Moshe Surchin, President of Keren Hatarbut.

Chapter 19
On a Magnificent Mission

Quite unexpectedly, I was invited to meet with Shazar, Soroka and Arye Bahir. The latter, who was newly brought into the picture, was an influential Party and Knesset member who, as the meaning of his name implies, contributed clarity and tranquility to our deliberations. In retrospect, I think it possible that the whole Bet-Berl story might have ended differently if he had been in charge! Shazar repeated Soroka's suggestion about my building a cultural and financial base for Bet-Berl in the U.S.A. and Canada. I would be the Dean of Foreign Studies and would have an opportunity to initiate valuable programs in a field that was so near to my heart. Ben Gurion too, they said, was very much interested in this mission. Upon its completion, I would direct the affairs of this department in general and be assured of a creative role at the Institute. I agreed without further ado.

To fulfill the mission effectively, I did some research on the objectives of the Institute as envisioned by its founders. I came across a statement by Berl that put in motion my thoughts about what Bet-Berl could accomplish in building bridges among Israel, the Diaspora, and the World. Berl said, "I have sleepless nights because of the many projects that could be accomplished were it not for the lack of people." I also came across a vision by Brachah Chabas, an editor of Davar and a disciple of Berl, "I see before me a long line of leaders, organizers of stae-building enterprises, path finders for our statehood — all of them are those whose character Berl cultivated, whose spirit he fortified and whose personal guide he was". I linked the two: Berl's cry for the need of leaders and Chabas' vision of its fulfillment by Berl's followers. I then spelled out for English readers Bet-Berl's origin and mission as follows: Berl Katznelson, one of the greatest and most revered leaders of reborn Israel, envisioned the creation of an educational and cultural center for the youth of the rising Jewish democracy — a center that would be free from the formalism of universities and the careerism of professional schools. A man of profound vision and practical acumen, he foresaw years ago the need for an institution which would cultivate intellectual and social leadership from among the free generation of youth that was emerging in the ancient-new Land of Israel. He saw the Exiles returning from countries of different languages, cultures, and ways of life. These individuals of diverse views and traditions would have to be molded into one homogeneous people who, together with the offspring of the firstcomers — the first Aliyoth — would be faced with the tremendous task of forging the independence and liberty of the Jewish people and with the building of a sovereign nation whose life would be based on the best traditions of their ancient civilization and on the cultural and spiritual values they had gleaned during their long centuries of life among the people of the world. Such nation-building tasks obviously require inspired and selfless leaders who would be cultivated in an institution dedicated to this high purpose.

Berl Katznelson did not live to see the fulfillment of his cherished ideal of founding a modern Bet-Midrash, which — like the Bet-Midrash of old — would be a stronghold and a treasure house of the soul and spirit of Israel. Several years after his death, his disciples and friends established the "Berl Katznelson Fund" for the purpose of bringing into life the idea of which their beloved teacher and colleague had dreamt. In 1947, the cornerstone of Bet Berl — "The House of Berl" — as the Katznelson Institute is lovingly called in Israel, was laid in the presence of the leadership of the labor movement and the Yishuv. On this occasion, Zalman Shazar, Minister of Education and Culture of Israel, gave a lofty characterization of the aims of the Institute, which aims are the embodiment of the thought and life of the great teacher whose name it bears.

Shazar saw in the establishment of Bet-Berl the opening of seven gates of knowledge and wisdom:

Heritage of the fathers, delving deeply into the life and thought of Israel's prophets and teachers in every age;

The gate of the world, creating a bridge between the thought of Israel and of the rest of mankind;

The gate of the exiles, for the study of the life of the Jewish communities of the Diaspora, past and present;

The gate of the homeland, the exploration of the geography, history and life of Eretz Yisrael.

The gate of social justice, the study of how to abolish exploitation, human servitude and war, and to insure human freedom, dignity and creativity.

The gate of sovereignty, the study of the ways and means of constructing, developing and safeguarding the State.

The gate of the perfect man, the continued laborious search for the good way of life.

(The explanation of the "Seven Gates" as given here is a summary that was published editorially in the Reconstructionist issued by the Society For The Advancement of Judaism, better known as the Reconstructionist Movement).

Armed with these lofty ideas and with a letter from Ben-Gurion to Eliyahu Eilat, Israel's ambassador to the U.S.A., I set out enthusiastically on a long and arduous road of laying the foundations for Bet-Berl's work in the U.S.A. and Canada.

As soon as my duties at the Institute were clearly delineated, I concentrated my thinking on a program that would address itself to two of Shazar's seven gates relating to my Department: "the gate of the world" and "the gate of the exiles". I came up with three main projects.

First, I wanted to put on a permanent basis the workshop for university students and to expand it to include students from a wider range of U.S.A. schools and from other English speaking countries.

Second, I wanted to establish an annual World Seminar for the interchange of ideas and experiences among scholars, scientists, authors and statesmen from various countries, primarily from the U.S.A., Canada, Great Britain and Israel. As the first theme for such a seminar I suggested "Israel as a Bridge Between Orient and Occident". The late forties and early fifties, when Israel enjoyed a comparatively calm period, free from Arab attack, brought to Israel many officials and students from African and Asian countries, who welcomed Israel's contribution to their early development in various fields of endeavour. We thought we would be relatively secure and free to devote our best efforts to constructive thought and effort. From the very beginning of modern Zionism, Jewish thinkers, poets and scholars envisioned the reappearance of their people as an independent nation not *apart from* but as an integral *part of* mankind. Universalism, in the spirit of the ancient Hebrew prophets, would be at the basis of Jewish revival and creativity. It therefore seemed natural for Israeli institutions of higher learning to make a contribution to the creation of a bridge between the thought of Israel and the rest of mankind. The Jewish people's "dwelling among the nations" of East and West for many centuries equipped them, we thought, to serve as a natural mediator between Orient and Occident.

Finally, I envisioned a plan to establish a model boarding-school for high-school students from English speaking countries. Our experiences at Bet-Berl and, even more so, with our children, had led my wife and I to the conclusion that serious thought should be given to the problems encountered by children from English speaking countries in their new life in Israel. I suggested a co-educational boarding school, to accommodate such new immigrants as well as students who would come for a year or two of studies, and a select group of Israeli students. Such an institution could serve a triple purpose: first, it could contribute to the creation of close cultural and spiritual ties between Israel and Anglo-American Jewish communities; second, the bringing together of American, Canadian, British and Israeli boys and girls would lead to a mutual understanding and appreciation of the life and problems of these countries and thus serve as a force in interpreting their cultures to their Israeli peers and vice versa; and, third, a year or two in such an institution, with a faculty of choice English speaking and Israeli educators, would facilitate the adjustment of new immigrants and enable them to acquire a sufficient knowledge of Hebrew prior to their entry into their regular schools.

A Shangri-La in Israel

The site of the Institute was ideal for these projects. In an article he published on the Institute, Dr. Voss described it thus: "one of the loveliest places in all of Israel is the Berl Katznelson Institute at Kfar Saba, not far from Petach-Tikvah. When Americans visit this garden spot, some twenty miles northeast of Tel-Aviv, they usually call it Shangri-La. Why not? It's an apt name. The lovely lawns and gardens, the shaded walks, and the several impressive buildings, fashioned after the modern architecture of the Haifa Technickum's Dr. Rattner, look like a welcome retreat from the atmosphere of Bedlam, Boomtown, and Babel which are Israel today. This unique educational center may become a pattern for Israeli education, and perhaps American, too." The buildings then in existence comprised only a fourth of the plan contemplated for the institution, but we were assured that additional buildings would be completed in time for the World Seminar, which was planned for the same period as other summer workshops in July 1951. The model boarding school, which was to open in Sept. 1951, was to be housed in a special building to be put up in close proximity to the Institution.

The saga of Bet-Berl merits a separate volume for the interesting and important lessons that could be learned from all the events leading from Berl's dream of a modern Bet-Midrash to its present status as just another post secondary-school offering even courses for typists. However, I shall confine my story to some of its American highlights.

Ambassador Eilat opened many doors for me. In his letter to Eilat, Ben Gurion had written: "We must turn the institution into *the center for the education of the Israeli and world youth*" (italics by the author). He referred to the University students, "including goyim", who had already studied in the Institute, and asked Eilat to put me in contact with influential persons "such as Felix Frankfurter". Ben-Gurion suggested to me that Frankfurter, the renowned jurist of the U.S.A. Supreme Court, be requested to serve as president of the Society of American Friends of Bet-Berl. It took but a call from Eilat for Frankfurter to receive me that very morning in his office at the Supreme Court. I was struck by the contrast between the simplicity of even the "highest places" in Israel and the awe-inspiringly stately U.S.A. Supreme Court buildings. When I was ushered into Frankfurter's office and saw the small, frail body of the brilliant jurist, I thought of the contrast between mind and matter, between the spiritual and the material. The hour I spent with Frankfurter was highly illuminating. He spoke of transitory and lasting values, of Israel's renewed sense of destiny and its impact on Jews like himself, and of his awesome duties as a member of the Supreme Court. Then he proceeded to explain why he could not possibly fulfill Ben-Gurion's request. He rose from his chair and pulled out from his filing cabinets copies of various letters rejecting invitations to serve on various bodies. As a member of the supreme court, he said, he must steer clear of anything that might someday bear even the least tinge of controversy. I detected from his words and demeanour, intangible though they were, some inhibitions by virtue of his Jewishness. As he accompanied me out of his office, he put his arm on my shoulder, saying, "like you, I am a melamed, and as a melamed I derived my greatest satisfaction".

I then came down closer to earth and recruited Rabbi Dr. Solomon Goldman of Chicago as the National President, and Rabbi James G. Heller as chairman of the Board. We next put together an impressive national board that included such distinguished individuals as philosopher Horace M. Kallen, educator William H. Kilpatrick, columnist Max Lerner, President of Brandeis University Abram L. Sacher, Rabbi Samuel Wohl, industrialist Fred Monosson, Dr. Nachum Goldman, President of Ampal Abraham Dickenstein, labour leader David Dubinsky and many others. Some of them made it clear they would not serve on an actively functioning national board and that all I could expect was the use of their prestigious names and their occasional help in enlisting the cooperation of certain individuals in various parts of the country. In Canada, we attracted such people as jurist Maxwel M. Cohen, justice Harry Batshaw, Major L.M. Bloomfield, Bernard M. Bloomfield, David Newman, Rabbi W. Shuchat, Dr. S.B. Hurwich, Eddie Gelber, Samuel J. Zacks and professor Sol Sinclair.

Ahead of me now lay the long, laborious task of establishing chapters in all the major cities of the U.S.A. and Canada, for without such active committees we could not get off the ground in the realization of our three projects. This proved to be the most difficult task. Bet-Berl was not known anywhere; people were inclined to shy away from joining new committees for fear of becoming involved in additional fund-raising schemes, and some hesitated at first to identify with a Mapai-sponsored institution. In all cases, especially in cities where I had no personal contacts, it was necessary for me to visit twice; I first had to persuade some influential individuals to convene a meeting for me on some future date, and I would then have to return a second time in order to organize the committee.

The "breakthrough" came mostly because of the great appeal to the World Seminar idea. Academics, communal leaders and theologians responded with enthusiasm. These are but a few examples: Robert Gordis, Bible scholar and Rabbi of Temple Bet-El of Rockaway Park, New York, "The Seminar idea is the most important I have heard of in the area of the creation of spiritual and cultural links between Israel and America. It has great possibilities and could open new and very interesting horizons". Rabbi Irving Miller, President of the American Jewish Congress, exclaimed, "It is a very important and wonderful idea".

We succeeded in organizing committees in Los Angeles, Chicago,

Cincinnati, Cleveland, Detroit, St. Louis, Minneapolis-St. Paul, Pittsburgh, Boston, Miami, Montreal, Toronto and Winnipeg.

Looking for Participants

Our very first priority in each city was to interest distinguished personalities in the World Seminar. The resulting publicity would enhance the prospects for the other two projects. The strategy was, therefore, to first ensure the participation of such individuals in the Seminar or, at least, to recruit them as members of the committee. I then addressed University faculty meetings as well as the Hillel foundations to publicize both the Seminar and the Students' Workshop. The high school project I took up with directors of Jewish Education Bureaus and with school principals. I learned quickly that attractive as these projects were, they would not be realized without the establishment of fellowships for scholars and scholarships for high school students. Having been prevented from conducting even a limited fund-raising campaign, our task was twofold: first, the local chapters would have to commit themselves to providing a specified number of annual fellowships and/or scholarships through contributions by a small number of philanthropists and/or organizations; and, second, to maintain a national office and defray local expenses. For this purpose, the Jewish Agency approved of our conducting limited annual membership drives in large cities. My personal distaste for "asking for money" was more than compensated by the insights I gained from my discussions with some of the most creative minds and by the knowledge I acquired about the state of Jewish life in the U.S.A.

Discouragement by a Jewish Academic in Chicago

The meeting in Chicago was to have been hosted by the national president, Dr. Solomon Goldman, but this plan had to be cancelled when Dr. Goldman was seriously hurt in an automobile accident, in which he lost an eye. The next would-be host, professor Louis Gottschalck of the University of Chicago, dropped out after receiving an invitation to spend some months in England. After much effort over a period of months, the meeting was finally convened by Dr. Samuel B. Blumenfield, president of the local College of Jewish Studies. The presence of Dr. Goldman, who recuperated sufficiently to attend, and other outstanding personalities and scholars, did not deter a prominent Chicago University professor from resorting to near-ridicule in his assessment of our plans for evolving an exchange program between Bet-Berl and American educational institutions. On the World Seminar idea he remarked, "What can great America learn from little Israel?!" I was literally amazed that this *Mah-Yafit* Jew was successful in diverting the whole evening to a useless discussion on Zionism and of Israel's scanty potentialities in the fields of research and science. Dr. Blumenfield later confessed to me it had been a serious mistake to invite a known opponent of Zionism.

Another disappointment resulted from my close look at the Chicago Hillel chapter. I was their guest at an Oneg-Shabbat where I lectured on the relationships between Israel and the Diaspora. My conversations with some of the students and the program preceding my lecture, opened my eyes, to say the least, to the lower than elementary level of the knowledge of Jewish things by university students and the shallowness of their cultural programs. They opened their Oneg-Shabbat with the lighting of candles hours after the start of Shabbat; the Brachah was recited with mistakes and great difficulty, and, of all things, they sang *"oifen pripitchick"* (an old childish Cheder song) in Yiddish, from which it was clear that they didn't know Yiddish either.

It was difficult for me to proceed from "kindergarten" to university level, so to speak. The thought then occurred to me, "highly university educated in general knowledge and kindergarten-trained in Judaism". After the lecture, a group of students invited me to a home for a *shmues* over coffee. The few hours I spent with them was a sort of an introduction to a general scenario that was to be repeated on various campuses: the small number of students belonging to Hillel, the anemic programs, and the lack of a clear philosophy and direction. In my discussions with Hillel directors, the defence was of the same type as of Sunday schools and synagogue youth clubs — "better than nothing", or "at least Jewish boys meet Jewish girls", and — in some cases — "They have at least a Jewish place to come to". Jewish leaders closed their eyes to the fact that it was almost futile to tend to branches when the roots and trunk had been neglected. The Hillel movement was not, of course, responsible for this neglect, and much credit is due to B'nai B'rith for doing many things that "are better than nothing". This lesson could have been learned through a comparison with Hillel chapters at Canadian universities, where participation was greater and the programs were much richer. This was due to the fact that, though involvement in Hillel even in Canada was greatly disproportionate to the number of Jewish students, many Hillel leaders and members were the products of day-schools (in 1949 there were very few day-schools in the U.S.A.) and comparatively better afternoon schools. Many years later, I said and wrote that if the relatively large sums invested in Hillel had been applied earlier to Jewish education, much more could have been accomplished in both Canada and the U.S.A. for and by a vastly larger number of students with a relatively much smaller overall expenditure. I left Chicago somewhat discouraged about the Bet-Berl plans and deeply concerned about the future of Jewish youth in America.

Encouragement by a Christian Nobel Laureate

My next visit served to restore my enthusiasm about our program. I cannot think of a more inspiring meeting than the one I had with Dr. Arthur Compton, a nobel laureate in physics. He was, at the time, President of Washington University in St. Louis, Missouri. Compton, his office, and the whole atmosphere were models of simplicity and informality. He greeted me with, "We have great expectations from Israel!" Here I had the singular opportunity to invite an answer from a great Christian to a small Jew's question. I paraphrased the Chicago academic's query, "What great expectations could America have from little insignificant Israel?" He looked at me in puzzlement. I elaborated: "You, a great scientist, belonging to the richest and most powerful nation, with the most abundant facilities for creativity and scientific progress, have great expectations from little, poor Israel which was just recently faced with annihilation and many of whose people are mere 'brands plucked from the fires'?!" Compton, who had been leaning on a window-sill, sat down in his chair and spoke as if to himself, "Man's greatest problem is the gap between his conquest of nature and his conquest of himself. Mankind's progress in the physical and material world by far exceeds his progress in the realm of the spirit. Israel's great contribution to humanity was in the domain of the spirit, in the realm of Man's struggle to conquer his *own* nature. Now that this ancient people has the opportunity to renew its national creativity in its own land, we have reason to look forward to a renewal of its contribution in an area that will determine man's fate; mankind's future is dependent more than ever before not on our efforts to master nature, but rather on our will and ability to gain control over our *own* nature". In essence, he said, we are faced with the challenge of achieving a synthesis between Science and Religion.

He therefore thought that Israel was the right place for an interchange of ideas among thinkers and scientists from various cultures. As for himself, he would make every endeavour to participate in the Seminar.

On the way back to my hotel, I was shaken out of my reverie by American and Israeli realities. The gap of which Compton had spoken was there before my eyes in the form of human degradation in an American streetcar that segregated between black and white. And as if to dramatize another gap, between sense and nonsense, I heard the radio in the streetacr blare out, "Give us your children! If you don't give them to us, we will take them". The accent and the tone were familiar. "Could it be?" I asked myself. "Yes, it could be and it is". With my own ears I was hearing chaver Granovsky, a Mapai member of the Knesset, uttering this stupidity in remote St. Louis. How little he understood if he thought he could take American children to israel against their parents' wishes! I learned later that his broadcast was stopped in the middle by his sponsors of the Histradut campaign

Mission Impossible without Fund-Raising

My terms of reference as they were presented to me by Ben-Gurion and Shazar called primarily for the creation of strong links between American institutions of higher learning and Bet-Berl and for the realization of our educational projects. Fund raising efforts were to be merely incidental. In no time at all, however, I found myself deeply involved in such efforts in aid of the Institute's operating budget and construction plans. There were some unpaid pledges that had been made to Shazar and others during their visits to the U.S.A. There were prospects for some large contributions, especially from labour unions which I was to pursue. With the active assistance of Ambassador Eilat, we received $25,000 from the International Ladies Garment Workers Union through the good offices of its president David Dubinsky. I met with other labor leaders, including Walter Reuther, from whom I learned that the composition of the unions had changed considerably since the times when they had had a large Jewish membership. Jews had begun to strike roots in other fields. A case in point was the amalgamated Workers Union. When I finally succeeded in meeting with its president Jacob Potovsky, he showed a negative attitude, not to Bet Berl but to our request for a contribution from his union, saying, "The union of which I am president is no longer mostly Jewish. A majority of its members are now goyim. There must be a limit to my appearances before them to ask for contributions for Israeli projects". We eventually received $5000 from them. The time and energy I spent in approaching some other organizations met with little success. They were already overburdened with commitments.

The worst headache was yet to come. Mr. Morris Schaver, a philanthropist and Histradut leader in Detroit, had pledged to Shazar a contribution of $50,000 towards the construction of the Bet Berl library, with the understanding, according to Schaver, that it would be dedicated to the memory of his father. Mr. Schaver claimed that the people in charge, not Shazar, were maneuvring to renege on this promise and instead to place a sign on a wall outside the building as a tribute to Schaver's contribution towards the library, in memory of his father. It was my task to appease Schaver and reconcile the differences. It took quite a few special trips to Detroit to straighten out this matter. I told Morris and Emma Schaver that a man like Shazar would see to it that his promise would be fulfilled. We then became close friends, and the Schavers promised to also furnish the library. They also spoke of the possibility that, if relationships with Bet-Berl would be in the spirit I have shown, they would help me persuade the two other Schaver brothers to devote to Bet Berl projects the $50,000 each of them had set aside in memory of their father. Encouraged by this attitude, I broached the matter to the brother who lived in St. Louis. Unfortunately, there was hardly a chance to pursue this matter further with him and the other brother, when things were again messed up. Mr. Soroka had asked Baruch Zukerman to tell Mr. Schaver that if additional funds were not forthcoming from the family, contributions would have to be obtained from other individuals, and the dedication of the library would then have to be shared with them. In spite of my pleadings that the Institute stood to lose some of its best friends, the issue was still unresolved in 1951 when I was no longer connected with Bet Berl. This whole affair gave me some psychological insight into the attitudes of "takers" to "givers". When I took up this matter with Soroka upon my return to Israel, it was difficult for me to contain my anger when he remarked, "What does the *chazir* (pig) want for $50,000?!" About twenty years later, this subject was revived vividly in my mind by an amusing incident in Tel-Aviv. Every day when I went down to Dizengoff St. to buy my morning newspaper, I came face to face with an old Yemenite woman who took up a permanent place near a large store, in pursuit of "contributions" from passarsby. I gave her my offering once or twice weekly. She received it with an air of gracious condescension, as if I should be grateful for her giving me the opportunity to perform a Mitzvah. Before we returned to Canada, my wife prepared a bundle of some clothes to give to this woman. I delayed taking it to her until the night before our departure. I rushed down to give it to her before *her* departure. She was already standing, ready to leave with the day's take. I told her I would not see her any more because I was leaving for Canada. She then exclaimed with an air of importance I find difficult to describe, "You are lucky you have caught me in time tonight, because, as you see, I was about to leave". Perhaps she gave expression unkowingly to the ancient Biblical law that assigned certain portions of the land's produce to the "have nots" as a matter of right rather than charity.

As the end of my mission was approaching, I was confident of the success of our projects. The Institute became known across the U.S.A. and Canada. Leading newspapers, including the New York Times, carried elaborate stories about its purposes and plans. Many prominent individuals lent their names to the Society in America, and leaders of various communities and Zionist parties became involved in its work. Directors of bureaus of Jewish education and school principals of major cities promised their cooperation in enlisting students for the model high school. Bet Berl became so popular that institutions other than the Hebrew Cultural Foundation of New York University, including the B'nai B'rith Hillel Foundation and the Union of American Rabbis (reform), approached us about holding seminars at the Institute.

There was, however, one very serious consideration that escaped me completely — the political situation and the realities in Israel. Something that had been to me little more than a word, *sachevet*, became a vivid reality. The literal meaning of *sachevet* is dragging, protracting (in Yiddish, *schlepping*); in other words, what is known in America as red tape. But to really understand the Israeli genre, one would have to be its victim. Answers to letters were delayed for months, requests for decisions on urgent matters were ignored, misunderstandings and misinterpretations were legion. I recalled a recommendation by Mendel M. Fisher, National Director of the J.N.F. in the U.S.A., that I be appointed as the J.N.F. representative in Israel in order to explain to the Israelis what Americans said in their communications, and vice versa. "We are two different worlds", he said, "and it takes one who knows both of them well to explain each to the other". The main obstacle was that the people who were officially in charge of Bet Berl bore the brunt of the problems of the country and were in no position to give Bet Berl the attention it needed. Thus, plans and activities that required experience in the academic field and, even more so, first hand knowledge of the American scene, were at the mercy of a person who had none of these, or even an elementary knowledge of English. I therefore started to have serious misgivings about our ventures. These were strengthened by a letter from Mr. Dan Pines, an editor of Davar who had been to America a number of times and served on the faculty of the New York University Workshop, in which he wrote, "The annual Seminar for American personalities is important in my eyes, but very difficult to implement. You surely know the personalities here and how impossible it is to pin them down in advance to a set plan of activity". In spite of my doubts, I decided to heed his final words on the subject, "Nonetheless, it is worthwhile to try, after sufficient preparation and investigation."

At this point, pressure began to be exerted on me to remain at my American post indefinitely. When I resisted the pressure, it was suggested that I return for the summer together with the University students, but leave my family in New York, just in case I agreed later to continue the work in America. Determined as I was to stand by my original agreement to devote only one year to Bet Berl's affairs in America, I rejected this suggestion. As a matter of fact, I wanted to "investigate" and reassass the entire situation before deciding whether to continue any connection whatsoever with Bet Berl, especially if it were insisted that I remain in America.

When I returned to Israel, the people around Bet Berl were so busy that the *sachevet* was at its height. The nominal board held no regular meetings, and I had to try to "catch" Shazar, Bahir or Ben-Gurion at the knesset. Since I lived in Ramat-Gan, it was arranged that I attend Party Central Committee meetings where I could get hold of one of them for a quick consultation either before or after the meeting. (At one of those meetings, I became aware more than ever before of Ben Gurion's high stature as a leader of all the people, without regard to partisan or sectarian interests. The issue was a long-standing controversy over the unification of the educational system under the jurisdiction of the state. There were still in existence separate education jurisdictions of the general Zionists, the Socialists and the Religionists. There was difference of opinion within Mapai on the unification issue. Ben Gurion favored one system under the jurisdiction of the State, which would still allow parents a free choice between General State Schools and Religious State Schools. There were very heated arguments for and against. Speaking with deep emotion, Ben Gurion advanced logical arguments against the fragmentation of the nation at its very foundation. He met with stiff, abrasive opposition especially from the kibbutz representatives. At one time, he turned to one of them with the question, "Why are you opposed to a unified system? Are you afraid your children will have to learn some of our sources, such as Mishnah? If they do, perhaps they will not become communists!" Someone sitting near me whispered into my ear, "The sons and daughters of some of these opponents are Marxists". Alas, Ben-Gurion did not carry the day that time. He did not sit down in his chair; he slid into it, exhausted and frustrated. However, he and others who valued national unity above parties were eventually successful in bringing education under the unified jurisdiction of the State.

Another crucial problem came up at that meeting. There was dissatisfaction with what some critics considered neglect of the youth. They claimed that there was a deterioration in the content and spirit as well as in the membership of the Histadrut Youth Organizations. A committee was appointed to investigate the situation and make recommendations. I sat near Israel Cohen, editor of the Mapai official organ *Hapo'el Hatsa-ir*. Both of us exclaimed at the same time, "Again the same people"! Again Sharett, again Babba Idelson, again individuals who are on many other committees. How will they ever be able to tackle fundamentally this difficult problem in addition to all their other burdens?! What is it that prevents them from involving other *chaverim* on such committees?!

I found myself running here, to the Knesset, and there, to the Party meetings, with few definitive results. I then informed Soroka of my decision to look elsewhere for a position. Before I had time to clinch one, I was summoned by Shazar and Bahir who "turned on all sides" to persuade me to return with my family to New York and continue my activities there. Again I was told that Ben Gurion too was of the same opinion. Their strongest argument was that my presence in the U.S.A. was essential to ensure the success of the projects and to consolidate the Society of Friends. I finally agreed to go alone for a maximum period of three months, with the clear understanding that one of my tasks would be to engage a replacement in New York.

I Get a Diplomatic Passport

We were all anxious for me to leave for New York as soon as possible. Since the validity of my passport had expired, I was to get a Diplomatic Passport, which could be processed in a few hours. It was thought that even with influential connections, it would take much longer to have a new passport issued by the ministry which was not in the Mapai orbit. A Diplomat's passport would also enhance the prestige of my mission. I was surprised at the Foreign Office director's question whether I had already decided on a Hebrew family name for use in my passport. He did not agree with me that Horowitz was a very venerable Hebrew name. When Sharett became Foreign Minister, he required all Diplomatic Passport holders to Hebraize their names. I was then told, "Sharet will never issue a passport in the name of Horowitz." I challenged him to pick up the receiver and ask Sharet. I could hear Sharet's loud admonition for asking such a question. When I had an occasion to relate the incident to Shazar, he threw up his hands and exclaimed, "What is the matter with this new generation of ours that they don't know the origin of this four hundred year old name and its Hebraization from the name Horvath. (See appendix for a short history of the Horowitz family.)

Ben Gurion Gives Me Instructions

My meeting with Ben Gurion prior to my departure was exhilirating and encouraging. He was in very cheerful spirits and told me he was especially fascinated with the World Seminar project. I was scheduled to leave the morning following the first day of Succot. Ben Gurion cautioned me that under no circumstances should I leave before talking matters over with Shazar who was recuperating from an illness in Tzfat. It was already *Erev Succot*; I pointed out that I could not travel to Tzfat and return before sundown. He told me to go and return by taxi, something I would never have thought of doing because of the long distance from Jerusalem to Tzfat. Upon my arrival at the hotel, I was told that "the honorable Minister" (he was Minister of Education and Culture at the time) was having his midday nap. The manager, who knew me and my family, exclaimed, "Rank Chutzpah!" when I told him to have Shazar awakened. He finally agreed because as a religious Jew he understood that I would have to be home before sundown. Shazar looked sombre but said nothing about my having caused the interruption in his rest. We discussed our American plans and agreed that the invitations to the World Seminar would be sent under his and Dr. Chaim Greenberg's signatures. Before taking leave, I apologized for having disturbed him. He smiled faintly and said, "*Nu, nu,* why did you?!?" When I explained that I do not travel out of town on the Sabbath or on Holidays, he remarked gleefully, "I did not know we had such observant members in our party, but I am glad we do!"

The three months I spent in the U.S.A. were devoted to meetings with additional prospective participants in the World Seminar, such as Dr. William Kilpatrick, Orway Tead and prof. Mordechai Kaplan. I was in touch with all the chapters, and revisited some of the cities where it was necessary to broaden and strengthen their committees. I also formed new chapters in Philadelphia and Baltimore. When the time came for me to return, I received a cable from the Secretary of mapai, Zalman Aranne, asking me "in the name of the Party" to continue to represent Bet Berl in America. My reply was an immediate and decisive "no". A few weeks later, Baruch Zuckerman invited me to his office to plead with me to reconsider my decision. He had told Ben Gurion, he informed me, that my presentation and interpretation of the Mapai philosophy and program to non-socialist elements was of even greater significance than my successful work for Bet Berl. It was a very difficult decision for me to make; I acquiesced, but only for a moment. As Zuckerman picked up the receiver to contact the Israeli Consulate to have them apply for an extension of my stay, I said to him: "I left important, interesting work in Canada to live with my family in Israel. If I bring them back and we continue to live here even only for a few years, our children's readjustment first to the U.S. and then once again to Israel will exact too high a price of them." I then proceeded to transfer my duties to my successor, Mr. Murray Pollokoff, who was at the time in the employ of the U.S. State Dept. in Washington.

The Sachevet Escalates

Upon my return to Israel in December 1950, I was faced with even more serious problems of *sachevet*, *schlep* and red-tape. There was no office-space available for me at the Institute and, in any event, Soroka and I thought it would be more expedient for me to work in tel-Aviv where I would have better access to personalities and facilities. Our months-long search for office-space was fruitless. There was no alternative but to request Leah Katznelson to put at our disposal a room in her apartment, which she did readily, rent-free. It was also very difficult to find a competent English secretary with a working knowledge of Hebrew. I had to impose on an old American friend, Ethel Kaizer De-Levi, who had been a secretary at the U.S. Consulate in Jerusalem. The rigorous demands of the job required just such a devoted and near-saintly person. It took about two months from the time I returned for my office to start functioning.

Martin Buber on Politicians

In the meantime, I endeavoured to line up Israeli participants in the World Seminar. Professors Hugo Bergman, Ben-Zion Dinur, Ernst Simon and other renowned scholars agreed to participate. I was cautioned about Martin Buber's probable negative attitude. It took over an hour of discussion to overcome his objections. "What have politicians like Ben-Gurion and Shazar to do with this type of Seminar?" I argued that they were not ordinary politicians, that they were highly learned persons who were motivated by high ideals, and that if Israel were an established, secure state, men like them, especially Shazar, would probably be in creative fields other than politics. Buber insisted that, whatever their merits, it was not appropriate for politicians to sponsor a seminar of thinkers and scholars. After I told him that men like Bergman, Dinur and Simon would also be involved, he somewhat reluctantly consented to participate too.

By and by, I was getting inquiries from America as to why the invitations to the Seminar had not yet been received. It was difficult, if not impossible to explain the entangled situations to people who were completely unaware of the political turmoil and the complexity of life prevailing in Israel at that time. Shazar had "resigned" as Minister of Education. There was talk of the government's impending resignation, and the people who were to be at the core of the Seminar were overwhelmed with problems. When I presented to Shazar the draft of the invitation, he refused to sign it. To my surprise that he would renege on a definite agreement, he reacted, "I agreed to sign the invitation in my official capacity. I am no longer the Minister of Education and Culture. Ask David (David Remez had succeeded him in that office) to sign it". I detected an undertone of anger about his political reverses. Remez, on the other hand, would sign "only at Zalman's request". It was therefore up to me to pose the problem to the *Zaken* (the "old-man", as Ben-Gurion was endearingly called), to whom I was to report on my activities in America.

Ben Gurion Reassures Me

I waited for Ben Gurion in the anteroom of his office. The moment he saw me, he greeted me with, "What do you bring from America, Horowitz?" He actually jumped up when I answered, *"Malchut Yisrael shniyah"*, (a second kingdom of Israel). "What, what; what did you say?" I told him that during poet Shin Shalom's visit in America, he acclaimed it as a Second Kingdom of Israel. Ben Gurion laughed loud and heartily. "Did he actually say that?! Where could I find a record of it?" I referred him to Shalom's article in the American weekly Hadoar, where he wrote about the great potential of American Jewry in the fields of cultural and social creativity and achievement. As I sat facing him in his office, he handed me a cable from Chaim Greenberg inviting him to speak at a colloquium of distinguished scholars at the Jewish Theological Seminary of America. "Why am I asked to speak at such a conference? Am I a scholar?!" (I did not tell him what Buber had said about him.) Somewhat embarrassed, I told him, "You surely know you are considered to be a man of the spirit." He came on again with the familiar Ben Gurion chuckle. He continued to chuckle while repeating, "A man of the spirit, a man of the spirit. Yes, perhaps I am a man of the spirit in the sense of *Meshuga ish harua'ach*", ('the man of the spirit is mad' (Hosea 9:7). That settled, I took the opportunity to criticize the official approach to Aliyah from America. I told him of the bitter reaction to the attack on Dr. Mordecai Kaplan by Eliyahu Dobkin (head of the Aliyah and Chalutz Dept.) who had told a group of youth leaders from America that Kaplan was an assimilationist and that his work was in the nature of pulling the wool over the eyes of the people. I told him of the damage that is done by such statements as Grabovsky's in St. Louis, "Give us your children", etc. I expressed my opinion that we must not negate the future of Jewish life in America, which is unfortunately the policy of the official *schlichim*. He looked at me with raised eyebrows and retorted, "In the long run, there is no future for Jewish life in America!" I gave up on that argument, and turned to the Bet Berl situation. I emphasized that the whole project was in jeopardy because of the stalemate resulting from Shazar's and Remez's refusal to send out the invitations and, even more so, because of the lack of prompt decision and action in various matters concerning Bet Berl. He said he would ask Zalman to sign the invitation. I requested that he do so without delay because rumours had it that Shazar would soon be going as ambassador to Moscow. Again I heard the Ben Gurion chuckle (almost cheerfully, this time) "Don't worry! Zalman is not going to Moscow." As I walked out of the door, Shazar was waiting behind it to enter. He asked me in a worried manner, "Did Ben Gurion say anything to you about me? What did he say about me?" I repeated only the part about signing the invitation. To myself I thought, "the frailties of the Great when their power is in the balance."

Imagine my consternation when Shazar told me a few days later that Ben-Gurion had not spoken to him at all about Bet Berl. I dispatched a letter to Ben-Gurion on Jan. 19, 1951, in which I wrote, "I wish to emphasize that our national and local committees in the U.S. and Canada announced that the Seminar would definitely be held the coming summer. If we do not carry out this program, it will influence not only our other two projects but all the activities of the committee. The various institutions and personalities with whom I was in contact as well as our committees will doubt our ability to implement any projects we undertake . . . . The invitations must be sent out without any further delay. Otherwise, I am afraid that our entire program will collapse."

What folowed put me in a whirl. The government resigned; everybody was infected with election fever, and time marched on without any decisive action. In the meantime two new elements appeared. On the one hand, Dr. Katch looked with disfavour upon holding the World Seminar at the same time as his workshop; on the other hand, commitments had been made without my knowledge for the holding of a workshop for Reform rabbis during that summer. The calls from America for immediate action became more and more insistent, and would-be participants started to change their plans. Realizing that it was too late for the project to succeed even if the situation were to change (which it did not), it was decided at my suggestion that the World Seminar be cancelled or postponed. As soon as this decision was taken, I informed all the committees that because of the impending elections to the Knesset and the World Zionist Congress, it would be impossible to hold the Seminar as planned.

The reaction was quick to come. In a cable addressed to me, Shazar and Soroka, Zuckerman and Polakoff wrote: "Repercussions to post-ponement of Seminar already beginning. Committees dumbfounded. Perhaps Seminar can be held in August after elections. Vital Soroka arrive immediately". Before the decision to postpone the Seminar, Soroka had expressed his desire "to see America". My conversations with Soroka about the U.S.A. and its American Jewish community had aroused his curiosity "to see for himself". (In one of these discussions, I said that we would yet pay a very high price for thinking that we already know all there is to be known about America. (It was at that time that "Hador", the daily Mapai newspaper, published as an editorial my article on "America Is Yet To Be Discovered"), and for failing to make a genuine effort to fathom the importance and ramifications of our mutual understanding and interaction. Soroka's tart response was, *"Anachnu metsaftsefim al America"*. The literal meaning is "we whistle on America", and the connotation is, "who gives a damn about America!" It sounded familiar. I recalled that shortly after the War of Liberation, Shimon Hacohen, a high Israeli military officer, spoke to our Hebrew speaking youth group in Montreal about the situation in Israel. One of the members engaged him in an argument about the relationships between Israel and the U.S.A. In the course of his remarks, Hacohen said, *"Anachnu metsatsefim al habayit halavan"*. "We whistle on the White House". His audience of teenagers were polite enough to refrain from telling him what they later expressed to me about his remarks.)

Although my personal opinion was that the trip by him at the expense of the Institute would be of no value whatsoever, I informed Zuckerman and Polakoff of Soroka's plans without mentioning at all my opinion. Their reaction was the same as mine, and they insisted that he should not come without the prior approval of the National Committee. Now that they were faced with the anger of various committees and individuals, they wanted him to come immediately in the hope that they would be able to have the decision on the postponement reversed. When he arrived, he resisted the pressure to proceed with the Seminar as scheduled, and they started to toy with the idea of postponing it to the end of August or even to the Fall.

I continued to receive letters of protest and "sympathy". The following are excerpts from a few such letters: Bernard M. Bloomfield of Montreal wrote, "It is an extremely disappointing situation ... I am rather 'on the spot' here." And he surely was! He had already announced in the Montreal Daily Star that K.C. Evans, Rector of Christ Church Cathedral, and Even R. Irvin, Associate Editor of the Star, would participate. In addition, he had informed the famous opera singer Madame Pauline Donaldo that she too would be going with a fellowship. Rabbi Julius Gordon and Sam Kadison of St. Louis wrote, "We know that if this comes as a shock to us, it comes as a bitter disappointment to you who has done such a magnificent job on a wonderful, albeit difficult project." The only person who did not protest was Dr. Max Nussbaum, President of the Zionist Organization of America. He reassured me that, "We will do all we can to make this undertaking a success", and stated, "As much as I, too, regret the postponement of the World Seminar, I agree with you that it was the only logical thing to do. An election atmosphere is not coducive to the task we are trying to accomplish." Little did he and others know of my certainty that the Seminar could have been held successfully as scheduled were it not for the general chaotic situation around Bet-Berl.

The turmoil about the Seminar, and the erosion in the confidence of the committees affected seriously the efforts on behalf of the high school. To add to the difficulties, Soroka decided on his own (while he was in New York) that the latter project would be implemented only with a minimum of twenty students. Little did he understand that to recruit twenty teenagers of the same grade for a new venture of this kind was a most unrealistic expectation. The result was that some committees started to return contributions, and school principals and parents abandoned the project.

I came to the conclusion that the chaotic situation at Bet-Berl would continue as long as it remianed the bailiwick of one person, and as long as there was not a continually functioning, active committee on an ongoing basis. I decided to withdraw completely from the Institute, but found that it was more difficult to resign than to be engaged. Shazar and Bahir did not respond to my letters of resignation. It was impossible to get a hold of them, and Soroka insisted from America that I deal with them. To bring the matter to a head, I wrote Shazar, Bahir, Ben Gurion and Soroka that on the 15th of May I would walk out of the office and would bear no more responsibility for any of the Institute's affairs. Bahir must have been too busy to keep an appointment with me, and I failed to reach him by phone. I finally cornered Shazar at his home on a Friday night. I spoke to him frankly about what I thought was the general malaise of Bet-Berl. In reviewing our planned projects, I brought up again the need for special projects to facilitate the adjustment of English-speaking pupils. I mentioned my own children's difficulties in that area. He raised his hands towards heaven and said dramatically, "Tell your children to be happy they have come home!" Turning to my resignation, he expressed his concern about the future of our work in America. I told him that since both the World Seminar and the high school project would not come into being that year, there was ample time to find somebody else. In any event, I was not prepared to make any more sacrifices, and I was not leaving Bet-Berl in the lurch. In addition to the American office, there was now an office and a competent secretary in Israel, so that the work could continue. He disagreed, and told me angrily, "If you leave Bet-Berl, I will never speak to you again." When I told him my decision was irrevocable, he walked out of his home and left me there alone. I sat there in a daze until I decided to walk out too. About a week later, our paths crossed again at the Jewish Agency building. He greeted me as if nothing had happened.

Some months later, Polakoff too resigned. New overtures were made to me, especially by Baruch Zukerman, that I resume my activities for Bet-Berl in America, but I rejected all of them. As far as I know, the whole American program collapsed thereafter. In 1972, I visited the Institute and found very little resemblance to what its founders had envisioned and to what it was when it was founded. I tried to engage the director in a conversation about what had happened to the American program. He seemed to be completely disinterested. All I could get from him was, "I did hear something about an American program in the past, but I really know very little about it."

Chapter 20
On a New Trail

A Contrast Between Educators and Politicians

Before I had a chance to look elsewhere for work, I received a wire from Dr. Alexander M. Dushkin that he would come to Tel-Aviv to meet me about a position at the Hebrew University. Although it was not within the ken of "bridge building", I was at first attracted to the offer he made me to become the Director of the University's Education Department. Without thinking about the problems of moving again, I accepted in principle, on condition that I take a week to survey the functions of the office and the duties that would be assigned to me. Two factors deterred me from following this new course. The University and its adminstrative offices were scattered in different parts of the city, because the University's original home on Mt. Scopus was occupied at the time by the Jordanians. The Education Office was a "loner" in a building that housed commercial offices. As I've always loved to work with and around people, being isolated there with just a secretary was not exactly to my liking. The second factor was even more serious. During my meeting with the head of the department, Dr. E. Rieger, I became convinced that my activities would be almost completely administrative. I therefore informed him at that time of my negative decision. Whereupon I was invited to a meeting with the Rector, Dr. Schwabe, who made every effort to dissuade me from my decision. I told him I would think about it. Following my meeting with him, professor Akiva Ernst Simon of the Department's Faculty, with whom I had a closer relationship, added his influential voice by offering two inducements: I would be assigned a teaching course in the Department as an exception to the rule requiring lecturers to hold a PhD degree. He would also recommend my pariticipation in an exclusive Talmud study-group which included the president of Israel, Yitzchak Ben-Zwi, and Professor Assaf of the Supreme Court. Both these admittedly interesting prospects were not sufficient to bring an end to my search for "bridge building" or for actual educational work. Without my asking, I received promptly a week's salary plus expenses and a letter expressing the Department's "unanimous regret" about my negative decision. This episode was rather soothing medicine. It served to contrast educators and politicians!

Good for Everything or Good for Nothing

I decided to take a break and go to the city of my birth, whose charm and tranquility are conducive to meditation. During one of my visits to Toronto, I had discussed with Ben Lappin, now professor of Social Work at Bar Ilan University, the possibility of our establishing a private summer camp in Israel for English-speaking children. I recalled this plan and presented it to the mayor of Tsfat, Moshe Padatsur, one of the 'last of the mohicans' who knew well my family's centuries-old connection with the city. I told him the truth when I said I had occasionally thought of my duty and desire to help in the revival of neglected Tsfat, which had been, in my childhood, one of the main centers of Talmudic scholarship and Jewish life. I asked him whether we could get some free land on which to build the camp and some other incentives such as an exemption from taxes until the camp would be well established. He referred me to Yoseph Shprintzack, Speaker of the Knesset, who was said to be especially interested in the development of the city. Said the mayor, "You know Shprintzak, he knows your Tsfaser background, and you are an influential member of Mapai (the mayor was a Mizrachi leader), so that he is the person who should be ready to help in the realization of such a project." When I caught Shprintzak some weeks later in Jerusalem, he told me, "There are so many more important things for you to do than establishing a summer camp!"

When I returned home, I found a wire (a private telephone was a rarity in those days even much more than today) from the Mapai central office that Zalman Aranne wanted to see me immediately. When we met, he proposed that I take charge of the election campaign in the Tel-Aviv district. Ben Gurion, he said, was worried about losing ground there and wanted us to put forth our best efforts to ensure our success. The following conversation ensued: "Zalman, it seems that you want Mapai to lose the election!" Somewhat irritated, he retorted, "This is no subject for jesting!" "Chaver Aranne," I said, "I've never been involved in any election campaign; I do not know at all the conglomerate of people that make up the population of the district, and I don't even know how to get around in the city of Tel Aviv. If I undertake this task, Ben Gurion and the party will really have something to worry about." "We know you and your abilities very well; only recently you carried through successfully a very difficult undertaking, and we have full confidence in you." To entice me, he added, "If we win the elections, I will become the Minister of Education and Culture, and an important role will be assigned to you in the Ministry." "Zalman," I said, "I have worked all my life in the field of education, and my interests and abilities lie only therein." He rose from his chair, perspiring profusely, and retorted angrily in Yiddish, "We have a theory *'az einer toig, toig er tsu alles, un az er toig nisht, toig er oif kapores'*," (a juicy Yiddish saying meaning if one is good, he is good for everything, and if he isn't good, he is good for nothing.) Said I softly, "That is why many things *toigen by unz oif kapores*, (are good for nothing with us)." Nonetheless, I agreed to give it a try.

When I entered the campaign headquarters, and heard the hubbub of the strategists, I had serious doubts whether I was the right person to put and hold together the various parts of the campaign machinery. I made a genuine effort at this difficult task, but when I read clearly the skepticism on the faces of those I was to direct, I determined to opt out before being thrown out. When I reported my failure to Aranne, he said in a resigned tone, "You reject whatever we offer you! What *do* you want?" (The editorship of "Hador", Mapai's daily newspaper, was one of these offers. When I pointed out to Aranne that my entire experience as an editor consisted in the production of weekly and monthly Hebrew columns in two Canadian newspapers, and that I would have much to learn before I could assume responsibility as an editor of a daily newspaper, he tried to influence me by telling me that I would work with an editorial board consisting of such people as himself, Ben-Gurion, Sharett and Golda Meir.) "I want very much to work for the building of bridges between Israel and the English speaking Diaspora." He brought our discussion to an abrupt end with, "We offer you positions that are of the highest importance to us, and you talk to me about nonsense!" As I was leaving, he murmured, "I doubt that I will ever again make any offers to you".

What transpired later was ample evidence of my correct judgement. Ben Gurion asked Levi Eshkol to give his personal attention to the Tel-Aviv situation. He in turn assigned this task to a group of top Histradut and mapai leaders each of whom was to assume a special campaign function. Much to my surprise, I was invited to its first meeting. Starting clockwise, the chairman allotted a task to each one of the group. When he reached me, he paused and looked at Aranne as if to ask, "Who is this fellow?" Aranne mentioned my name and suggested that I be in charge of preparing the campaign material, such as slogans and leaflets. It was a really difficult effort for me to declare in that august company that they would not like what I would write and I would not write what they would like. The chairman looked at Aranne in astonishment as if to say, "What is *he* doing here!!" Embarrassed, Aranne said, "Leave Horowitz to me; I will speak to him later about a task for him." I never heard from Aranne again about the elections.

My experiences with Bet-Berl and the party brought to light the contrast between Mapai as I had known it in the thirties and as it was now. I was convinced it would be good for the nation if Mapai were not to lose the election, but to get a really good jolt. I voted for the Liberals.

Working with Young Sabras

Having had enough of bureaucracy and politics, I turned again to my first love, education. I applied to the Education Department in Tel-Aviv. When I informed the head of the Department, Dr. Meroz, that I held no M.A. degree (a prerequisite for high school teachers), he said, "an ordained Rabbi with your background and achievements has more than the equivalent of an M.A." That was pleasing to my ears, but I thought it unfair that teachers from outside Israel were given increments for only half of their years of experience. Without bargaining, I merely made the observation that such teachers would be paid for double their number of years of experience if those who made the rules knew how much more difficult it was to be a Hebrew teacher in the Golah. One official suggested that I be appointed as a supervisor, but the head of the department thought that a supervisor would have to be well acquainted with the situation in the field and that principals would not accept a newcomer who had not gone through the Israeli educational mills. I agreed with him. Furthermore, I knew I would not find satisfaction in supervising ("snoopervising") others' work. (I should point out, in this connection, how preposterous it is to have Israelis as supervisors of Canadian and American schools). Finally, I was appointed principal of Municipal High School "D". Since high school education was not compulsory at the time, students of well-to-do families attended private secondary schools. To provide high school education at a nominal fee for highly qualified students who could not afford the private high school tuition, certain municipalities established special schools, one of which was High School "D". The entrance requirements were quite rigorous. To begin with, only graduates with at least a B in all the five major subjects (Hebrew, Bible, mathematics, history and English) were eligible to apply for admission. All the candidates would then be given a series of tests, and only those with the highest results were admitted to fill the available vacancies. The municipal secondary schools were therefore the best in the country.

When registration time came around, I asked my secretary, a very authoritative person, who had been in charge of the defense of Jaffa during the War of Liberation, about the procedure for enrolment. She looked puzzled and said, "Candidates come, some with and some without their parents, and wait in line for their interview with you". I noticed that there was not even one bench or chair in the corridors. She looked surprised when I asked why a schedule of appointments was not set up for the candidates and why there were no seats for them in the corridors. I told her to invite daily by mail an equal number of candidates at fifteen minutes' intervals and to make sure to have seats for those who would be waiting in the corridors. With a benevolent look, she remarked, "This is not America; it won't work here!" It worked so well that I won the respect and confidence of parents and students alike.

The Bane or Boon of "Protektsyah"

Protektsyah (pull), also known as Vitamin "P", was probably the most popular word, and the reliance on *protektsyah* was almost universal. Israelis defended this practice by pointing out that it was a means of breaking through the walls of bureaucracy and *sachevet*, and it thus made life somewhat easier. Almost everybody was in a position, at one time or another, to give it and/or take it; "you make life easier for me and I will make it easier for you".

I was now in a position to give it, but I was one of those Westerners who was going to change things! My first clash was with an uncle who sought *protektsyah* for his niece. He presented to me a letter from the Chief Supervisor of the schools under the jurisdiction of the Histadrut, Yaakov Niv, introducing the uncle as an influential member of the Mapai Central Committee, and asking me to "try" to help him. To my query whether his niece had received B in all the major subjects, he responded, "If she had, why would I be here?" I told him in no uncertain terms that I would not deviate from the rules, and that, as a central figure in the Party, it was his duty to encourage adherence to rules and regulations. Grabbing the letter out of my hand, he said in a fury, "I will complain about you to Ben Gurion!" I had the last word: "To Ben Gurion you will go?! He has no jurisdiction whatsoever here. You can even go to the Minister of Education. I hope you do!"

That evening, I met Niv at a social function. I asked him why he had sent to me somebody seeking *protektsyah*. His reply was short and clear, "I knew you wouldn't give it to him!" The second and last such incident happened with a highly placed police officer who had been my student at the Police Training School in the early thirties. He passed by the classroom where I was teaching. Recognizing me, he started walking towards my desk. I told him to go and wait for me in the office. He was still waiting when I finished my lesson. My secretary told me: "Officer D. was very happy to learn that you are the principal of the school and was sure that you would admit his daughter even though she does not meet all the requirements". She told him, "not this principal!" Turning to the officer, I said, "She is absolutely right, and you, as an officer of the law, should be opposed to infraction of the rules". He blushed, accepted the verdict gracefully, and thanked me. I thought: "I hope I will never need *his protektsyah*".

The curriculum consisted of compulsory subjects and of other approved subjects selected by the principals. Since the school had originally been under the jurisdiction of the Labour Movement, there had been no such subjects as Mishnah and Aggadah. I decided to introduce Aggadah and the History of Zionism in the second and third years respectively. In the fourth year, I introduced Mishnah and the History of Zionism and the Labour Movement. These subjects were not popular among the students, nor did any of the instructors relish teaching them, either because of their unpopularity or because the teachers were unqualified. The task therefore devolved upon me. The graduating class was mature enough to accept my explanations of the importance of a knowledge of Mishnah and the history of Zionism and the Labour Movement. It was harder to overcome the negative attitude of the third year students to the study of *Tzionut*. The general trend both of educators and students was to break away from the past, to disdain the Galut, to concentrate on the present. This does not apply of course to the religious schools, where studies such as Mishnah and Aggadah are an integral part of the curriculum. To the independent minded Sabras, studying Zionism meant reliving and rehashing the humiliations and sufferings of their ancestors in the despised Galut. In large part, it was the result of the teachings and preachings of the preceding generation, that Galut was sickness and ugliness. As Bialik had expressed it: "My father is Black Poverty, bitter Exile is my mother; but it is not the wanderer's staff, nor the beggar's wallet I fear; for seven times more cruel, more terrible than these is life itself, the life that knows no hope, no radiance, the life of a hungry dog, fettered to its chain — O, curse upon you, Life that knows no hope!" *Tzionut* took on also the connotation of preaching, and the proud Sabras, the sons and daughters of those who laid the foundations of the new State and fought to liberate and secure it, were not in need of any preaching. Unfortunately, this trend was carried to extremes and estranged the new generation, including many teachers, from Hebrew sources other than the Bible, as well as from the life and problems of the Diaspora. And that had certainly not been the intention of Bialik and other Galut negaters!

The strongest objection, however, was to Aggadah. "Who is interested in outdated ancient literature!." I made a "bargain" with the class. I promised that if the majority still objected to the subject after a few months' study, we would substitute for it another one entirely to their liking. With classes in those days of necessity very large, with up to sixty students per class, naturally we had a sprinkling of Marxists. One of them, a sprightly fifteen year old girl, was sitting right opposite me. We were in the midst of a story when she suddenly burst out, "This story contains such profound wisdom of life!" I took advantage of this moment to ask the class whether they agreed to continue with the subject for the rest of the year. The response was a unanimous, enthusiastic "Yes!"

(Years later, when the negative results of this attitude showed themselves in the life of the people, the Education Dept., under the direction of the Minister Zalman Aranne, introduced a program of *Toda'ah Yehudit* in the General State Schools. *Toda'ah Yehudit* means "Jewish consciousness" ', referring to knowledge and appreciation of traditional Judaism and of the close links between Israel and the Diaspora.)

Education with Social Activity
Is Like Swimming without Water (John Dewey)

Generally speaking, education in Israel was innovative and progressive in the sense that it sought and pioneered new methods and was in touch with new ideas and developments. High school education therefore included required participation in *chugim* (clubs) that met after studies. Our school had a choir, dramatic and dance groups, and a band. My suggestion to form a club for studying the life and problems of Diaspora Jewry was met with skepticism by the faculty. "That will be the day! You are really naive if you think you can interest young Sabras in this type of activity". Students chose their *chugim* at a general assembly. When I proposed what the faculty thought would be met with complete indifference, I too was astonished at the response. It was one of the largest and most interesting groups. We met weekly at dinner in a private restaurant-room. Each time, we had a guest speaker who described to us Jewish life in his country of origin. The many questions he was bombarded with proved that Sabras were not necessarily indifferent to their people outside of Israel!

A Surprise Visit

One day a student came running breathlessly to inform me that the Minister of Education, the Mayor, and the director of the Tel-Aviv Education Department were waiting in the courtyard for permission to enter. Flabbergasted that they would ask for permission, I rushed out to meet them. Dinur apologised for not having informed me in advance of his visit. He had come to Tel-Aviv unexpectedly, and the mayor had suggested that he visit one of the municipal schools. The graduating class was the first they visited. Since classrooms were crowded and chairs were scarce, I asked some students to bring in just enough chairs for the guests. Dinur refused to sit down unles a chair was brought in for me too. It was pleasing to see how the questions and answers flowed freely and informally in a tension-free atmosphere. When none of the students could answer one of Dinur's questions, he remarked, "Surely, this is a common sense question?" He was greeted by a chorus of voices, "They do not teach us common sense here!" In explaining our program to our guests, I mentioned the Chug for the study of Diaspora Jewry. Dinur was greatly pleased, and remarked, "would that all high schools would have such Chugim!"

Running a School by Consensus

I liked very much the system I found in the school with regard to relationships between the principal and the faculty. While the principal was the highest and final authority, he and the faculty constituted a sort of governing council. Every Friday, when classes were held only until noon, we met after lunch for as many hours as was necessary to review the events of the week, to discuss problems and air differences of opinion, to hear teachers progress reports and to make decisions. Theoretically, controversial issues were to be decided by majority vote, but in practice our deliberations resulted in consensus; a vote was required only once during the whole year.

Strictness or Leniency

This one vote concerned a grave matter. Somebody had broken into the teachers' room and stolen some examination papers. One of the *Mechanchim*, (literally, educator, a form-teacher to whom students could turn not only for counsel but also for help) undertook to discover the culprit, a task I would never know how to go about. I did not press the sleuth to disclose to me how he had achieved this feat. I was glad, however, that no promise for leniency was involved. I suggested that the student be suspended for a year. Opinions were sharply divided, and it took many meetings to resolve the issue. The final meeting took place at Cafe Kassit (a hangout for writers, actors and artists) and lasted until about three A.M. I mustered all my authority and persuasive powers to influence the decision for strictness. To the pleaders for leniency I explained thus my unusual firmness in this particular case: We are now building the foundations of our new state. If we ignore these early symptoms of disrespect for law and order and if we close our eyes to small acts of corruption, they will gradually infest our society and turn us into another Levantine state. As educators, I said, we must reject the attitude of Levi Eshkol (he was then Treasurer of the Jewish Agency), who, when the first incident of embezzlement occurred at the Jewish Agency, showed leniency by quoting the Biblical saying, "Thou shalt not muzzle the ox when he treadeth out the corn" — (Deuteronomy 25:4). I turned a deaf ear to the many pleas, including that of the supervisor of the school, that I reconsider the decision. When I visited Israel in 1972, I asked one of the teachers whether our decision had been implemented after I left the school at the end of the year. He told me I was naive; the student was reinstated shortly after the new principal took over!

(I want to believe that Eshkol would feel deep remorse were he alive today to witness how that small theft may have set the stage for the present big thieveries. According to my brother-in-law, Itamar Pilpel, district court judge in Tel-Aviv, an injustice was and is still being done to Eshkol by misinterpreting his statement. Judge Pilpel claims that Eshkol meant: in an organization as large as the Jewish Agency it is not always possible to "muzzle the ox", etc.

Back to Canada

For a while it seemed that my family and I were striking roots in Israel. I liked very much the work with Israeli youth. I loved their candor, their simplicity, their integrity, and their serious attitude to life. My relations with the faculty were completely harmonious, and some of them became close friends of my wife and myself. We adjusted to the *tsena*, the severe austerity that prevailed in the country; that did not enter at all into our decision to "take up the wanderer's staff" again. This decision arose out of an entirely unexpected situation. Our younger boy, Yigal, assumed quickly the characteristics of a Sabrah. He was at the age when he was not concerned with politics or social phenomena. He turned out to be tougher than his Sabrah friends. He beat up those who taunted him as "Americani", and quickly became the leader of the "gang". Not so our eldest son Gadi. He was extremely sensitive and more mature intellectually than his peers. From an early age he had taken an unusual interest in political ideas and parties. He resented deeply the negative attitude of certain leftist Israeli circles to America. We once received a letter addressed to "Dr. Horowitz". Thinking that I had been addressed erroneously as "Dr.", I opened it. It was a letter of thanks from the editor of Hamaarav, a pro-American monthly, for an article lauding the American way of life which "Dr. Horowitz" had translated from English. The editor had been impressed with the quality of the translation and had published it in his magazine. We were baffled until Gad revealed to us that it was his doing. He was critical of many aspects of life in Israel. He once expressed himself: "these are Hebrew speaking Greeks" (meaning, of course, Hellenists). Because of his tendency to introversion and shyness, it took some time before my wife and I became aware of his intense unhappiness. When we did, he strongly pleaded that we return to the U.S.A. or Canada. We became convinced that there was no alternative for us but to heed to his pleas. (Twenty years later he told us that on the day of our departure he had had serious doubts about whether he really wanted to leave.)

In the meantime, word reached us that the situation at the Calgary Hebrew school had seriously deteriorated. Among other things, the Hebrew speaking youth movement and all its activities, including Camp T'chiyah, had ceased to exist for some time after the Malamuts accepted teaching posts in Winnipeg. The chairman of the Board of Education, Nathan Safran, wrote to ask for my assistance in obtaining a new principal. The Board in Calgary was very happy when I informed them that my wife and I were ready to return to the school. And thus, in 1952, started our second period of service in Calgary.

Chapter 21
Striking of Roots Accelerates

Is a Day School a Panacea?

When we returned to Calgary in 1952, the day school had already a five year history. Yet, the academic level and the entire atmosphere had deteriorated considerably. During the years of my agitation for the establishment of a day school, I had emphasized so strongly that it would not be a panacea that some people considered me inconsistent. I pointed out that there were other essential elements in an effective educational process and that the primary factor was the quality and dedication of the educators. There was a danger, I said, that the importance of these other elements would be minimized because of the glorification of the day school per se. In short, I said, only with *every thing else being equal*, was the superiority of a day school indisputable.

I had a deeper knowledge and better understanding of Calgary than of any other Jewish community. As well, my absence from the city for a number of years afforded me an extraordinary opportunity to delve into the causes of the changes that had been wrought in the short span of six years. There were four main factors involved. One of them was an old problem, the shortage of teachers, and the others were new developments.

The old world teachers were gradually disappearing from the scene, and there were no other really qualified ones to take their place. I described this situation by revising the Hebrew expression, *"mikol habba el hayad"*, (anybody that comes to hand) to *"mikol hanitkal baregel"*, (anybody one's feet bump into). In other words, the situation was so desperate that there was no alternative but to engage as teachers individuals who happened to know a little Hebrew or who were mere graduates of an elementary Hebrew school. In those days, persons could get teaching positions simply by virtue of being Israeli or by having spent some time in Israel. Thus, the school had only two qualified teachers when we returned. When I refused to re-engage an unqualified person, I was told that the children liked him better than all the other teachers. It was easy to find the reason. He would devote much of his time to discussing sports and telling stories that had nothing to do with jewish education. He would also occasionally treat the children to ice-cream.

The deterioration was also manifested in the discipline area. I found it necessary once to take the most drastic step I had ever taken as an educator, in order to re-establish the authority of the principal and staff. A certain student was once so disruptive and provocative that I decided to expel him from the school. His rich family threatened to withdraw all its support not only from the school but also from all other Jewish organizations. All the pressure that was brought upon me to reinstate him was in vain. The President, Charles Waterman, for whom I had great respect and affection, strongly pleaded that I rescind my decision. Never even for a second did he try to use his authority. He merely discussed with me the possible repercussions of this incident. When I explained to him the greater dangers to the school of the breakdown of authority and of bowing to intimidation, he understood and approved of my action. The family continued its support not only to other organizations but also to the school. Some years later, at a chance meeting between me and the student, he approached me, shook my hand, and declared, "I now understand, Rabbi, that you were entirely right!"

The New Developments

One new development was that the school became less of an organic part of the community. It was certainly not any more the center of Jewish life. Second, a new generation, mostly Canadian born, was providing the children for the school. In the past, a very small number of the pupils took piano lessons: Now, the younger parents wanted their children to take up music, dancing, etc. and to become boy and girl scouts. This was difficult to accomplish when children attended Hebrew school late in the afternoon, or in the evening, and had to devote the rest of the time to homework from two schools. That, in my opinion, was one if not the main reason for overcoming the objections that many people had harbored against day schools in Calgary and in other cities. These parents still wanted their children to receive a Jewish education, but all concerned — leaders, educators and parents — were fully aware that the best resources and efforts were given to the general studies. In many cases, the Hebrew program was gradually watered down, and it became increasingly difficult to bear the financial burdens of the two programs. We never used the term "parochial school" in Western Canada. We did not want to be and were not parochial. Without apologies, we stressed that a day school was essential for a more effective educational program and for allowing our children time for play and recreation.

Third, the people who had clamored for a "modern" Rabbi had won the day, so that there was now a "spiritual leader" to contend with. Some of the leaders of the new congregation, who tended to assimilationism, had enough political acumen to engage a modern orthodox Rabbi as their first "spiritual leader", in order to gain the support of some of the traditional and national elements. Ironically, an orthodox Rabbi allowed himself to be used by those who wanted a mere Sunday school education for their children. To justify his support for a Sunday school, he used the bugaboo of secularism "upon you, Jews of Calgary". This specious argument was most infuriating, as our community schools were much more religious than congregational schools and very much more religious than Sunday schools. When I confronted him once with this anomaly, the Rabbi defended himself by saying it was better that he, rather than a reform Rabbi, was their leader, that he would influence them to change their attitudes. His influence was so great that once they felt sure of their hold on a significant part of the community, they shunted him aside and quickly replaced him with a "conservative" Rabbi whose approach and activities were clearly detrimental not only to the school but to the entire community.

The New Rabbi

Our hopes of being able to work in harmony with a conservative Rabbi were quickly dashed. In his sermon on Rosh-Hashannah, he declared that Jews were a religion, not a people; that Jewish identification was only through the synagogue, and that such people as Ben-Gurion and Sharett were Israelis but not Jews.

I felt I had to make some gesture of protest, and I and my family walked out of the synagogue. Other people followed us. It was clear to us that our school and community were headed for turbulent times. The rabbi started to campaign against the school. He insisted he would establish a Sunday school in competition with the day school and was rash enough to claim that he could accomplish in a three-day-a-week afternoon school much more than our five-day a week Day school. My first opportunity to present publicly my diametrically opposed view about the relationship between Jews and Israelis came when I addressed a Hadassah meeting, which was usually representative of all sections of the community. I was sure the Rabbi's wife would quickly convey the message to him and awaited his reaction. He sent me a nasty letter which made it clear that we could "live in harmony" only if we would agree to follow the leader.

The community split wide open. Our differing philosophies continued to agitate people in their homes. Families divided on the issue at meetings and even in the streets. The upshot of it all was that the Rabbi went to such extremes that even many of his followers became aware of the damage he was causing their congregation, and "let him go" in the middle of the year. The night before he left, people from "both sides of the fence" were present at a social gathering in honor of Israeli

Ambassador Michael Comay. I noticed the Rabbi was engaged in a conversation with him. He was trying to convince Comay he was not Jewish. When Comay extricated himself, he walked straight up to me with the question: "Who is this nut?!" I clinched my explanation to Comay with, "he is not an ordinary nut; he is a nut of a Rabbi". I was not at all surprised when I read some time later an interview with him in an American newspaper from which it was clear that he belonged to the rabid anti-Zionist "Council for Judaism".

The situation had not been lacking altogether in humor. One of the gimmicks the Rabbi had used to entice people to his Friday Night services was to honor them on occasions such as birthdays and wedding anniversaries. (These gimmicks are now apparently common practice in Conservative and Reform synagogues.) He would ask all members of the family to stand up while he sang their praises. He would conclude the ceremony with the priestly Benediction. The Rabbi was so short that he would habitually raise himself to his toes when he stretched out his arms to intone the Benediction. One Friday night, he looked especially comical. All the members of the family he was blessing were so tall that his arms were parallel to their chests. The head of this family, a pillar of the community, had once told me that he was an atheist. At the end of the Service, I asked him how he, an atheist, could lend himself to such a farcical spectacle. "Rabbi Horowitz", he answered, "don't you realize we are playing games? It is about time that you too start playing!"

On another occasion, many of our students and some adults were gathered at the home of Mr. and Mrs. I. Gurevitch for the monthly Oneg-Shabbat of our Hebrew speaking groups. One of the members of the Rabbi's congregation walked in on us smoking a large cigar, something that was then absolutely taboo on Shabbat even at a gathering in a private home. He puffed continuously on his cigar as he said, "I have just come from the Rabbi's Service. He explained to us that Judaism is only a religion." The cigar smoker chuckled while he repeated several times, "Judaism is only a religion."

The Best of Doctors are Destined to Purgatory (Kidushin 82)

This bitter struggle exhausted me mentally and physically. I developed cramps in my legs. At times, they were so severe that they interfered with my normal walking. Upon examining me, my doctor pronounced "Buerger's disease". Having never heard of this disease before, I asked the doctor to explain it to me fully. He snapped, "you want me to explain in a few minutes what took twenty years to learn!" His tone in explaining the little he did, prompted me to remark, "Dr., you apparently think that a Rabbi should not be too concerned about going so soon to the 'here-after'!" He was so certain about his diagnosis, which was confirmed by two other doctors, that when I suggested he should refer me to the Mayo clinic in Rochester, Minn., he said, "If you have money to throw out, go ahead!" I had resigned myself to what I thought was my fate until I made one of my frequent visits to Joe Joffe's store. (A young priest by the name of Father O'Bourne was one of the friends I acquired at Joe's store. We would exchange quips, anecdotes, etc. On this occasion, Joe was trying to cheer me up with an effusion of jokes. He told Father O'Bourne the story about the priest who told a Rabbi he didn't know what he was missing by abstaining from eating pork and the Rabbi's reply was that *he* didn't know what *he* was missing by not having a wife. Noticing Father O'Bourne's slight embarassment, I told him, "Why don't you tell Joe that the priest had the last word?" They both looked at me expectantly, when I told them the version that occurred to me at that moment: "Father O'Bourne," I said, "tell Joe that the priest told the Rabbi, "Try it my way; it is even better". Father O'Bourne laughed even more hilariously than Joe.)

I loved to go in there for a chat with Joe Joffe, a wonderful, ever-cheerful human being. There would almost always be there some other non-buying customers who came to enjoy the balmy atmosphere. Noting my sad countenance, Joe asked me for the reason. When I told him, he insisted that I go immediately to Mayo. "If you don't, I'll take you by the ears and put you on the plane." I did. The verdict of the head of the Department of Circulatory Diseases was, "If you have Buerger's, Rabbi, then I too have Buerger's". For reassurance, I asked him how it was possible that three physicians would have made such a grave error. He explained that it was a rare disease, that my symptoms were characteristic of Buerger's, and that those doctors probably never saw such a case. Some people advised me to sue my doctor, but I dismissed it with the above Talmudic statement.

Revival of Hebrew Youth Movement

The new developments made it more difficult to revive the youth activities than it had been to originate them when there was no Rabbi in the community. Nonetheless, we did succeed in reviving all of them, including Camp T'chiyah. Our youth movement was strengthened by the existence of a Hebrew youth organization in Edmonton and by the closer links between the two schools. Students from Edmonton started to attend Camp T'chiyah, and our annual Hebrew youth rally was now sponsored jointly by the two organizations.

Our ranks were enlarged and strengthened by a positive new development. Some of our graduates became actively engaged in our work in Calgary and in other Western cities: Yale Joffe and Ephrayim Kettner became Treasurer and Board of Education Secretary, respectively, of the Calgary Talmud Torah; Yaakov Chetner became principal of the Edmonton Hebrew School, and Zwi Sherman, Vice principal of the

Vancouver Talmud Torah. Graduates who did not move out of Calgary formed an Alumni Association, and some of them lent leadership and direction to the Hebrew youth movement as well as to Young Judaea. One of these former students, Ziporah Shwartz (Fay Smolensky), a graduate of the Jewish Theological Seminary, joined our teaching staff.

Another significant development was the return of Dr. Carl Safran to Calgary in the capacity of Consultant Psychologist of the Calgary School Board. He became the Consultant Psychologist of our school as well, and played an important role in our school and community.

A Proposal to Unite the Hebrew School and the Peretz Shule

Leaders from both sides started to think of the possibility of bringing about some form of unification between the Peretz Shule and the Hebrew School. The anti-Zionist, anti-religious tendencies of the Peretz Shule had become a thing of the past, and both schools were faced with increasing financial difficulties. We proposed that the general studies programs should be completely amalgamated. As to the Jewish curriculum, there should be parallel classes with separate Talmud Torah and Peretz Shule programs. There could also be certain joint activities, such as holiday celebrations and sports. The other side was adamant in its stand that the Jewish studies program should also be completely amalgamated. The two institutions still continue to exist separately!

Events Repeat Themselves

When I returned to Western Canada, the Igud and Keren Hatarbut were still struggling along separately in the East. The Western Educators Council was no more in existence, and the Igud and Keren Hatarbut could do little with their meagre funds. At the first opportunity, the schools in the major Western cities revived the regional setup and affiliated officially as a unit with both organizations. We renewed the annual conference. The first took place in Calgary during May 28-30, 1954. We reviewed fully the situation in the West, and resolved, "to coordinate as much as possible the activities of the various communities and to undertake joint educational and cultural projects". We took upon ourselves to establish at least one adult Hebrew course and a Hebrew speaking youth organization in each city. We also decided to have the regional chairman and others visit each community at least once annually; to hold a yearly workshop for teachers and a youth rally; to endeavour to turn T'chiyah into a regional camp, and to organize a lecture series with outstanding speakers from the U.S.A.

An Executive Board representative of all the larger centers was elected, with the following officers: Rabbi Horowitz — Regional President and Consultant-Supervisor of the schools; Nathan Safran —

Chairman of the Executive; Irvin Lipsky and Dr. N.F. Gropper — Vice Chairmen, respectively, for British Columbia and Saskatchewan; Max Katzin — Treasurer; and Morris Greenberg — Secretary. Later, Dr. A. Kravetz, Chief Rabbi of Winnipeg and Principal of its Talmud Torah, was elected Honorary President, and Rabbi Arthur Chiel, Spritual Leader of Cong. Rosh-Pinah in Winnipeg, was named Vice-President of the Region. It was also decided that all principals and presidents of the larger schools would automatically be members of the Board.

Realizing that the financial burdens of the schools would make it impossible for us to accomplish much without the help of a national organization, we asked Keren Hatarbut and Igud for an allocation to help us meet our financial obligations. It took much effort and a great deal of correspondence to finally receive some financial help from them. We often found ourselves without any funds, because the remittances from the head offices were slow to come. At one time, Irvin Lipsky and I threatened to resign and to concentrate our efforts on our own schools and communities. When the miniscule budgets of both organizations, especially that of the Igud, were revealed to us, we agreed to carry on.

It became clear to us at the conference that the new developments referred to in the description of the situation in Calgary applied more or less to the entire region. We, therefore, found it necessary to include among our resolutions:

"We view with alarm and deep regret the new trend among certain groups in Western Canada to water down Hebrew education by decreasing the number of hours and days devoted to the instruction of our children. We are especially perturbed by the apparent desire on the part of those groups to establish Sunday schools at a time when many communities and congregations in the U.S.A. are realizing increasingly that Sunday school education has resulted in the tragic loss of a great part of two generations of Jews in that country. We appeal to those people to learn from the tragic experiences of American Jewry and to desist from their endeavours, which will lead to the undermining of the work of the established schools in our communities. We call their attention to the views of educational experts that the five-day-a-week schools are the barest minimum for imparting to our children even a small part of the vast treasures of Jewish civilization and culture, for the preservation of any type of positive Jewish living in this country, and for the mental and emotional health of our children.

In keeping with the principles mentioned in the previous resolution, we hereby resolve that no school affiliated with our organization shall prepare for Bar-Mitzvah any pupil who has not had at least three years of continuous study in a five-day-a-week school. We appeal to all Rabbis and congregations that they should not allow Jewish life to be a mockery by allowing Bar-Mitzvah ceremonies to be held in their synagogues for children who have had no Jewish education. At the same, time we suggest that special consideration be given to children from country-towns, where no Jewish schools are in existence.

Western Canada — An Important Reservoir

In Montreal and Toronto, our leadership consisted almost entirely of individuals who would have been considered Haskalah followers (followers of the Enlightenment Movement) in the old country. A few of them were somewhat fluent in Hebrew, some understood the language, and some had a special liking for it. They did not hold any important positions in the Zionist organization or other national organizations. The Hebrew Movement was their social and cultural niche. In Western Canada, on the other hand, Zionist officers readily assumed the leading roles in the Keren Hatarbut branches: L. Pekarsky, Dr. E. Wershof and A. Estrin in Edmonton; William Guss, M. Wolochow and N. Gould in Calgary; Roy Calof, David Secter and G. Skulsky in Winnipeg; Dr. S. Kraminsky, J. Schwartzfeld and S. Promislow in Regina; Rabbi Z. Gotthold and M. Aarons in Saskatoon; Drs. P. Coodin and Weisstaub, Shimon Kirsch, and Saul Laskin in Fort-William. In every one of these cities (except for Regina where the temperature was forty-one below zero and there was a one-time performance of Macbeth) large audiences attended the public meetings I addressed on "Jewish Life in Canada After the Establishment of the Jewish State". (During my address, in Regina I was distracted by the smiles and whispers in the audience. After my speech, a woman took out her mirror and said, "look into the mirror and you will know the reason for the whispering". I was alarmed when I saw my right ear double the size of my left ear. It was so frozen I might have lost part of it without immediate treatment.)

All the newly organized branches made financial commitments to the national office. I do remember that not all of them could meet their obligations because of their struggles to maintain their local Hebrew schools and activities. The Calgary branch distinguished itself more than any other in the financial support it gave to the movement. Thanks to the efforts of Morris Wolochow, who directed the welfare office on a voluntary basis, the welfare-fund — the only one in the country — made an annual allocation of five hundred dollars to the Keren Hatarbut.

Oh, For Yesteryear's Volunteers

My main purpose, however, was to lay the foundations for a cohesive national organization, to introduce Hebrew activities where there were none, and to strengthen those that were already in existence. In Edmonton, for instance, it was not necessary to organize Hebrew courses. Messrs. Goelman and Kaliger were already conducting a Bible class and a beginners course respectively. We succeeded in initiating Hebrew studies in all the other large centers, including Saskatoon and Fort-William, thanks to the voluntary spirit of the principals and teachers: E. Malamut and Y. Walker in Calgary; Ben-Zion Bendel in Regina, where the courses were attended primarily by senior Judaeans; J. Huberman in Saskatoon, and S. Kirsh in Fort-William. All of them gave their services without receiving any remuneration. In general, *all* the work in Western Canada was accomplished by volunteers.

During this tour, it became evident to me that without trained, knowledgeable Hebrew-speaking youth leaders, branches of the youth movement would not endure even in cities where there were good day schools. We therefore planned to have as many Westerners as possible attend Massad in order for them to gain experience in youth leadership. In the meantime Calgary and Edmonton were the only two centers where the work of Hebrew *chugim* was uninterrupted. I was particularly pleased with the continuation of all the projects of the Hebrew Youth Movement in Calgary, under the leadership of Ephrayim and D'vorah Malamuth and of some of its original founders. It was surprising to me that Winnipeg, though it had one of the best schools, experienced difficulties in maintaining a Hebrew Youth organization. The possible explanations are that the local school did not concern itself with youth activities and also that available capable leaders were all involved with Habonim and Young Judaea which were in their heyday at that time. Fortunately, there was a large and very active dramatic group (the only Hebrew children's theatre in Canada), established and directed by Biela Lepkin under the auspices of the Talmud Torah. At my suggestion, they agreed to form the basis of a Hebrew Youth organization and to affiliate with the national Hebrew Youth Movement. In 1948 Mrs. Lepkin organized a small Hebrew camp with a nucleus of Young Judaean leaders and members of the Hebrew theatre. This was made possible by Roy Calof who put his large summer home in Gimli Manitoba at the disposal of the group for several weeks. This successful venture sowed the seeds of Winnipeg Massad, although it was not to come into being until four years later. That year saw also the inauguration of a vocalized Hebrew column in the Winnipeg Jewish Post, under the auspices of the Keren Hatarbut and the editorship of Biela Lepkin.

Out of the Mouths of Babes and Sucklings
Hast Thou Founded Strength (Psalm 8:3)

As I made my rounds from city to city and from school to school, I was often exhilirated (after suffering from the fatigue of meetings and campaigns) by the gems that issued "out of the mouths of babes". In one class, a seven year old told in Hebrew about God's command to Abraham to leave his country and go to Canaan. I asked him whether Abraham obeyed God. "Yes," he said, and he proceeded to relate how Abraham took his wife etc. etc., and his *kippah* and went to the land of Canaan. After a teacher in a third grade of the Winnipeg Talmud Torah introduced me as "the supervisor from Montreal", a little fellow asked me (in 1960) "are you a Jewish English-Canadian or a Jewish French-Canadian?" I often regretted that I did not have the time or presence of mind to record all such gems with the view to publishing a book on "From the Mouths of Babes in Hebrew Schools". I hope that some day a teacher, or teachers will undertake this task.

Why Keren Hatarbut and Igud?

The absurdity of having two separate organizations with the same objectives came into full view during my visits in Western Canada. Time and time again I was reminded by my colleagues of the decision that had been taken by them in 1945, when I had been chairman of the Hebrew Educational Council, to affiliate with Keren Hatarbut only if it would eventually amalgamate with the Igud. This matter came up because my tour was sponsored by both organizations. The part-time Igud director, Mr. Shmuel Lerner, could not go on an extended tour because his main position was as principal of the Shaar Hashamayin Hebrew school in Montreal. I was asked what part of me represented which organization, and why I didn't have a separate *kipah* (skull-cap) for each of them. (It was a common occurrence in those days for individuals to hold offices in several organizations. It happened at times that an individual who presided at a meeting of one organization would remain in the same room at its conclusion to chair the meeting of another organization. The story goes that one such multiple chairman took off his *kipah* at the end of one meeting, put on another one, and remarked, "Now I shall doff my Talmud Torah kipah and don my Mizrachi kipah.") I pointed out that my visits and evaluations of the schools were on behalf of Igud. This sounded more than ridiculous in places where I had served their schools for years and whose officers could not care less whom I represented. I told them I had not changed my mind about the need for a united movement for the advancement of Hebrew education and culture, but now that I was on the scene in Montreal, I was confronted with realities that could not easily be changed. Nonetheless, I promised, I would continue to work towards the goal of unity.

In order to preserve educational integrity, unity, and harmony in our communities, we strongly favor that Hebrew schools should be community-wide institutions and should maintain absolute autonomy in their work and activities."

Our identity of purpose and united efforts bore significant fruit. We did carry out our program almost in its entirety, and our activities focused public interest upon the centrality of the school in the community. We succeeded in arranging lecture-tours by such noted educators and scholars as Yehuda Ya'ari and professors Avraham Halkin, Samuel Blumenfield and Rafael Patai, who assisted us in bringing to the fore our philosophies of education and Jewish life. My frequent visits to the larger centers served to give our schools a sense of unity and of belonging to a national movement.

The affinity of ideas and approach among all the principals of the larger centers contributed greatly to the harmony and success of our endeavours. Rabbis Kravetz and Chiel were enthusiastic advocates of Day Schools and of the primacy of a national-religious educational system. The Principal of the Edmonton Talmud Torah, Yaacov Chetner, and the Vice-Principal of the Vancouver School, Zwi Sherman, were graduates of the Calgary Hebrew High School and of the Jewish Theological Seminary. Avraham Assaf, a highly qualified and experienced Israeli educator, was Principal of the Vancouver Talmud Torah. The Spritual Leader of Saskatoon, who was also the Principal of its Talmud Torah, Rabbi R. Adler, was a nationalist-Hebraist, and the Principal of the Regina school, Zwi Horwich, was a native Torontonian with a rich Hebrew background and with experience in youth leadership and as Director of Camp Massad in Winnipeg.

Several months following our conference, the Winnipeg office of the Canadian Jewish Congress decided to convene a Western educational conference of their own. Invitations were sent out to individual schools, and the Western organization of the Igud — Keren Hatarbut was completely ignored. When It became clear that our affiliated schools would not participate, I was accused of preventing them from attending. In a letter to Mr. Meyer Averbach, Secretary of the Winnipeg Congress office, dated August 13 1954, (followed by a more elaborate letter to Mr. David Slater, Chairman of the Western Division), I wrote in my capacity as Western Igud Chairman: "I cannot participate as a representative of our school. We, as the other schools in the West, are affiliated with the Igud. We held a conference about two months ago and elected an executive committee, which adopted a concrete program of activities. We must abide by the decisions of the National Executive, which decided against participation in your conference."

"I personally am of the opinion that there certainly are an area and a possibility for cooperation with other organizations in general and with the C.J.C. in particular. Had you invited the Western Division of the Igud, I would have contacted all the members of our executive and suggested that we participate as a unit. I am almost certain they would have supported my suggestion."

"When I was in Montreal several days ago, Mr. A. Kronitz told me that the National Committee of the Igud was invited by you to the conference and decided not to attend. It is too late now for me to try to influence them to change their decision, as their leading members are out of the city."

"I enclose a copy of the resolutions adopted by our conference. I shall be glad to recommend to our executive to consider the possibility of cooperating with another organization or organizations in the implementation of our program, if we will receive concrete suggestions from you in that direction." We never heard again from the office of the Canadian Jewish Congress.

Congress versus Igud

When the C.J.C. in Western Canada first disagreed with the Hebrew Educators Council about the role of the Congress in the field of education, the Igud was not yet in existence. In the mid-fifties, the Igud had already been in existence for over a decade, and the controversy shifted to Montreal. The Igud, especially if it had united with the Keren Hatarbut, could have developed into a coordinating agency for all the national religious schools in the country, but it was never given a chance to really get off the ground because of the skimpy allocations it received from both the C.J.C. and the Zionist Organization of Canada. The Igud leadership tried valiantly to convince Congress to recognize it as the organization representing all the national religious schools, but Congress was adamant in its stand that the Igud should limit itself to specific activities in Quebec and perhaps also in the Maritimes. The directors of the Igud, Chaim Spillberg, and of the Keren Hatarbut, Aryeh (now Leon) Kronitz, turned to us to strengthen their case vis-a-vis the Congress. It was Mr. Kronitz who wrote us that, "The Congress apparently wants to take under its wing all educational matters, and it makes it difficult for the Igud to exist". He referred to a letter by Mr. Saul Hayes, according to which the Congress was engaged in the field of education in Ont. and in Western Canada and that there was no need for Igud activities there. Our reaction was that, "The activities of the Congress office in Winnipeg during the past two and a half years were limited to sending us monthly a few copies of World Over and, on several occasions, also material for holidays, which arrived a few days before or after the holiday. We pointed out that the holiday material was prepared by the Igud, and we failed to understand why it had to come to us via the Congress office in Winnipeg. The Igud's stand was best summarized, in a letter of January 5, 1955, by its President, Mr. S. Silver, to Mr. Saul Hayes: "Whereas your letter of December 24th speaks of Jewish education in general, the Igud emphasizes Hebrew education. The essence of our work is to maintain and promote the spirit of Hebrew learning wherever we can and in which ever way possible. The schools which are affiliated with us are of special Hebraic and religious nature, and no matter whether these schools happen to be in Montreal, Western Canada, the Maritimes, or Ontario, they demand and deserve our constant vigilance."

Our executive decided at its meeting on February 23, 1955: "It was unanimously decided to give our fullest support to the National Executive of the Igud in its stand that it is absolutely essential to maintain the Igud as the *national association of all Hebrew schools across the Dominion*; that its work be expanded and intensified in all regions; that the Canadian Jewish Congress be strongly urged to give adequate financial support to the igud; that only the igud can represent our schools, and that the assistance of Congress to our schools can and should be given to and through the Igud as the properly constituted representative of all Hebrew schools in Canada."

At the same time, we referred again the Igud and Keren Hatarbut leadership to the resolution of our Western conference that: "In order to insure the success of our endeavours for the strengthening of Hebrew Education and Culture, and in order to eliminate unnecessary duplication, we most strongly urge the Keren Hatarbut and the Igud to be formed into one united and strong body." We stressed once more that a united, strong national organization would be in a much better position to obtain the support and cooperation of both the Canadian Jewish Congress and of the Zionist organization.

"Change of the Guard" at Keren Hatarbut

When we held our annual conference in May, 1955, the Western Igud-Keren Hatarbut had already struck firm roots. In addition to the active participation of veteran school principals and officials, new dimensions were added to our work. New generation Canadians, including graduates of the Calgary Hebrew school Frank Ketner and Yale Joffe; Morris Greenberg, and Ben Shapiro, became concerned not only about the future of their local schools but also of Igud-Keren Hatarbut. Subjects other than organization and curriculum were given serious consideration for the first time. A brief description of the agenda will be an indication of the wide spectrum of interest that had been engendered: "The Philosophy and Content of Our Education" was discussed by me; Rabbi Kravetz spoke on "The Place of Zionism and Israel in Our Education"; Yaakov Chetner on "The Teaching of Israel as a Special Subject and by Integration with Other Subjects"; Dr. Carl Safran on "The Psychological Aspects of Hebrew Education"; Chaim Brandwein on "The Teaching of Israel Through Chumash"; Nathan Safran on "The Place of Our Schools in the Community"; Hymie Baltzan on "Our Perennial Problems — Finance, Teacher Shortage, etc." The deliberations were closed with my presentation of "A Program For Our Region".

At this conference, Aryeh Kronitz, who was one of the guest speakers, brought me quite a surprise. He had resigned as National Executive Director of Keren Hatarbut to take up the position of Principal of the Shaare-Zion Day School in Montreal. On behalf of the executive, he asked whether I was interested in reassuming my old position with the Keren Hatarbut. My answer was affirmative, provided the Calgary Talmud Torah would release me from my commitment to serve there for another year. A few days later, I received a wire offering me the position.

I was surprised but heartened that my former students on the executive were among those who were, at first, the most stubborn in their refusal to release me. I pleaded the cause of the national movement and my strong desire to advance its fortunes. The reaction was: "We have to think first and foremost of our own community", to which I silently agreed in view of my long experience with the tenuous relationships between head offices and peripheries. They finally agreed when I undertook to go at my own expense to some of the largest centers in North America to find a successor acceptable to the executive.

I immediately thought of Rabbi Israel Silverman, a graduate from the Jewish Theological Seminary of America. I went to New York to appeal to him for the cause of Hebrew education in a community with whose achievements and potentialities he was well acquainted. I told him he would receive in his first year a few thousand dollars more than I did in my last year, and a thousand dollars more than I was to receive as director of a national organization!

My Keren Hatarbut salary was to $7000. It was the second time I was "bamboozled". When the offers were made to me for my first and second tenures, I agreed to receive the salaries of my predecessors. I eventually discovered that both times the directors had received additional "fringe" amounts. . .

After listening to me for a long while, he said, "I am not the idealist you are. I have to think of myself and my family." The clincher was when he told me smilingly he had even rejected the invitation of Calgary's Conservative Congregation to serve as their Rabbi, though they offered him a much higher salary... His explanation made it clear to me why a Rabbi preferred preaching to teaching...

Since the Igud had no candidates for us, I continued to search in New York and even went as far as Chicago. In the end, I succeeded in recruiting Rabbi Dr. G. Davey of Montreal for the position.

Chapter 22
Keren Hatarbut Becomes A National Movement

A Preview of Massad

I was asked to substitute as director of Massad for two weeks for Mr. Kronitz who was to attend the World Hebrew Congress in Jerusalem. When I arrived at the camp a few weeks after its opening, I was told that everything was running smoothly and that my presence was required just as a sort of supervisor during the director's absence. It turned out to be my most difficult camp season. The director returned only about a week before camp closing. All my effort to contact him before then were in vain. In the end, I was glad I had had this opportunity to observe the situation first hand and to learn what not to do in the future. One of the things I learned was that an Israeli, especially without prior camping experience in America, should not serve as a head counsellor, no matter how dedicated he was. In the early fifties, the Jewish Agency had not yet started to send camp personnel to Canada. As in the case of teachers, nondelegated, inexperienced Israelis were engaged as counsellors because of the shortage of Hebrew speaking personnel. We therefore had serious problems with some of the Israelis on the camp staff.

Igud and Keren Hatarbut Unite

When I resumed my duties as Keren Hatarbut director, one of my highest priorities was to bring about the unification of Igud and Keren Hatarbut. This task was now easier because Igud had already been practically starved financially. After preparing the ground for what some termed the "take over", the Keren Hatarbut national convention, which took place in Ottawa during March 7-9, 1956, decided to bring about "the full amalgamation of Igud and Keren Hatarbut." Following a few meetings with representatives of the Igud, the decision on the amalgation was finalized at a special meeting in September 1956. The only opposition came, surprisingly enough, from the outgoing Keren Hatarbut director. At first, Melech Magid, too, argued strongly against amalgamation, but when the vote was taken, his voice was among the overwhelming "yea's". When I asked him, there and then, what made him change his mind, he remarked humorously, "I have been in favor of amalgamation all the time, but I wanted to give Horowitz a hard time! Why should he be free from the hard times I and other principals get from our bosses!" I joined in the laughter.

There was practically nothing to "take over" from Igud, except all the files and program materials. Its tiny office had been located at the C.J.C. headquarters, and the office equipment was Congress property. There was a heated discussion about a new name for the unified organization. The Igud leadership insisted on the retention of the name Igud. The compromise agreed on was: *"Keren Hatarbut — Igud Ivri Lechinuch Vetarbut BeCanada"*. It was not easy to arrive at a consensus that both "Keren Hatarbut" and "Igud" be omitted from the organization's English name — Canadian Association for Hebrew Education and Culture.

Soon after the amalgamation, a concerted effort was made to establish regular contacts with all Hebrew educational institutions in the country, including those that were not directly under our supervision, in order to ascertain the practical ways in which we could help them. The response was ample evidence of the need and value of a national coordinating agency. Numerous schools of all types approached us for information and advice, for help in obtaining principals and teachers, and for various materials and teaching-aids.

When the amalgamation was decided upon, it was generally understood that Mr. Chaim Spillberg, who had borne for years the brunt of Igud difficulties, would become a co-director of the organization. He insisted, and I concurred fully, that the functions of director should be divided between us, and that we should both be completely independent in our respective areas. The committee, however, was firm in its opinion that there could be only one over-all director. To my deep regret, Mr. Spillberg withdrew. He did so in a most gracious manner.

Looking for an Assistant

Even before the amalgamation, the increased activities and our ambitious plans to turn Keren Hatarbut into a veritable national movement necessitated the appointment of an assistant to the director. There was no point in advertising for candidates because of the shortages referred to previously. As if from heaven, a young Israeli knowledgeable immigrant, Dov Parshan, appeared on the scene, and we engaged him, in September 1956, to assist in our activities in Montreal so that I could be free to travel to various parts of the country. A year later, upon Mr. Parshan's resignation, we recruited Chaim Brandwein, an Israeli scholar and highly qualified teacher (now professor of Hebrew Literature at Brandeis University), to serve primarily as a consultant-supervisor of our affiliated schools.

Mr. Brandwein was serving at that time as a teacher at the United Talmud Torahs in Montreal. When I discussed with him the possibility of his working for Keren Hatarbut, he assured me he was free of any commitments to the Talmud Torah for the forthcoming year. Although Mr. Magid confirmed this, I was uneasy about taking away an excellent teacher from one of the best schools in the country. I convinced myself, however, that Mr. Brandwein's services would be put to better use in the wider field presented by Keren Hatarbut. Some time later, I saw Mr. Magid at Israel's Independence Day Celebration at the Israeli Consulate. Since Mr. Brandwein had assured me he had decided to leave the employ of the Talmud Torah in any event, I told Mr. Magid I thought he should be pleased that Mr. Brandwein would benefit all our affiliated schools. Mr. Magid's outburst was so vehement that people around us were startled. He rose from his seat and shouted at me, "What you have done is unforgivable; you have taken a good teacher to do something of little value. This is the end of our friendship." As it turned out, Brandwein worked for us only one year, Magid withdrew from active participation in Keren Hatarbut, and I lost a wonderful colleage and friend. Magid never gave me a chance to tell him he was right. During my work with the schools in later years, I became convinced that especially in the Golah, where teachers of Brandwein's calibre are hard to come by, there is no task that can even remotely compare with the educator's work in his classroom. As to supervision, it is the last and least on the priority scale. I had hoped to tell this to Magid even if I would have had to force myself upon him, but, alas, he passed away before I had a chance to do so.

Strong Bonds with Jewish Agency and Brit Ivrit Olamit

The rapid progress in our work was largely due to the strong bonds of understanding and cooperation that were forged with the Department of Education and Culture of the Jewish Agency and the Brit Ivrit Olamit (World Hebrew Movement) during my visit in Israel in 1956. At that time, Shazar was the head of the department of Education and Culture of the Jewish Agency; Dr. Y. Mehlman was its director, and Nachum Levine served as the director of the Brit Ivrit Olamit. The three of them were deeply concerned about Jewish life in the Diaspora, and were ready to lend their full support to those who were laboring in the fields of Hebrew education and culture. It was Shazar who, at a Zionist congress, dramatically reversed the oath "If I forget thee o Jerusalem" (Psalm 137) to "if I forget thee o, Diaspora". It was thus during that visit that we laid the foundations for the projects that were to revolutionize our work in Canada:

In 1955, the Jewish Agency sent at its expense a noted Hebrew scholar to teach Bible to senior campers at Massad. Since I was substituting for the director that summer, I had occasion to observe that, to say the least, it was a misplacement of talent and resources to bring a scholar all the way from the Hebrew University for a task that could have been adequately fulfilled by any competent local teacher. As a matter of fact, the great discrepancy between the levels of the scholar and the campers created serious disciplinary problems. I therefore persuaded Shazar and Mehlman to make three thousand dollars available to us for laying the foundations of a serious, permanent leadership training institute in conjunction with Massad.

We discussed fully all the ramifications of our plans to embark on a teacher-exchange program. (On that occasion, we arranged for the very first time for an Israeli teacher to come to Canada with the authorization of the Jewish Agency. At the request of Mr. Kronitz, who was in urgent need of a teacher, I made arrangements with Mr. J. Jacobi to proceed as soon as possible to Montreal to take up a teaching post at the Shaarei Zion day school, where he served for many years.) We also reached an agreement about Mr. Aharon Rosenne's impending visit to Canada, which — as will be seen later — revolutionized our methods of teaching Hebrew to adults.

Most encouraging was the knowledge that the Jewish Agency would support us financially. Although in a real sense this method of obtaining funds was beneficial, because the people we dealt with in Israel understood better our needs and priorities, it was discouraging that the "Canadian Jewish community", whether through the Z.O.C. or the C.J.C., was not mature enough to invest adequately in projects fundamental to the preservation and development of Jewish life in Canada. There is no doubt in my mind that there would now be less Hebrew day schools, no Massad camps, and considerably fewer adult Hebrew courses; that there would never have been a National Hebrew Youth Movement; and that Jewish life in general would now be much poorer were it not for the existence of Igud-Keren Hatarbut for over three decades. It therefore seemed preposterous to me that we should have to get money that was contributed by Canadian Jews, by sending it first all the way to Israel, and by expending money, time and effort in bringing some of it back for our own essential educational needs. At the same time, it required some measure of understanding and cooperation on the part of the Canadian Zionist leadership to be supportive, though grudgingly and slowly, of our general aims. Moreover, this supportiveness was by far greater than the Hebrew Movement in the U.S.A. succeeded in gaining from the Z.O.A. In any event, I left Israel with a strong feeling that funds for our projects would be forthcoming, though no promises of definite amounts were made.

Essentials and Priorities

Upon my return with the good news from Jerusalem, we set out to determine the essentials and priorities of our program. It was no simple task to map out the details, because we seldom knew in advance the financial base upon which we could build. We followed the path of action without waiting for definite assurances, and certainly not for the money to be in our coffers. Our priorities were clearly in this order: Schools, Camps, Youth, Adult Education.

Schools — The First Line of Action

Our ultimate goal was to unite all the Hebrew schools around a national organization that would set policy, plan and implement programs, establish authority and discipline, endeavour to solve the problems resulting from the perennial teacher-shortage, and, in general, to muster all our creative powers for the enhancement of Hebrew education. The situation in the country was not conducive to the speedy realization of this vision. In Montreal, schools guarded jealously their separateness and independence. They therefore resisted even the establishment of a bureau of Jewish education. Although they cooperated with Keren Hatarbut, they did not seem ready to come under the roof of a national agency. In Toronto, the Director of the Bureau of Jewish education, Dr. J. Diamond, was involved in Keren Hatarbut activities in all areas except formal education. He was of the opinion that any coordinating authority would have to come under the aegis of the C.J.C. Unlike some others, who politicked and zigzagged according to the direction of the winds, Dr. Diamond was completely honest and steadfast in his stand.

I therefore did not serve as supervisor-consultant in the Toronto schools. However, the principal of the Associated Talmud-Torahs, invited me from time to time to visit the school and discuss with him its situation and problems. I was always impressed with its high scholastic standards, the seriousness and knowledge of the students, and the devotion of the high calibre teaching staff. If this fine institution had had an elaborate students' activity program, Toronto might have had an active Hebrew youth movement, and might have been able to prevent the demise of Massad in Toronto, as did the leaders and graduates of the Hebrew youth movement in Montreal. Such a program was, of course, lacking in all other schools, including those of Montreal, where the youth movement was initiated and nurtured by the Keren Hatarbut.

In the small centers of Ontario, a special education department of C.J.C. had been functioning for many years. Its director, Dr. Joseph Klinghoffer, worked in cooperation with Keren Hatarbut in such areas as Hebrew Writers Week, Hebrew Month, and the Summer Seminar for Teachers. The schools of Ottawa and Fort William-Port Arthur, though in Ontario, were always affiliated with our organization. In the Maritimes, there was no semblance of any regional setup. It was therefore natural to begin in the West, where Keren Hatarbut-Igud had struck deep roots.

A Historic Conference

For years, we referred to the Regina conference, that was held during April 25-27, 1957, as an historic event. It was historic in the sense that we all considered it a precursor of and a model for National Unity. For three days, the authoritative representatives (presidents, chairmen of boards of education, principals and teachers) of the six major Western communities deliberated on every aspect and problem of their schools and of the region. All the sessions were held at the Hebrew school, and continued from early morning to late at night. We did not even go out for lunch or supper, but had short breaks twice a day when the Ladies Auxiliary of the congregation provided us with light meals. Many of us continued the discussions until the wee hours of the morning. The region was strengthened by the participation of additional young Canadians such as Joseph Putter, Harry Krolick, Dr. Nathan Gropper, Prof. M. Steinberg, David Isman, Ben Shapiro and Eddy Yuditzky. The following excerpts from the official report will explain why we all considered it the most fruitful Hebrew educational conference that had ever been held in Canada:

"The comprehensive curriculum and teachers' guide (consisting of 91 pages), prepared and issued by Head Office, was adopted as the basis of the educational program of the major schools;

A basic salary scale was worked out, and will be presented to the boards of the various institutions for their consideration and approval;

It was decided to obtain and replace principals and teachers in consultation with Head Office. Schools will not engage new principals and teachers without prior clearance with Head Office;

Non-certificated teachers will be required to attend our Summer Seminar until they receive teacher certification from the authorities of the Seminar. Qualified candidates from Europe and Israel will also be required to attend the Seminar, in order to acquaint themselves with the situation and teaching methods prevailing in Canada. Increments in salaries will be given to teachers attending the seminar.

The educational consultant of our Organization will serve as the official supervisor of these schools. The tasks of the supervisor will also include preparation of educational materials, uniform tests, and revision of curricula, in close cooperation with the principals and teaching staffs of the schools.

It was decided to develop Maimonides College into a Day High School and Teachers' Seminary, which will serve the entire West. This institution will be under the joint auspices of the Winnipeg Talmud Torah and the Keren Hatarbut. *An all-day Grade Eight will be opened for the academic year 1957-58.* An educator of high calibre has already been invited from Israel to teach in this institution, at no cost to the Talmud/Torah.

The presidents, the chairmen of the boards of education, and the principals of all the schools in the Region will constitute the Executive Committee of the Western Region, *which will determine its own policies in consultation and cooperation with Head Office.*

The lasting benefits of this conference were evidenced by the region's continuous progress, by the adherence of all the schools to the principles set forth unanimously by their representatives, and by the continuing alternate annual conference or workshop as a permanent feature.

The conference was not entirely devoid of discordant incidents. We were aiming at unanimity in all our decisions. A principal of one of the best schools persisted for some time in his opposition to importing teachers from Israel. He had had "bitter" experiences with an Israeli couple. While they were good teachers, their superior attitude and lack of understanding of our realities made for disharmony in the school and community. I pointed out that the teachers, who would be official emissaries of the Jewish Agency would be responsible not only to the school but also to Keren Hatarbut and the Jewish Agency. Furthermore, I said, I had stressed to Shazar and Mehlman the need for preparing such teachers adequately, preferably in Canada, for their important mission. He was finally convinced to make our decision unanimous.

In my address at the Oneg-Shabbat I stressed the emotional and psychological aspects of our educational process, which is based on the triad of God, Torah or culture, and nation. Paraphrasing Achad-Ha'am's statement "more than the Jews preserved the Sabbath, the Sabbath preserved the people", I said that a good Hebrew education does more for the emotional health of our children than they do for the preservation of our people. To emphasize the point, I said that, as an educator, my concern does not start with God, Torah, and nation, but rather with the emotional and mental health of the child. It was therefore essential, I said, that our schools should be places of joyful experience for our pupils. Our schools would thus help to create the necessary motivation for the children's identification with God, Torah, and nation. The local Rabbi (orthodox) jumped up in fury to express his astonishment that I, a Rabbi, and the son of "Reb Yeshaye" at that, (somehow, orthodox Rabbis would now and then invoke "Reb Yeshaye" in our discussions on Judaism) should deny God and Torah. Rabbi Kravetz signalled to me to let him deliver the reply. In his inimitable calm and witty manner, he made it clear that, whether you agree or disagree with Rabbi Horowitz on his educational approach, he most certainly did not deny God or Torah. Rabbi Horowitz thinks that if you start from the child, it will lead more successfully to God, Torah and nation. Apparently wanting to have the last word, the local Rabbi stated, "a Winnipegger told me that Mr. Joe Putter, Board of Education Chairman of the Winnipeg Talmud Torah, was discriminating against religious teachers". Joe seemed to enjoy himself when he quoted none other than Rabbi Kravetz that a so-called good secular teacher was to be preferred to a poor religious teacher.

Now that the West had achieved a comprehensive program for unified action, we turned our attention to the Maritimes with a view to developing a similar setup. We had been in touch with all the communities in the area and placed some teachers in a few of their schools. I then visited Halifax, St. John, N.B., and Glace Bay, N.S. to acquaint myself with the situation first hand. As in other small Jewish communities, the burden devolved on a few individuals who did the best they could to maintain a school under, to say the least, difficult circumstances. Qualified teachers were harder to come by in that region because of the small size of the schools and their limited finances and facilities. To top it all, there had been no contact between schools, and every community laboured in isolation. As I visited the schools and spoke with the leaders, I wondered how much better the situation could have been if they had been given the necessary attention and help by a national organization.

As a consequence of my visit, all the schools in the area affiliated with Keren Hatarbut. Rabbis, school officials and principals became involved in its activities. Dr. Charles Oler, Board of Education chairman of Bet Israel's Talmud Torah in Halifax, was elected Regional Keren Hatarbut Vice-President. He, Rabbi Herbert Dobrinsky, Dr. Philip Simon of Glace-Bay, and D. Lubin of St. John, N.B. were the moving spirits of the region. The schools received all the services of Keren Hatarbut, including annual visits by the consultant-supervisor and, occasionally, by the national director.

Educational standards improved gradually. Especially fortunate were St. Johns, Nfld. and the Halifax Talmud Torah. By sheer coincidence, we were able to place in St. John's a teacher (Mr. Avraham Eisenberg) of a calibre that could be found only in some of the best schools. He did much for the community during the few years he stayed there. Halifax was in the midst of what seemed to be a futile search for a suitable principal when I received word from Zwi Horwich, who had gone again to live in Israel for a few years, that he wanted to return to serve in the field of Hebrew education in Canada. His years of service in Halifax were a blessing not only to its Talmud Torah but also to the development of Keren Hatarbut activities in the region.

By 1963, Keren Hatarbut had struck roots in the Maritimes, whose communities were then well on the way to becoming a vital, cohesive unit with Keren Hatarbut. During March 29-31 of that year, we held in Halifax a most successful regional conference, which augured well for the future. It adopted officially the principles and program of the Western region. There was already even talk of establishing a day school in Halifax. The progress of the region was reflected in the wide participation of its leadership in the gathering and in the Conference Agenda, which included such subjects as "Education For Jewish Living in Canada" (Rabbi A. Horowitz), "A Suggested Unified Curriculum for the Maritimes", (Zwi Horwich), "New Methods of Teaching Hebrew" (Ben-Zion Fishler), and "An Educational Cultural Program for the Maritimes" (Rabbi A. Horowitz, A. Feder, and Drs. C. Oler, S. Silver, and P. Simon).

As was the case throughout Canada, Keren Hatarbut served also at this conference not only as a catalyst, but also as a unifying force among divergent religious groupings. Delegates were delighted to see the representatives of Orthodox and Conservative congregations working together in harmony for the advancement of Hebrew education and culture.

The once flourishing Jewish community of Quebec City, where so outstanding an educator as Moshe Surchin had been school principal, was in a category by itself. Its geographical position prevented it from becoming part of a regional organization. At the invitation of its spiritual leader Rabbi Bernard H. Walfish, I visited Quebec for the first time at the end of 1956 to evaluate its educational program. A few months later, I was invited by the Community Board to discuss the entire situation with a view to ascertaining the ways in which Keren Hatarbut could be of help to them. We then included their school among our affiliates and offered them all our services, including visits by our consultant-supervisor.

Israel Answers Our Call for Teachers

As the teacher shortage reached crisis proportions, we called upon the Education Department of the Jewish Agency to initiate the teacher-exchange program I had discussed with them during my visit in 1956. We were also motivated by our conviction that even if there were no shortage, it was essential to employ a certain number of Israeli educators in our schools, "in order to bring Israel's spirit and influence to our children and to make a contribution towards our cherished goal of building cultural-spiritual bridges between Canadian Jewry and the State of Israel".

The Jewish Agency responded promptly and delegated to Canada eight teachers; four for Winnipeg, two for Edmonton, and two for Ottawa. At the same time, we made extraordinary efforts to recruit additional teachers especially for the small communities.

Surprisingly enough, we encountered opposition from two sources. Some local teachers were afraid of the competition that might result from a massive influx of teachers from Israel. Their fears were quickly allayed when we pointed out to them that such a situation was not likely to arise in our lifetime...

The stronger opposition came from the Education Committee of the C.J.C. Its chairman, Mr. Shamai Ogden, and Dr. Samuel Levine, its Secretary, called at our office some months following the Israeli teachers' arrival. The discussion started on the wrong foot. As I remember, it went thus:

— Who gave you permission to invite teachers from Israel?

— The Keren Hatarbut decided to initiate this project.

— The Congress is opposed to it. Why didn't you ask for our approval?

— Since when does Keren Hatarbut, an independent national organization, have to receive the approval of the Congress? What has Congress to do with the work of Keren Hatarbut anyway?

— Congress is the Parliament of the Jewish people in Canada.

— I do not recall ever having been given the opportunity to vote for my representative to this parliament.

I suggested that we discuss this matter as representatives of two independent organizations. We then proceeded to consider the possibilities of Keren Hatarbut affiliating with the Congress. We agreed on making the following recommendations to our respective organizations:

a) The Keren Hatarbut to form an integral part of the National Education Committee of congress and to participate in all its activities;

b) Keren Hatarbut to be accepted as an agency active in formal Jewish education for schools which are officially affiliated with it. No field services of the Keren Hatarbut would be required nor rendered for schools not affiliated with the Keren Hatarbut;

c) Congress field services to be avaialble to schools in Canada and communities which are not affiliated with the Keren Hatarbut and which wish to avail themselves of such services;

d) A common program be developed for joint action in areas of common interest, such as teacher welfare, etc;

e) The National Conference on Jewish Education to be all inclusive and to encompass every group interested in and working for the strengthening of Jewish education in Canada in whatever way it may be;

f) Full recognition be given to youth and adult activities of the Keren Hatarbut as an integral part of the all-out effort which the National Education Committee will make to strengthen youth and adult education."

Our executive approved these recommendations pending ratification by our next national convention.

There followed some correspondence between us and the Congress office on this matter. Unfortunately, the Congress did not respond with any action to bring about what might have been a fruitful partnership for the benefit of Hebrew education.

At a later time, following Mr. Brandwein's appointment as Director of the Jewish Teachers Seminary, he, Dr. Levine and I discussed the possibility of joint Congress and Keren Hatarbut sponsorship of the seminary. Regretfully, this did not materialize either.

The Israeli teachers were so successful that by 1963, within a period of six school years, we had brought over about seventy teachers from Israel, not including those who were invited directly by the Toronto Bureau of Jewish Education beginning in 1961, contrary to the agreement with the Jewish Agency that all such teachers be processed through Keren Hatarbut.

When we embarked on the teacher-exchange program, it was clear it would have to be centralized through one national office (the same as it was in Israel), in order to bring an end to competition and "raiding" between schools, to keep tabs on both schools and teachers, to facilitate visa processing (the Canadian Immigration Department, which was most cooperative, complimented us on our efficient coordination of this process), and — last but not least — to prevent the introduction into Canada of the party "key"-system prevalent in Israel. As a matter of fact, the director and, some months later, also the head of the Torah Department in Israel called at our office to persuade me to agree to the establishment of a liaison office of their own for the invitation of teachers through their department. I argued that it was not at all necessary to have two departments to serve the small Canadian Jewish community, that it would make for undesirable competition and disharmony, that the additional expense could be put to much better use, and — above all — that it had been made clear to our schools that we would follow their instructions regarding the department through which they would want us to invite their teachers. The Jewish Agency generally adhered to this agreement, so that we were in a position to report at the end of 1959 that, "this service has contributed greatly to the alleviation of the acute shortage of qualified teachers. It has given the schools, which have availed themselves of this very essential service, a feeling of security and relaxation; it has stabilized the situation in almost all the schools affiliated with our organization, especially in Western Canada, where educational institutions have been almost rid of the constant shifting of teachers, "raids" from other schools, and the fear of being left without teachers. Institutions that are in need of teachers, and are ready to make the necessary efforts, can now have the assurance that there is a national organization in Canada which will spare no efforts and leave no stone unturned in order to obtain for them qualified and experienced teachers."

The first "crack" appeared, as mentioned, in Toronto in 1961, when the Jewish Agency "forgot" our agreement. The next and more serious one came after the passing of Chief Rabbi Kravetz, when his successor ignored completely the Keren Hatarbut and started to invite teachers directly through the Torah Department.

Chief Rabbi Goren Assails Israeli Teachers

Some years following the initiation of our teacher-exchange program, I received an urgent request from Shazar to send him a comprehensive report on the Israeli teachers in Canada. The Anglo-Jewish press in the U.S.A. had reported a bristling attack by Rabbi Shlomo Goren on the Israeli teachers in the U.S.A. He claimed that they were not religious and that their general behaviour was not in harmony with the communities they served. Ben Gurion, too, I was told, was deeply disturbed and asked for a full report from the department of Education and Culture of the Jewish Agency. The gist of my reply was: I do not know how many East European teachers would be considered religious in accordance with Rabbi Goren's requirements. The general criterion in Canada was — attending Services on the Sabbath (very few attended on weekdays), refraining from driving on the Sabbath, and other such public manifestations. I knew teachers who were genuinely and fully observant, I knew a larger number who complied reluctantly, and I knew others who tried their very best to circumvent restrictions on their freedom. Generally speaking, Israeli teachers were free from the stifling atmosphere of East European communities; they had a strong sense of security, independence and professional pride. They were thus likely to be less apprehensive of what some individuals might think or say. From my own observations, I could attest that they knew how to conduct themselves in a manner that would not damage their relationships with the schools and communities, which, — by the way — differed widely in their outlook on "religious" matters. In any event, I said, we had no complaints whatsoever about any irreligious behavior. Aside from two serious disputes, there was generally extraordinary satisfaction with their work. Their work was invaluable in raising the standards of Hebrew education and in infusing a new spirit and enthusiasm in the schools and communities they served.

The two confrontations referred to: One case concerned the teacher assigned to Maimonides College in Winnipeg, who was also designated as the Keren Hatarbut representative in Western Canada. He was in constant conflict with the local Keren Hatarbut committee and ignored their decisions. He claimed that he was the highest and final authority by virtue of his being "the emissary from Jerusalem" ... We finally had to request the Jewish Agency to recall him. As a result, the department of Education did not delegate a replacement at its expense, and the Keren Hatarbut had to make good its financial commitment to Maimonides College out of its own budget.

The other case related to an excellent teacher in Vacouver. He claimed that the committee was not living up to the terms of their agreement. Al Gelmon, Chairman of the Board of Education, exercised unusual patience and tact, and even agreed with my comment that "where there is a choice between an excellent teacher who is somewhat troublesome and an ineffective one who never disturbs the committee's equanimity. I would readily be troubled a little..."

In my correspondence with the teacher, it was evident that it was difficult to put up with his arrogance and abrasive manner. In my attempt to assist in reaching an amicable solution, I tried to explain to the teacher our realities, and pleaded with him to show some patience for the sake of our "sacred work". His swift reaction was: My name is Amige, meaning my nation is proud. I am a proud independent Sabrah, who "whistles" on you, the Keren Hatarbut and your values. He used the word *Metsaftsef*, whistle, the colloquial meaning of which is to deride. In my final reply to him, I repeated my advice that he patiently and peacably seek an amicable solution. I added, "If you whistle, others too could whistle," and — quoting from High Holiday liturgy — the disagreement will end in *"Eilu Ve'eilu Betsiftsuf Metsaftsefim"*, these and those will whistle together. (The translation in the prayer book is "whisper", referring to "all created beings who shout with joy and whisper together, The Lord Shall Be King." The colloquial connotation is "we will whistle on one another"...) The matter was settled agreeably, but the teacher went on to greener fields at the end of the year.

Advancing Teachers' Qualifications

Igud's most significant contribution was probably its Summer Seminar and Yemei Iyun (workshop), which were nurtured in their early years by Chaim Brenman, Shmuel Lerner and Chaim Spillberg. The Seminar was held for four weeks in the Laurentians, away from the hustle and bustle of the city. It served primarily teachers from smaller communities who were given an opportunity to increase their knowledge, to learn new teaching methods, to exchange views and experiences with colleagues from across the country, to add to their repertoire new Israeli songs and dances, and to enjoy, at the same time, a relaxed and pleasant social atmosphere. The workshop took place in Montreal for a few days following the Seminar. It was intended for principals and educators from Montreal, Toronto and nearby communities.

Following amalgamation, this program was augmented with teachers workshops (primarily in the West and, some years later, also in the Maritimes) and, for some period, with special weekly seminars for Montreal educators who wanted to enhance their knowledge and improve their teaching methods. This Seminar was conducted by Chaim Brandwein.

Following the 1957 Regina Conference, the Summer Seminar fulfilled another important function. It provided non-certified teachers with the opportunity to continue their studies until such time as the Seminar authorities and the supervisor, who observed them at work in their schools, recommended them for certification by the Keren Hatarbut. Attendance at the seminar was obligatory for uncertified teachers of our affiliated schools. During the period of 1957-1964 about eighty teachers from about forty schools of thirty communities participated in one or more seasons of the Seminar. In all, about 175 teachers were accommodated during this period and a significant number were awarded permanent Teacher-Certificates.

The faculty and lecturers included noted scholars and educators such as L. Leideker, professors Samuel Blumenfield and Waxman, Shimon Dunsky, Aharon Rosenne and Ben-Zion Fishler. Members of the Israeli Diplomatic Corps lectured on Israeli life and culture. Much was added to the life of the institution by such popular singing instructors as Miriam Denburg, Emmanuel Bach and Yehuda Weinberg. The closing exercises developed into a widely celebrated annual cultural event in the Laurentians.

Crossing a Bridge to Israel

In 1958, we initiated another project of advanced studies for teachers, and for strengthening cultural links with Israel. A group of ten teachers from various parts of the country formed a Canadian section of a large Conference and Tour Project sponsored by the Department of Education and Culture of the Jewish Agency in New York. They spent three weeks in study and tours in Israel, and participated in the World Conference on Jewish Education convened by the Department of Education of the Jewish Agency. We also started to encourage young teachers to spend a year or more at the Chaim Greenberg Teachers Institute in Jerusalem. The first one to go there was Shimon Rein for the academic year 1960-61.

The Bible — A Cornerstone of Jewish Life

The Bible returned Home with the Return of the Exiles. It occupies a primary place in the education and spiritual life of modern Israel. The Israeli Bible Society inaugurated an annual Bible contest for adults in which participated contestants from all parts of the country. Later, it included participants — Jews and non-Jews — from other countries. Its popularity is so great that it has been compared to the Super Bowl game. Thousands of people flock to these contests, which are held in the presence of the Prime Minister, the Chief of Staff, top government and communal leaders, and many scholars. Ben Gurion and Shazar were among its greatest enthusiasts.

Popularizing the Bible in the Diaspora

In 1960, a Bible Contest was introduced by the Department of Education and Culture of the Jewish Agency in Jewish schools in the U.S.A., and by the Keren Hatarbut in Canadian Hebrew schools. It became one of the most popular and successful annual projects. Canadian students have distinguished themselves from time to time at the Finals of the North American Contest held in New York.

In 1963, the Israeli Bible Society, in conjunction with the Ministry of Education and the Jewish Agency, inaugurated a World Bible Contest for teenagers, held annually in Jerusalem. We learned about it from the press, and did not plan to participate because of financial limitations. A few months before the contest, I received an urgent message from Dr. Samuel Blumenfield that Shazar thought it was important for Canada to participate in the First World Bible Contest. When I told him that we could not afford it, he suggested that the Jewish Agency, the Israeli Consulate in Montreal and the Keren Hatarbut should each cover a third of the expenses. I immediately contacted the Consul General of Israel, who told me in an angry tone that as far as he was concerned there was no such contest, because he had not been directly contacted about it. I pointed out that we too had no prior direct information and no one should stand on ceremony about such an important project. He was adamant in his refusal to have anything to do with it. We therefore had to obtain a third of the expenses from a few individuals.

Canadian Teenager Crowned First World Bible Champion

I started to search for a student with sufficient Bible knowledge who would be ready to make the trip on short notice. I came upon the name of David Goldmitz, a former Massad camper, who had scored First in our Canadian contest in the previous year. Since David was a student of Herzliah High School in Montreal, I enlisted Melech Magid's help in persuading David's parents to allow him to make the trip. We were happily surprised when we were cabled the news that David, who was the youngest of the contestants, tied for first place and became First World Bible Champion, together with an Israeli contestant. I personally was profoundly disappointed that Canadian "organized Jewry" showed much less interest in this "score" than it surely would have shown had David scored in a national ball game. Even my Keren Hatarbut president thought I had gone overboard by visiting David at his home to congratulate him and his parents.

Keren Hatarbut Moves to a New Home

The small building at 5815 Jeanne-Mance, which had come as a salvation a decade earlier, had now become grossly inadequate even as administrative headquarters. It was not only drab, dark and depressing, but the rooms were also too small to be used as classrooms for Hebrew courses. When our President, Solomon Gordon, visited me in my office upon my resumption of the directorship of the organization, I remarked about the comparatively luxurious offices and facilities I had enjoyed in Israel. He remarked caustically, "In Israel, they have a rich uncle..." This time, Mr. J. Margulis, the treasurer, came to the rescue. Largely through his efforts, we secured new headquarters at 5234 Clanranald Ave. (across the street from the Chevrah Kadisha-B'nai Jacob synagogue) which was more suitable also because of its central location. However, while the problem of lack of office and classroom space was partially solved, the lack of a hall for lectures and social acitivities continued to hamper us.

He Came to Learn but He Taught

Another incident pointed up the crucial need of bridging the gap of understanding between Americans and israelis. I was discussing our plans with Daniel Bell, then editor of Fortune Magazine. We spoke about U.S.A.-Israeli relations. By way of illustrating the "I know it all" attitude of Israelis he had met, Bell pointed to the chair I was sitting in, saying, "A few weeks ago I had another Israeli guest sitting in this chair. Eliezer Livneh (one of the better intellectual Mapai theoreticians) was here to speak to me about the U.S.A. He said he had been asked by Ben-Gurion to spend about a year here in order to learn at first hand about American life and institutions. He therefore wanted to hear from me about certain matters and problems. Without giving me a chance to open my mouth, *he* proceeded to tell *me* all about America! He came to learn and found himself teaching!

Bell too thought the World Seminar was a worthwhile project. He agreed to attend if time and prior commitments would permit.

A Responsive Lady

The montreal committee was one of the most productive, thanks largely to the enthusiasm and cooperation of its chairman B.M. Bloomfield and his brother Major L.M. Bloomfield. They went to work immediately, and endeavoured to enlist the support of various synagogues and fraternal organizations in setting up scholarships. Major Bloomfield arranged for me a meeting with Lady Davis, a philanthropist and benefactor of educational institutions. He cautioned me to refrain from speaking to her about financial contributions. I assured him that I personally never discuss such matters with individuals I try to interest in Bet-Berl. My meeting with Lady Davis was a memorable one. She was keenly interested in Israel's progress, and asked about its educational and scientific institutions. She evinced an interest in our projects, especially in the World Seminar. We parted without any mention of specific contributions for the Institute. I was then invited to meet her a second time. This time, she inquired what she could do in support of our program. I suggested she might consider awarding a fellowship for a distinguished Canadian scholar to attend the Seminar. She decided there and then to do so.

In 1973, many years after the demise of the grandiose Bet Berl plans, the Lady Davis Fellowship Trust came into operation. Its main stated objective is "to make the cultural heritage of ancient and modern Israel, its achievement and development, state building, scholarship, science and education widely available and known to people from both technologically advanced and evolving societies. By providing the means for scholars of various disciplines and nationalities to study, perform research, or teach at the Hebrew University of Jerusalem or the Technion in Israel, it hopes to serve that objective, and to advance the interests of international scholarship and of higher education in Israel.

During 1973-77, the Lady Davis Fellowship Trust made 214 awards, "aiding young scientists and scholars from Israel and abroad in furthering their training and research, and bringing to Israel a number of established academics from various disciplines who, as Lady Davis Visiting Professors, have used the support of the Fellowships both to pursue their research and to participate in Israel's scholarly and scientific life, thus contributing to that cross-fertilization of ideas and outlook envisaged in the Lady Davis Fellowship Trust's charter".

This single trust fund is a salutary example of the achievements that result from the faith and devotion of such people as the Bloomfields, who were the moving spirit behind a fund made possible by the understanding and generosity of a great lady.

˙ Our search for the best possible candidates for the Institute brought to light several incidents of *Kin'at Sofrim* (scholars' jealousy). The most noteworthy of these incidents was when Baruch (Barry) Margulis came to my office to interview and "size me up" in order to decide whether it would be worthwhile for him to attend the Institute. A Hebrew school principal had told him it would be a waste of time for a serious and bright student like him ... Baruch graduated from the Institute, was active in the Hebrew Youth Movement, and rose to the position of head counselor, before he proceeded to specialize in Bible studies at Brandeis University and at the Hebrew University in Jerusalem. He married a Sabrah, and is now on the faculty of Haifa University where he teaches Bible.

Institute Grows Seven Fold in Seven Years

Following the first year of its existence, the *Machon Le'madrichim* (as the Leadership Institute was called in Hebrew) was moved to Massad Alef primarily because of the inadequate facilities at Massad Bet. As the registration for the second year had already reached fifty(!!), it was necessary to build three new bunks in Massad Alef.

Convinced that we were facing a period of growth both in the camp and the Machon, I proposed that we build a second camp unit (acorss the road from the original camp-site) specifically for the accommodation of the Machon. My proposal was first met with opposition from some of the Massad Board members. Their two strongest and apparently valid arguments were: How can we assume the financial burden of a new camp while we have not as yet paid the outstanding debts for the old one?

Furthermore, where will we get the personnel for another camp when we find it difficult to staff the existing camp? My reply that "we will have to borrow the necessary funds and that we will train our own staff" was received with sarcastic smiles. One member, Mr. Chaim Maizel, went even so far as to declare: "This is not 1946. We are all older now, and you, Rabbi Horowitz, are also too old and tired, (I was forty-five years old at the time) to undertake such enormous tasks!" I told Mr. Maizel; "Speak for yourself! I am not at all old and tired, and am ready for the challenge". The Board was bold enough to borrow about thirty-five thousand dollars and to proceed at once with the construction of the new camp.

A Song of Dedication

Beyond all expectations, the new camp was completed in time for the 1958 season. The official dedication was one of the most memorable I have ever witnessed. The site was beautifully decorated. Canadian and Israeli flags and appropriate posters adorned the gates and the buildings. It was a joy to see the hundreds of campers, their parents, and hundreds of guests streaming towards the platform that was built out of doors for the occasion. Some of those who had laboured for the realization of what seemed a dream had tears in their eyes at the sight of over a thousand children, youth and adults rising as one to sing songs of dedication. Leaders of the Keren Hatarbut and of the Montreal Jewish community expressed their elation about the emergence of an important new institution for the cultivation of future leaders. The Consul General of Israel, Dr. Michael Simon, stated that he was nearly moved to tears to see and hear so many boys and girls speaking Hebrew and imbued with the spirit of our National Rebirth.

We soon had two completely self-sufficient camps, camp Emek for elementary-school pupils, and Camp Galil for high-school students. At age fourteen, campers entered the Machon, which was now based on three seasons of intensive training. In addition, they were required to attend the Leadership Institute in the city throughout the three years of preparation. When I first explained these requirements to the Machon candidates, I was challenged with the argument, "You always tell us that we can participate in activities of the Youth Movement without any obligation to attend the Leadership Institute in the city. You always say that you believe in freedom and self-motivation. Now you are telling us that we must attend the Machon in the city". My answer was, "You don't have to do anything, but if you want to be on the camp staff, you have to prepare for your chosen tasks just as teachers, nurses and doctors have to prepare for theirs."

Both Camp Emek and Camp Galil made rapid progress. By 1963, they reached a total of two hundred and forty-nine campers, a hundred and eight of whom were members of the Machon.

Our problem now was not a shortage of campers, but rather a lack of space for the accommodation of their increasing numbers. I could have reminded the committee of the arguments we had had upon my return to Massad, when I had been absolutely opposed to continuing the practice of engaging a paid canvasser or canvassers to recruit campers. I had insisted that the only way to succeed and grow was by making our camps so good that kids and parents alike would "knock at our doors"...

Financially, the camp started to make a significant annual profit, even after deducting a substantial amount for "Depreciation of Fixed Assets".

In very large measure, the camps succeeded because the kids started to think of them as *their* camps. Campers knew they could look forward to becoming junior counselors and counselors and advancing to higher positions, even as high as head counselors and directors. The general spirit was so enthusiastic that Massad competed with the most prestigious camps in the Laurentians. Campers were aware that theirs was not a private camp for personal profit but a vital institution that really belonged to them and to future generations. Massad therefore excelled not only in the educational and social areas but also in sports. Our kids won in almost all sports games they played against camps whose purpose or specialty was sports!

By the early sixties, we already provided the entire staff (except for the occasional specialty counselor or counselors) for Massad Alef and the Machon, and we could already spare some for other camps. Nor did we have to look frantically anymore for directors from the U.S.A. Our own *Massadnicks* took over completely. Some of those who held the highest positions during that period were: Dr. Chaim Solomon, now a resident of Israel; Israel Rosenberg, now practicing law in Israel; Moshe (Norman) May, LL.B. Chairman of the Canada-Israel committee; Yigal Horowitz, nuclear physicist on the faculty of Ben Gurion University at Be'er-Sheva; Yitzchak (Irwin) Cotler, Professor of International Law at McGill University, and Baruch (Barry) Margulis, now on the faculty of Haifa University.

Bine'Areinu U'Vezkeneinu Nelech — With Our Young And With Our Old We Will Go (Exodus 10:9)

"And he shall turn the heart of the fathers to the children,
"And the heart of the children to their fathers" (Malachi 3:24)

As in other areas of our activites, we used every possible opportunity to bring together parents and children. The Camp Reunion had been held in previous years (primarily for campers) at the Adath-Israel Hall. It became too small to contain any longer the increasing numbers of campers. Moreover, we turned the affair into a celebration by and for the campers and their parents. The Reunion was therefore shifted to the Ball Room of the Mt. Royal Hotel until it too became inadequate. The Queen Elizabeth Hotel then became the scene of our annual reunion. By the early sixties, about a thousand children, youth and adults participated in what developed into one of the most outstanding cultural events in the community, which was given wide coverage in the media, including television. The scramble for admission tickets was so great that we had to limit them to a fixed number for each family. The program consisted of two parts. Adults and children first met in separate halls. Campers and counselors "relived" some of the season's highlights, while parents had the opportunity to socialize, to hear reports and make comments. The doors of the adjacent salons were then opened and the entire audience was treated to an appropriate program, which included an outstanding feature every year. One year saw the presentation of a Hebrew play, *Cherev Shlomo* (King Solomon's Sword), which had been directed at camp by an Israeli creative dramatist, Mrs. Biela Lepkin. The campers' acting, their Hebrew diction and fluency, and the dazzling costumes and scenery (products of the camps' arts and crafts workshop), made a tremendous impression upon the audience. Another year, we invited Shlomo Carlebach to make real *freilech*, to lift our spirits even higher with joyous, ecstatic chassidic songs. Another time, a 16mm sound film, "A Dream Came True", was featured. The film unfolded the history and development of the camp through the reminiscences of a young man who had been a camper in Massad from the first year of its existence and rose to the position of its head counsellor. It was filmed at Massad by Mr. Tolly Reviv, producer of Tolea Films Inc., who charged us only for materials and labor.

Massad Bet

Some of the factors that contributed to the phenomenal success of Massad Alef were absent in Toronto. Mr. Wilfred Gordon, Q.C., who was President of Massad for a number of years, was wont to say: "The fellows in Montreal are big heroes. Let them lend us the national director even for one year only, and we will show them what we can do!" While the lack of a full-time director made it impossible for the Toronto camp to make the same strides as the Montreal camp, Toronto suffered from additional impediments. In Montreal, both Keren Hatarbut and Massad were led by one and the same Board. To most of its members, the Hebrew Movement was their first, if not their only, love. In Toronto, where Keren Hatarbut and Massad were managed by diferent Boards, people like Wilfred Gordon, Sam Sigler, Leon Sharon, David Newman, Rose Hersh and Abe Richmond were deeply involved, some more and some less, in other organizations. That may be one of the reasons that they could never muster enough support to engage a full-time director.

And the absence of a person who could devote all his time to the Movement was probably an important factor in their failure to develop and maintain a strong, permanent Hebrew Youth Movement. The camp committee did put forth much effort within the limitations of their situation, and the camp did make continuous progress, slow though it was. By 1963, the committee succeeded, with the assistance of a loan from the Z.O.C. and a Keren Hatarbut subsidy, in building a new recreation hall and in improving some of the facilities. For a while, it seemed that the committee had gained new impetus and that the camp would continue to progress. However, in my final official report (dated August 12, 1964), I had to report "with great regret that Massad Bet was not opened for the season of 1964. It should be mentioned that inspite of the continuous help and financial assistance by head office, the committee in Toronto did not succeed in interesting a sufficiently large and effective group of people who could assume the obligations necessary for the maintenance and development of the camp."

Massad Gimel

Winnipeg was fortunate to have a few people to whom Massad was their first love. If it be true that an institution is the extended shadow of one person, Massad Gimel was the extended shadow of Leona Billinkoff. In 1960, the three-week camp season was extended to two three-week camp periods, and the number of campers reached a high point of about a hundred and seventy. About twenty-five applicants had to be turned away in 1962 because of lack of space. That year, the camp was officially incorporated as a branch of Hebrew Camps Massad of Canada. In addition to the devoted, hard-working committee who, among other things, succeeded in raising annually about five thousand dollars for scholarships, the camp benefitted from the cooperation and financial assistance of the local Zionist Cultural Institute, conceived and headed by Sam Drache, Q.C.

Massad Gimel was also fortunate in having a continuous leadership in the staff and programming areas. Gad Horowitz, who had received his initial experience in Massad Alef, became the Program Director in 1959, served as assistant to director Ben Zion Cohen in 1960, and continued as director from 1961 to 1965 inclusive. According to Leona Billinkoff, it was he who created and nurtured the camp program, which continued to serve as the model in succeeding years, and it was during that period that the Hebraization of the camp reached its zenith. Keren Hatarbut contributed to Massad Gimel's great success by providing it with various educational materials, by granting scholarships annually to some of its senior campers to enable them to attend the National Leadership Institute and to participate in the Youth Tour to Israel. These boys and girls then became an asset to the camp by serving on its staff. In the early sixties, we started to send to Massad Gimel annually, at our expense, one of our brightest and most capable youth leaders. In 1961 we delegated Chaim (Charles) Dalfen, now Vice-President of the CRTC, to serve as assistant director. In 1962, we sent Yaakov (Jack) Brandes, now psychiatrist at Mt. Sinai Hospital in Toronto, to act as assistant director, and in 1963 we sent David Brandes, now a film maker in Los Angeles, to serve as Drama Director. All three were of great value to the Camp program.

The Challenge of Youth

"Train up a child in the way he should go,
And even when he is old he will not depart from it" (Proverbs 22:6)
The real meaning of this proverb is lost in the translation. The Hebrew *"al pi darko"* means in *accordance* with *his* way. In the Hebrew original the effectiveness of a youth's training depends on whether it is done in accordance with his abilities and desires; in the English translation it is the "trainer" who alone determines the "training" process. Guided by this exhortation and by the Talmudic statement that "only the lesson which is enjoyed can be learned well", we took into consideration the capacities, needs and desires of our youth in the formulation of their program. We also had to take into account the motivations and interests of teenagers who were members of the Movement without any involvement as campers or future counsellors in Massad.

During the summers when I was unable to personally direct the camp or the Machon because my attention and presence were needed also in our other summer projects, I spent between two and three weeks at camp, in order to interview all the members of the machon and camp staff. I discussed with all of them, individually, the extent of their participation in the activities in the city, the type of camp work they wished to prepare for, and the role — if any — they wished to play in the youth movement. Those who were continuing their formal Hebrew education, I advised to participate in such groups as drama, choir and dancing. The others, I advised to give priority to study and discussion groups. All those who aspired to serve at camp were required to take courses designed for training in camp and youth leadership.

I used to look forward to these meetings. They afforded me an opportunity to become more closely acquainted with our young people. They were free to spend as much time with me as they liked, to express their opinions about the camp and the movement, and to offer suggestions. The atmosphere was completely informal; we kibbitzed and exchanged quips and anecdotes. I recall my conversation with a fourteen year-old who told me that since he was going to continue his formal Hebrew education, he would be able to attend only the leadership course, adding, "but I will not give up the dance group." At that, I remarked,

"Apparently you like girls!" His big, beautiful, dark eyes lit up as he exclaimed emphatically, "Rabbi, we *all* like girls! The only difference is that some of us admit it and some of us don't". (I was once criticized by the orthodox camp director for walking around the camp grounds without a *kipah*. I asked him which was the more serious offence, dancing with girls or walking around without a *kipah*. When he gave me the right answer, "dancing with girls," I asked him, "Why then do you dance with girls?" "That," he chuckled, "I like too much to forego!" "In that case," I said, "yours too is a 'religion of convenience'. You make your selections and I make mine.")

Just as the Youth Movement played an important role in Massad's success, so did Massad contribute greatly to the flourishing of the Youth Movement. It grew so rapidly that by 1963, it reached a total of about three hundred high school and university students. All the studies, lectures and activities were, of course, conducted in Hebrew, except the course in Child Psychology (relating to camping), which was given by Dr. Douglas J. Wilson in English, because there was at that time no psychologist in montreal who could lecture in Hebrew. If there were today a Hebrew Youth Movement in Montreal or elsewhere in Canada, many graduates of Massad and the machon could lecture in Hebrew on a variety of subjects. As to psychology, I can think at the moment of Dr. Peter Shizgal in Montreal, Dr. Jack Brandes in Toronto, Susanna Dalfen (Cohen) in Ottawa, and Dr. Shulamit Denburg (Dalfen) in Hamilton.

We also started to involve our youth in our adult activities. For example, one of the main features at the oneg-Shabbat at our National Convention in 1960 was a symposium by Sarah Rafman, Yitzchak Cotler, Baruch Margulis and Moshe May on "Canadian Jewish Youth As We See It". Dr. Samuel Blumenfield, who spoke that evening on "Our Youth — Will It Remain With Us?", observed that the calibre of the participants in the symposium and the presence of so large a number of Hebrew-speaking youth might indicate part of the answer to his question.

Most youth organizations of such scope commanded the services of a full, or, at least, part-time director and of paid youth leaders, but our ten different groups, which met regularly once weekly, and all the other activities such as Ongei-Shabbat, Holiday celebrations, and Winter Seminars in St-Agathe, functioned effectively without any paid help. (One of the ten groups consisted of younger campers. Yerachmiel Cohen, at that time a young counsellor and now acting curator of Jewish art at the Israel Museum in Jerusalem, organized and led it on his own initiative.) Furthermore, group and discussion leaders from within the Hebrew Youth Movement, such as Dr. Chaim Solomon, Norman May, Irwin Cotler, Leah Kilbrick and Nurit Oko, volunteered their free services. Only professional lecturers and teachers received honoraria.

If the fact that we did not pay our youth leaders did not affect our activities, the shortage of funds to pay the professionals, and the lack of adequate headquarters did hamper our work seriously. I was once both pleased and embarassed when Mr. Yoseph Shapiro, Director of Brit Ivrit Olamit (World Hebrew Union), visited us in Montreal and offered what amounted to a token contribution. I told him of our financial difficulties and "homelessness", and that we would have to discontinue the youth choir because our meagre budget made it impossible for us to maintain it. A few days later, he was a guest at our annual Simchat Torah Celebration, where he witnessed the presentation of certificates to twenty eight graduates of the Machon, who, together with other members of the Youth Movement, presented a beautiful Hebrew program to an audience of hundreds of people, about a hundred and fifty of whom were high-school and university students. He was so impressed that he made a "special effort" to grant us the five hundred dollars we needed for the continuation of the choir. I was embarassed that financial help had to come to us all the way from Jerusalem, but was pleased that it did come... However, the greatest obstacle, especially in our youth work, was our "homelessness". I quote from my official report of december 31, 1962:

"...Everybody speaks piously about the importance of our youth and the necessity for continuing their Hebrew education. Well, Keren Hatarbut has succeeded in gathering around itself many teenagers and young people who are ready to be part of a youth movement, one of whose main activities consist of Hebrew studies, such as Tanach, Hebrew Literature, Zionism and Modern Israel. This is no mean achievement, and we did not come by it easily... And the sad fact is that — with all the beautiful and costly buildings of the Jewish community in Montreal — there are no adequate accommodations for the Hebrew Movement and particularly for its Hebrew youth activities. A few examples will suffice: 1) Ongei Shabbat must be held in Private homes because of the lack of our own hall; 2) it took us about three months until we succeeded in obtaining — at a proper rental — a room for our dance group; 3) we hope secretly that not all the members will come to the Sunday discussion meetings, so that the small rooms will accommodate all the participants (unfortunately, our prayers are not always answered!); 4) our kids succeeded in obtaining the hall of a local synagogue for their Annual Chanukah Celebration. After all preparations had been made, they were told they could not have the hall, because there would be a wedding a few days later and the people in charge did not want to be bothered with cleaning the hall again. These conditions create many unnecessary difficulties and affect seriously our youth work. This is not said in the spirit of criticism of other organizations, but rather to emphasize that, unless something is done — and soon — what we have won through very hard thinking, planning and work will be lost to us. We have decided to record it here, because this Report is submitted to all individuals and organizations that bear or should bear the responsibility for the Hebrew Movement"...

The situation did not change. Lectures that were co-sponsored with other organizations were held in their halls. The others continued to take place at various congregations. With the assistance of Rabbi David Roth of Chevrah-Kadisha-Bnai-Jacob, its doors were opened to most of the activities of our youth movement.

Building a Youth-Bridge to Israel

As early as the second year of Massad's existence, when I was convinced of its permanence, I started to speak about the importance of sending some of our youth for a summer of study and experience in Israel. Our National President, Moshe Surchin, cautioned me against initiating this project because he thought it would affect attendance at Massad. I told him that there are enough children and youth for more than one Massad and for visits to Israel! Exactly a decade later, in 1958, I broached the matter to the *shaliach* (emissary) of the Youth and Chalutz Department. I told him it would be necessary to offer partial scholarships, especially to participants who would have the additional cost of transportation from distant cities to Montreal. He immediately promised an allocation of three thousand dollars. A few months later, when I informed him of our success in organizing a group of seventeen boys and girls for the visit, he confessed that he had been hasty with his promise because he hadn't really believed we would be able to recruit the required minimum of fifteen. Although he now had the problem of getting the allocation, he would make every effort to fulfill his promise, which he did.

That summer, for the first time in three years, I allowed myself to take a week's vacation. I gave my telephone number to my secretary but told her to call me only in case of emergency. It didn't take long before I got an urgent call from her that parents were demanding the immediate return of their children because of the deteriorating security situation in Israel. We were ready to fulfill their wishes, but the kids wouldn't budge. They phoned their parents to reassure them of their safety. They came back full of enthusiasm and inspiration. They pointed out, "with sadness rather than with pride", that they were the first and only *Hebrew speaking* youth group from the Diaspora to have visited Israel. The people in charge there had complimented them on their knowledge of Hebrew and Yahadut, their seriousness and their general conduct. Becuase of their knowledge of Hebrew, they were in a much better position to understand the life and problems of the country and to communicate with Israelis in their own language. Some of the kids commented on the difficulties of non-Hebrew-speaking groups in realy understanding what was happening around them, and "on the tragedy of a people without a common tongue".

A Summer in Israel Equals Two Seasons in Massad

When we started the Israel Youth Tour Project I recalled my statement ten years earlier that a season at Massad was preferable to a whole year even in a Day School. Upon the assessment of the effect the Israel Tour had on the group, I expressed my opinion that a summer in Israel was worth two seasons at Massad. My view was confirmed recently when Ross (Avraham) Rudolph of Edmonton, now Professor of Political Science at York University in Toronto, allowed me to read the detailed diary he had kept during the duration of the Project. It revealed not only the knowledge, the insights and the experiences this adolescent gained, but even more so the profound sense of identity it gave him with the rich ancient-new culture and spirit of his people. I venture to say that if a study were made today of the more than a hundred youngsters who participated in this project during 1958-64, it would be found that what they learned and experienced in Israel broadened their horizons and helped them "find themselves" when they were on the threshold of their search for a synthesis of their Canadian and Jewish identities. As to those who later chose to build their future in Israel (it would be interesting to know how many of them made this choice), it would be found that their initial visit contributed to their striking of permanent roots in their adopted country.

Revolution in Methods of Teaching Hebrew

During my visit in Israel in 1956, when we inaugurated the teacher exchange program, I met Mr. Aharon Rosenne, a master teacher of adults and a pioneer in the development of the now famous Ulpan methods of teaching Hebrew to adults. I was surprised when he made what seemed to me the presumptuous statement that by using his methods, one could enable students to carry on simple conversations in Hebrew by imparting 500 basic words in a short period of four weeks of intensive study. His conditions included: the students should be complete beginners; a commitment to do their homework faithfully; two-hour sessions six days weekly, and a maximum of twenty students in each class. I took up the challenge and, through further negotiations with the Department of Education of the Jewish Agency, they agreed to make this experiment in *Canada*, "because the Hebrew courses there are better organized and centralized than in any other country in the Diaspora."

Mr. Rosenne was loaned to us for a period of three months, with the idea that he should spend one month in Montreal, one in Toronto and one in Winnipeg. (Rosenne stayed only two weeks in Winnipeg. He had to return to Israel for personal reasons. His work was continued by the Israeli exchange-teachers.) We abided by all his conditions, save one. We could not resist the clamour of candidates to attend his courses. In Montreal, we exceeded the maximum of twenty by ten, in Toronto they accepted forty two, and in Winnipeg they settled for thirty seven. There was unanimity on Mr. Rosenne's exceptional success. From Toronto, Joseph Klinger wrote, "Mr. Rosenne's method has been very successful here, and there is a great deal of interest on the part of many people to take an intensive course in Hebrew. We are now about to open two new *ulpanim* and are introducing his method in all our classes." The Winnipeg report by Mr. Melvin Fenson, read in part: "The class was an exceptional success. The questionnaires filled in by the students indicate unanimous enthusiasm." Upon the completion of Mr. Rosenne's course in Winnipeg, thirty two of the original thirty seven continued to study Hebrew twice weekly. Reporting for Montreal, I can say that the replacement of the old method, which was based on translation and grammatical drill, by Mr. Rosenne's live conversational method, opened a new era for our Hebrew courses. No longer did we have the many dropouts in the middle of the year; students had a sense of achievement because of the focus on conversation, and ever larger numbers continued to take advanced courses, including Bible, Hebrew Literature and the course leading to the Jerusalem Examination. Because the emphasis shifted to living conversational Hebrew, we succeeded in bringing together all the students for various joint affairs and Holiday celebrations, where they presented their own programs entirely in Hebrew.

While in Montreal, Mr. Rosenne gave a series of lecture-demonstrations that were open to all teachers in the community. Incidentally, only by paying the instructors of our courses half of their regular fee did we prevail upon them to attend Rosenne's lessons throughout the month, in order to master his methods.

Hebrew Self-Taught

In view of Mr. Rosenne's unusual success, I suggested to him that he prepare a special text-book for use in our courses. The text he prepared, "Hebrew Self-Taught", is based on his book "Elef Milim" and contains five hundred basic Hebrew words. The lessons are in the form of conversations, and each lesson is preceded by a translated and transliterated vocabulary-list. As its title suggests, the text was intended also for people who could not attend classes, including those who lived in small communities where no teachers were available. The book was so popular that its first edition of two thousand copies was soon out of print. To meet the increasing demand for it, we published a second edition in 1962. Until this day, I recommend this book especially to students who wish to acquire a rudimentary reading and speaking knowledge in a short period of time. The book, which was first published in Canada by the Keren Hatarbut, is now obtainable only in its U.S.A.

edition, consisting of two parts of two hundred and fifty words each, from the Histradut Ivrit of America.

In 1962, the Department of Education and Culture of the American Zionist Council produced twelve T.V. films of Hebrew lessons with Rosenne as the teacher. We acquired them, televised them in Montreal, and offered them for use to all our branches.

Our joint program with the 'Y' started with two classes and grew to seven within two years. Our partnership was not confined to Hebrew courses, but expanded to lecture series, exhibits, holiday celebrations, and special events that attracted hundreds of people. The C.J.C. joined us in sponoring some of these outstanding cultural events. The 'Y' took on a new look. Hebrew speech, music, dance and drama were heard within its portals. The peak in our partnership was reached in March 1960 when Mrs. Evelyn Shapiro, chairman of the "Y's" Education Committee, dedicated a special room at the Snowdon Branch "as the initial stage in the development of a center of Hebrew learning and culture and of a section of Hebrew books in the library, to be developed jointly by the 'Y' and Keren Hatarbut". On that occasion, attended by an audience of over three hundred and fifty, one of the adult Hebrew classes presented a dramatic reading; the Hadassah choir and soprano Belva Boroditzky presented Hebrew musical selections; the dance group of the Hebrew Youth Movement staged Israeli dances, and Ehud Ben-Yehudah, son of the father of modern Hebrew, Eliezer Ben-Yehudah, spoke on "Hebrew From Cradle to Statehood". It is noteworthy that Arthur Rotman, who is now Executive Vice President of the Jewish Welfare Board of America, is doing much, with the assistance of the Department of Education and Culture of the Jewish Agency, to make Hebrew an integral part of his organization's program.

Hebraization of the Diaspora

The Department of Education and Culture of the Jewish Agency and the Brit Ivrit Olamit declared the Tenth Anniversary of the State of Israel as Hebraization Year. Their communications spoke of "Hebraizing the Diaspora". They envisioned masses of people learning Hebrew, and suggested that we focus our efforts on "entire families studying in Hebrew at their homes". Knowing our realities better than the armchair strategists in Jerusalem, we proceeded to formulate our own plans. We communicated with our branches and with all the congregations and schools in the country. We offered them our assistance in organizing as many Hebrew classes as possible "as a gift to the State of Israel" (the slogan used by the Israeli sponsors), on its Tenth Birthday. In Montreal, we mailed a special letter, with enclosed registration cards, to approximately ten thousand five hundred homes. And we embarked on an intensive campaign to publicize the project through the media in general and the Anglo-Jewish press in particular.

As a "gift to Canadian Jewry", the sponsors sent us at their expense four *ulpan* experts to help us in the implementation of the project during a period of six months. We delegated one of them, Yitzchak Yod Cohen, to Toronto, where he was active in the whole sphere of Keren Hatarbut activities. In addition to conducting *ulpanim*, he became the moving spirit of several Hebrew speaking groups (named after Elizer Ben-Yehudah), which were formed largely through the efforts of Hadassah leaders Helen Smolack, Rose Dolgoff and Rose Ehrenberg. The Central Zionist Region, too, through its representatives Mr. Leon Sharon and Dr. George Liban, Chairman of Hebrew Culture Activities and regional Executive Director respectively, contributed to the success of the project. Largely through the efforts of Yoseph Klinger, Toronto excelled, in some years even more than Montreal, in the number of adults who studied Hebrew, exceeding at times the three hundred mark. The Hebrew speaking *chugim* , which afforded their members an opportunity to make use of their Hebrew studies, were so popular that Mr. Cohen was requested to remain in Toronto until 1963 when two new *Chugim* were established on his initiative.

A Rewarding Association With the Y.M.W.H.A.

Even before Mr. Rosenne's "revolution", I proposed that we enter into a partnership with the montreal Y.M.W.H.A. in our adult education program. We had to first overcome the opposition of Melech Magid amd Aryeh Kronitz. They argued for "guarding our independence", and spoke of the danger that "the 'Y' would enter into competition with Keren Hatarbut and eventually swallow it". The consensus was that we would not get very far if we persisted in our not-so-splendid isolation. as to the danger of the 'Y' competing with us, I quoted from Numbers 11, 29, "Would that all the Lord's people were prophets", adding that if and when the 'Y' were to compete with us in the spreading of Hebrew, it would be one of the greatest triumphs of the Hebrew Movement.

Our association with the 'Y' was one of the most pleasant and rewarding of Keren Hatarbut's relationships with other organizations. The top officers of the 'Y'; Executive Director Harvey Golden, Program Director Arthur Rotman, and Group Work Director Dr. Leonard Levine, (now on the faculty of McMaster University) showed an extremely positive attitude to Hebrew Language and Culture and did much for their advancement within their organization. This was evidenced also by the fact that as many as fourteen members of the "Y's" staff were among the first to respond to our call to study Hebrew during the "Hebraization Year". It is interesting that there was no response at all from any other major organization except for the National Executive Director of a major organization who first enrolled but later withdrew because "people would learn about his being illiterate in Hebrew". At least he was embarrassed... (He did "one better" than a top employee of the Z.O.C. who told me in an almost boastful manner, without my touching on the subject at all, "I am not ashamed to tell you that I don't even know the Hebrew alphabet, but that doesn't prevent me from being a good Zionist".)

In addition to the 'Y', Shaarei-Zion Congregation was one of our major partners in the spreading of Hebrew in Montreal. Edith Linetzky,who was one of our excelling students who achieved the Jerusalem Certificate, devoted much of her time and effort to making Shaarei-Zion Congregations second only to the 'Y' in the number of Keren Hatarbut classes and students. In general, Shaarei-Zion and its spiritual leader Rabbi Moshe Cohen were most cooperative in allowing us the use of their facilities for other activities as well. We also sponsored adult courses jointly with Congregation Bet-Zion, Adat-Israel, Chevrah-Kadisha, and Young-Israel of Montreal and of Chomedy.

Chapter 23
Achievements, Frustration and Debacle

My final two years with Keren Hatarbut constituted the apex of our achievements. Ironically, they ended with frustrations and defeat. By the early sixties, all our projects and institutions had struck firm roots in Canadian Jewish life. Even in the area of formal education, where we were unsuccessful in bringing all the schools of all regions under the roof of one coordinating agency, there was general recognition and appreciation of the Keren Hatabut as the sole representative of the Department of Education and Culture of the Jewish Agency, so that national coordination was achieved almost entirely at least in the Department's wide sphere of activity. We arrived at a modus vivendi with Dr. Diamond of Toronto regarding the teacher-exchange program. While he was free to negotiate directly with the Department in Israel, he agreed to seek our approval and to process immigration requirements through our office. Mr. Kronitz, who persisted (though a member of the Keren Hatarbut executive) in his stand that formal education was the domain of the C.J.C., was told politely by Dr. Mehlman to invite teachers to his school through the Keren Hatarbut office. When our Executive learned that Rabbi Witty of Winnipeg was ignoring the Keren Hatarbut and inviting teachers through the Torah Department, some members suggested that "we take action". My reaction was that our services were offered only to those who were our willing partners, and that we should not waste valuable time and effort on ideological conflicts.

Hebrew courses for adults continued to exist in fourteen centers and to thrive in most of them. In the academic year 1963-64, there were about nine hundred students (exceeding the number of even the "Hebraization Year") attending over fifty-five classes across the country. The most outstanding achievement that year was scored by Winnipeg, with a total of a hundred and eighty registered students. This success was due in part to the efforts of Mr. Melvin Fenson, who was then part-time director in Winnipeg.

The Institute for Hebrew Studies in Montreal, whose foundations had been laid in 1958, attracted many adults and youth who were offered, in addition to Hebrew language at various levels, such courses as Bible, Modern and Contemporary Hebrew Literature, History, Zionism and Modern Israel, and Pedagogical Workshops for Teachers. Hebrew studies in Montreal had become so popular that A.N. Eigner wrote in his column "Confidentially Yours" in the Canadian Jewish Chronicle: "The Keren Hatarbut has been spending a busy summer, with its Massad camps, teachers summer school, seminar and Ulpan courses. The inroads of the Hebrew language into our way of life are becoming more and more impressive, thanks to the efforts of this organization in its program of popularizing Hebrew culture, including the language. HEBREW LANGUAGE CLASSES ARE ALMOST AS POPULAR AS GOLF AND CHA-CHA LESSONS AMONG THE YOUNG MARRIED SET...".

Hebrew speaking *chugim* met regularly in Vancouver, Winnipeg, Ottawa, Montreal, Halifax and Toronto. The Hebrew Youth Movement had branches (some of them with occasional interruptions) in Montreal, Toronto, Winnipeg, Calgary, Ottawa and Edmonton.

Ben-Zion Fischler was assigned to the *ulpanim* in montreal. When the four experts had arrived from Israel, I had asked them in what communities they wanted to serve. While three of them expressed their preferences, Fischler was clever enough to say, "I will go wherever you send me". It was not because of this response of his that I decided to keep him in Montreal. I sensed that he had potential in areas other than *ulpanim*. He turned out to be an excellent language teacher. Upon observing him in action, I likened him to a master symphony conductor. During that year, we reached in montreal as many as nineteen classes with an actual attendance of several hundred students. Ficshler did remain with us initially for two years. He served successfully in various areas. He conducted workshops for teachers; he gave demonstration lessons in the *ulpan* method; he visited some of our affiliated schools; he directed our teachers summer seminar for one season, and one year he led our youth tour to Israel. A year after he returned to Israel, when we had failed in our endeavours to obtain an assistant national director, Shazar and Mehlman responded favourably to our appeal to disregard the rule restricting *shlichim* to two years of service in any one country and to assign him to us for an additional two years. His second tour of duty with us was just as successful as the first. The other two teachers were delegated to two communities each; Alizah Shoshanni conducted *ulpanim* in Vancouver and in Halifax, and Emanuel Keren in Calgary and Saskatoon. These are but a few excerpts from several of the glowing reports we received about the success of all these *ulpanim*. Dr. Charles Oler of Halifax — "The enthusiasm is overwhelming!"; Rabbi H. Dobrinsky of the same city — "We shall long remember the great contribution the *ulpan* program made to our community"; Mrs. H. Landa, Secretary of the Board of Education of the Saskatoon Jewish community — "Mr. Keren also inculcated us with a deeper understanding of the problem of Israel and even succeeded in opening our minds to our own problems. Sending men of his calibre to Saskatoon speaks well for our future relations and will do much to strengthen and expand the role of the Hebrew school here."

Ulpanim were also held in Victoria, Edmonton, Regina, Fort William, Windsor, London, Ottawa, St. Catharines, Quebec City, Glace Bay, St. John, N.B., and St. John's, Nfld. Our efforts bore fruit. Over eight hundred students studied Hebrew that year in large and small centers.

Our Women Added Charm

In addition to playing an important role in all our work, Hebrew-speaking women formed a special Women's Hebrew-speaking Group under the name of *Chen* (meaning charm) which they borrowed from the acronym *Chail Nashim* — Women's Corps of the Israeli army. Mrs. J. (Chavah) Gotlieb was the founder and moving spirit of this active group. Some of its other leaders were Miriam Denburg, Rachel Yagod and Mrs. Pearl. All their regular meetings, lectures, holiday celebrations and social affairs were conducted in Hebrew. On special occasions, such as the celebration of Israel's Independence Day, joint programs were sponsored by Chen and the other three Hebrew speaking women's groups — "Ivriah" of Hadassah, "Rachel Yana'it" of the Pioneer Women, and "Tekumah" of Mirachi.

A Historic Milestone

Seven years after the revival of the Noar Ivri and the establishment of the Leadership Institute, there were already many who had outgrown the Youth Movement. Most of them were academics, graduate students, and professionals. It was a challenge and an opportunity to test the depths and strength of the roots we had planted, by organizing them into a Hebrew speaking club. The founding dinner meeting was held October 8, 1962 with an attendance of about fifty members. The guest speaker, Prof. Akiva Ernst Simon of the Hebrew University in Jerusalem, spoke on "A Philosophy of Life for the Young Hebrew Intellectual in the Diaspora". He referred to the establishment of the club as "an important historic event the like of which I had not seen in any other part of the Golah". Solomon Gordon and David Finestone, who were present at the founding meeting, remarked to me jubilantly, *"Lazeh pillalnu"*, this is what we prayed for! "We can now be confident that there is hope for our future." When Mr. David Rivlin, the Consul General of Israel addressed them at one of their monthly dinner meetings on "Israel — a Three Way Bridge", he was so impressed that he spent many hours with them after the lecture. He wrote me an enthusiastic letter, from which a few quotations are in order here: "I hasten to express with great joy my profound impressions of this group that you organized ... It was for me a refreshing experience ... Young faces — when are we privileged with such! ... genuine and frank discussion of basic problems, conducted in Hebrew which all understood and participated in with exalted spirit ... I am grateful to you for this evening ... This group of fifty members should be consolidated into a nucleus that could serve as an example to many others ... I suggested that they should arrange such meetings at the consulate together with Israeli students, to which they agreed with enthusiasm." The Moadon Ivri, as it was called, did not rely solely on guest speakers. They had more than ample intellectual power to serve themselves as lecturers, discussants and debaters. I was especially impressed with a debate on "Resolved: Complete Jewish Living is Possible in the Diaspora". There were no judges and no decision on the winners, but I thought the Israeli students Yoseph Elan and Yochannan Friedman were beaten by Canadians H. Steinberg and David Lewittes who were living proof to me that complete Jewish living in the Diaspora was possible. Norman May, the moderator, delighted me with his fluent, high level Hebrew. (At this meeting I had the fatherly satisfaction of hearing my own Canadian-born son, Yigal, conduct the discussion freely in Hebrew.) When professor Simon addressed the club a year later, he confessed to me that he had not been utterly confident about its permanence. I do not know what happened to it eventually, but it still existed in 1964 when I left Keren Hatarbut.

Our Partnership Widens

In our desire to enlarge and deepen Keren Hatarbut's influence in the general Jewish community, we seized every opportunity to reach out to additional congregations and organizations. This enabled us to sponsor such personalities as Professor Simon. I do not remember whether Rabbi Wilfred Schuchat, spiritual leader of Sha'ar Hashomayim Congregation, first suggested to me or I to him that Keren Hatarbut and the Culture Foundation of the Sha'ar Hashomayim Men's Association sponsor jointly two annual lectures, one in Hebrew and one in English. In those years, Professor Simon visited N.Y. annually during the High Holiday season. Since Rabbi Schuchat and I were among his admirers, we extended to him a standing invitation to be our guest for the last days of Succot as long as he continued his visits to N.Y. We thus started a tradition that Professor Simon was the guest speaker at our Simchat-Torah celebration, which was held simultaneously with the Graduation Exercises of our Youth Leadership Institute. Both the Hebrew and English lectures attracted large audiences who were fascinated by Professor Simon's erudition, wit and charm. The lectures and cultural evenings we sponsored jointly with other organizations were in addition to our Duchan Ivri (literally, Hebrew Platform), the Hebrew lectures that were given periodically by some of the most outstanding scholars, authors and lecturers from the U.S.A. and Israel.

Hebrew at Sir George Williams University

Up to 1961, Hebrew had been offered at Sir George Williams University (now Concordia) as a classical language. The only connections between the University and Keren Hatarbut were the two annual prizes awarded by the latter to the two most excellent students in Hebrew language. At the initiative of the head of the Foreign Languages Department, Professor James Whitelaw, we met to discuss the ways in which Keren Hatarbut could be of assistance to the department. Professor Whitelaw told me he had been embarrassed and somewhat amused, at times, when individuals called him to offer themselves as instructors or to recommend some teacher in preference to some others. As a result of our meeting, there developed a close and rewarding relationship between us and the Department. The first step was to accord Hebrew the status of both a classical and a modern language. Upon my recommendation, Ben-Zion Ficshler and Ze'ev Bloom (the latter a graduate of Sir George) were engaged as instructors. We also offered the department our facilities (educational materials, audio-visual aids, etc.). The university in turn made available to us its Language Laboratory for demonstration lessons to the teachers of the Keren Hatarbut courses. When Mr. Ficshler returned to Israel, I became in charge of the Hebrew studies and taught Hebrew 421 (Bible and Modern Hebrew Literature) until I left Montreal in 1964. The number of students increased significantly and reached a total of about one hundred.

An important development was the recognition by the university of the Jerusalem Certificate for two credits for Hebrew 211 and Hebrew 212. This was the first time a university agreed to grant credits for a foreign language taken at an institution other than a recognized university. Students now had an additional incentive to attend the Keren Hatarbut Jerusalem Certificate class. The other privileges enjoyed by holders of the Jerusalem Certificate included admission to the Hebrew University without examinations in Hebrew and Yahudat, credit towards a Teacher's Certificate and eligibility for positions in the public sector in Israel without the requirement of passing Hebrew language tests. In my final year at the university, there was a very significant development. The teaching of Hebrew Language and Culture was put on the same level as all other modern languages. Hebrew 211-Day was increased from two to three times weekly, Hebrew 211-Evening from two to four hours weekly, and the Language Laboratory Class became compulsory for students of the 211 courses. In addition, the university offered Intermediate Hebrew (212). Bible and Modern Literature (421) was scheduled as an annual instead of a biennial course.

In view of the progress in the Hebrew studies, I suggested that the university authorities open a section of Hebrew books at the university library for the use of the Hebrew language students. Following lengthy negotiations, the university agreed to start with a limited section primarily because of lack of space at the library. For me it was a "Yom-Tov", a day of celebration, when we presented the university with the initial installment of Hebrew books, consisting of Bibles, Mishnah, dictionaries, Hebrew classics, and Modern Hebrew Literature. These books were a gift to the university from the Keren Hatarbut and the Department of Education and Culture of the Jewish Agency. The ceremony was attended by university officials and department heads. It was conducted by Principal Robert C. Rae, Chief Librarian Keith Crouch, myself, and the Consul General of Israel, Mr. David Rivlin. It is interesting that, although invitations were sent to presidents of major Jewish organizations and prominent Jewish leaders, the only ones to attend were Mr. Allan Bronfman, President of the Canadian Friends of the Hebrew University; Mr. Milton Klein, Q.C., M.P., and the Director of Hillel, Rabbi Samuel Cass. The president of the C.J.C. sent a congratulatory telegram and the president of the Z.O.C. did not respond at all.

"When a Tzadik Departs Glory and Splendor Depart." (Breishit Rabba) A Tribute to Rabbi Avraham Kravetz

When Rabbi Kravetz passed away early in 1962 there passed with him much of the glory and splendour he had bestowed upon the Jewish community in Winnipeg in general and on Hebrew education in particular. The verse in Isaiah (3:10) "Say ye of the righteous, that it shall be well with him" is interpreted homoletically in the Talmud, (Kidushin 40) "Say ye that he is a good tzadik", a good righteous-man. The question is then posed: "Is there a tzadik who is good and a tzadik who is not good?" The answer, says the Talmud, is: "If he is good to Heaven and good to people, he is a good tzadik; if he is good to Heaven but bad to people, he is a bad tzadik". Rabbi Kravetz was a good tzadik! Though he was chief Rabbi of the orthodox community, he never paraded his orthodoxy; he never used it in controversial subjects, and he always discussed issues on their merits. He was in love with education, and treated it as a basis for understanding and unity rather than a divisive force in the community. In a word, he represented and served K'lal Israel, the totality of Israel. He was wise, subtle and clever. That is why I took to him the very first time I met him. That is why there was a genuine affinity between us. We stood on the same ground where education was concerned, although we both knew well that we stood on different grounds on ritual interpretation and practice.

Rabbi Kravetz was one of the few principals who made a lasting impact on many of his students, and influenced some of them to enter the service of the Jewish Community. The most outstanding of them is Rabbi Edward M. Gershfield, a renowned Talmudic scholar who received his Ph.D. in Jewish and Roman Law from Oxford University in England. He is at present Associate Professor at the Jewish Theological Seminary of America. His wife (née Tobby Helman, a grand-daughter of Chief Rabbi Israel Kahanovitch) was also a student of rabbi Kravetz.

It is interesting that all the seven students he influenced to enter the Rabbinate serve in the U.S.A. A measure of his purely educational approach is that he did not direct them either to an Orthodox or to a Conservative Seminary. Three of them, Rabbis Gershfield, Malcolm Thomson, and James S. Diamond were ordained by the Jewish Theological Seminary. The others, Rabbis Harold Karp, Chaim Roswasky, David Silverman and Philip Kirshner, were ordained by an Orthodox Seminary or Rabbi.

As far as is known to me, the only other community that "produced" a Rabbi in Western Canada is Regina, whose Sol Hyman — a student of my brother Sol — went on to study at the Jewish Theological Seminary in New York, and is now spiritual leader of the conservative congregation in Edmonton.

Rabbi Kravetz's passing was a great loss not only to Winnipeg but also to theKeren Hatarbut that we both envisioned as a creative, unifying force in Canadian Jewish life. It was therefore with a sense of awesome responsibility that I proceeded, at the request of the Board of Education of the Winnipeg Talmud Torah, to search for a successor worthy of Rabbi Kravetz. I approached some men of outstanding scholarship, character and experience. I did not consider it my prerogative to make definite recommendations but rather to convey facts, the opinions of colleagues who knew the candidates, and my personal impressions of them. My report, however, pointed in the direction of a *Torah U'mesorah* (a coordinating orthodox educational agency) candidate who, I thought, would be the most likely to continue in Rabbi Kravetz's tradition. It was a freak of fate that I had to leave for Israel to participate in the World Hebrew Congress before the matter was settled.

I have heard many times the cliche "things will never be the same again", etc. In the case of Rabbi Kravetz and Winnipeg, things have indeed never been the same again... He was rooted in Winnipeg "like a tree planted by streams of water" (Psalm 1:3); what followed was a procession of comers and goers... There was even one who didn't know Hebrew, and there was one who had to leave in the middle of the year. To me personally Rabbi Kravetz's passing was a great loss and one of the severest blows in a period that was to see my sad separation from the movement I loved and nurtured.

When I visited the school in September 1978, it was a short time after the arrival of Dr. Yoseph Levannon, who had left his position as

Director of the College of Jewish Studies in Detroit, to become head of the institution in Winnipeg. My impression, later confirmed by Dr. Fischel Coodin, a member of the School Board, was that Dr. Levanon's arrival marked the beginning of a new revival for the Winnipeg Talmud Torah.

At about the same time, we suffered two more losses by the passing of Mr. Eli Shuchat, a founder of Keren Hatarbut and Massad and one of their staunchest supporters, and Mr. David Aisenberg. Mr. Aisenberg had devoted many years to Hebrew education, first as principal of the Regina and Calgary Talmud Torahs and later as an effective and popular teacher in Montreal. As camp manager of Massad Alef for thirteen years, he worked with singular devotion to the physical maintenance and development of the camp. He belonged to the minority of East European teachers who dared to flout communal bosses and to stand up for the rights of the Hebrew teacher. In the mid-forties, when the Hebrew teachers' lot in Montreal was generally a sorry one, Mr. Aisenberg told me he was about to organize a strike against the Talmud Torah. I cautioned him that the strike would surely faily because the Talmud Torah boss was too hard a nut to crack. Aisenberg was misled by his sense of dignity as a teacher and by his intense feeling against injustice. He said to me with strong conviction, "We will not give in until we win". It didn't take too long for the strike to collapse, and Mr. Aisenberg found himself teaching at Sha'arei Zion...

Winnipeg Talmud-Torah Impresses Mosheh Sharett

Rabbi Kravetz, who passed away in the prime of his life, lived to see some of the fruit of his labour, but was denied the pleasure he would have felt in witnessing a historic event which was largely made possible by his work. When Moshe Sharett visited Winnipeg in the interests of the U.J.A. a few months after Rabbi Kravetz's death, Mr. Sam Drache, founder and Chairman of the Zionist Cultural Institute, organized an event that, as far as I know, was the only one of its kind in Canada, if not in the whole of North America. He arranged with Premier Roblin to host a "Hebrew Happening" in the Manitoba Legislative Building. Under the joint auspices of the Cultural Institute and Keren Hatarbut, Sharett met with and addressed an audience of about two hundred and fifty, two hundred of whom were high school and university students. ("The key to the invitation to this gathering was solely competence in Hebrew conversation".) A lively discussion on various Jewish subjects echoed in Hebrew in the Manitoba Legislature. The event was covered by the Winnipeg Tribune, CBW-TV and several radio stations.

The next day, Sharett had a singular treat at the Talmud Torah and the J. Wolinsky Collegiate. Mr. Melvin Fenson wrote in his column in the Israelite Press. "Mr. Sharett marvelled at the *"Ya'ar Shel Yadayim"* (forest of hands) that shot up for each reply. He wrote in the school guest book, "I am profoundly impressed with the high standards of all the classes", and commented, "distinguished *individual* students are not unknown to me in my travels around the globe, but the uniform high level of achievement in Winnipeg exceeded anything I have ever seen". The N.Y. daily newspaper "Der Tog" later reported that during his visit in N.Y., Sharett spoke with enthusiasm about Winnipeg, where he had found a "poetic atmosphere" in its Hebrew school.

Rabbi Kravetz was denied the pleasure of another outstanding occasion when Ya'akov Herzog, Israel's Ambassador to Canada, presented the Jerusalem Certificate to as many as thirteen students of the Hebrew High School who passed the Jerusalem Examinations sponsored by the Keren Hatarbut. The ceremony was televised by CBW-TV. If my memory serves me right, the Winnipeg and Vancouver students constituted a majority of those who passed the examinations that year in the U.S.A. and Canada.

It should be pointed out that Israeli teachers had already been members of the Talmud Torah faculty for six years and that they had made a major contribution to the higher educational standards and to the "poetic spirit" in Winnipeg, as they did, to a larger or smaller degree, in all institutions they served.

Vancouver is Part of Canada

In a previous chapter I mentioned that in the late thirties and early forties mid-Westerners considered Vancouver an extension of Seattle and that those who moved from Winnipeg and other centers to Vancouver in the forties and fifties contributed much to the enrichment of Jewish life in the city. By the early sixties, Vancouver could not be mistaken as anything other than an integral and vital part of Jewish Canada. The Day-School had become known as one of the best in the West. The Zionist Organization and Young Judaea thrived under the direction of Leo Marcus and his successor Al Gelmon, both of whom showed a keen interest in the progress of the Day-School. They themselves studied Hebrew and encouraged others to do so. Marcus cooperated fully with the Keren Hatarbut, and Gelmon became one of its moving spirits in the West. One of the best things that ever happened to Vancouver was the decision of Winnipeggers Shimon and Mona Kaplan to move there. They took over the struggling, deficit-ridden Western Jewish Bulletin and transformed it into a profitable business as well as one of the best Anglo-Jewish weeklies in the U.S.A. and Canada. Kaplan became a pillar of the Hebrew Movement. It was due to his enthusiasm and the efforts of such people as Dr. and Mrs. L. Komar, Dr. B. Goodman, Mr. C. Leonoff, Mrs. D. Frankenburg and Mrs. M. Thal that the Hebrew courses developed into the "Vancouver Hebrew Institute" consisting of seven classes with an attendance (in 1963) of eighty six students, many of whom were high school and university students. Their *Chug Ivri* was one of the most successful in the country. My last fond memory of Vancouver is the "First Educational Retreat" conceived and organized by Kaplan in the Summer of 1964, under the joint auspices of Keren Hatarbut, the Talmud Torah and the Zionist Organization. I served as Resource Speaker. The retreat was attended, among others, by some of the younger leaders of the Talmud-Torah, Canadian Jewish Congress. Zionist Organization and the Bond Drive. We spent many hours (from Saturday night to Sunday evening) in informal discussion of various aspects of Canadian Jewish life. I and some others continued our discussion throughout Saturday night ... It was hailed by the participants as a very instructive and rewarding experience. I know it was continued the next year (after I left Canada) because Kaplan asked me to help him get Dr. Blumenfield as the Resource Speaker.

Seek Ye Out The Book and Read" (Isaiah 34:16)

It is no secret that "the people of the book" have neglected the Hebrew book in the Diaspora. In 1963, the Department of Education and Culture of the Jewish Agency and the Brit Ivrit Olamit called upon Jewish communities throughout the world to organize a Hebrew Book Week in order to revive interest in Hebrew sources and to promote Hebrew books in the Diaspora. Keren Hatarbut was the first to respond to the call. We invited the Consulate General of Israel and the YMYWHA to join us as partners in sponsoring Hebrew Book Week in Montreal. The official opening, on April 21, 1963, in the large 'Y' auditorium was attended by an overflow audience of about seven hundred. Although the Week was dedicated to the Hebrew book, we decided to use the three languages spoken by Jews in Canada. As chairman, I welcomed and introduced in French the Honorable George Emil Lapalme, Minister of Cultural Affairs and Attorney General of the Province of Quebec. The other speakers I introduced in the languages they spoke. Brief speeches were delivered in English by S.S. Gordon, S.H. Levine and J.M. Frank (Presidents, respectively, of Keren Hatarbut, the 'Y', and the Z.O.C.); Michael Garber, President of the C.J.C., spoke in Yiddish, and it was agreed between me and Mr. David Rivlin, the Consul General of Israel, that he speak in Hebrew, but he was so carried away in English that he forgot to use even one Hebrew word ... The Hadassah choir and the Montreal Mandoline Ensemble presented a musical program, and a member of the Hebrew Youth Movement, Chanah Schaffer, recited in Hebrew a chapter from the Bible. Two things soured somewhat the success of this beautiful affair: my open irritation with the Consul General who disregarded completely the language to which the week was dedicated, and an indiscretion of mine that pained me for a long time afterwards. Joseph Frank sincerely expressed his appreciation of Keren Hatarbut and promised his fullest cooperatioon. In my response to his remarks, I said in Yiddish, *"Fun zein moil in Got's oieren"*, the literal meaning of which is from his mouth to God's ears, which could be taken as sarcasm. If there be any justification for such an indiscretion, it was the frustrations I had experienced that year in our negotiations with the Z.O.C.

The 'Y' building teemed with young and old who visited the Book and Art Exhibits during the week. The books, many hundreds of them, were provided by Sifrei Yisrael Inc. of N.Y. and by the Israeli Consul and Trade Commissioner in Montreal. The Exhibit included a special section of books and educational materials published by Keren Hatarbut. Most of the books were sold during the week. The opening ceremonies and the exhibits were covered by the media, including T.V.

We Pin Our Hopes on Dynamic Zionism

In reviewing briefly the Z.O.C.'s policy towards the Keren Hatarbut, it should be borne in mind that it did not result from the general will of a large, informed rank-and-file, expressed through its elected leadership. The Z.O.C. attitude to Keren Hatarbut was dependent largely on the individuals at the helm, who, in turn, were influenced by their backgrounds and associations. Sam Schweisberg, Eddy Gelber and David Newman, for example, could identify almost completely with the aims and program of Keren Hatarbut. Unfortunately, they were not at the helm when the time was ripe for an identity of purpose between the two organizations. Others, like Michael Garber, represented a different view. In an interview with J. Medresh (Canadian Jewish Eagle, July 3, 1962), Mr. Garber stated, "I do not believe in the Hebraization of the Diaspora. It is unnatural. The same is true of Yiddish. If Jewish languages are to be studied at the expense of Jewish content, of Jewish knowledge, it is unnatural and of no benefit". (For my view on the value of Hebrew, see Appendix on the role of Hebrew). Nevertheless, because of his democratic nature and fair-mindedness, he had a positive attitude to Keren Hatarbut. When he was president of the Z.O.C., he always responded readily when we requested him to meet with us to discuss our relationships. At one of these meetings, Mr. Maizel plunged into an ideological discourse. "Mike" cut him short gently: "Mr. Maizel", he said, "we hold different views, and we are not going to change them by discussing them yet again. Keren Hatarbut represents a certain segment of opinion in the Zionist constituency. As such, it is entitled to and will receive my support". He then turned to me with the question:

"Horowitz, how much do you need?"

"Fifty thousand dollars!"

"If you want to get fifty thousand, ask for more."

"I prefer to be straightforward and ask for what we really need."

"It does not work that way. If you ask for fifty thousand, you will get less."

We followed his advice, and eventually got fifty thousand!

When Mr. Lawrence Frieman was elected president, Solomon Gordon and I called at his office to congratulate him and to bespeak his cooperation. He received us with the cheerful declaration, "I am not against Hebrew, but I am still against Day Schools!" Mr. Gordon told me later that I had been unpolitical when I reacted with "I am certain, Mr. Frieman, that you are not against Chinese either". Joe Frank never discussed ideology and always promised his help. It is thus with individuals that we chiefly dealt.

Gradually and laboriously, our relationships with the Z.O.C. became closer and better. At its 1960 convention (October 29-November 1), the Z.O.C. adopted the following resolution:

"Be it resolved that this Convention express its satisfaction with the significant progress that has been made by the Keren Hatarbut of Canada during the past two years in the fields of formal Hebrew education, Hebrew camping, youth activities and adult education.

The Convention reaffirms that Keren Hatarbut activity is an essential and integral function of the Zionist movement and that the Keren Hatarbut of Canada should constitute an educational-cultural arm of the Zionist Organization of Canada.

The Convention urges the National Executive to develop closer relationships with the Keren Hatarbut by means of the exchange of representatives on the national, regional and local executive bodies of each organization and the integration of the Keren Hatarbut program with that of the Zionist Organization of Canada.

The Convention urges the National Executive to give consideration to the provision of financial support of the Hebrew movement adequate to meet growing needs of expanded activities in the Hebrew educational field throughout Canada."

On the whole, the Z.O.C. Executive abided by this resolution. In our negotiations, first with Max Malamet and later with Sol Granek, we came to believe more and more that the Z.O.C. was ready to change its role from Keren Hatarbut patron to full partner in the advancement of Hebrew education and culture in Canada. This change, we thought, would be brought about by two main factors. With the transfer of fund-raising to the U.J.A., education and culture could give the Z.O.C. a new raison d'etre that it badly needed. The second and no less important factor was the success of the Hebrew movement and its increasing influence on Canadian Jewish life. The legend that the Messiah was born before the destruction of the Temple, that the remedy was present before the illness, thus applied to this new situation. The Keren

Hatarbut, which had been started by individual Zionists, could now provide the basis for a dynamic Zionist movement.

World Hebrew Movement Girds for Action

The Brit Ivrit Olamit, which had been envisioned by its founders as a world movement for the advancement of Hebrew education and culture in the Diaspora, had been seriously hampered by its limited financial resources. In the late fifties, Nachum Levine was appointed as its director. He was fired with the ambition to turn it into a real movement with active branches throughout the Diaspora. He visited various countries to acquaint himself with the situation and lay the groundwork for such a central organization. In my many and long discussion with him during his visit in Canada, he evinced a profound understanding of the vital role of the Hebrew Rennaissance in stemming the flood of assimilation. He did not tire from repeating that the future of Israel depends greatly on its cultural, spiritual impact on the Golah. He was one of the few who did not harp on Aliyah and understood that it too was dependent on conscious and conscientious Jews who would identify with the revival of our nationhood. Alas, he passed away before he could see even the beginnings of such a Renaissance.

With the appointment of Yoseph Shapiro as Levine's successor, there was a renewal of Levine's vision and plans. In August 1962, a World Hebrew Congress was convened in Jerusalem. It coincided with our new relationship with the Z.O.C. and filled our hearts with hope for the future. The congress was attended by delegates from all over the world. Outstanding Israeli personalities, including President Yitzchak Ben-Zwi, Zalman Shazar, Mosheh Sharett and Aba Eben, participated. There was a real euphoria about the great things to come.

Canada was represented by one of the largest delegations, which was the only one to include representatives of a Hebrew Youth Movement, Shoshannah Cohen (Dalfen) and Shachna Cohen. Our delegates came from Vancouver, Calgary, Edmonton, Winnipeg, Toronto and Montreal. I was elected to the presidium, and our delegation played an important part in the proceedings.

High tribute was paid to the achievements of the Keren Hatarbut and "to the unique spirit of cooperation and support it received from the Z.O.C., a condition which is the exception rather than the rule in most other lands of the Diaspora." One of the warmest receptions was accorded to the Hebrew speech by seventeen year old Shachna Cohen. An indication of Keren Hatarbut's singular role in the World Movement was the election of as many as eight of its leaders to the World Executive.

The resolutions dealt with the ways and means of intensifying Hebrew Education and promoting Hebrew language studies throughout the Diaspora. One significant resolution was "TO OBLIGATE ALL ZIONIST

We Had a Dream

Encouraged by what we thought was the beginning of a new era for Zionism in the Golah, we continued to dream and hope that Zionism would no longer be relegated to a "corner in Jewish life", that it would become a vital and creative force in the life of the Canadian Jewish community. We continued our negotiations with the Z.O.C. with enthusiasm.

During all these negotiations, it was clear to all concerned that the Keren Hatarbut must continue to function as an autonomous body even after its "incorporation within the framework of the Z.O.C." With this in mind, we convened a National Council meeting in order to decide on the terms of amalgamation we would propose to the Zionist convention. Fifty nine members of our National Council, representing twelve communities from coast to coast, devoted two sessions to a comprehensive discussion of the pros and cons of the proposed new association with the Z.O.C. Their unanimous decision on the basic principles of the partnership was presented to the Resolutions Committee of the Zionist convention. We left ourselves the option to call a special national convention to consider any new terms that might be proposed by the newly-elected Zionist Executive if we found them to be at variance with our basic proposals.

Our participation in the Zionist convention was larger and more intensive than ever before. I was a member of the panel at the Session on Education. Moe Bauman, David Finestone, Wilfred Gordon, Chayim Maizel, Louis Rudolph and I served as members on the various convention committees, and Maizel was elected as one of the two Eastern Region Vice-Presidents.

Because of our status as beneficiary of the Z.O.C., we did not participate in the electioneering for any of the presidential candidates. We did hope, however, that Sam Drache would be elected president or a member of the triumvirate that he proposed to replace the presidency. Drache had shown an unusually keen interest in education and culture; he had created the Zionist Cultural Institute, and had extended his support to Massad and other Hebrew projects. For some years prior to the change in the climate within the Zionist leadership vis-a-vis the Keren Hatarbut, he followed with profound satisfaction the progress of the Hebrew movement. In our many conversations on Zionism, he identified completely with our philosophy and program. In his offer to serve as a member of a "troika", he intended to dedicate himself to the educational and cultural aspects of the organization. Unfortunately, his proposal was rejected by the convention. What followed from that moment up to the possible decision to liquidate the Z.O.C. (according to its national president Rabbi David Monson) is an important subject for the historian of Canadian Jewry.

Much as we regretted that Drache would not be the architect of the new relationship between the Z.O.C. and the Keren Hatarbut, we were jubilant when our proposals for the new partnership were incorporated fully in the following resolution adopted by the Zionist convention:

Resolution on Keren Hatarbut, adopted at the 36th National Convention of the Zionist Organization of Canada, held in Toronto during November 2-6, 1962.

"This Convention approves the resolution adopted by the outgoing National Executive of the Z.O.C. to incorporate into the Z.O.C. the Keren Hatarbut, subject to satisfactory arrangements being agreed upon between the two organizations.

This Convention notes with pleasure the following resolution adopted in Toronto on November 2, 1962, by the Keren Hatarbut:

"The National Council of the Keren Hatarbut, at its meeting in Toronto on November 2, 1962, with the participation of representatives from various parts of the country, unanimously resolves to authorize its National Officers to consummate negotiations with the Zionist Organization of Canada on its proposal 'to incorporate the Keren Hatarbut within the framework of the Zionist Organization of Canada', it being clearly understood that the following conditions will form the basis of an agreement for a close partnership between Keren Hatarbut and the Z.O.C. in the field of Hebrew Education and Culture:

1) That the Keren Hatarbut continue to function as an autonomous body;

2) That it continue to be governed by its own bodies, such as its National Convention, National Council and Executive Board;

3) That co-ordination of the activities of the Keren Hatarbut, and of the Z.O.C. in the field of Education and Culture be achieved through reciprocal representation in equal numbers on the National, Regional and local bodies of the two Organizations;

4) That, while the Zionist Organization may require that the general budget of the Keren Hatarbut should be approved by the Executive Board of the Z.O.C., the Keren Hatarbut should remain free to determine priorities within the general limits of its budget.

The National Council of the Keren Hatarbut commends Mr. Lawrence Freiman, President of the Zionist Organization of Canada, and its Executive Board, for their initiative and endeavors to make Hebrew Education and Culture the basis of Zionist work in Canada, and welcomes a close association between the Zionist Organization of Canada and the Hebrew Movement, with a view to providing the necessary means for the extension of Keren

Hatarbut work to all Canadian Jewish communities and the intensification of all cultural activities, especially in the field of formal education.

This Convention directs the incoming National Executive to pursue, with all possible seriousness and vigor, attempts to bring to an early and successful conclusion the negotiations with Keren Hatarbut, for incorporation on a basis satisfactory to both organizations."

The beginning of the End

Mr. B.M. Weiner was sitting near me when the Resolution was adopted unanimously. Noticing my satisfaction, he handed me the following note, which disturbed somewhat my equanimity: (translated from Hebrew) "The partnership between the Zionists and the Keren Hatarbut is now a fact. *Mazal Tov!* As a delegate, I too have agreed, but I have misgivings and feelings of uncertainty. I am thinking of the Talmudic saying 'A common pot is neither hot nor cold', because the water is neither too hot nor too cold to prevent some guy from sticking his unclean fingers into the pot and causing confusion and ruin. By whom? By those politicians whose garb is Zionism but whose purpose is what is known as cheap politics." Since Mr. Weiner's note ended with, "what is your opinion?" I told him we should approach the new opportunity with confidence and hope. Alas, Mr. Weiner's apprehensions were not unfounded./

What followed was a most painful period for me. It took me years to overcome its traumatic effects.

Soon after the convention, Keren Hatarbut appointed a committee to negotiate with the Z.O.C. on the terms of the proposed partnership. It took almost a year before the Z.O.C. proceeded to deal with the matter. I received my first shock when a proposal that had never been mentioned before was sprung upon us at the very first meeting, on September 30, 1963. While the resolution of the Zionist convention stipulated clearly that "*coordination* of the activities of the Keren Hatarbut and of the Z.O.C. in the field of education and culture be achieved through reciprocal representation in equal numbers on the national, regional and local bodies of the two organizations", we were now faced with a completely new proposal: "the establishment of a board consisting of twelve representatives of each organization, which shall *be the ruling body* on all matters of policy and budgets and all phases of Keren Hatarbut activities, excluding Camp Massad, it being clearly understood that the budget of the Keren Hatarbut shall first be submitted for ratification to the National Executive of the Z.O.C." We did not reject the idea of a new board, but we proposed seven principles as a basis for the board's work. The three most crucial points were: 1) While the total Keren Hatarbut budget would have to be ratified by the Zionist Executive, the priorities would be determined by the joint Board. 2) While the Z.O.C. Executive and the combined board would have jurisdiction over funds allocated by the Z.O.C., allocations of the Jewish Agency for specific projects would continue to be under the jurisdiction of the Jewish Agency and the Keren Hatarbut. 3) "We consider it of utmost importance to guarantee the continued non-partisan and non-sectarian nature of the Keren Hatarbut. For this reason, we consider it crucial that the ZO.C. shall appoint to the combined Board only officials and members of the Z.O.C. (which is also non-partisan in nature) who are not officers or officials of Zionist parties, in order to make sure that no political considerations, pressures, or interests shall enter into the work of the Keren Hatarbut."

Our proposals were made in a letter dated October 23, 1963. We received no response at all! Instead, we received a letter on December 12 asking us "to supply the names of our board members".

I have often expressed the hope that some university scholars with a good Hebrew background will some day devote their theses to various aspects of Canadian Jewish life and history. I hope that someday such research will be done on the role the Z.O.C. and the Keren Hatarbut played in Canadian Jewish life and on the circumstances and developments that brought about their eventual demise.

(Some years after my resignation from Keren Hatarbut, I was told that a fire at its headquarters had destroyed all the records of the organization. Fortunately, I kept copies of reports, minutes, memoranda, correspondence, etc. All these materials are available at the Public Archives in Ottawa, under the "Horowitz papers, Call number MG 31 H 103".

Since I was not on the scene from 1964, after which the period of decline started, I shall only outline here briefly the reasons that led to my resignation:

Even before our negotiations were completed, a report appeared in the Z.O.C. Bulletin that a joint Z.O.C.-Keren Hatarbut Board was a fait accompli.

When Mr. S.D. Granek was asked why he had not replied to the Keren Hatarbut proposals, and why there had been no further negotiations, he read from the minutes of the meeting of the national executive of the Z.O.C. of December 8, 1963 wherein Mr. L.J. Shine, speaking on behalf of S. Gordon, Keren Harabut president, stated: "It is time to abandon letter writing and get on with the job. He feels it would be advisable for the Z.O.C. to appoint its twelve members and let the Keren Hatarbut appoint its twelve members." Mr. Gordon later explained that had had left the meeting in the middle because he felt ill; he asked Mr. Shine to act on his behalf, and told him about the brief we had submitted; he instructed him to state that Keren Hatarbut would agree to a fifty-fifty representation on the joint Board but that it would insist on the remaining six points; he believed that the two bodies would meet again and that the negotiations would continue. It was also brought to my attention that while Mr. Maizel strongly opposed the Zionist Organization's position at Keren Hatarbut meetings, he "went along with the boys" at te Zionist Executive meetings, which he attended as a vice-president of the Z.O.C. Eastern Region. It therefore became clear to me that, to say the least, some of our members were working at cross purposes. Dr. Charles Oler, in resigning from the negotiating committee, gave expression in part to my feelings about this state of affairs. He wrote to me: "...The special characteristics of moral and ethical rectitude cannot easily be molded to fit particular circumstances — so that I find myself belonging to a small concert of men who mean what they say and say what they mean ... Under no conditions of compromise could I agree to the establishment of a committee which would direct the work of a cultural and educational service body, if its members would be drawn from the many political Zionist groups on the Canadian Zionist scene. This would of necessity equate your vital work, purpose, responsibility and deep seated hopes, which by their very nature can never be multilateral, with those special political aspirations... The high aims of Keren Hatarbut with its broad horizons must not and dare not be constricted and choked off by the inevitable machinations of the known party system... I cannot compromise on the original purpose set forth by the Keren Hatarbut and must therefore disqualify myself from any further negotiations of the committee".

Even before there was any agreement, the Zionist Executive proceeded to appoint its twelve representatives to the Joint Board. From my previous experiences with some of these people I knew that, to say the least, much of our time would have to be devoted to controversy instead of constructive work.

In all our negotiations, both sides always spoke of a partnership with the Z.O.C. At no time did anybody mention the United Zionist Council (consisting of the Z.O.C. and all Zionist parties) as a partner. Even before there was any agreement, partisanship was injected by pulling out from the hat the bugaboo of Keren Hatarbut's "secularism". When people would refer to the success of Keren Hatarbut, I would always emphasize that our success was in large part due to our freedom from politics. Now the spectre of political maneuvring became very real to me.

Finally, my resignation was prompted by the fact that, in the end, the Zionist Executive categorically rejected the three crucial points mentioned above, and our top leaders in Montreal (to the consternation of most of our workers throughout the country who were far from the "front line") did not take a strong stand against the distortion of the nature of the new association as originally envisioned by both the Z.O.C. and the Keren Hatarbut. In his letter of "acceptance" of February 3, 1964, (hastened no doubt by the threat that "unless an immediate agreement was reached between the two organizations, the Keren Hatarbut would not receive an additional penny for 1964") to Mr. S.D. Granek, Mr. Maizel was naive enough to state: "We are satisfied with your assurance and explanation that all twelve of the Zionist appointees to the Combined Board will serve as persons without party or sectarian considerations just as they do on the National Zionist Executive. We are confident that all representatives from your organizations will be such as to eliminate any possibility of political considerations, pressures or interests".

I recalled the conversation I had had with Eddy Gelber in 1957. Eddy was already living part of the year in Israel and part of the year in Toronto. I visited him to consult him on matters relating to Keren Hatarbut, Z.O.C. and C.J.C. He warned me that, inspite of our achievements, the foundation would someday be taken from under our feet "because Keren Hatarbut lacked a strong political base." At that time, it was beyond me why we were in need of a political base...

All or Nothing

Mr. Gordon and some other members, notably David Finestone, Moe Bauman and Nathan Roskies, did not give up easily. Mr. Gordon even went so far as to plead with my wife not to let me resign. A committee met with me a few times to try to convince me to rescind my resignation. They offered to increase my salary from eight thousand five hundred to fifteen thousand dollars and to deposit a certain amount annually for a retirement fund (as if money were at issue). I made the following suggestion: Since I detested and was not good at the game of politics, a new national director should be engaged. I would be fully in charge of Massad, the Leadership Institute, the Hebrew Youth Movement and any other Montreal or national projects that we would agree upon. I would be satisfied with the $8,500 salary and would direct Massad Alef without any additional remuneration. Mr. Gordon seemed to be amenable to this suggestion, but after consulting with his top advisor Mr. Maizel, he came back with "all or nothing". I then made my resignation final. I concluded my last report (August 12, 1964) as follows:

"I believe that those of us who have worked with me for many years will readily understand that it was not at all easy for me to arrive at the agonizing conclusion that I cannot continue to serve as the National Director of the Hebrew Movement in Canada and that I must, therefore, leave my life work after about twenty-five years of service in the field of Hebrew Education and Culture in Canada. Without going into detail about the reasons for my leaving Keren Hatarbut, I should say — in the mildest and briefest terms I can — that in my opinion, the new set-up is contrary to the resolutions of the National Conventions of both the Keren Hatarbut and the Zionist Organization of Canada. I am convinced

— and I am not alone in this conviction — that complete amalgamation, or as it was put at the first and only meeting of the Joint Board, that "the Keren Hatarbut should be the Hebrew Department of the Zionist Organization of Canada", is not in the best interests of the Keren Hatarbut or of the Zionist Organization. Now that this set- up is a fait accompli, I wish it well, and hope I shall be proven wrong in my assessment of the new situation."

I Left "B'shen Va'ayin"

I was really and truly shocked when I was told I would not get any severance pay because it was I who resigned. I reasoned that I had been engaged by an independent Keren Hatarbut; my resignation came as a result of the imminent complete change in the Keren Hatarbut's structure, and it was therefore my prerogative to decide whether or not I agreed to work for this new organization. I also pointed out that I had been satisfied with a low salary throughout my years of service, that I had received no fringe benefits whatsoever, and that I had never received any extra remuneration for teaching courses or for conducting projects during the summer, when people in my profession took one or two months of vacation. All arguments and pleas for fairness and justice by many people (spearheaded by Sam Kaplan of Vancouver) I had worked with fell on deaf ears. I left B'shen Va'ayin. Biblical law enjoins a master to free a bondsman whose tooth or eye he destroyed. The phrase *Yeitsei B'shen Va'ayin* has taken on the connotation "to go out with great loss".

(It is noteworthy that "newcomers" Moe Bauman and Harry Linetzky, not my erstwhile Hebraist colleagues, were responsible for the increment in my salary from seven thousand dollars to eight thousand five hundred. They took the initiative by asking me one day (a few years before my resignation): "Rabbi Horowitz, we notice that you are still receiving the low salary you started with in 1955." They looked at each other in bewilderment when I said, "We have to do so much with our small budget that I have tried to keep administrative costs at their barest minimum". They persuaded me to allow them to recommend an increase from $7000 to $8500.

Months later, when I was in Montreal to attend the wedding of one of the graduates of our Machon, Zehavah Bauman, Mr. Gordon agreed that the decision about severance pay was unfair and that he would "see to it" that justice be done. But he must have succumbed to those who apparently sought sweet (or is it "bitter") revenge...

Obviously, I was fearful about the longevity of the Keren Hatarbut. However, it never occurred to me that the Z.O.C. would ultimately suffer the same fate. Years after my resignation, I came across a document which surprised me no end. Months before the 1962 Zionist convention, the Zionist National Executive was considering a demand by

Mosheh Sharett that the United Zionist Council should become the supreme Zionist body in Canada. The strongest objection came from Sam Drache and Joseph Frank. At the meeting that dealt with this matter, Frank stated that Sharett's demand was part of a grand design to force all Zionist parties into one monolithic group; that if the Z.O.C. acceded to this demand, it would go out of business; that it was going to face increasing pressures, and should never let its guard down. It was therefore beyond my comprehension why Mr. Frank, who was president of the Z.O.C. at the time of the *shiduch* between the Z.O.C. and Keren Hatarbut, "let his guard down" and welcomed party representatives to the wedding... The contents of the above mentioned document led me to believe that Mr. Lawrence Frieman contributed to setting the stage for the scenario which eventually brought about the fulfillment of Mr. Frank's prediction. Ironically, this was done by the son of parents who had a major share in building and nurturing the Z.O.C. (See chapter 7, "A corner in our life", for a possible explanation).

The Final Touches: Habimah Comes to Montreal

My endeavour to bring *Habimah*, the national theatre of Israel, to Montreal was a refreshing break from the stress and strain of politics. It was no mean task. We first had to convince their U.S.A. agent that a performance in Montreal would be profitable. That achieved, we realized that it was financially too risky to "go it alone". There was the additional motivation to involve other major organizations in such a significant cultural event. We convened a meeting of representatives of Hadassah, the 'Y' and B'nai B'rith. It was harder to convince them than the agent that *Habimah* would attract enough people and would not incur a financial loss. Some doubted whether there were enough people who would understand performances in Hebrew. It was *davka* the Hadassah representative who voiced the strongest conviction that performances in Hebrew would not be successful. She therefore doubted whether her organization would participate in such a risky venture. "It would be different, of course, if they were to perform in Yiddish", she said. ((Hadassah President Mrs. Mandy Roskies later assured me that their representative at the meeting did not represent Hadassah's attitude to Hebrew.) In the end, Keren Hatarbut and Hadassah committed themselves financially and sold very many tickets. The 'Y' cooperated in the sale of tickets and in publicizing the event. Both Habimah performances, *Hadibuk* and *Shesh Knafayim La'echad*, drew capacity audiences. The actors, their spokesmen, and, later, the Israeli press, hailed Habimah's performances in Montreal as "the most successful in America from every viewpoint".

Before leaving Montreal, I completed the organization of all summer projects, recruited all the necessary teachers, and did the groundwork for all the activities for the coming year. I made extraordinary efforts to obtain an asistant national director (a position that had been vacant for two years!), Mr. Y. Lipsitz, Principal of the Talmud-Torah of London, Ontario, so that there should be somebody in charge at Head Office until a national director could be engaged.

I then said Shalom to Keren Hatarbut!

Chapter 24
Herzliah Hebrew Teachers Institute of America

Teachers are Guardians of the City

In the Jerusalem Talmud (Tractate Chagigah 81), the story is told that three scholars came to a certain place and could not find a teacher or a scholar. When they requested to see "the guardians of the city", they were directed to the police. The Rabbis wondered, "These are the guardians of the cty? Scholars and teachers are the guardians of the city!" Believing as I do that educators are the guardians of society, my appointment as dean of Herzliah Hebrew Teachers Institute in New York was, in a sense, in the nature of "the Messiah was born before the Destruction", (see Chapter 23). It restored my spirit. The new challenge left me no time or strength to brood about the recent debacle.

Herzliah Hebrew Teachers Institute was founded in 1921 and was chartered by the University of the State of New York in 1923. A permanent charter was granted in 1946. The Institute was a charter member of the American Association of Hebrew Teachers Colleges, and its graduates are licensed by the National Board of License. Colleges and universities throughout the United States recognize work done at Herzliah for transfer credit. Subjects taken at the Institute are also recognized for advanced graduate credit by the Board of Education of the City of New York.

Herzliah was established by Mosheh Feinstein, a Hebrew scholar and poet who created a non-hyphenated institution for the training of teachers for Klal Yisrael, for the entire Jewish community, not just for Reform, not just for Conservative, and not just for Orthodox. Its emphasis was on ancient and modern Hebrew sources, on the National Revival and on Hebrew scholarship, with Hebrew as the language of instruction throughout. Feinstein surrounded himself with Hebraists like Daniel Persky, Eliezer Leideker and Avraham Halevi. Though beset with the financial problems that are endemic to an institution without a denominational or "political base", it developed into one of the most successful and respected teacher training institutes. Its many hundreds of graduates serve not only Hebrew institutions of various types and levels throughout the length of the U.S.A., but also in Israel, Canada and other countries.

3780 Teachers in Sixty Years!

It is a measure of the cultural poverty of the American Jewish community that, according to 1964 statistics, only about 3800 teachers had been graduated from the six teacher seminaries in the U.S.A. during the sixty years of their existence. Herzliah had contributed about twenty percent of the toal of these graduates during *forty years* of its existence! Many of its graduates became principals, Rabbis, educational consultants, directors of education bureaus and centers, teachers in the public high school system, and professors in colleges and institutions of higher Jewish learning.

Herzliah was thus the type of institution where I could find meaning and fulfillment and where I could finally strike permanent roots. I had heard about its years of decline and financial struggles. I knew that its rehabilitation and revival would require time and great effort. Dr. Azriel Eisenberg who, like a *Nachshon*, leaped to the rescue of the institution (and pulled me along with him), revealed to me as much as he knew about its ailing condition. (Legend has it that when the Israelites reached the Red Sea in their flight from Egypt, they were afraid to step into the water. Whereupon *Nachshon* jumped into the sea and the Jews followed him. The word *Nachshon* thus took on the meaning of a brave person who does not hesitate to face challenges and risks.) I followed *Nachshon* because of the assurance I was given of the full support of such people as Dr. Emanuel Neuman and the noted philanthropists, brothers Abraham and Jacob Goodman who had practically rescued Herzliah from complete collapse in recent years. I was further promised that a sum of $50,000 would be deposited in the bank for that academic year, so that I could devote myself entirely to laying the foundation for the rehabilitation of the institution.

Dream and Reality — A Twain That Seldom Meet

When I appeared for work the first morning, on a typical New York hot, humid August day, my sense of humor stood me in good stead. I noticed that all the windows were firmly locked with chains. I turned to the secretary with the question, "is the situation so bad that measures have had to be taken to prevent me from jumping out of the window?" Lacking a sense of humor, she proceeded to explain with a straight, sombre face that the state of the windows was only one of the many building violations that would have to be corrected. Indeed, I was harassed time and again by court summonses before we succeeded in ridding ourselves of that stumbling block. The three-storey building was situated in a centrally-located, sightly spot on ninety-first Street between West End Avenue and Riverside Drive. Looking at it from the outside, it was impossible to know how neglected it was on the inside.

Among other things, it needed very badly a few coats of paint. The institution was so poor that Dr. Eisenberg had to obtain a gift of paint without which our superintendent would have been helpless... The office too would have been helpless if Dr. Eisenberg had not put at our disposal some of the facilities of the Jewish Education Committee. For example, when our mimeograph machine became completely useless, our material was mimeographed at the J.E.C. office. Later, Dr. Eisenberg made us a gift of one of their old mimeograph machines, and it took quite some time until we could afford a new one. Worst of all, most of the $50,000 that was supposed to have been available for the operating budget had been used for payment of old debts. Old accumulated debts continued to preempt a significant part of our budget. Instead of devoting myself completely to "rehabilitation", I had to spend hours on the phone every day urging individuals to send us their contributions (in some cases, ahead of time) in order to pay salaries on time.

Give Me Neither Poverty Nor Riches (Proverbs 30:8)

The author of Proverbs' request of God not to give him poverty lest he be poor, and steal, and profane His name, comes to mind when one considers how poverty can lead to obfuscation of reason and perversion of justice.

A veteran instructor who had retired because of a heart attack wanted to know why he had not received any payment on account of the retirement benefits he had been promised. He was surprised that I did not know anything about it. He had nothing in writing but he told me that when an authoritative officer had visited him at the hospital, he had promised him two thousand dollars annually for life. When I broached the matter to that officer, he pleaded Herzliah's poverty. I argued that if such a promise had been made, poverty was no excuse whatsoever. During our exchange of opinions as to whether or not the pledge should be honored, the officer blurted out: "Had I known he would recover I would not have made the promise. Now that he is well again, let him work!" (The instructor was past his retirement age.) The pledge was honored!

A case in point about the obfuscation of reason was the notion that the faculty need not be invited to the Annual Dinner. When I observed that my tally of the guests list exceeded that of the person in charge of the ticket-sale (because mine included the faculty), he was amazed at my taking it for granted that they should be invited. "Let those who want to attend buy tickets." In order to win this case, I had to declare that I would not attend if the faculty, as well as the super and his wife, were not invited.

What was it that prompted such an attitude? The individuals who expressed it were not niggardly; they were, in fact, honourable gentlemen. It was not, in my opinion, solely the poverty of Herzliah. It was due in great part to the mentality about the "portion" the Lord has assigned to the *Klei Kodesh*, to those who serve Him in this world. After all, they will get their due portion in the Hereafter...

Since there was no "retreat", I set out to design a plan of action for both the financial and the academic spheres. We found it necessary to revise the curriculum, which was deficient in some essential subjects. We could not remedy the situation without reducing the number of hours in other subjects. I found that, in the absence of a dean for some time, the faculty had apportioned the teaching hours so as to ensure a maximum number of hours to certain faculty members. Much of the time of the first faculty meetings was taken up with my endeavours to convince some of them to "sacrifice" willingly some hours so that we might add such subjects as Education, Psychology, Methodolgy, History of Zionism, The State of Israel, and Contemporary Jewish Life, with special emphasis on American Jewry. It is noteworthy that even in New York we could not find a pyschologist with sufficient fluency in Hebrew to lecture on psychology. Fortunately, we found an Israeli psychologist, Miriam Bar-Lev, who was working at one of the universities on her doctoral thesis, to fill this vacuum.

As in other educational institutions, we were bogged down at times by tradition and inertia. The story of which Bel Kaufman is the heroine well illustrates this situation. The author of "Up The Down Staircase" took an examination for her teaching certificate. She had to interpret a poem by Edna St. Vincent Millay. Her examiners failed her; whereupon she wrote to Miss Millay and described her interpretation. Miss Millay's reply was that not even she could have interpreted her own poem that well. Miss Kaufman, (a granddaughter of the famous author-humorist Shalom Aleichem) sent the examiners a photostated copy of Miss Millay's letter. The examiners did not reverse their decision! Instead, they decided TO USE IN FUTURE EXAMINATIONS ONLY THE WORKS OF DEAD POETS! I have told this story many times to authors, educators and academics. So far, no one has guessed what the examiners' decision was.

To restore the academic prestige of Herzliah, which had suffered following Moshe Feinstein's resignation, the Board appointed an Ad Hoc Advisory Committee consisting of the Dean, Professor David Sidorsky of Columbia University, and Drs. Samuel Blumenfield, Azriel Eisenberg (the chairman of the Committee), Emil Lehman and Judah Pilch. This committee dealt with such matters as the introduction of a program of Practice Teaching under competent supervision and guidance, the upgrading of the librarian's position from part time to full time, and the tightening of the entrance requirements, which had been somewhat lax in recent years.

The committee was also faced with the problem of the high school division, where the decline had been even more serious than in the institute. The fact that its thirty one students came from about twenty different schools in every borough in New York and Long Island was sufficient evidence that it met the need, small as it was, for a high level secondary school. Moreover, such a school was essential as a "feeder" for the Teachers Institute. On the other hand, the financial limitations made it extremely difficult to maintain a school whose thirty one students consisted of four different levels. The committee brought its influence to bear on the Board to hold out for a better future.

Not by Studies Alone

Believing that a teacher-training school should be not only a place of study but also a center of life and activity, we organized a student council that became an integral part of the Institute. It served as a link between the student-body, the faculty and the administration. It sponsored holiday celebrations, cultural events, and social gatherings, to which were invited also alumni and the general Hebrew-speaking public. It published a Hebrew newspaper, and offered assistance and guidance to students. For me, the greater significance of these activities was in providing the students with a training ground for learning by doing in an essential sphere of the educational process. In addition, we organized *ulpanim* at various levels.

Im Ein Kemach Ein Torah
Where There is no Bread There is no Torah

Perhaps there is not as much Torah as there should be because it is totally dependent on *kemach*, which, in my experience, is much harder to come by than Torah. And such was my experience also in Herzliah.

For the financial rehabilitation of the institution, we turned our attention in a number of directions: Eleven additional influential people were added to the Board of Directors with a view to widening the circle of contributors. The renewal of the Annual Dinner netted about twenty percent of that year's budget. Through the efforts of Libby and Molly Goodman and Dr. Miriam Freund, a Women's Section was established; it made a significant financial contribution already in its first year. Since Herzliah served the entire American Jewish community, we applied for assistance to over two hundred welfare funds throughout the country. Although the initial response was not at all encouraging, it did provide prospects for the future.

Alumni Association

Herzliah's alumni were spread throughout the U.S.A. and Canada. They included personalities such as Rabbi Stuart Rosenberg of Toronto,

Professor Ezra Spicehandler of Hebrew Union College, Dr. Avraham Holtz of the Jewish Theological Seminary and Professor Barzilai of Columbia University. An Alumni Association was reorganized under the leadership of Martin Tananbaum, chairman; Dr. and Mrs. Donald Gribetz, and Dr. Lloyd Gartner. Their stated aims were "to further the ideals and programs of Herzliah; to assist in its development, and to serve as a social and cultural fraternity for its graduates and former students". They contacted all the alumni whose addresses were available, and set out with confidence and enthusiasm to build the Association. Although they could not make an immediate, significant financial contribution, they did establish a potential for bringing Herzliah to the fore as an important national institution, for the recruitment of students, and, ultimately, for substantial financial support.

With all that, we could not balance the budget without chopping off $13,000 by reducing the office staff and by my volunteering to take the place of a member of the faculty who was leaving for Israel on a year's leave of absence. These measures had to be taken at a time when I and the office should have been enabled to devote ourselves to the rehabilitation process.

Moshe Sharett to the Rescue

All these steps could remedy the situation only for a period of transition from what was, at best, "a hand to mouth" existence to a financially secure future. I came to the conclusion that this could be achieved only if one or two major organizations were to assume part of the resonsibility for the maintenance of the institution. Since Sharett was at the time the head of the Jewish Agency, I turned to him for help. At the same time, I followed the road of "proper channels" and wrote also to Mr. Yitzchak Harcavi, the head of the Education and Culture Department of the Jewish Agency. I was confident that they would appreciate the special significance of Herzliah and come to its rescue. And so they did.

Sharett responded immediately that he would help us get an allocation from the Jewish Agency. Moreover, in one of his letters he wrote me, "I hope I will be able to visit the U.S.A. in 1965 and will then devote special time and effort to Herzliah". He also stated that he would ask Dr. Emanuel Neuman, a foremost Zionist leader, to fulfill his obligations to the institution. To my regret, Dr. Neuman was always preoccupied with other matters.

Great was our joy when we were later informed through proper channels of the Agency's $12,000 allocation for its fiscal year March 1965-66. This, we thought, meant that our budget would be augmented by $24,000 annually because of the pledge of the Tarbut Foundation — the Goodman brothers — to match the Jewish Agency's allocation, in addition to their $12,000 annual contribution. Through the efforts of the Goodman brothers and Mendel Haber, the president of Herzliah, the Z.O.A. "adopted Herzliah" and promised an annual $12,000 allocation.

I had intimated to the Board that I would renew my one-year agreement with the institution only if I were given an opportunity to devote my primary attention to its academic needs and to the development of the Alumni, the Women's Section, etc. Now that the budget seemed to be secure, we started to plan a strategy that included the recruitment of students for the high school, the prozdor (preparatory to the Institute), and the teachers institute. We also contemplated the establishment of a permanent leadership training institute in partnership with the Z.O.A. We even started negotiations with a university for the establishment of a joint program that would enable us to grant the B.A. degree in addition to the Teachers Certificate. As a first step, we planned to meet the requirement of the Committee of Hebrew Teachers Colleges that teachers certificates would be granted only upon the completion of at least two years of general studies at a recognized college, in addition to the prescribed Herzliah curriculum. In view of the acute shortage of suitable teachers for Hebrew High Schools, we planned a special program for the training of such instructors.

Herzliah Re-Accredited

In 1966, the Committee of Hebrew Teachers Colleges decided on the visitation of all its member-colleges in order to determine their eligibility for re-accreditation. The visitation of Herzliah was assigned to Dr. Eisig Zilberschlag, President of the Boston Hebrew Teachers College, and Dr. Hyman B. Grinstein, Dean of the Yeshivah University Teachers Institute. Their report encouraged us greatly. Stating that "Rabbi Horowitz is doing an excellent job in the face of difficult odds", they recommended "that in view of the fact that a great attempt is being made by him and the members of the Board of Trustees to bring back the glory which was once Herzliah's, that the school should be re-accredited".

Meigara Rama Lebeira Amikta (Chagiga 5)
From a Great Height to a Deep Pit

This Talmudic expression describes the situation that prompted me to decide to withdraw from Herzliah. To make a long story short, Sharett became seriously ill, and passed away about a year after he had written me what he would do for Herzliah, and our letters to the Jewish Agency for the renewal of the allocation went unanswered. At best, our "foster father", the Z.O.A., acted more like a step-father. It was very difficult to extract from them the money they promised. The President told me that because of their financial difficulties he could not meet my request for a monthly remittance of a thousand dollars. To show his good faith, he instructed the Comprtoller in my presence "to remit $1000 to Herzliah within one week." *Nine weeks later*, I wrote the president, "As you know, my repeated calls to your Comptroller, and his repeated promises, have been to no avail, so that now — nine weeks following our meeting — we have not as yet received the $1000 promised at that time..." At the same time, the Tarbut Foundation informed us that the total annual contribution of the goodmans would be $12,000 instead of the expected $24,000. As the "devil's advocate", I explained to my angry colleagues that the Goodmans were probably concerned that, in view of the new circumstances, Herzliah's financial burdens might again devolve upon them.

Mendel Haber and Abraham Goodman, in particular, tried to persuade me not to resign. In the meantime, a new element entered into the picture. While Herzliah's difficulties were financial, the Jewish Teachers Seminary (for training Yiddish teachers) enjoyed financial stability but lacked sufficient students. Some people suggested that an amalgamation of the two institutions would solve their problems. As a matter of fact, when I discussed Herzliah's situation with Mr. Rechavam Amir, the Director of the Education and Culture Department of the Jewish Agency, he told me, "If you want to save Herzliah, unite with the Jewish Teachers Seminary". I failed to verify whether Mr. Amir's view had something to do with the fact that the Jewish Agency did not continue its allocation to Herzliah and that the amalgamation was ultimately effected. The Herzliah Board had not taken any official decision before I left the institution, but from private conversations with some of its officials, I became convinced that although some were against the merger, (the strongest official objection came from the Alumni Association), the fate of Herzliah had already been sealed primarily by outsiders ... The Herzliah activists who considered the amalgamation inevitable tried to convince me not to resign because the united institution would consist of Hebrew and Yiddish departments, so that as head of the Hebrew department, I would be in a position to preserve the principles and character of Herzliah. I told these people that I had rejected an offer in 1939 to become the head of this same Yiddish seminary because of my opinion that Hebrew, not Yiddish, was "the wave of the future". Obviously, I would not involve myself now (a quarter of a century later) in an institution in whose future I had even less faith than in the future of Herzliah. One of my colleagues used another approach, "The amalgamated institution will surely last at least until your retirement, so what do you care, Aron?" My reaction to that was: "You must be kidding; you know me well enough to realize that I would not be guilty of such rationalization".

In my letter of resignation, I made it a point to mention that the Z.O.A., upon which we had pinned so much hope, "cannot be relied upon to fulfill its commitment to Herzliah."

About a year after my resignation, the amalgamated institution came into being. I am not at all familiar with the history of its short existence. I do know that Dr. Eli Goldstein, an American-born physician with an excellent knowledge and fluency in Hebrew, who had joined the Herzliah Board during my tenure and who cherished its objectives and principles, contributed much of his time, substance and ability to keep the institution alive. It lasted for about a decade. In 1978, its existence could not be justified any longer. It merged with Turou College, a baccalaureate-granting institution whose program *does not include the training of teachers*. Thus came to an end the dreams and efforts of two institutions which were to train teachers for the future, at a time when both the U.S.A. and Canada are dependent on the continuous flow of teachers from Israel.

Chaim Nachman Bialik's anguished cry *"Re'itichem bekotzer yedchem"*, I have seen you in your helplessness, could certainly serve as a fitting epitaph for the fate that has befallen Herzliah and the Jewish Teachers Seminary. (See chapter 4, for a clue to this situation.)

The Jewish Education Committee of New York

The Lack of Continuity

From teacher-training I went to secondary Jewish education. I joined the staff of the Jewish Education Committee (now known as the Board of Jewish Education) in New York. My functions were to direct the department of Secondary Education, to supervise personally the high schools in Long Island, and to serve as principal of Marshalliah Hebrew High School. I had known about the dismal situation in the high school arena in both the U.S.A. and Canada, but I was astonished to learn that only about two percent of elementary school graduates (or more correctly, Bar-Bat Mitzvah products) went on to study in high schools in New York, and that, already at the end of the first year, the attrition was about fifty percent.

Following a study in depth of the Jewish Education Committee's role in meeting the challenge in this area, I discussed a plan of action with Rabbi Eliezer Rosenfeld, the then Executive Vice-President of the organization. His response and approach encouraged me in pursuing with confidence a new largely-uncharted course in an arena that, at certain moments, seemed overwhelming.

Saving an Old Institution

My terms of reference called for the liquidation of Marshalliah Hebrew High School. Euphemistically, the "liquidation" was referred to as "the transfer of full responsibility" to the schools where Marshalliah classes were held, but none of these was prepared to assume the responsibility. Marshalliah had been founded in 1913 by Dr. Samson Benderly, a foremost pioneer and architect of a coordinated Jewish educational system in New York. It had been the largest afternoon high school in New York. Through the years, it graduated many hundreds of students, a large number of whom have played important roles in all areas of Jewish life. By 1966, when I became its principal, the number of its students had dwindled to a hundred and sixty-five, partly because the shift of the Jewish population to new areas. The J.E.C. administration therefore decided that it could not justify any longer the comparatively large expenditure for its maintenance at seven far flung locations in Brooklyn and the Bronx.

My submission called for Marshalliah's continuation under all circumstances. I argued that if it did not exist, I would favour its establishment even with a hundred students. I mentioned a few less essential items that could be eliminated instead. I recommended that the seven units be restructured into two viable units, one in the most central place in Brooklyn and the other in the Bronx. I pointed out that Marshalliah still enjoyed a special status qualitatively. Its hours of instruction were six weekly for grades one and two, and eight for grades three and four, as compared with a *maximum* of six hours even in the best afternoon high schools, and its educational level was the highest of all afternoon high schools under the supervision of the J.E.C. Two viable branches would enable us to institute some important changes that could serve to develop Marshalliah, first as a successful pilot institution, and, gradually, as a model afternoon high school. The development of a model school, I said, was an essential task of a catalyst organization such as the J.E.C. towards the building of a vital Hebrew high school program in metropolitan N.Y.

Developing a Vital High School Program

The general plan of action for the Department was based on the premise that one of the basic reasons for our failure in this area was the fact that students entered high school without adequate preparation academically, and without being conditioned emotionally and socially for embarkation upon a four-year course of high Hebrew education, resulting in a very high rate of dropouts, especially in the first and second years. As an initial program, I recommended:

Preparation and development of educational materials and media, which will be truly suited to the needs, realities and opportunities of our generation.

Development of a porgram of various activities, which could gradually bring into being an active high school youth movement.

Day camps, whose specific goal would be to serve as a living laboratory for the preparation of senior elementary-school students for entry into the domain of high school education. I would *begin* — as an experiment — with one such camp, in a carefully selected area, for two distinct groups: a) students who are about to enter the graduating class of elementary school, and b) students who will be entering the first year of high school.

Visits to Israel: "On the basis of first-hand knowledge and experience, I say without hesitation that the gradual development of a program of visits in Israel by high school students, with studies and activities geared to our *high school realities and needs*, will contribute much to the development of an effective High School Movement. In this area, I would start with students who will be entering the fourth year of Hebrew High School".

In addition, we suggested a recruitment program that included: regional meetings of principals and teachers of graduating classes to plan recruitment programs best suited to their respective areas; separate meetings with pupils and parents of graduating classes of elementary schools; invitations to them to visit high schools and to attend their graduation exercises; involvement of students of graduating classes in social activities of Marshalliah and other high schools; an extensive-intensive recruitment campaign through the media and congregational bulletins; and an effort to convince Rabbis to devote their sermon on Shabbat Shel Pessach, designated as Hebrew High School Day, to the importance of Hebrew High School education.

This plan was developed with the active assistance of the J.E.C. Staff Committee on Secondary Hebrew Education and with the cooperation of the Commisssion on Secondary Hebrew Education under the chairmanship of Judge J. Gellinoff.

A Vietnam Casualty

We were well on the way to implementing our plans when we were interrupted by a totally unexpected turn of events. The Student Council we had organized in Marshalliah had initiated a program of informal educational as well as social and recreational activities. Its first highly successful project was a three-day Seminar-Conference that was held on a farm during the spring vacation. Once again I saw the value of learning by doing. The strenuous work and the sleep-deficit (discussions, singing and dancing lasted into the wee hours) did not spoil in the least my elation with the serious discussions by adolescents of Jewish and world problems, with their intelligent appraisal of their Hebrew education, with their proposals for the creation of a Hebrew high school youth movement, and with their general behaviour and respectful relationships. We had also started to "put the pieces together" in the Department as a whole, when the spectre of Vietnam hit us suddenly like thunder. Our youngest son Asher was graduating from high school in the midst of the Vietnam war-turmoil. We were vehemently opposed to the war and we were afraid that he would, sooner or later, be drafted. Since we wanted to avoid the possibility of his becoming a draft-dodger, our thoughts turned again to Canada. Although I could not think of any suitable position I might get in Canada at that time, we were determined to return there at all costs.

It was one of my most agonizing decisions; I gathered the courage to inform Rabbi Rosenfeld that I was forced to leave him in the lurch just as we were getting off the ground. My association with him had been harmonious, enjoyable and highly rewarding. I admired his intellectual integrity, his sincerity, and his openness to new ideas and challenges. I enjoyed being part of a group of colleagues who worked as a team in cooperation and mutual respect. It was therefore most difficult for me to leave them, especially my closest co-worker Matityahu Mosenkies. Rabbi Rosenfeld was shocked, and refused to entertain the idea of my leaving at the very beginning of my work. When he realized that to me and my family it was a matter of *Piku'ach Nefesh*, of vital concern, he suggested that I take a year's leave of absence. I agreed with enthusiasm.

Before Rabbi Rosenfeld reconciled himself to my leaving, he emphasized that he had agreed on continuing with Marshalliah as a test-case. In view of the new development, he could not see how this could be done without somebody who understands the situation thoroughly and who is determined to implement the new plan. I persuaded him to entrust this task for one year to my assistant Morris Sugarman who had a singular talent in working with adolescents.

As a postscript to the subjects of *Hemshech*, of the lack of continuity in Jewish education, I should emphasize that it is a most crucial problem in the Diaspora. It is a measure of the poverty of what we call "Jewish life" that, while a proportionately much higher number of Jewish youth go on to study at institutions of higher learning, the number of those who continue their Jewish education past elementary school level is a mere trickle throughout North America. How could we seriously speak about Jewish survival and creativity if most of the forty percent who receive some kind of Jewish education abandon it even before they reach the stage of adolescence! (According to the Board of Jewish Education office in Toronto, about eleven percent — 600 out of 5600 — of day school graduates continue their studies in high schools, including *yeshivot*, in Toronto, 1978-79.) Obviously, there cannot be a vital Jewish community without Jews who are fortified with knowledge, understanding, feeling and a desire to preserve and develop a lasting, meaningful Jewish life in the Diaspora. There, therefore, seems to be very little hope for the future if we do not give of our best thought and effort to the solution of this problem. Furthermore, the fact that about ninety percent of day school graduates do not go on to high school should sound a general alarm about the effectiveness of our present educational system. The fact that even the day school fails to motivate Jewish children to continue to grow in their Jewish knowledge and understanding should bestir us to take a good long look at *the roots* — at the philosophy, content and methods of our present educational "establishment".

Chapter 25
From Stem to Roots

A Typical Afternoon School

When Azriel Eisenberg learned that I was going to Hamilton Ontario for a year, he said smilingly, "This will yet be your greatest challenge..."

Beth Jacob Religious School was a typical three-day-a-week institution, where pupils attended classes six hours weekly. Although the general starting age was seven, older children were admitted to grade one, so that here too there was a mishmash of ages and levels of comprehension. The curriculum was as spiritless as in other such schools. The teachers, mostly unqualified, used the translation method, and the texts were largely archaic. In these matters, there were no surprises.

There was, however, a surprise of another sort. The school was housed in an old shabby cottage, where the children were crowded in small rooms, and most of the desks were old and unsuitable. I had not seen such an inadequate "school house" anywhere in Canada or the U.S.A. In fairness, it should be mentioned that the congregation had broken away from the communal school several years earlier and was therefore forced to use makeshift quarters until its planned school-wing could be built. It was surprising, though, that rather expensive improvements to the synagogue were given priority over the building of the school.

This was the first time I was directly in charge of a three-day-a-week school. Even as Keren Hatarbut consultant-supervisor, I dealt mostly with five-day-a-week afternoon schools. The West had pioneered the day school; it was the last to succumb to the truncated afternoon program that had started earlier in the East, and most of the Keren Hatarbut affiliated schools were in the West. I remember my shock when Magid informed me that his institution too had gone the way of other such watered down schools.

My wife, who had been teaching in a three-day-a-week school in Montreal, had strong opinions on the possibility of teaching children to speak even the simplest Hebrew in this type of school. She argued that it could not be accomplished because the little time given to Hebrew was compounded by even more serious realities, such as the intervals between lessons; the intervention of the many holidays and vacations;

There was, however, another instance of my under-estimating the the fact that the children came to Hebrew school when they were already mentally tired and restless; the unsuitable text books; and the generally low motivation of both parents and pupils. (An extreme example was the case of a pupil who, when asked why she had been absent the previous day, explained that her mother promised her that if she would behave at home, she would not have to go to Hebrew school the next day.) I suggested that we were presented with a good opportunity to experiment by endeavoring to change as much as possible as many of the realities as possible.

We gave our attention first to the elements of time and curriculum. We proposed the addition of a mandatory year of study by establishing a two-day-a-week preparatory class for six year olds. To prepare the ground for opening this class the next year, we engaged an experienced kindergarten teacher with the idea of preparing the five year olds emotionally and socially for that class. The kindergarten met for two (and later for two and a half) hours on Sunday mornings.

From past experiences I knew that principals, Rabbis and education committees often hesitated to make "radical changes" for fear of stirring up opposition in the Community or congregation. We therefore awaited with interest and some anxiety the parents' response to this "bold" decision. The result confirmed the opinion I had expressed many times in many places that parents would be receptive to new ideas and programs if they were presented with clarity and conviction. Only one grand-father, one of the "founders of the congregation", phoned me to ask whether I had the right to dictate to parents when their children should start Hebrew school. He gracefully accepted the verdict when I explained to him that we were motivated by the desire to have a normal, effective school of which he "as a founder could be truly proud"....

To normalize the situation caused by age disparities, we initiated a coaching program that enabled us to upgrade the Hebrew knowledge of older children and transfer them to their proper age-groups. This program served also for students who were in need of individual attention, for those who had to "catch-up" because of absences, and for new-comers to the city.

New Methods and Teaching Aids

During a visit at Beth Zedek in Toronto, I observed an audio-visual method of teaching Hebrew, *B'yad Halashon*, developed by Re'uven Yalon, an Israeli linguist with teaching experience in the U.S.A. I decided to experiment with *B'yad Halashon*. Since this entailed an expenditure of a few thousand dollars, I cautiously proposed to the Board of Education Chairman to plan the inclusion of this item in next year's budget. (My past experiences apparently made me over-cautious about expenditures.

committee's readiness to meet unexpected budgetary items. Our agreement with one of the Israeli teachers provided for payment of one-way fare for one year's service, and return fare for a longer period. She decided to return at the end of the first year, even though this meant she would have to borrow the money for the return trip. When I put her case to chairman Jordan Livingston and his co-chairman George Levinson, I was very pleased when they agreed immediately, and without question, to my recommendations that the school finance her return trip as well.) After I explained to him its merits, he responded with, "What are you waiting for, Aron? Go ahead immediately". The chairman, Jordan Livingston, could serve as a model of the ideal education chairman. He had none of the symptoms of "bossism". He always appraised himself of the realities and of the potentials for improvement. While he wanted to understand fully every suggestion, he was aware, and so stated, that it is the professional educator who, in the final analysis, must be entrusted with decisions regarding the content and methods of the educational process. He was possessed of the necessary patience and tact to hold together all the parts that made up the school jigsaw-puzzle. If all our communities were blessed with such leaders, Jewish education would have much greater chances for success in all areas.

We discarded the old text books, and invited an expert to train our teachers in *B'yad Halashon*. Since it was not suitable for grades one and two, they used other new materials and teaching-aids, including film-strips and Shalom Alef. which was prepared for the Diaspora by the department of Education and Culture of the Jewish Agency.

While *B'yad Halashon* was an improvement over the old textbooks, it fell short of our expectations. As soon as we learned about another audio-visual method, *Habet Ushma*, which was hailed by the educators who were already using it as superior to *B'yad Halashon*, we suggested to the Adath-Israel Day School to join us in inviting an expert to train our teachers in that method. I could not come to any firm conclusion about *Habet Ushma*, because it was introduced only a year before we left Hamilton. Nor was I in a position to arrive at a definite opinion about whether even good three-day-a-week afternoon schools could produce Hebrew speaking students. Our graduates did achieve much greater comprehension in Hebrew, and some could carry on a simple basic conversation. More important, a significant number were motivated sufficiently to continue to study the language. I continue to believe, however, that American children could be trained to speak Hebrew even in afternoon schools where there is an awareness of its importance and a readiness to equip the school with all the elements that are essential for the achievement of this goal. (See appendix "The Role of Hebrew in Jewish Education".)

A Curriculum Alone Does Not a School Make

The attitude of the pupils was generally apathetic. To create student motivation, we inaugurated an activity program that enlivened the school and encouraged the student-body to become partners in our scheme of things. To begin with, we turned Sundays into activity-days for all pupils from grade two and up. As in other afternoon schools, Sunday had been another day of book-learning. On the approach of holidays, pupils would be pulled out from various classes to rehearse for holiday programs, interefering thereby with the normal course of study. At best, some teachers would prepare class presentations that seriously interrupted normal class work. We therefore devoted Sundays to such activities as arts and crafts, drama, singing, dancing, prayers, and — for older students — also *sichot*, discussions on contemporary subjects. Except for prayers, which was obligatory for all these grades, pupils were free to choose any two of the other activities. Grades two to six were divided into a junior and a senior group. Each activity thus involved pupils from more than one grade. This made it possible to change the Sunday schedule from two shifts to one, so that attendance for all pupils was from ten to twelve. Although we engaged specialists for some of the activities, we still effected a saving of a substantial amount of money, which was applied for improvements in other areas.

A few months after the inauguration of the new Sunday schedule, it became clear that two hours were insufficient for three activities. In our desire to increase the time by a half hour, we were faced with two problems: How the children and the parents would react, and a financial problem, as institutions are invariably sensitive about increasing the budget in the middle of the year. I was pleasantly surprised when all the ten instructors of the Sunday program readily agreed to work the additional half hour without pay. I was just as pleasantly surprised at the reaction of the children when I informed them of the increase in time at a general school assembly. I put it to them this way: "Some of you have justifiably complained about the short activity periods. I have good news for you. The teachers have volunteered to give you another half hour, so that starting next Sunday each period will be increased by ten minutes." The hush in the hall was broken by two students. A girl complained thus: "I used to be absent most Sundays, because my parents took me to Toronto to visit my grandparents. Then you came and said, 'No Sundays, no weekdays'. Now my parents will have to wait for me until *half past* twelve." She sat down quietly when I told her that her parents wouldn't mind waiting another half hour for such a good cause. A boy (Neal Livingston, who is now a film-maker) asked whether the increase would apply also to the Bar-Bat-Mitzvah class. The expression on his face did not reveal to me whether or not he was pleased when I told him "they especially should be appreciative of the additional time". We heard no complaints whatsoever from any of the parents.

The Bar-Bat-Mitzvah Panic

The Bar-Bat-Mitzvah panic starts at least a year before the Great Event. People in various places actually spoke to me about the Bar or Bat-Mitzvah of their children when they were still in the primary grades. (Jewish "creativity" in America even invented a verb form for the word Bar-Mitzvah both in English — to be "Barmitzved", and in Hebrew — "*Lebarmetz*".) Bar-Bat-Mitzvah candidates thus absent themselves from Hebrew classes during the year, in order to take Bar-Bat-Mitzvah lessons. The new Sunday arrangement helped us in solving this problem. One of the activities consisted of a Bar-Bat-Mitzvah class, where all the year's candidates were prepared for the occasion, which has been turned into the pinnacle of Judaic educational attainment. The girls were prepared for a joint Bat-Mitzvah performance. This was one of the outstanding annual events, because the girls were taught to chant beautifully some of the prayers by the congregation's excellent cantor, Mr. Henry Zimmerman.

Sundays were also used for student council activities. Council meeting were held at the school in the form of luncheons. They dealt primarily with projects and activities in which the student-body was directly involved, such as Junior Congregation, celebrations, library, school newspaper, outings, and visits to places of interest out of town. Students could also air their grievances, offer criticism, and make recommendations through the Student Council.

A New System of Student Evaluation

A serious problem in Hebrew education, particularly in afternoon schools, is the fact that pupils are often discouraged by the slow pace of achievement in Hebrew language studies. The old marking system evaluated primarily the knowledge attained by the student. Very little account, if any, was taken of the pupils' aptitude. Pupils with low marks in "knowledge" quickly lost interest because of lack of confidence in their ability. They could never make the Honor Roll, where it existed, even though they might have excelled in other areas. I often found myself trying to persuade children that they were not "dumb"... We therefore experimented with a credit system we designed for the evaluation of the whole child. It was based on attendance, effort, progress, conduct, service, involvement in activities, and participation in junior congregation. Those who achieved eighty percent of the credits made the Honor Roll, which was published in the monthly congregation bulletin. The emphasis was not on competition but rather on individual effort and attainment. Our experience was that this approach induced serious slow learners to make greater effort to make progress also in their Hebrew studies. At the same time, no child was denied recognition and reward because of lesser achievement in "knowledge" or in any other area.

The success of the credit system led us to the creation of a "B'nai-Moshe Honor Society", starting with grade three. The name was adopted following a discussion with the senior students on the role of the B'nai Moshe Society (founded in the early days of modern Zionism by Achad Ha'am) in the revival of the Hebrew language and culture. Pupils who obtained an average of eighty percent for the year became members of the Society. A special event was held annually for the initiation of members. They were awarded pins with the inscriptions "B'nai Moshe" in Hebrew and in English; bronze pins for the first year, silver for second year, and gold for third year. Those who maintained membership up to graduation received Bibles with silver or gold plated metal covers from Israel. Without saying it out loud, I wondered whether the congregation would have expended the necessary sums of money for these costly prizes if they had not been donated by Mr. George Pollock.

Another project that contributed to higher motivation in studies and greater interest in the school was the annual visit to New York. At first, participation was limited to honor students, who received partial scholarships for the trip. At the request of the student council, we later included other pupils without giving them any scholarships. The New York project was quite a treat for youngsters from far-away Hamilton. They visited outstanding places of interest; they had their meals at famous kosher restaurants, including one that featured Israeli food and entertainment; they attended a popular Broadway play. It was quite an experience for them to be received at the United Nations by the Canadian representative, who addressed them briefly and answered questions on Canada's role in the U.N. They were also received at the Israeli Consulate.

Other highlights were their visits at the Jewish Theological Seminary and the Jewish Museum, where they were especially impressed with the rich collections of rare old books and ancient artifacts. They were all "eyes and ears" when we showed them the sights of the East Side, which had once teemed with Jewish life and institutions. I had a personal "kick" when I could point out places where I had studied, prayed, and dined when I was a Rabbinic student. These visits had an impact on their "Jewishness" and on their identification with their school and congregation. Of no less value was their togetherness for three days; the tension-free atmosphere, the shared experiences and the cemented friendships. They continued to speak enthusiastically about the trip for years to come.

The Perennial Problem of Continuity

My suggestions for finding a formula for post Bar-Bat-Mitzvah studies were met with the usual scepticism, but I was encouraged by the Rabbi and the Board of Education Chairman to try. The meeting I had with graduates of recent years resulted in two groups that met for two-hour-sessions on Sundays. Rabbi Israel Silverman's group discussed the Parashat Hashavu'a, the weekly portion of the Pentateuch. My group concentrated on simple Hebrew readings and conversations. We started with *Lamatchil* and advanced to *Omer*, two vocalized newspapers published in Israel for new immigrants. This group gradually progressed until they were able to study some of Achad-Ha'am's essays in Hebrew.

Passover on Television

The new developments changed significantly the atmosphere in the school; they enhanced the interest of the members of the congregation, and they heightened the motivation of both parents and children. They all took special satisfaction when forty of our students appeared in a television program on "The struggle for Freedom". The successful results of the Sunday activities were in full view through the participation of the choir, and the dance and drama groups.

A few months after we started our work in Hamilton, we were requested to renew our contract for at least another four years. We were again faced with the problem of staying or moving. In the meantime, we learned that if we returned to New York, our son would still be liable for the draft, even if he remained in Canada. We agreed to stay on condition that the congregation should employ only qualified teachers and that work on the new school-building should commence without any further delay. Because of the continued shortage of qualified teachers, I was authorized to go to Israel to obtain such teachers. Our staff thus consisted of experienced Israeli instructors, some of whom we succeeded in recruiting in Canada. This enabled us to restrict the "B'nai T'filah", (who had previously served also on the regular teaching staff), to the Bar-Bat-Mitzvah classes. (A Ba'al T'filah generally conducts some of the prayers and serves as the Torah reader. In some congregations, he also serves as a teacher.)

It took much longer to resolve the housing problem. It was encouraging to know that a substantial contribution by Mr. and Mrs. Larry Goldblatt, in honor of his parents George and Jessie, would make it possible to go ahead with the construction of the school building. (The Goldblatts were generous, unassuming and deeply involved in communal life. George Goldblatt was a venerable gentleman. He was one of the last of a generation that combined some of the best values of the old country and the new one. He cherished learning and revered educators and scholars. I was once touched by a Chassidic quality manifested by Abby Goldblatt, a nephew of George Goldblatt. As he, the Rabbi, I, and some others were once walking home from the synagogue, we noticed an old lady carrying two heavy bags. She was a familiar figure at our synagogue because she always carried with her what people said were "all her possessions". Abby Goldblatt went over to her, gently took the bags off her hand, and carried them all the way to her home. We all heard stories about Chassidic Rebbes who went out of their way to help the poor and the weak. This time it was not a Rebbe, but the congregation preisdent who emulated a Rebbe.) However, the building was not ready for the next school year. Technical delays and strikes prolonged the construction process, so that classes and activities had to be held in halls and corridors for a whole year.

An Unstructured High School

My experience in the high school arena in New York led me to the conclusion that it was unrealistic to expect many graduates of even the best afternoon schools to embark on a four-year high school program. Already at that time, I had started to think in terms of a non-structured high school, where students would be free to study any number of subjects of their own choice. Hamilton presented a good opportunity for such an experiment. I discussed the idea with the graduating class, and told them they would be free to suggest subjects of interest to them. At the same time, we offered a full high school program for those who wished to go on to higher Jewish learning. The response was beyond our expectations. All that year's graduates took one or more courses, and some registered for the full program. It is noteworthy that a few of these students tired of formal studies in the second year, but requested that I allow them to help in the office and the library because they "loved the atmosphere of the school", and did not want to part from it entirely. Some students "made the grade", received entrance credits for Hebrew, and continued to study Judaics at universities in Toronto and in other places. One of them, Shimon Albert, went to study at the Hebrew University in Jerusalem. His sister, Bracha, recently received a Leonard Wolinsky scholarship for study at the Hebrew University. Some of the excelling students became assistants to our teachers.

Confidence or Apathy

A source of frustration was the lack of interest on the part of parents in becoming directly involved in our work. We failed in all our endeavours to establish ongoing communication and dialogue with them. The reaction was almost always "you don't need a parents-teachers association. We have full confidence in you". I often wondered whether it was more apathy than confidence...

Praise But No Prize

Our experiments and achievements were noted by the head office of the United Synagogue Education Commission. If my memory serves me right, I was told by Mr. Livingston that we had won much praise for our high standards and achievements, but we could not qualify for the annual prize because we did not use the Commission's curriculum...

Youth Without Deep Roots

In my Keren Hatarbut years, I was occasionally invited to speak at United Synagogue Youth meetings and regional conventions, but I knew very little about this organization. In Hamilton, I had the opportunity to become acquainted with their program. It was mostly social, and educationally shallow. It suited the products of Sunday schools and the run of the mill afternoon schools. In reading about and listening to suggestions for improvement, I thought of the story about the manufacturer of a four-way cold remedy who discussed with his salesmen the recent serious decline in the sales volume of his product. One of the salesmen popped the question, "Why don't you invent a six-way remedy that will fight colds just as ineffectively!" What can be said about such organizations is what is often said about Sunday schools, "better than nothing". Here is another theme for research: Where are now the thousands of U.S.Y. graduates? What are they doing, and what is the degree of their involvement in Jewish life?

I cannot say that our efforts with the U.S.Y. in Hamilton met with great success. The results were certainly not commensurate with the efforts. I personally concentrated on the high school students in the hope that they would change the situation in the future.

Some Diversions from Hamilton and the School

After Montreal and New York, it was difficult to adjust to life in Hamilton. It was therefore a welcome relief to take on some additional duties in Toronto. The first year, I taught Achad-Ha'am in Hebrew at the College of Jewish Studies at Beth Zedek Congregation. A year later, the principal of the United Synagogue Day School, Dr. Aaron Nussbaum, asked me to serve as Consultant-Supervisor of that institution. My wife and I thus spent Fridays and Saturdays in Toronto. During my four years at the school, I gained some insights into the "external" (parent pressures, television, influences of the "street", etc.) and "internal" (quality of teachers, teacher-pupil relationships, committee interferences, etc.) perennial problems of even a good day school. One thing became clearer than ever: Canada does not provide the type of qualified and experienced teacher that is essential for the true success of our educational institutions, be they afternoon or day schools.

Because of my bitter experiences with politicians, I kept away from entanglements with organizations. I could not, however, resist the requests of a colleague at the United Synagogue Day School that I speak at a meeting of a Zionist book club of which she was chairman. It was a very stormy winter night, so I was doubly surprised when I saw the president of the Z.O.C., Mr. John R. Devor in the audience. I did not touch at all on any controversial issues. However, during the question period, I was reluctantly drawn into an argument on Jewish activity or inactivity on the university campus. I thus found myself reiterating a statement I had made many times in many places, that we were already paying a high price for the Zionist organization's neglect of that front. Mr. Devor confronted me with the familiar question, "What comes first, another bomber for Israel, or the university campus?" I suggested that an investment in educational work on the campus would not have to be at the expense of another bomber for Israel. I offered to indicate what budgetary items could be eliminated or reduced in favour of this important task. He accepted my challenge, and promised to send me a copy of the budget. I am still waiting for it...

I Saw a Picture of Adam

I was invited to speak on Judaism to the grade seven students at one of the public schools in Hamilton. I mentioned that the unity of God is a fundamental principle in Judaism, and that the unity of man is a corollary of that principle. I quoted from the Bible that, "God created man in his own image", (Genesis 1:27), not Jew, or Christian, or Moslem, but "man", all men. One of the students asked, "If God meant us all to be equal, why did he create Adam white?" To my rejoinder, "how do you know that Adam was not created black or yellow?", the student declared, "I saw a picture." What struck me even funnier was that nobody laughed!

Why Don't You Accept Jesus?

I was guest speaker at a Reunion Meeting of the staffs of some Protestant summer camps. One of the young women asked me, "You are such a nice person, why don't you accept Christ?" I explained that Judaism precludes belief in any divinity other than the one and only Creator. I also mentioned that, according to Judaism, the "good life" is of overriding importance and that "the righteous of all nations will have a share of the world to come". To end the discussion on this subject, I pointed out that they and I practice the faith that we were born into and that we didn't arrive at our religious "truths" on the basis of a comparative study of all faiths. The person who wanted me to accept Christ then asked me: "Do you mean to say, Rabbi, that if you had been born a Christian, you would now be of the Christian faith?" My reply, "most likely!, as well as if you had been born a Jew, you would most likely now be of the Jewish faith," agitated some of them, while others told me later that it provided them with food for serious thought...

The End of Another Chapter

The last few years in Hamilton were most boring for me and my wife. The school was running very smoothly, and there was little for us to do in the dull cultural and social atmosphere of a city that suffers in part from its proximity to Metropolitan Toronto. We did not want to even consider extending our stay there. We turned again to Israel.

Chapter 26
Aliyah, Yeridah and Self-Righteousness

Aliyah, immigration to Israel, is probably one of the most bungled areas in the history of modern Zionism. From the very beginning, the approach of Zionist leadership seems to have been to implant in the hearts of Jews a feeling of guilt for not immigrating ("ascending") to their ancestral land, and to justify "non-kosher" means of inducing them to go there. And some of these means have ranged all the way from the ludicrous to downright dupery. At first, I doubted the varacity of a story in a book, *History of Zionism*, about the antics of a fellow named Yehudah Kopleman, who was sent to Bialystok, Poland, to induce some of its people to settle in Petach-Tikvah when it as founded in 1878 (today a town of about 100,000, ten miles from Tel-Aviv). The author describes Kopleman as a strikingly handsome and charismatic figure who could "move mountains" with his oratorical power. He addressed his gaping audience, who had gathered in the largest synagogue, thus: What are you doing in Bialystock? Why don't you come to the veritable paradise that is Petach-Tikvah? The land is so blessed there that we reap its produce without much effort. The watermelons are so huge that a family can live on half a melon for a whole week. And do you know what we do with the shell? It is so big and strong that a whole family uses it was a rowboat to sail on the Yarkon River. Imagine how beautiful and wonderful it is to see the people of Petach-Tikvah sail the Yarkon, with song and joy, on Friday afternoons before ushering in the Sabbath. And the same shell is not used twice. What for, when there are so many of them!" Well, some of the Bialystock Jews acted like *Chelemer* and proceeded to Petach-Tikvah, where they found arid land, want and disease.... The Kopleman story came to mind as I came in contact with contemporary Aliyah stories. Kopleman's yarn characterizes, though grotesquely, the attitude and methods of the *shlichim* (emissaries) and bureaucrats of the Jewish Agency's Aliyah Department. No less ludicrous and harmful are the concepts and statements of Zionist and Israeli spokesmen on this crucial problem for the future of Israel. Many years ago, I read about a meeting of Zionist leaders in Jerusalem where Israelis taunted Americans with the familiar question, "Why don't *you* send *us* your children?" Dr. S. Margoshes, who reported on this incident in his daily English column in the New York Yiddish newspaper *Der Tog*, countered with, "improve conditions and change your methods, and we shall then send you our children!" What unbelievable naivete! Israelis will demand and the Margosheses will send! Aliyah has become such an obsession that otherwise sensible individuals are guilty of innumerable nonsensical utterances of which the following are mere examples: When the Likud came to power, the new Minister of Immigration and Absorption, who was of course about to revolutionize the Aliyah Department, presented his case this way to the vice-chairman of an American Rabbinical organization: There are three thousand Jewish communities in the U.S.A. At present, we get from your country only three thousand *olim* a year, one immigrant per community. My suggestion is: let the communities commit themselves to an annual minimum quota of one family per community. This in itself will quadruple the number of immigrants, as there are on the average four members in every family. Wheher out of politeness or out of similar naivete, the Rabbi responded by promising to take up the suggestion with his organization, in order that it could be adopted as a binding decision (*Ma'ariv 11.8.77*). This nonsense calls to mind the story from Greek mythology that the birds received with enthusiasm the decision of some people to build a city in the air. A noted columnist, Levi Yitzchak Hayerushalmi, writes in Ma'ariv of October 26, 1978: "The Jews of the Diaspora do not feel as if they live in the Golah, in exile. Perhaps the original sin is in the substitution of the word Diaspora for Golah". Unbelievable! Jews don't go to Israel because of the use of one word instead of another! It is thus not at all surprising that a Mapam member declared in the Knesset years ago, that if he had the power, he would force all the Jews to come to Israel! Nor is it surprising that the Israeli press has been scolding Menachem Begin for not demanding Aliyah from American Jewry. Very simple! Menachem Begin will demand; he will utter the *Shem Hameforash*, the Divine Name, and the exodus from America will follow....

If not "making Aliyah", as the phrase goes, is a national sin, then *Yeridah* (descent), emigration from Israel, is tantamount to a national crime. No less a reasonable person than former Prime Minister Yitzchak Rabin referred to *yordim* as *nemushot*, the decadent. One can understand and sympathise with those who look askance at people who weaken their beseiged country by leaving it, but one can neither understand nor condone name-calling by responsible leaders who should realize that abuse alienates these people and does irreparable damage not only to Israel but to the Jewish people as a whole. It most certainly does not deter *Yeridah*!

Victims of Bureaucracy

I am writing this with a very heavy heart. I have asked myself many times, "why tell this story; what good will it do?" I have decided to record it, because I do not believe in "cover up". Perhaps it will come to the attention of the powers that be and will contribute, even if a little, to fundamental change in this subtle and crucial area. (Only this week, a friend of mine wrote me that his son had "experienced an astonishing amount of red tape when he arrived in Israel as an immigrant, and his used clothing and personal effects were taxed in spite of his papers to show he was considered exempt".)

A few years before we left Hamilton, I learned that Israeli citizens must return before December 1970 in order to retain certain "rights" relating to customs, mortgages, etc. Since we were committed to the congregation in Hamilton until the end of the 1972 school year, and since we were not clear about our status, we inquired from the Department of Immigration and Absorption in Jerusalem as to whether we would be considered "returning residents" or "new immigrants". (Under Israeli law, an Israeli has the status of a returning resident even if he has lived for many years in a foreign country and adopted its citizenship. In our case, there was some doubt because we left in 1952.) We did not ask for, nor did we expect "special consideration". I had hoped to work in my favorite "bridge-building" sphere in Israel for four years, up to the time I would be eligible for Pension and Social Security. This would be possible, from a financial point of view, only if we had the status of new immigrants. Otherwise, we would go to Israel upon our retirement.

For about two years, we could get no response about our status. I made a special trip to Montreal to request Leo Marcus, Executive Vice President of the U.I.A., to find out for us. In his sincere desire to help, he did something I had neither asked nor expected. In a letter to Uzi Narkiss, Director general of the Aliyah Department, he wrote:

"In the history of Canadian Zionism, the name of Aharon Horowitz is recorded as having been one of the great leaders of the Movement. His contribution to the cause of Zionism and his personal sacrifices on behalf of the creation of the State of Israel are unparalleled. It can be said with certainty that the existence of a viable Zionist Movement in Canada today is due largely to the dedicated efforts of Rabbi Horowitz throughout the years...

I would be grateful to you, both personally and officially, if you would present this matter to the Special Committee dealing with veteran Zionists, at the earliest possible moment, and if you could see your way clear to endorsing his special requests."

Narkiss responded with, "I promise you that Mr. Horowitz will receive the utmost care and consideration." His promise was followed by a letter from the Assistant Director General which stated clearly: "We have informed our representatives in Canada that Rabbi Horowitz will be entitled to all rights of a new immigrant." It took about two and a half months of telephone calls and letters to the "representative in Canada" to get him to confirm this by sending me a copy of his letter to Jerusalem in which he wrote: "I am beginning to process his immigration with all the rights of a new immigrant." We then set out on a road that led to a most difficult and traumatic year.

Our troubles started already on our way to Israel, when the Aliyah representatives on board the ship declared that we would *not* have the status of immigrants! Upon our arrival in Israel, problems followed difficulties, and difficulties followed problems. When I finally got to Uzi Narkiss about midway on this road of agony, one of his remarks was, "You can write a book about us". Indeed I could; but I do not wish to relive all those bitter experiences, and will recount only some of the most salient facts.

To say the very least, we were given "the run around" from office to office and from city to city for about half a year, before it was finally established that we were *not* "entitled to all rights of new immigrants", but only to limited rights by virtue of the fact that we left Israel before the 14th of July 1952. (These "limited rights" would not even enable us to purchase essential appliances without payment of the exorbitant duty and luxury taxes). In the course of the long run-around, we were humiliated a number of times. Most painful: an official of the Immigration Department told me, "every official in our department will consider you a traitor because you left in 1952."

My meeting with Uzi Narkiss was of a similar nature. Without looking at me, he opened and read his mail while talking to me. Here is the gist of our conversation:

"What is the problem?"

"The problem is that Mr. Lahav assured me that my status was that of a new immigrant, but it now appears that this is not so."

"What is the problem? You lived in Canada for so many years, so you must have plenty of money."

"I wasn't in business in Canada. All my efforts were devoted to Hebrew education and Zionism."

"So, we will give you a medal."

"Tell me Mr. Narkiss, what is the reason for this boorish attitude?"

"Well, you could write a book about us."

He called in and presented the case to Mr. Lahav, who said that he had written the letter to Mr. Marcus on the basis of the information he had received from the Government Department of Immigration and Absorption. (The Immigration Department of the Jewish Agency and the Absorption Department of the Government often work at cross-purposes). Lahav then assured me that I would get a regular immigrant's certificate within a week. I phoned *a few weeks* later, and was told that Mr.

Lahav was not any longer with that department and that they did not know where I could reach him...

During one of my long waiting-sessions in one of the offices, I entered into a conversation with a Russian immigrant. "Mark my word", he said, "not many Russian Jews will continue to come here. It is not what they give us or don't give us; it is not the people in Israel; it is the attitude of the damned bureaucrats". What is most disturbing to me is the self-righteousness of those who deal with and write about this issue. Never and nowhere have I heard or read that any of these people pause for a moment to search their own minds and hearts for at least part of the reason that most Russian immigrants go elsewhere, and that there is only a trickle of olim from America. It is always "they", the Russian Jews, the American Jews, etc., who are the culprits.

My harassment by the Aliya bureaucrats left me little time or energy to look for a position. I had been engaged as director of a department of a certain institution of higher learning while I was still in Hamilton. The letter of appointment stipulated that my salary would be fixed upon my arrival. I had no idea that salaries in Israel were made up of different parts, such as housing, transportation and telephone. When I discussed my salary with the personnel manager, he pronounced: You will receive nothing for transportation because you have no car; you will have no phone (it takes years to get a phone in Israel), so you will receive nothing for a phone, and you will get nothing for housing because you will be living with your son. To my question "What makes you think I would stay with my son?", he replied, "You have a son here, so we took it for granted you will stay with him". I told him I did not understand what all these things had to do with my salary. His explanations made it clear to me that "these things" made up a very substantial part of the salary. It was not, however, this "comedy" that prompted me to withdraw. I reached this decision following a serious conversation with my predecessor; in the course of his explanations of the workings of the department, he claimed that even though he had a family, he would under no circumstances continue to work there because of the boorishness of the personnel manager.

Later, I met with a high official of the Israeli Education Department. I had first met him during a previous visit in Israel, and from the letters he had written me afterwards, I had very good reason to believe that a position would be available for me in the newly created department for the Diaspora. Upon my arrival at his office, I learned that an American Rabbi had recently been appointed to an important position in that department. When I expressed my surprise that a person who had very little to do with education had been put in charge of such important work, he told me with a broad smile on his face, "He is really not interested in this department. He came to Mr. Arye Pincus (the then head of the Jewish Agency Executive) with a proposition to create a public relations department. Since neither the Jewish Agency nor we were prepared to establish now such a department, we suggested that he should in the meantime take charge of the position in our department."

Our Kafkaesque experiences led us to the decision to return to Canada. When I told a close friend about our decision, he commented, "You have been shuttling between Canada, Israel and the U.S.A. for decades. Will you ever strike permanent roots in one of them?" I replied, "I have lived, worked and have relatives and friends in all of them; I love the three of them, and there is no contradiction whatsoever in continuing to shuttle..."

There was one welcome break in the whirlwind. I was invited by the Ministry of Education to leacture on Jewish life in the U.S.A. and Canada to inservice teachers who were candidates for teaching positions in North America. The person in charge rejected outright my suggestion that we divide the large number of candidates into groups and that I conduct with them informal discussions, with special emphasis on the country to which each group was being sent. "No", he said, "I want you to give *frontal* lectures!" It was the first time I heard the expression "frontal lectures". However, although I met with the two large groups in Tel-Aviv and Haifa, I was "frontal" as little as possible. We exchanged views and experiences about *Moledet* (Homeland) and Diaspora. I learned much about the thinking of the new breed of Israeli teachers. I believe that they got some insight into Jewish life in America, and we all had some fun with anecdotes about what makes both sides tick. I recall an especially hilarious moment when a female teacher asked me, "How can you speak with so much reverence about a religion that enjoins males to recite daily a *Brachah* thanking God for not creating them females?" I shot back, "I do not recite such a *Brachah*. I recite every day, sometimes even more than once a day, 'Blessed art thou Lord our God, King of the universe *for creating woman!*" I asked the young woman who had posed the question whether she would henceforth recite such a *Brachah* in reverse. When the merriment subsided, we discussed, of course, fully the meaning of this *Brachah*. I would have loved to do this work on a permanent basis, but I understand that the entire Diaspora Department of the Ministry of Education lasted but a few short years.

About two months before our departure, I visited with an old friend, Mr. Yonah Ettinger, who was also a shuttler between the U.S.A. and Israel. He was a very influential person, and was reputed to be Dr. Nachum Goldman's "right hand man". When he heard a small part of my story, he immediately phoned Mr. Arye Pincus who suggested that we meet at my earliest convenience. When *he* heard my story, he called in his "trouble shooter" for immigration matters and told him in my presence to straighten out the affair without delay. Reading my skepticism on my face, he observed, "You apparently don't believe that the problem will be solved; you will see that it will!" As he was seeing me to the door, I commented, "Although I have already made arrangements to return, I shall change my plans, but I am afraid, Mr. Pincus, that the realities are so cockeyed that even you will be unable to remedy the situation". He didn't...

During my long entanglements with officialdom, I was practically cut off from colleagues and friends. An invitation to the World Bible Conference at President Shazar's residence therefore came as a welcome relief. At first, I hesitated to attend because I had not been in touch at all with Mr. Shazar during the eleven months of my stay in Israel. I was sure that the whole affair would inevitably come up if I were to converse with him. Nonetheless, I decided to go and to try to avoid meeting him. But already at 'the opening session, which was attended by hundreds of people, he noticed me sitting on the very last row and beckoned me to come over. Since he was surrounded by many admirers, I was hoping our conversation would be too short to go into personal matters. He, however, asked me whether I had come to stay and why I had not contacted him. I blurted out that I had indeed come with the intention of staying but would be returning in about two weeks. He asked "why, why", and told me to meet with him soon after the conference. Later, as I was talking with Dr. Alexander Dushkin, I felt a tap on my shoulder. I looked around and faced Shazar. He started questioning me about the reasons for my decision to return to Canada. When I stated my reasons very briefly, he asked me why I hadn't sought his help, and insisted that I come to see him, adding, "two weeks is sufficient time to do something".

I was faced with a very difficult dilemma. I could not ignore his wish that I see him. On the other hand, I was already conditioned emotionally against staying; I was afraid he would succeed in "doing something"! Following some very agonizing meditation, I decided to write him a letter and mail it on the day of my departure.

The gist of the letter was: "I have been perturbed ever since our conversation at your home. I appreciate greatly your attitude to me and your readiness to help. I should perhaps have communicated with you as soon as I encountered the irresponsible and insensitive attitude of bureaucrats. But — as I told you — I felt strongly that the President of Israel should not be bothered with such matters... There surely is a subjective side to my sad "saga", but as far as I am concerned, it is immaterial now whether the objective or subjective is the overrriding factor in this sorry affair. The bitter reality is that my wife's and my suffering was so great *davka* when we returned to our homeland to work for the ideals that motivated us all the years of our life in the Diaspora... The sorrow is not only because of personal grievance, but because of what seems to be a general situation...

I now dread the reopening of this painful chapter. I simply do not have the emotional strength to recount all that has happened. I therefore deny myself the "blessing" of your intercession..."

On my way back to Canada, I could not help but feel a deep nostalgia for the economic-social ethos, the idealism, and the comradeship of the simple life of the Eretz Israel of the thirties. I recalled what I had told Shazar in 1952, "Little foxes spoil vineyards (The Song of Songs 1:15) and you close your eyes."

Nevertheless, I was aware at that time, as I am even more so today, of the tremendous burdens, stresses and strains of a people, including the bureaucrats, whose very existence is under constant threat. I was confident then, as I am confident today, that this is but a passing phase and that, with the coming of peace, Israel will yet fulfill its destiny.

Chapter 27
Striking Roots, Northern California Style

"No person lifts a finger on earth without it being decreed in heaven" (Tractate Chulin). Whether or not one interprets the above quotation to mean that the Lord literally directs each person's actions, my "call" to Petaluma, California, came as suddenly and unexpectedly as if I had been catapulted to another planet; it was a sharp diversion from the nature and content of my life work. An orthodox Rabbi would most certainly say that the above quotation applies to this abrupt change in my life.

In the beginning it was a bewildering and somewhat shocking experience, although I had already been partly conditioned to it by the year I had spent at the school of an old and pretigious congregation in New York. My work in Canada had been almost entirely in the milieu of nationally conscious and, in most cases, religiously oriented Jews. I had known about and even encountered some assimilationist tendencies, a rising rate of intermarriage, and some general erosion in the structure of the family, the school and the synagogue. By and large, however, all this was happening outside of my ken of interest and activity. In Petaluma, I often found myself thinking and — at times — saying out loud, "This could not happen in Canada"! In actuality, I was given a preview of that which I had felt and stated many times could occur *even* in Canada if the emerging new trends were not stemmed by extraordinary efforts of analysis, diagnosis, prognosis and action. My two years of living and working in and with the Jewish community of Petaluma and district brought home to me also the serious danger of the continued neglect of such outlying communities by all national organizations, the conscious and unconscious needs and quests of many of the people of these centres for self-identity and for meaning in their Jewishness, and the possibilities of stemming the tides of estrangement and *escape*. I was reminded of the neglect of the small communities in Western Canada that I had witnessed when I would make my annual rounds of them during the late thirties and the early forties.

As I became increasingly aware of the realities of second and third generation American Jews who were denied what we consider to be the benefits of an intensive Jewish background and education, I recalled and understood better my father's statement that he should have left Tsfat (Safad) "to serve Jews in the *Galut* as a matter of duty" rather than have been driven by financial circumstances first to New York and later to Winnipeg. What my father failed to realize, and what our so-called world and national leaders have only started to understand faintly even now, is that the Jewish nation has lost many of its numbers during the past two or three generations largely because of its leaders' failure to comprehend that "service" such as that of my father, myself and others should have been conceived, planned and directed by world and national bodies. The future historian will find — after exhaustive research and study — that what was accomplished in the field of education in Canada and the U.S.A. in the twenties, thirties and forties was mainly due to accidental circumstances and individuals.

So, referring again to the quotation at the head of this chapter, I came by mere chance to a community that was in dire need of help, but about which the "great" world and national organizations were completely unconcerned, except when campaign times came around.

It is not my purpose to write even a sketchy history of the Petaluma Jewish community. Its uniqueness is perhaps underscored by the University of California's grant to two young scholars to research and write the history of the Jewish community. My purpose is to record my experiences, observations and evaluations as they relate to the struggle for survival of outlying Jewish communities in Canada and the U.S.A., indicate some of the lessons we could derive from their past and present realities, and to suggest some remedies. I shall therefore include as an appendix the program of studies and activities I introduced in Petaluma, as in most cases the people in charge of similar communities — including the Rabbis — are confronted with the very difficult problem of maintaining a viable and effective educational program, but do not possess the expertise and experience to cope with the situation.

Although the Petaluma Jewish Community is about 100 years old, and its present Community Centre marked its 50th Anniversary in 1976, I found — when I arrived there at the end of 1974 — a small building, comprised of a hall with a seating capacity of about 250, clubrooms to accommodate 50-60 persons, a shabby and inadequate Kindergarten room and a chapel with sixty-five seats. There was no office for a Rabbi or a Principal, no secretary, and only a pay-phone. The club-rooms consist of a small hall, which is equipped with a sliding partition to divide it into two classrooms.

I was somewhat embarrassed when the president of the Ministerial Association called on me — without prior notice — to welcome me to the community. Whether or not Rev. Herbert Bauck had this thought, it struck me that he might have been puzzled by the seeming inability of a hundred-year-old community, with a membership of about 85 families and a potential membership of about 300 families who reside in the era, to provide adequate facilities for its educational, cultural, social and religious functions.

To understand the present realities in that area, we should look back for a brief moment to the roots that brought forth the present shaky tree The early Jewish settlers, who came mostly from eastern Europe to make a new life for themselves and their children, were — in the main — leftists: socialists, bundists, Yiddishists and even some communists. What united them was an intense hatred of the capitalism they had experienced in its most oppressive forms in Russia, Poland, etc.; their desire to live in a free society, where they could develop their own modes of economic and social life; their deep faith in the socialist revolution, and their conviction that they could maintain their Jewish identity by preserving the Yiddish language, and by creating a tightly knit enclave to replace the European ghetto. Most of them engaged in raising chickens, and thus contributed to the area's development into "the egg-basket of the world".

They did *not* need a synagogue or a Rabbi. All they required was a place to meet for lectures, discussions, literary readings in Yiddish and social events, and where they could transmit their "secular" values to the new generation. They therefore built for themselves a "centre". The existing chapel was added later by new arrivals, Zionists — mostly socialist Zionists — and "Americanized" families. It is significant that the leftists' opposition to the addition of the synagogue was overcome by their realization that by having a religious congregation in the building they would be exempt from property tax.

Some of these old settlers are still so enamored of "Mother Russia" and its "Communist Paradise" that — in spite of the Kremlin's barbaric hostility to Jews, Judaism and Israel — they continue to cling to their deep faith in the communist Millenium. Following a Warsaw Ghetto Memorial meeting, where I spoke of the rising evil of Communism and Arabism, one very affable gentleman called on me to protest, also in his comrades' names, against my "insulting remarks" about Russia. And when we met the following year to plan the annual Memorial Meeting, one of the representatives of "The Yiddish Cultural Group" alluded to the sins of the past and seriously suggested that, instead of criticising the Kremlin, the meeting should protest against antisemitism in America! This old lady — who looked like a typical Yiddishe Babe — and her "comrades" evoked my sympathy much more than my disdain. Fortunately, there are very few of them left and they are mostly harmless.

As more and more American-born families moved into the area — to escape the pressures and high cost of big-city living — the clamor for a Rabbi grew increasingly. Without going into detail about the rifts between the "old" and the "new" and among factions within these two general groupings, the old gradually receded into the background — so much so that the leftists do not meet any longer in the center — and the young took over. At first, they engaged the services of a series of part-time Rabbis, none of whom lasted no more than half a year. Fortunately, there was in the community a layman — Mr. Irving Newman — with sufficient knowledge, skill and experience to serve as a "caretaker" spiritual leader for a number of years. After looking unsuccessfully for an ordained Rabbi during an extended period, events moved quickly following a chance conversation with my brother Sol, Rabbi of neighboring Vallejo, and I became the first full-time Rabbi of this unique and disoriented community.

To get some idea of the overriding effect these early settlers had on the development of the Jewish community, we have but to take a quick glance at the Vallejo Jewish community, a mere 20 miles east of Petaluma. Although its membership is not larger, and its potential membership from the peripheral towns is much smaller, the Vallejo Jewish Congregation "boasts" a large beautiful synagogue, a large hall equipped with attractive and comfortable furnishings, a separate wing for its school, a spacious modern kitchen, and a residence for the Rabbi. True, Vallejo now has a larger number of professionals and —say the Petalumans — a significant number of prosperous people, but the gap between the "assets" of the two congregations is so vast that the situation in Petaluma must be attributed — at least in part — to the leftist element who did not follow the pattern of the general congregational development and therefore remained — to a large extent — outside the mainstream of American Jewish life. True, Vallejo has had a very talented and energetic Rabbi, my brother Sol Horowitz, who for the past 30 years has been the spearhead of this thriving and vital community. But one wonders whether both the inheritance and heritage the young generation found in Petaluma would have been much greater and richer were it not for the fact — in part at least — that the old settlers "did not need" and did not have a Rabbi during most of the years of the existence of an organized Jewish community. The fact is that it is the younger people, who have moved in recent years into the area, that have given it a new lease on life. While a Rabbi per se is not yet an absolute assurance of a vital and creative Jewish life, the young people realize that they do not stand a chance without a Rabbi.

Believing as I do that *the school* should be the foundation of a community's purpose and life, I turned my attention first to study the situation and to do what was possible within the limits of the local reality, which — sad to say — was much like the reality in outlying centres in the U.S.A. and Canada.

The appendix dealing with this school may seem to some as too detailed a description of the situation in one particular community. It is, however, essential for an understanding of conditions as they prevail in many — if not in most — afternoon schools. I therefore believe and hope that the approach and program we developed in Petaluma will serve as a guide for other schools that are confronted with similar problems. For example, I found the situation to be more or less the same as in an afternoon school in New York, where I served as principal in 1973-74 — in addition to my position there as the consultant-supervisor of the Day School. However, in Petaluma I was free to reorganize the whole structure of the school, so that it became the centre of most of the community's life and activity.

The fact that the children became the main focus of the Congregation contributed much to its vitality and progress. The pupils' desire to attend Friday-night services and to actively participate in them brought to the synagogue many parents who would otherwise not have attended. One Friday every month, the pupils conducted the service entirely on their own, and were free to plan its form and content.

Gradually, more and more adults participated in Shabbat and holiday services by offering readings, recitations, etc. The children's repertoire of Hebrew songs increased constantly, so that they enlivened religious and cultural events with their singing and — sometimes — dancing. The synagogue thus turned into a live and vital force also for some of those who were not interested "in the ritual aspects of Judaism".

Having been averse myself to the Rabbinic sermon, I made it clear at the outset that I would not sermonize, pontificate, or preach. The Rabbi's function, I submitted, was to teach by analysis, interpretation, discussion and example. It is for the individual to select, accept or reject — to be *with it* or *without it*! The Service was therefore usually followed by a "teach-in". The concluding Oneg Shabbat was participated in actively by the children (the younger ones were kept busy elsewhere during the "teach in"), some of whom adorned the "head table" in place of the officers and leaders. The informal atmosphere, free of pretension and artificiality, gave the participants a sense of belonging and even of family. Non-Jews who attended these gatherings expressed their delight with the genuine simplicity and friendliness of the people.

The question has probably already occurred to the reader: In the light of the near-idyllic picture I have painted, why the bewilderment and shock referred to earlier? I was bewildered, because within about one month of my arrival I had had three presidents. The president who had negotiated with me resigned because of family reasons, the newly elected one moved to another city, and I found myself working with a brand new *Nasi*, albeit a very good one. It was very difficult for me to orient myself — in the beginning — to the purposes, the goals and the workings of a community which — to say the least — was lacking in cohesion and clear direction. It was then that I first observed that much of American Jewry can be likened to the Tower of Pisa... It mostly leans... (It is a sad commentary indeed that very many belong to one or another congregation — orthodoix, conservative, reconstructionist, reform —

without really understanding their different philosophies...) For the congregation was neither orthodox, nor conservative, nor reform, which is true of many congregations, even though they may bear one of these labels. Its resources were very meager, so much so that I often had a genuine desire to contribute to its coffers... It took about six months to convert some space to a Rabbi's study, to install a telephone, and to make other necessary improvements. It is true that there was a small building-fund, but it was "untouchable". There was strong opposition, for quite some time, to using it even for essential improvements to the existing building, although the chances for erecting a new one were very remote. At one Board meeting, when this issue was discussed, I related the story about the old woman who was found moaning in the rubble of her home at the time of the London Blitz. Somebody discovered a small bottle of scotch in the ruins and urged the victim to take a sip. Whereupon she cried: "Oh! No! No! Don't touch that that! I am keeping it for an emergency!"

Later, — as I understood the difficulties the congregation faced — I came to have a very high regard for its leaders as well as for many of its members. In all my forty or so years of work in three countries I had never seen so much readiness for any type of voluntary work. One of the members came forth to offer her free office services, and actually worked first 2 and later 4 hours daily for almost a whole year until a paid secretary could be engaged. Members performed all kinds of tasks, including hard physical work at night and on Sundays. I was once really impressed with a sight I could never have witnessed anywhere else — the president (Larry Tenzer) sprawled on his hands and knees as he was laying the carpet in my study. It occurred to me, when I thought of other congregations I had known, that too much affluence in most of them had tended to keep away their members — especially the youth — in more than one way... I thus came to like — and, sometimes, love and admire — these unpretentious and genuine young people. (The president and other leading board members barely reached age thirty!), who — although not fully aware yet of their aims and motivations — were sincerely searching for Jewish meaning in their lives and for their true identity as American Jews. They gradually won the confidence and respect of the older leaders and members, which acted as a catalyst and a leaven in the slow but sure process of the coalescence and unification of the community.

I was shocked at first by such phenomena as the president's wife being an unconverted Lutheran who attended our religious services and was more active in the congregation than many Jewish women; by an active non-Jewish board of education member who always eagerly volunteered her help, whose husband was not Jewish either and whose children attended our Hebrew school not only on Sundays but also on weekdays, and — on the negative side — by people who were "ashamed"

of their Jewish birth and engaged in all sorts of acrobatics to escape... I
later came to understand and empathize with all these people — even
with the escapees for whom I had mostly pity — with their
disappointments and disillusionments, with their bewilderment because
of the lack of a meaningful Jewish education, and with their earnest
quest for Jewish roots for themselves and their children. I soon learned
that most of the converts and their children were practising Judaism to a
greater extent than many of the born-Jews. I came to realize that these
people, as well as many disoriented born-Jews, needed understanding,
patience and subtle guidance.

Lest the reader get the notion that I am recommending and perhaps
even commending these phenomena, I should stress that my purpose is
to describe a situation that has already become a solid reality in many
places, especially in the U.S.A.; that the remedy is not to scoff and
condemn, but rather to understand, to sympathize and to bring
"sweetness out of the bitter"... My main purpose, however, is to sound
an alarm of *"things to come"* in Canada if we fail to comprehend fully the
decisive role of education, and the urgent need for its transformation
into a *living* and *vital* process. I shall therefore relate here some of my
experiences — both the dismaying and the heartening:

Not all the following incidents occurred in Petaluma. Occasionally, I
would be called upon by people from towns without a Rabbi, or by
persons whose Rabbi would not have anything to do with matters that
are not stricttly in accordance with the Halachah. Let me start with one
of those: (These are mere examples of many others):

A Case of Compassion

The voice on the phone was hesitant and disturbed. Would I conduct a
"Service" at his home for his dead father, who had already been interred
in a Christian cemetery, because "he wished to 'rest' side by side with his
late Christian wife". His father "had not been religious, did not go to
Synagogue for many years, and died of cancer following years of
suffering and voluntary isolation from family and friends". Why then did
he insist on a religious service in his memory? The response brought to
mind the inscrutability of the human mind and the intangibility of the
heart: "Before his death my father made me vow that I would hold such a
Service". Why didn't he apply to his local Rabbi? He had, but his plea was
abruptly rejected. Since this was my very first experience of this nature, I
asked him to call me back in a few hours. After agonizing soul-searching,
I felt that I must fulfill his request as a pure matter of human compassion.
I asked myself — as I did many times during my encounter with my new
realities — whether my rejection would tend to enhance and sanctify
religion or "the name of God", or whether it would push "a Jewish soul"
further into the mire of confusion and estrangement.

That Rabbi's insistence on clinging strictly to every custom, and his outright refusal to consider this man's special case, brought to mind the following Talmudic discourse in Babba Metzia (30:2). Rabbi Yochanan said: "Jerusalem was destroyed because they judged in accordance with the law of the Torah". Says the Talmud: "This statement is perplexing. According to what law should they have judged if not by the Torah?" And the Talmud answers: "Because they judged strictly according to the Torah and did not go beyond what the law requires", i.e. they did not temper justice with mercy. I concluded that to adhere strictly to every custom in those Northern California realities would contribute, to paraphrase the Talmudic statement, to the "destruction" of Judaism.

On the way to his home out of town, he talked much about himself, his parents, his feelings about Judaism and Israel. But what rang in my ears — in the torrent of words — was *"Aval asheimim anachnu"* — the fault is more ours than his. For these confused and "lost souls" were — in large measure — the fruit of our neglect, of our failure to comprehend and to deal with the realities of a *new World and a new Culture*.

His home was full of people, young and old. I later learned that most of them were of various Christian denominations. His wife — and, of course, his children, according to Jewish Law — were not Jewish. At the conclusion of the service, consisting — partly in Hebrew — of appropriate Psalms, one of his uncles, a religious-nationally conscious Jew who had come from Los Angeles for the occasion — whispered into my ears: "What you have done now is in the nature of *Kiddush Hashem* — the santification of the name of God. Sensing my puzzlement, he told me his nephew was an adopted and only son whose religious parentage was unknown. "Had you rejected his pleas, his estrangement would have been total and final. Now there is some hope..."

On our way back to Petaluma, what was mostly a monologue continued. Although he was not religious, never participated in religious services, did not give his children a Jewish education, he still considers himself Jewish. He reads a lot about Judaism and about Israel. When his children grow up, he would "tell them all about it"... In taking his leave, he made the point that I had never mentioned payment for my services. I recalled the anger of bereaved persons who — as they informed me — were deeply hurt that "how much it would cost" was the first thing certain Rabbis mentioned when called upon to officiate at funerals of non-members of their congregations.

Why Was I Always Afraid of Jews?

It was late at night when the choking voice of a bereaved father told me that his young son was dying and wanted to speak with a Rabbi. Upon my arrival at the hospital about 60 miles from Petaluma, I learned that the young man was dying in the most tragic circumstances. He was in terrible agony and could hardly whisper. After I made several attempts to "reach" him somehow, he mustered his last strength and cried out aloud: "Why was I always afraid of Jews?" He repeated this anguished outcry several times. I left without having reached him. I had a profound feeling of failure — I felt a deep sorrow that I could not give some solace to an anguished soul...

I could not sleep that night. I could not shake off the gnawing thought that the neglect and failure referred to above had something to do somehow with the desperate outcry of a young man who was not given the opportunity to really know himself and his people and could not find any meaning — even in his last breath — in the life and destiny of a nation millions of whose children had died *al kiddush hashem*" (the sanctification of the name of God)...

The nurse who tended him in his last moments told me later that he had not really asked for a Rabbi. He had asked the psychiatrist, "What will happen to me after I die — *Is that the very end?!*" The psychiatrist, true to his detached "scientific" approach, responded that he did not know, that he should ask his Rabbi. Little did the psychiatrist know that the one he was supposed to help somehow in his last moments of life, did not have a Rabbi either.

"Confusing", Sometimes "Amusing"

People seem to wonder how intelligent and educated Jewish students find their way to such fringe "movements" as *"Jews for Jesus"*, *"Jesus Freaks"* and the *"Moonies"*. Very seldom have I heard parents and Rabbis attribute this phenomenon — even in part — to the lack of a real understanding of Judaism, resulting from the neglect of Jewish education and the failure to attune it — in many places where it exists — to our times and needs. Parents usually blame the university, the loss of confidence in society and its leaders. Rabbis point an accusing finger at parents who did not bring their children to "worship" in the artificial, formal synagogues — a la "the family that prays together stays together". Aside from the question whether the synagogue, in its present form, can fulfill youth's yearning for understanding, meaning and involvement, these Rabbis and parents do not realize that *education precedes the Synagogue*, that without an intensive and vital Jewish education, *there will be no Synagogue* or any other Jewish institution. Here are just a few samples of my experiences not only in Petaluma but also in other parts of the U.S.A. Some are "amusing", some sad, some "confusing", and some somewhat heartening and hopeful.

He Didn't Mention Jesus

We were enjoying ourselves at an engagement party. A man sitting across the table described a wedding ceremony of a Jewish friend's son. It took place in a Unitarian church, with a protestant minister officiating. With glee in his voice, the man exclaimed: "The minister didn't even mention Jesus!" To him, the facts that neither one of the couple had converted to the other's faith and that the name of Jesus was not mentioned were comforting, reassuring, and perhaps even welcome. At first, I refrained from entering into an argument at an especially joyous (perhaps because both the boy and the girl were Jewish) celebration. When the person's jubilant voice continued: "That's what's happening all over!", I baffled him (afterall, wasn't I a *modern Rabbi*?) with my categorical statement: "Thank God that's *not* what is happening all over. It's happening only where Judaism has completely disintegrated!" In my heart, I was not very sure...

A Prayer for a Wedding

A member of our congregation whose late father — though a Zionist, had been one of the founders who had no need for religion or a synagogue, asked me to provide her with a "Jewish prayer" for a wedding. She apparently was ashamed or embarrassed to disclose to me what I already knew, that her son was to be married by a Unitarian minister (presumably, he would not make mention of Jesus either!) to a girl who had not converted to Judaism. She must have desired to assuage her feeling of guilt by having somebody — perhaps the minister — recite a "Jewish prayer". That, of course, would make it *kosher*. She was ruffled and indignant when I told her that a Jewish wedding ceremony consists in its entirety of Jewish prayers...

Afraid of the Name Jesus?!

It is indeed pitiful that the proverbial empty statement "I am proud to be a Jew" is bandied about by some people when they think they identify with Judaism merely by rejecting other faiths and recoiling at the sound of the name Jesus. I was the Baccalaureate speaker at a High School graduation ceremony, held at the United Church of Christ. There were only a few Jewish students among the graduates and a handful of Jewish parents at the service. The ministers — apparently in deference to the Rabbi and Jewish parents in the audience — used only prayers from the Psalms and readings from the Old Testament. Two Christian students, however, presented a duet in praise of "Jesus the Saviour". At the conclusion of the Service, a Jewish student told me with pride that he had expressed his chagrin to the person who was in charge of the program for having allowed this song to be included in the program. The Jewish student was surprised when I told him *he* was wrong. Afterall, I pointed out, about 99% of the graduates and audience were Christian, the event took place in a church, the ministers refrained from using purely

Christian prayers, the speech of the Jewish student, who sang the praise of Judaism, was not censored. What rhyme or reason, then, in censoring the Christian students' presentation? To me, it seemed rather sad that a Jewish student who had received no Jewish education, never attended any religious, cultural or social event during the entire period of my stay in that area, apparently thought he was "a good proud Jew" by denigrating somebody else's faith. He seemed to be completely unaware that while the Christian students gave expression to a "we believe", his contribution was an "I do not believe" — in other words, Judaism not through affirmation and real identification, but thru negativism. His father later told me he was convinced his son's teacher was antisemitic. How and why? She would always address herself to his son — the only Jew in the class — for answers to questions about Judaism or Israel! This man had gone so far as to protest to the principal and demand that the teacher "refrain" from "picking" on his son. Father and son mistook a natural assumption that a Jew would be informed about his people and culture for the bugaboo of anti-semitism. Isn't this Jewish "pride" in ignorance! Is this possibly one of the roads to anti-semitism!...

Yiskor Judaism

One of the main reasons for the precarious financial situation of the community is the large number of residents who say they are not religious (as if a Jewish community is merely another religious denomination), and do not therefore send their children to "Sunday school", or who do not disclaim religion but insist that because they have no children and/or do not care about ritual, they should not be expected to support the congregation. Some do agree they should pay for services rendered to them occasionally, while many others are quite ready to let others "foot the bills" even when they avail themselves of certain Jewish community services. One such incident occurred on Yom Kippur. It was just before Yiskor (a prayer for the deceased) when one of the officers whispered into my ear: "There is a woman outside whose family doesn't belong to the Congregation and never contributes anything to the community, but insists on being admitted for Yizkor without a ticket." Should he yield, contrary to the Board's decision to adhere strictly this year to the rule that no one — unless financially unable — be admitted without a ticket? Believing as I did that it was high time to put an end to a situation that allows a majority of the area residents to bear no responsibility for the maintenance of the congregation, I suggested that he use is own judgement. (I was reminded of the mother who preached to her little boy that "God put us here to help others", to which the youngster retorted, "and what are the others here for?") In my opinion, which I stated later unequivocally, the officer used sound judgement in refusing to admit her. Well, well, *"Oi abroch!* (What a furor!) Some people took strong objection to such a sacreligious act. "My God, where are we coming to when we deny a person the sacred duty of reciting the Yizkor Prayer?" These people didn't realize that the community was nearly bakrupt because it tolerated for too long a time a situation whereby many residents of the area availed themselves of community services and benefits without assuming any financial or other obligations essential for the maintenance of the Congregation. Much patience and tact was required to convince the protesters that Yizkor is not the only,or — as some of them thought — the most sacred Jewish duty, and that Jewish law and tradition require every Jew to support his community if he is financially capable of doing so.

Camps Massad Flourish

Camps Massad served not only as educational institutions where children and youth learned by living. Their influence radiated to the schools. Their pupils returned to their studies with increased knowledge, with much better fluency in spoken Hebrew, with greater motivation, and with a real sense of achievement. In an indirect way, Keren Hatarbut's most significant contribution to the revitalization of Hebrew education could thus come through a network of vital camps in all regions.

In 1955, Massad Alef, in Montreal, had reached a static situation. It could not make any further progress not only because of its physical limitations, but alo because of its dependence on U.S. personnel. Massad Bet, in Toronto, was faced with even greater obstacles. Its facilities were far from adequate; it was still based on two monthly seasons; and it had to look to Head Office for financial help. Massad Gimel which was established in Winnipeg in 1953 through the efforts of David Secter, Frank Marantz and Joseph Putter, was still dependent on the rental of a camp site, and had not yet succeeded in extending its three-week camp season. And Massad Bet and Gimel were even more hampered than Massad Alef by the lack of experienced staff.

For a short term solution, we still had to look to the U.S.A. Avraham Zimmels, a young American Rabbi who had been connected with Massad Alef for four years, first as sports director and then as head counselor, was elevated to the position of camp director, in which capacity he served with distinction for a number of seasons and made a significant contribution to its success. For Massad Bet, we recruited former Canadian David Sidorsky, a teacher of philosophy at Columbia University. Although he served only for one season, he left his mark on the educational program of the camp. One of the serious problems of Massad Bet was the constant change of directors who served for only a season or two, and were not otherwise connected with Keren Hatarbut work. A new period of intensified activity began in Toronto in 1956 with the appointment of Yosef Klinger as director of Keren Hatarbut and Massad Bet. Having had previous experience at Massad Alef, he spent his first year at Massad Bet as camp manager and acquainted himself first hand with its situation and potentialities. He then served as its director for six consecutive years. The fact that he could now give his attention to the needs of the camp throughout the year added a large measure to its stability and successful development.

For Massad Gimel, a new era started with the appearance on the scene of Leona and Alec Billinkoff. It was largely through their efforts that a majority of the shares belong to Massad. (Legally, the property in owned by "The Massad-United Zionist Organization", but a rented camp-site became the permanent property of Massad), and that its physical facilities were renovated, remodeled and developed into what they are today. Massad Gimel too suffered from a constant turnover of directors. Those who served it in its early period (Eddy Yuditzky, Zwi Horwich, Rabbi Judah Stamfer and Avraham Paritzky) either left the city or wanted a break from their year-round educational work.

Massad and Youth Movement Become One

For the long term solution, it was obvious to me that we would have to revive the Hebrew Youth Movement, develop it into a permanent training ground for leaders, and treat it as the continuation of Massad life in the city throughout the year. The camps, in turn, would have to serve, in part, as workshops for the cultivation of the leaders and members of the youth movement. In a word, the success of the camps and the youth movement would lie largely in their interdependence and interaction.

I started to meet regularly with a group of former youth leaders in the hope that they would agree to serve as the leadership of the new youth movement. Because of their wariness of publicity and their skepticism, my meetings with them were first held almost stealthily, until we were discovered by Solomon Gordon. He drove by the Keren Hatarbut office late one night. Observing a light in one of the rooms, he came in to check, and caught us "red-handed". He understood my reason for treading cautiously... The immediate, positive result of these meetings was the return of some of them to Massad. At the same time, we proceeded to lay the foundations for a National Leadership Institute as an integral part of the camp and the youth movement. We did it with the three thousand dollars that had been allocated by the Jewish Agency for delegating an Israeli teacher to Massad. We awarded scholarships to fifteen excellent Hebrew high school students from Montreal, Toronto, Ottawa, Winnipeg and Calgary, who devoted a whole month to study, discussion, and varied activity in a camp setting. Although it would have been much more convenient for me and the participants, as well as less expensive, to conduct the Institute at Massad Alef, we decided on Massad Bet, in order to help it financially and to boost its morale.

A Wedding on a Mountain

A strikingly attractive couple walked into my office in an almost furtive manner. I immediately sensed they thought they had a very serious problem. They had lived as man and wife for about six years, and now they wanted to get married. To my query, "What is the problem? Is one of you not Jewish?", came the response — in a subdued chuckle — "Eisenberg and Rosenthal (fictitious names) not Jewish?!" They proceeded to tell me they wanted the Ceremony to take place on the mountain they had purchased near Boonville, about two and a half hours drive from Petaluma, where they were in the process of building their home with their own hands. He had been a peace-corps volunteer in Turkey (here he mumbled that perhaps he should have volunteered to help in Israel); at one time, he had been in charge of the T.V. program Sesame Street, and later decided to abandon city-life for "living with nature" on their beautiful mountain. She was a high school teacher, and from our ensuing conversation, I sensed that her desire for marriage was greater than his. At this point, I inquired about their reason for wanting to get married now. They looked at one another, and answered almost simultaneously, "to please our parents". When my wife and I arrived on their truly magnificent mountain, we were met by a person (non-Jewish) whose entire appearance made us think of the Patriarchs or Elijah the Prophet. We soon learned that he too had chosen to live on a nearby mountain, in communion with nature. With great satisfaction, he showed us the wedding present he had presented to the couple — the staircase to their home he had built with his own hands.

Since all the other guests were relatives, we set out in search of two Jewish males witnesses, not at all an easy task in that area. The bridegroom thought of one possible witness, and we rushed down to town to recruit him for the task. It took some hard thinking before he recalled that the pianist at an area nightclub (that is to be found even in far-out places!) was also Jewish. When we located him at his home, I pondered — "The theme of my book — Which? *Without Roots, Striking Roots,* or *Scattered Roots*? Here, in what I would refer to in Hebrew as *Harei Choshech* — in a remote (in more than one sense) place, we find a pianist who received an intensive Jewish education in a New York Yiddish school and who obviously took great pleasure in treating us to a torrent of Yiddish songs he played on the piano. I could not help but feel that the young man was ambivalent about his performance in the presence of a Rabbi and his non-Jewish friends, and his manner betrayed *his* awareness of the seeming dissonance in the strange atmosphere that was suddenly injected into his home. *Speaking of Jewish dispersion*, of scattered roots...

Thinking of *dispersion*, I experienced a strange — if not bizarre — feeling of confusion, memories from the far (*how far?!*) past, intermingling thoughts about Judaism, Christianity, Agnosticism, and Atheism, escape and estrangement. The remote mountain suddenly became the symbol of the barren, lonely, groping, fleeing American Jew...

The ceremony was held in a fascinating and romantic setting with an arc serving as a *Chupah* (canopy), and with the cackling of geese, turkeys and peacocks providing the background music. Most of the guests were non-Jewish, unmarried young couples, some of whom told me they were so impressed with the beauty and simplicity of the ceremony that they would want me to officiate at their weddings if and when they were married. I looked at the crosses dangling on the nearly bare chests and thought about the strange phenomenon of crosses at a Jewish wedding ceremony.

What is heartening and hopeful about the *Wedding on the Montain* episode? A desire to please parents, an awakening Jewish spark, a glimpse into the beauty of Judaism by Jews and non-Jews, and the appearance of the *mountain couple* — who knows after how many years — at the next High Holiday Services...

"A Person Without Torah Cannot be a Pious Man" Avot 2:6

(Lack of knowledge and piety do not dwell together)

Unusual as it was in the smaller centers in Northern California, we had a Minyan (a quorum of ten males for holding public prayers) on Shabbat mornings, partly thanks to some university students who would appear from time to time. I soon learned that most of them could not even read Hebrew. Yet, they would sit through the 2-hour service (conducted entirely in Hebrew) with obvious reverence and awe. I befriended them, of course, and endeavoured to understand what it was that awakened their "Jewish spark". I could not reconcile, at first, the contradiction between displaying the *Talit Katan* (vest-like garment with four fringes worn at all times by Orthodox Jews) and riding a bicycle on Shabbat, or taking out a pencil during *Kiddush* in the synagogue to write down an address. on Yom Kippur, a group of them occupied the front row in the synagogue, some of them in white *Kitels* (robes), and injected some real Chassidic flavour by swaying to and fro, shutting their eyes at times in pious rapture. Imagine the agitation of some of the old people who witnessed — during the recess — the pencils in these students' hands as they wrote down my phone number in order to call me for information about the adult courses to be offered at our centre. Obviously, these young people are no hypocrites. They lack knowledge; they may be confused, but they honestly quest for meaning in life and seek genuine means of identification and involvement with their people. They are "the brand plucked from the fire" of the large army of those who have received no Jewish education at all, or received their *Lechem Haklokel* (shoddy bread) in the Sunday schools. What is heartening, however, is that many of them find the road back to us rather than to the Moonies, Hare Krishna, or other cults.

Meah She'arim'in Petaluma

One Shabbat monring, I rubbed my eyes in amazement when I saw a young man in the Chassidic garb of Mea She'arim entering the synagogue. He was strikingly handsome, and reminded me of some of the impressive figures of the Yeshivot in Tsfat and Jerusalem. He spoke an excellent Hebrew, but with an easily detected American accent. He had served in the Israeli army, was now doing graduate work, and was counting the days when he "could return home". After the service I was approached by Mr. Simon Jaffe, an erudite Hebraist (one of a kind in that entire area) who by an act of God or a quirk of fate was diverted from his way to The Land of Israel to live and have an impact on many lives in Northern California. With a gleam in his eyes, he informed me that the young man was a convert from far-out Boonville (remember the wedding on the mountain?) who could truly serve as an *Or La'no-ar* (a paraphrase of *Or'La'goyim*: a light unto the nations), "a light" unto estranged Jewish youth...

I Won't Intermarry!

A significant number of people approached me about converting to Judaism. Most of them were already married and had children. Some "could not accept Christian dogma, studied about Jews and Judaism, and considered conversion". I was delighted one morning with a visit by a young, charming student who wanted me to prepare her for conversion. Concerned that I might think her motivation was marriage to a Jewish boy, she stated categorically: "I have both Jewish and non-Jewish friends, I am not in love with any one of them, and I sincerely desire to understand and adopt Judaism!" Following a moment of silence, she added: "Of course, once I convert, I won't intermarry!"

These and other manifestations confirmed my faith in *lo alman israel* — Israel is not widowed (Jeremiah 51:5).

This faith in the continuity of Jewish life and creativity even in most difficult circumstances is made possible by individuals who are "infected" with the instinct for life — by those whose names were mentioned previously in this chapter and by an indefatigable, loveable Ann Barlas, one of the strongest "men" on the Board (a vestige of my "male chauvinism"); affable Ann Weinstock, Shelley Bauer and Chayah Eisenstein, whose love for Hadassah knows no bounds; the late Walter Weinstock, a chassid of the U.J.A. and of "unity"; Adrienne and Bob Lipman, responding to every beck and call; Sally and larry Levi, adorning their devotion with singular charm; Bernice Krulevitch, humanitarian par-excellence; Yoel Yagoda and Marcel Feibush, catalysts for peace and harmony; Lou Steinberg, in quest of ideas and reasons; and the sparkplugs of the Sisterhood Sharon Yagoda, Jan Tencer, Pat Feibush and Julie Steinberg.

At that juncture, my wife and I were enamored of Northern California in general and of our congregation and friends in particular. Why then did we leave? A clue will be found in the preface to this book. My few days in the hospital turned my attention to "ultimates". I wanted to devote all my time to writing this book, and my wife's and my desire to be near our sons grew increasingly stronger. But we still miss our friends and California.

Chapter 28
How Deep the Roots?
Perspectives and Projections

When I returned from Israel in 1973, my intention was to obtain *part-time* work in Toronto, in order to be able to write this book. I also planned to undertake a comparative study of the involvement in Jewish life and the simultaneous integration into Canadian life of individuals who are products of an intensive Jewish formation and of an equal number of individuals who are products of a minimal Jewish background and education. While still in Israel, I had been in touch with, among others, my friend Dov (Robert) Eisen, Q.C., who was enthusiastic about the possibility of my working in the field of Jewish education in Toronto. Soon after my arrival, I learned that the gates to a suitable and desirable position were closed to me for personal (one person) reasons. As for my planned creative projects, it became clear that the organized Jewish community was too poor to invest in such projects. One high official (a knowledgeable one) put it this way, "I am ready to support your comparative study, but our organization's grant would amount to no more than several hundred dollars. I am not prepared, however, to support your other project because I disagree with your philosophy." I turned to the Multicultural Organization, but the person in charge of the Toronto office at that time did not give me any encouragement. My subsequent stint in California therefore made it necessary for me to postpone writing this book until I returned to Toronto.

Try and Try Again

I turned again to the Multicultural Organization. This time, the person in chage told me she would refer my application to the head office in Ottawa. My determination to continue with the project was strengthened when I met Miss Judy Young, Literary Projects Officer of the Multicultural Program, after she had read the first two chapters of my manuscript. Miss Young is the type of person who radiates enthusiasm and encouragement. She not only promised to recommend my project, but said with conviction "Your book should be written and should be published". She also assisted me in getting a grant from the Explorations Program of the Canada Council.

Canada Revisited

For some perspective on Jewish life in Canada today, I visited some of the communities where I had worked, with a few interruptions, during the period of about four decades. I visited Edmonton, Calgary, Regina, Winnipeg, Montreal, Ottawa, New York, Albany, Hamilton, and some educational institutions in Toronto. (In Hamilton, I had a long conversation with the out-going principal, and reviewed with Mr. Jordan Livingston some of the events during my five years of service there. I had made arrangements to visit the school, but was prevented from doing so by the Rabbi's objection. This was the only time in my life that a school was closed to me. I was always more than welcome in the numerous institutions that I visited in Canada, the U.S.A. and Israel, especially in those which I had served.)

I interviewed about sixty persons, including Rabbis, Ministers, educators and communal leaders. Some of these interviews are recorded on tape and are available at the National Ethnic Archives section in Ottawa. In addition, I corresponded with individuals in cities which I did not visit.

A Complete Transformation

As I drove and walked about for several days in Winnipeg, I looked for traces of the Jewish community I had known in the mid-twenties. I could hardly find any. Everything was different: the synagogues, the Rabbis, the leaders, the schools, the organizations, the very life on the streets. Jews have obviously struck deep roots in Canada. Crucial questions loomed in my mind: to what degree have the Canadian roots replaced the Jewish roots; how strong are the Jewish roots; is there a conscious search for a synthesis between Canadianism and Jewishness; are there any visible expressions of such a synthesis? I recalled a lecture I had given, in the early sixties, to Jewish students at the University of British Columbia. Leo Marcus, who had set up the lecture, was puzzled about my subject, "I Am In Favour of Assimilation". The students too were baffled. I could hear a sigh of relief when I made my main point. Assimilation, I said, is good and desirable — nay, even mandatory — if we think of it as a process of absorbing the language, the culture, the ethos of the country in which we live. What we should guard against is *disintegration*, the process of decay that results from ignorance and abandonment of one's original language, culture and ethos. The challenge that should confront us, I emphasized, is to search for and achieve a coalescence, a fusion between the two, which fortunately draw their spiritual and cultural essence from the same roots. Now, as the thoughts of "what was", "what is" and "what might be", were going through my mind, the one big question was, "how deep are the roots and how far has the disintegration gone?"

I am not so presumptuous as to suggest that I can give the answer here, or even that I have found it. What follows will be mere thoughts, observations and indications, which will, I hope, stimulate thinking and searching.

First in line come (of course) the schools. A great debt is owed to the men and women of vision and courage who created the day schools. There seems to be a national consensus that were it not for these institutions, Jewish education would now be in a catastrophic state. Even opponents of yesteryear have recognized their great worth. This general change in attitude was aptly expressed by Chief Justice Samuel Freedman who, in my recent interview with him, told me: "My generation looked with some fear on the parochial school. There was the feeling that it amounted to a kind of voluntary ghettoization, that it was inconsistent with our obligation as Canadians to participate completely in the life of our country. We always coupled with that the obligation to remain good Jews, because as I have said more than once, to be a good Jew and to be a good Canadian are not antagonistic but concentric loyalties. They can and do coexist. We were wrong about parochial schools." He went on to say that he was happy his grandchildren are attending a day school and that he is "absolutely convinced that the experience will not in any sense make them less Canadian and that they would emerge with a far, far better background in the essentials of Jewish life".

In recent years, there has been a general growth in enrollment in day schools. According to the American Association for Jewish Education, the number of Jewish day schools in the U.S.A. and Canada has grown by more than eighteen percent in the past five years. In the U.S.A., about one fourth of the *reported* student enrollment was in day schools in 1975-76, compared to one seventh in 1965-66. In addition to new "converts", day schools gained some of the losses sustained by afternoon schools. As a matter of fact, many more parents would give their children a day school education if they could afford its high price-tag.

On the whole, the Day-Schools I visited in Canada seem to be fairing well, but I have found that there has been a general decline in standards and achievement in the Hebrew department. One cause may be the greater pressure exerted by the present generation of parents to insure the primacy of the general studies. Other causes are probably the incipient erosion in the Jewish family structure and the effects of the affluent society on children and parents alike.

But what of the afternoon schools? Are the pupils fated to continue to receive the type of education that can not possibly prepare them for Jewish life and its challenges in the Diaspora? Their situation will not improve without imaginative, innovative and daring leadership, without a *concerted national* effort to overcome the problems that beset them, particularly the state of isolation of the smaller communities. Regina and Saskatoon can serve as examples. Both of them still have a Jewish population of about two hundred families, but from the standpoint of Hebrew education, they are gradually declining to the status of such small communities as Prince Albert and Moose-Jaw in the forties. During my interview in Ottawa with Senator Sid Buckwold of Saskatoon, he said, "our Talmud Torah is now barely hanging on." When I visited Regina about ten days before the High Holidays (in 1978) they were still making efforts to obtain a Rabbi, and the school was awaiting the late arrival of a new teacher from Israel who had been recommended by her predecessor prior to her departure at the end of the school year. (Another indication of the direction of the "new winds" is the fact that a city like Regina does not now have a kosher butcher.) David Isman and Victor Samuels, veteran leaders in all phases of Jewish life, lamented (as did leaders in other centers) the absence of guidance and concrete help from a national or regional organization. My own firm conviction is that, although the day schools in the West are holding their own, the disappearance of the national and regional Keren Hatarbut has brought back the state of isolation that I found in the West at the end of the thirties and in the Maritimes as late as the mid-fifties.

Israel's Greatest Contribution

In my considered opinion, Israel's greatest contribution, quantitatively and qualitatively, to Canadian Jewish life during the past two decades has been made by the many hundreds of Israeli teachers who have served in our schools across Canada. It can safely be said as an understatement that Israelis constitute the majority of Hebrew teachers in Canada. Wherever I went, I found either that Israeli teachers are in the majority or that they reach nearly one hundred percent of the teaching staff. According to Mr. Yaakov Burke, Principal of the Junior High School of the Associated Hebrew Schools and of the Hebrew Academy of Toronto, his institutions would have to be closed, were it not for the Israeli teachers. As a matter of fact, even the Hebrew Teachers Seminaries could barely exist without their Israeli students. To be sure, it is not healthy for a community to depend so much on teachers from another country, but it is they who save the situation so long as our Canadian Jewish community cannot or will not provide its own teachers.

New Trends

In recent years, we have started to follow in Canada a trend that originated in the U.S. many years ago. Mainly, perhaps, because of the shortage of personnel with rich Hebrew backgrounds, schoool boards have come to the conclusion that a school principal does not necessarily have to be a *Hebrew* educator. In some places, he does not even have to be able to speak Hebrew. I recall the tragi-comical story told to me by one of my former students. I took it as a grotesque joke until she swore to its truth.

She was in the midst of a lesson in a Sunday school in the New York area when the principal made his first appearance in the class. The students greeted him with the song *"Heiveinu Shalom Aleichem"*. The principal then turned to the children: "Do you know, children, the meaning of Sholom Aleichem? It means I bring you greetings from the great Jewish author Sholom Aleichem". After the class sang *"Artzah Alinu"*, the principal said "and now, children, let us sing the Olinu song — *"Olinu leshabeiach..."* Unbelievable?! In my opinion, Hebrew education in Canada will be seriously affected if this trend continues. For a principal is not merely an administrator. He should be well versed in Hebrew; he should be familiar with Hebrew sources; he should be able to give direction, motivation and inspiration to his staff; he *himself* should be able to evaluate Hebrew educational programs as well as teachers and pupils. The assignment of teachers to these tasks is most undesirable. Aside from the fact that they cannot possibly replace an effective principal, they are usually Israelis who are sent by the Jewish Agency for a period of two years. When assuming their duties here, they are not familiar with Canadian realities. Even if they learn enough before the end of their tenure, they have to be replaced by other novices, so that the school suffers from the lack of even minimal continuity. In my opinion, an Israeli in the role of principal, supervisor, or even Hebrew curriculum director in a Canadian school can be likened to the guide who was hired by an American to guide him on an intensive tour of Quebec. When they got lost somewhere in the woods, the tourist expressed his surprise that one who was recommended as the best guide should not be able to find his way around. To which the guide replied, "I am really the best guide in Maine, but not in Quebec!"

Financial Dependence

Another dangerous trend is the movement toward financial dependence of Hebrew schools on provincial governments, which is already a fact in Alberta. The Jewish school boards in that province have welcomed a development that reduces considerably their financial burden. They feel confident that the fact that the government bears the cost of the general studies department will not detract from the quality of the Hebrew department, but I personally have seen the first signs of its inherent negative potential. Modern hebrew schools discarded the translation method many years ago. To my surprise, I witnessed an Israeli teacher using this method in a good day school, in a class where the level of knowledge was far below par. The embarassed teacher explained the reason: The class includes recent newcomers from other cities whom the school must admit because of its new status as a public school under the jurisdiction of the provincial Department of Education. It is true that those pupils receive extra coaching, but their significant number retards the normal progress of the class.

The big question, however, is: What guaranteee is there that some new government will not withdraw some day its financial support? The resulting crisis could endanger the very existence of such schools. In Calgary, I asked the leaders of the school whether their fathers, who preceded them as the leaders of that very school, would have agreed to the partnership with the government. All of them answered with a categorical "no!" They justified themselves by pointing to the present enormous cost of maintaining a day school. True enough, but the financial ability of their fathers was proportionately much more limited than the ability of the present generation to bear the total cost of the school.

In one city, a parent reminisced about her student days. In order to attend summer camp, she saved the ten cents her father gave her daily for bringing his breakfast to his store. Sometime later, she told me that today's children are not so diligent and conscientious as they had been in her generation, but she insisted that her children do their homework regularly. She told her son that if he would not do his lessons, he would not go to Hawaii for the next school holidays! While this must surely be an isolated case, it does shed some light on the general difference between the economic situation then and now.

To me, dependence is more dangerous in the long run than any other factor. A striking example is the Histradut Ivrit of America as compared to its Canadian counterpart. The Histradut Ivrit used to be envious of the Keren Hatarbut in Canada because the Keren Hatarbut's was funded almost entirely by the Z.O.C. Although the Keren Hatarbut's range of activities and achievements were much greater, the Histadrut Ivrit continues to exist as an independent organization while the Keren Hatarbut is no more. (To the best of my knowledge, Toronto is the only city where Yoseph Klinger continues some of the Hebrew activities under the name of Keren Hatarbut.)

To use an amusing illustration, in the comics, Dennis the Menace says to his pal Joey, "my folks say this is my room but they forget that it is in their house..."

Since the school has become a room in the house of the Education Department, the latter have imposed, so far, at least one requirement that has very little if any relevance for the Hebrew department. The B.A. degree is a prerequsite also for Hebrew teachers, so that a teacher who is fully qualified to teach all subjects in an Israeli elementary school is not qualified to teach in the *Hebrew* department in Alberta, unless he or she takes courses towards a B.A. degree! (In Israel, elementary school teachers are trained in special seminaries, where they study for two years following graduation from high school). Furthermore, one principal has already been forced out of his position because he was not prepared to go back to school to take courses towards a B.A. after about a quarter of a century of successful service as principal of his institution. A school in Alberta advertised recently for a principal whose knowledge of Hebrew and Yiddish culture would be "desirable but not a prerequisite"! This can only compound the difficulties caused by the continuing shortage of Hebrew teachers.

Sons and Daughters

It is encouraging to note that, generally speaking, graduates of day schools send their children to day schools and that many sons and daughters continue the communal work of their parents. Here and there, we can even find native Canadians as principals of Canadian Hebrew schools. In Ottawa, Rabbi Yaacov Kaploun, Director of Education, told me, "Your Massadniks are a source of invaluable support and strength to our school." I was particularly pleased to hear among the names he mentioned those of Prof. Avivah Freedman, daughter of Rabbi Baruch and Shoshannah Kravetz, and of Dr. Eliyahu Rabin, son of Rev. J. Rabin.

My visit in the Ottawa school brought back old memories. When I had visited there for the first time in the early forties, classes were held in the basement of an old building. Rabbi Baruch Kravetz, who became the school's principal in 1939, gave it his undivided loyalty and devotion until he passed away in 1956. In addition to being principal and teacher, he had to send out the bills and actually collect the money because the school did not even have an office. He also had to train his teachers. When he was offered the principalship of the Winnipeg Talmud-Torah, where he could have had much "greener fields" in every respect, he couldn't part from the institution he had nurtured with great effort from a small afternoon school to a large modern day school. Instead, he recommended for the position his younger brother, Avraham Kravetz. Preoccupied as Baruch Kravetz was with his school, he, together with Rev. J. Rabin, were the spearhead of Keren Hatarbut work in Ottawa. More than most school principals, he understood that his institution was but a link in the chain of a national movement. He was also one of the few principals who was fortunate, though, to have his wife, Shoshannah, as a partner in all his work, both as a teacher in the school and as an activist in Jewish public life.

In Montreal, Yechiel Glustein serves as educational director of Sha'ar Hashomayim and, in recent years, has played an important role in Jewish education organizations. His brother, Rabbi Moishe Glustein, is a Rosh Yeshivah of Yeshivah G'Dolah Merkaz Hatorah (a native Canadian

Rosh Yeshivah augurs well for Orthodox Jewry), and has contributed much to its progress and growth. Leona Laxer, originally a graduate of the Winnipeg Peretz Shule, later became a protege of Rabbi Avraham Kravetz, graduated from the Herzliah Hebrew Teachers Institute in New York, attended Keren Hatarbut summer seminars, and is now principal of the elementary division of the Winnipeg Talmud Torah. In Toronto, a graduate of the Associated Hebrew Schools, Mr. Joseph Rosenfield, is now principal of their general studies departments. Two Calgarians, Yaakov Chetner and Zwi Sherman, served for many years as principals in Western Canada: the former in Edmonton, and the latter, first in Vancouver and later in Calgary. Unfortunately, they have recently withdrawn from the Jewish educational field. I am convinced that this loss to Jewish education in Canada could have been prevented by a central authority, a national organization on the alert and in touch with happenings and developments throughout the country. It is a pity that an investment of many years of study and experience has been allowed to go by the board because Jewish education in Canada is very largely left to chance.

In some places, graduates of the local school form a significant segment or even the majority of its board of directors. This is especially the case in Calgary, where sons have taken over from their fathers. Al Rubin, Charles Waterman's son-in-law, and (later) his son Dave Waterman stepped in as president after the passing of Charles Waterman. They saw the school through years of financial difficulty, and have continued to give it their full support after withdrawing from the presidency. During my recent visit there, I saw the Waterman spirit still at work: The music teacher of the school, Mrs. Chetner, (wife of Dov who is one of its most devoted graduates) told me that during a casual meeting with Dave, he inquired about her work in the school. When she told him she could do much better with some costly musical instruments the school could not afford, he said, "Go ahead, buy them and have the bill sent to me." The president, Mr. Joseph Spier, Q.C., is a graduate of the school; Frank Kettner, grandson of Shaye Jaffe who was president and Board of Education Chairman for many years, is now Board of Education Chairman; Yale Joffe, whose father was Treasurer for a long time, served in the same capacity. All of them, as well as other graduates, are deeply involved in communal Jewish life and are devoted to their alma mater.

CAMPS MASSAD

Massad Alef

Before leaving for California, I was deeply shocked when I read in the Canadian Jewish News (October 25, 1974) that "Camp Massad was forced to close its doors, but Camp Hagshamah has received a reprieve". The recommendation to close Massad was "reluctantly" justified by Menachim Roytenberg, who stated, "How can I, in all honesty and with a clear conscience, continue to permit the Jewish community to subsidize a camp that simply isn't flickering ... when that same Jewish money is so badly needed in the life and death struggle of the state of Israel". But, it was decided at the same meeting and by the same people to reopen camp Hagshamah! And the reopening of this camp was defended by Col. Joel Wolfe, President of the Z.O.C., Eastern Region, who said, "the decision was made to reopen the camp because we cannot afford to have a Zionist youth movement camp closed. It will prove to be a tragedy for the Jewish community of Montreal, and it would hurt the Zionist Youth movement of Young Judea drastically". *Hebrew Camp Massad No, Young Judea Camp Hagshamah Si!* It is true that enrollment in Massad Alef had dropped to about sixty in 1971, but, although it had picked up to about ninety five in 1973, the Z.O.C. did not consider it worthy of a chance for a new lease on life. I could not contain my tears when I thought of the death of an educational institution that had contributed so much to Canadian Jewish life. I told my wife, "I feel as if a child of mine has died".

I underestimated, however, the deep roots of Massad Alef. How great was my joy when I learned after I returned to Toronto that Massad had been given a new lease on life by none other than its graduates! Fortunately, its founders had had the foresight to incorporate it as a company, so that it was not included in the take-over of the Keren Hatarbut by the Z.O.C. A group of former Massadniks prevented the Z.O.C. from closing it by assuming full responsibility for its continuance!

Massad Revisited

It was with excitement and great expectations that my wife and I planned our visit to Massad in the summer of 1978. We were reminded of our pioneer days when we were told that the camp office had to be moved to the home of Dvorah Tonchen (Wexler), who had been a camper in the first year of Massad's existence. Later, the *shaliach* of the Youth and Chalutz Department, Yehudah Grossman, put at their disposal one of the rooms in his office. He too had been at Massad, as a camper-waiter, in its first season. The early days came to mind also when the President, Professor Mordechai Yalovsky, former camper, Machon graduate and Hebrew Youth Movement leader, recounted to me his committee's financial problems. It was no easy task to embark on the revival process. The assembly hall in the Galil unit of the camp had collapsed, fire had taken its toll of some bunks, and most of the facilities were in need of repair and renovation. And here they were, and still are, a group of young academics and professionals facing a financial burden they could not possibly cope with if left to their own resources. The only old-timer to whom they could look for some help was David Finestone, whom they honoured at the camp's twenty fifth anniversary celebration. The Canadian Zionist Federation (!) and the Allied Jewish Community Services had rejected their pleas for assistance. It is astonishing that the Canadian Zionist Federation which, according to many informed people, spends significant sums of money on fringe activities, cannot find even a small place in its huge budget for an essential Zionist educational institution. As to the A.J.C.S., according to Professor Yalovsky, its Executive Vice President, justified his organization's denial of help to Massad by his lack of confidence in the future of camping. That does not, of course, prevent them from subsidizing other camps! Moreover, the rapid increase in enrollment in Massad by over fifty percent proves the baselessness of the projections of some professionals, just as the past phenomenal success of Massad disproved the pessimism of some of its leaders in the late fifties.

Nor was there a Mr. Gold in sight to come forth with substantial loans. A few years ago they did obtain a $10,000 loan from the Jewish Agency, but that did not go very far. It was pleasing, however, to learn that Mr. Gold's grandson, Danny, who was also a camper from the very first season, continues to give his financial support to the camp although he now lives outside of Canada. At the same time, it is disappointing that here too the names of the founders are quickly forgotten. I remember Isaac Gold's statement to me that the decision to name the hall after him pleased him greatly not because of the honour conferred on him but because his descendents "will identify his memory with Massad." But, alas, nothing in Massad now bears the name of Isaac Gold.

All this was forgotten temporarily when we saw the children at their various activities. The spirit and vitality of Massad were in evidence everywhere. The singing in the dining hall was just as lively and enthusiastic as it had ever been in this happy camp. When I was asked to speak about "then" and "now", I was moved to tears and was unable to complete words of nostalgia and joy.

In spite of the dificulties that beset the new pioneers, we left the camp with a feeling of confidence in its future. A group of young people who have succeeded, in a short few years, in improving significantly the camp's facilities and in increasing the enrollment from a hundred to over a hundred and fifty, will not surrender to difficulties. At the same time, I am issuing a plea to all former Massadniks and to those who cherish Hebrew life and creativity to extend their support to this Hebrew jewel in the Laurentians.

On the bus back to Montreal, we met a counsellor from Pine Valley camp. I asked her whether the Massadniks still beat Pine Valley in most of the intercamp sports games. "They sure do", she said, "so far, they have done it in nineteen out of twenty games!"

Just as Massad progressed in its heyday simultaneously with the growth of the leadership institute and the Hebrew youth movement, so did its decline coincide with the disappearance of the Hebrew youth movement and its leadership training program. The camp thus has had to rely again for the bulk of its staff on the U.S.A. and Israel, as was the case before the leadership institute and the youth movement developed their own leadership. It is to be hoped, though, that with the renewal of the Machon program, Massad will soon be able to rely again, in part at least, on its own resources. Perhaps, the Hebrew Youth Movement too will be renewed.

Massad Bet

It will be recalled that Massad Bet had not been opened for the 1963 season. When I was in Hamilton, I learned that it had started to function again but with even greater difficulty than in the past. In 1977, I read in the Canadian Jewish News (Nov. 11, 77) that, in announcing the camp's closure, Mrs. Rose Hersh "would not elaborate on Massad's fate other than to say she had personal reasons for closing down operations". To complete as much as possible the story of the birth and death of an important educational institution, I requested Mrs. Hersh to help me fill in some of the gaps.

To me personally, the beginning of her story was of special interest. At the conclusion of Massad Alef's first year, I had stated that the effectiveness of elementary Hebrew schools and the continuation of Hebrew education on higher levels could be insured by the proliferation of Hebrew speaking camps. I said that I could foresee a time when a school as large as the United Talmud Torahs of Montreal and/or a group of smaller day schools would combine their efforts to create summer camps as integral extensions of their educational programs. Mrs. Hersh apparently had such a plan in mind when she purchased the campsite in Torrance, Ontario with the intention of turning it over to the Associated Hebrew Schools in Toronto. Since the "Associated" was not ready to assume this responsibility, the camp became Massad Bet of Keren Hatarbut. When the situation became so precarious in the early seventies that the camp was about to collapse completely in 1972, Mrs. Hersh made a special trip to Montreal to plead in vain with the Z.O.C. for Massad's life.

She then decided ("unwisely", as she said) to operate it on her own, in the hope that the Z.O.C. or some other organization would eventually step in to insure its existence as a Hebrew speaking camp. Since this did not happen, and she could not carry the burden any longer, she finally decided to close it down in 1978. If my views regarding the potential impact of Hebrew speaking camps on the formal educational process are even partially valid, it would be a boon to the Jewish community in

Toronto if all the day schools were to combine their efforts to revive Massad Bet as an overall community project. The C.J.C. could certainly play an important role in such an endeavour. According to Mrs. Hersh, Massad Bet is now probably the best equipped and most beautiful Jewish campsite in the area. I have heard it argued that camp Ramah meets the needs for Hebrew camping in Ontario, but this is not so. First of all, one such camp is certainly insufficient if Hebrew camping is to develop as an extension of formal schooling. Secondly, Ramah is not a strictly Hebrew *speaking* camp. Its focus is more on studies, and its program is therefore geared more to students of afternoon schools than of day schools.

Massad Gimel

Massad Gimel's good health and stability is due in large measure to the continuity in its leadership for about a quarter of a century. During my recent visit in Winnipeg, I was told that Leona Billinkoff intended to retire completely from the camp. I expressed my concern, but she assured me of the camp's permanent, deep roots. Knowing Leona as I do, I felt, without telling her so, that it would be impossible for her to withdraw completely from something she had helped so much to nurture. Now, seven months later, I am happy to include here her projections for the coming season and the future: Although she will not continue as administrator, she will still be heavily involved on the board and all the committees. She will be handling a great deal of the fund raising, which brings in many thousands of dollars annually for scholarships and improvements. The new administrator will be a former camper, Sophie Tapper (Ingberman), who has given up a job with a bank, at a financial loss, in order to serve her alma mater. Most of the members of the board are Massad graduates. The chairman is Dr. Richard Boroditsky, former camper and head counsellor; the vice chairman, Arky Berkal, former camper, counsellor and director; the secretary, Fagie Krieger (Rosner), former camper and counsellor. The new director is Jeff Ross, the fifth Massad graduate to serve as its director. The other four were Gad Horowitz, Arky Berkal, Anne Wagner and Jack Boroditsky. The outlook for the coming season is excellent, and registration is moving very briskly. Of special significance is the fact that Massad Gimel continues to train its own staff.

Massad Gimmel, the only Hebrew speaking camp west of Toronto, stands out as a tribute to the steadfastness of a dedicated group of individuals who cherish Hebrew education and creativitiy.

Youth

Winnipeg and the West were once alive with Zionist youth organizations and activities. I knew of the complete disappearance of the Hebrew youth movement, even in Calgary where it had originated. My inquiries about Young Judaea in various places elicited answers such as, "very little", "non existent" and "dormant but not dead". I was not surprised, because even when it had been sponsored and supported by what was at the time the largest and strongest Zionist body, the Z.O.C., Young Judaea was beset with many problems and crises. Now that its parent organization is in the process of liquidation, and there is not even one Judaean camp left in the whole region, there is a real danger that it will soon become completely extinct, at least in the West. What there is of Jewish youth activity, I was told, is centred largely around B'nai-Brith and some synagogues. I discussed this development with former Judaeans, particularly with Aliza Poskanzer (Flaum), a native Winnipegger and social worker, who had been deeply involved first in Young Judaea and later in Habonim, and has raised her own children in Winnipeg. In comparing the present with the past, I asked: "Is there a feeling of Jewish life today as there was then?" Her answer as, "no, there isn't. There is really no youth movement. There is a synagogue youth. They go to conventions, and participate in Jewish life the way their parents do. It's a very social thing. It's rooted in a day-to-day life of this community — dances, dinners, etc. I don't think the content and the Jewish knowledge are terribly deep."

It came as no surprise to me to learn about the existence of a Lubavitcher youth organization and summer camp in Winnipeg. As is well known, Lubavitch has succeeded of late in extending its influence in various areas of Jewish life. However, by its very nature, Lubavitch can reach very limited numbers and only in large centers. There obviously still remains a vast vacuum to be filled if Jewish youth is to be guided and cultivated for meaningful and intensive participation in Jewish living.

Zionism

I put the question of Zionism and organizational Jewish life "then" and "now" to many people. The excerpts that follow represent samplings of their views. For background, I start with Noah Witman. He arrived in Winnipeg in 1927, at about the same time I did, but he has lived there continuously and has witnessed the tremendous changes that have taken place during the past five decades. For many years, he was also a sort of troubador-ambassador throughout the small communities in the West. He brought to Jews in far flung places a taste of Yiddish and Hebrew song, folklore, humor and his own Yiddish verses that were usually parodies of Jewish life. I remember especially his song about "Samelle the Bar-Mitzvah *ingelle* (little boy) who will repeat his *Maftirel* and *speachelle* like a parrot." For some years, he was also owner-publisher of the Israelite Press, and has persevered in his effort to keep Yiddish alive by various means, including a weekly radio program. Through his

Travel Bureau, he is in contact with people throughout the West, and has his finger on the Jewish pulse in the area.

In the main, his was a sad story: "It was an altogether different life. We had in Winnipeg about fifty organizations and *landsmancshtafen* (societies). The language was Yiddish — completely. I don't know whether we now have two or three of these organizations ... We had a very active Canadian Jewish Congress, and I think Winnipeg was one of the few cities, or perhaps the only city where elections to the Congress were actually held. Now, we hardly hear about the C.J.C. ... Zionist life consists only of campaigns. There are no Zionist club meetings; there is nothing ... I am told that intermarriage has reached over thirty-five percent — imagine, over thirty-five percent intermarriages in Winnipeg! ... There is no Jewish life anymore in the small communities. Here and there are still a few Jewish families. I don't think their children receive any Jewish education ... Jews who come in to my office don't understand even one word of Yiddish! ... I don't feel optimistic ... I am afraid that only the very religious Jews, such as the Lubavitcher, will keep Judaism alive...."

Without being pessimistic, Dave Waterman of Calgary used the following hyperbole in expressing this metamorphosis: "Probably, we were one step out of the ghetto while our children are a thousand years out of the ghetto!"

"It is not all bad"

My interview with Senator Sidney L. Buckwold took place in his office at the Senate. I have known him since he was Regional President of Western Young Judaea. As a matter of fact, I thought then that if he had lived in Winnipeg, there would have been much greater harmony and cooperation between the youth and the Z.O.C. At a time when the day school was under attack, he understood its "very important contribution to Jewish life".

Senator Buckwold, who has been involved in Jewish life all these years, opened his remarks by reminiscing about the late thirties, when Zionism was very much alive in Western Canada. "At that time", he said, "Jewish youth took two directions; a few of them became communists, many became Zionists. Both had an appeal. I became a Zionist, and it has been a meaningful experience for me". In comparing that period to the present, Senator Buckwold observed: "We lived a Zionist life in Saskatoon. We had so many Zionist organizations that there was something going on almost every night of the week. We had a Histradut group, a Mizrachi group, a University group, a Zionist Council, etc. That has disappeared. Hadassah, though, is still very strong ... I think we have lost the philosophical and inspirational aspects of Zionism ... We are now faced with the realities — no more philosophies ... Zionism is expressed now more by financial commitments. I think that the inspiration for Zionism and the real love and support of Israel is almost self-generating now rather than coming from our organizations. I haven't felt their influence....

The community in general lacks leadership, but I am delighted that some of the young people are taking over the responsibilities, and we could have some revival... We are not able to interest our many academics and intellectuals, though some of our marvellous University people *are* dedicated to the Jewish community..."

On Israel's influence, Senator Buckwold said: "Although Israel has not had the great impact I had envisioned as a Judaean in 1939, people have developed a keen interest in Israel and are thrilled by what is going on there. That has made them better Jews. Also, Israel *has had* a significant cultural influence on the many young people who go there for short periods of time ... What of the future?: I am not writing off the Jewish youth. No, it isn't all bad ... I am not entirely optimistic, but I am not completely pessimistic either ... Jewish life will not disintegrate. It will perhaps not be the kind of Jewish life you and I would like to see, but I think it will go on in a different way..."

Money Raising Overshadows Everything Else

Not only Witman and Senator Buckwold saw fund raising at the core of Jewish organizational activity. With whomeever I spoke and wherever I went, I heard this refrain. It was best summarized by Yale Joffe of Calgary: "Cultural life is almost nonexistent ... Money raising overshadows everything else. It even tends to divide the community. Top givers meet and hear the best speakers who come to raise funds ... These distinguished people are very rarely heard by the community in general."

A Change in Leadership

A possible clue to the shift of emphasis to fund raising was given by Chief Justice Samuel Freedman of Winnipeg. Justice Freedman has never confined his work to the judiciary or to the Unversity of Manitoba when he served as its president, nor has he limited his interest and participation in Jewish life to the West. He has been in touch with Jewish affairs on a national level, and has made his mark on various institutions and organizations.

In discussing the changes that have taken place on the Jewish scene, he observed: "It seems to me that what has happened in Canada, and I think in the United States and in South Africa and in England, is that leadership has tended to be equated with subscription capacity. Leadership is gone to the businessman. Who were the leaders in Jewish life fifty years ago? They were the Chaim Weizmans, the Shmarye

Levines and the Rabbi Stephen Wises. Where are their counterparts today? Today their place has been taken by the successful businessman who moves among the circles of people of that class, also successful, and is able therefore to raise money from them. He, himself, will be a good donor and he will be a good canvasser, a good worker. In fairness, I want to make it clear that I am not speaking critically of these businessmen who have assumed the role of leadership in Canadian Jewish life. In a way, the time called for that sort of thing. What was needed was money, and the academic or professional person was not the type of individual who could meet that challenge. And also, in fairness, I think I should add that there are and always have been and I suppose always will be successful people who give only a minimum of support to good causes, so that we should be thankful for the leadership that we have got, albeit it may not be on a moral, spiritual or intellectual level."

The Wisdom of Yefet in the Tents of Shem

The Talmud (M'nachot 9) speaks of a fusion between the wisdom of Greece — descendants of Yefet — and the teachings of Israel-descendents of Shem. Translated into modern terms, the reference clearly is to a quest for a synthesis between Western and Judaic cultures.

To me, David Newman, Q.C., is a unique example of a person who is deeply rooted in the cultural sources of his people and of his adopted country. When he arrived in Canada in 1924, at age thirteen, from Bochnia, Galicia, he had already attained a comparatively high level of biblical and Talmudic knowledge. His uniqueness lies in the fact that he is one of very few Canadians of his generation who developed into a Talmudic scholar without becoming a Rabbi, a phenomenon that was widespread in Europe and is still a fact among orthodox Jews in Israel. As mentioned before, for every Rabbi there were hundreds of Mevinim, or Talmudists. Such scholars sometimes surpassed even Rabbis in wisdom and knowledge. In that tradition, Newman continued to increase his Talmudic knowledge as a student of Rabbi Judah Leib Graubart while he was pursuing his general studies in Toronto schools. Equally remarkable, he has continued to be a student of the Talmud all these years, and until four years ago he delivered a weekly Talmudic *Shi'ur* (discourse) at the Torah Va'avodah synagogue. At the same time, he is well read in modern Hebrew literature, and speaks Hebrew fluently. Furthermore, he has found time to serve the general and Jewish communities in leading positions in various areas and at the local and national levels. His observations and opinions are therefore of special interest.

On the question of Zionist organizational activity "then and now", his story was not much brighter. He cited some examples: Of the Men's Zionist Clubs that existed in Toronto in the past, there now remains only the Ajalon Lodge. In those days, every meeting of the Zionist

Organization in Toronto was preceded by a short Shi'ur, conducted by various members. Young Judaea was strong not only in numbers but also in cultural substance. Manny Brown and he met weekly with all Judaean club-leaders to review in depth the subjects they were to discuss with their charges. Those things are no more. In the early forties, there were in Toronto about 600 Judaean members divided into forty groups as compared with 150 members divided into four age-groups today.

On the relationship between Israel and the Canadian Jewish community: If ever there was any justification for the existence here of different Zionist groupings, there certainly is no rhyme or reason now in the diffusion of our efforts and limited financial means in different directions. We have no right to advise or tell Israelis how to run their affairs, just as they have no right to tell us what is good for us in Canada. Our Jewish community, locally and nationally, should be able to look after its affairs, including those concerning our support of and relationships with Israel, without a Canadian Zionist Federation. "That is certainly not needed now; it's a waste of money," since there is today only an insignificant number of Canadian Jews who are not Zionists.

"*Shomer Mah Milayil* — 'Watchman, what of the night? (Isaiah 21:11), What does the future hold for us?" A person with David Newman's Jewish background, erudition and insight must have faith in *Netzach Yisrael Lo Yeshaker* (Samuel 1:15,29), that God will not abandon Israel. "There is the negative side, but there is also much of the positive. While it is tragic to have lost so many of our young people, there is also an upsurge among them to return and to keep to the fold. In Toronto, for example, the orthodox have made significant progress, and are filling some of the gaps..."

On the subject of the over-organization in our Jewish community structure, there was near unanimity that the Canadian Zionist Federation is now superfluous.

With full knowledge that no price is awaiting me for my attempt at imitating the Peter Principle, I have formulated the "Horowitz Principle": "The size of the roof-organization is by far disproportionate to its underlying structure, and the roof continues to expand even as the structure shrinks." To use the new expression "umbrella organization," the umbrella expands as the drought intensifies."

I believe it was Dr. Chaim Weizman who answered the question "What will happen to the Zionist Organization after the establishment of the state of Israel," thus: The paid officials will make sure that it continues to exist.

It seems logical that now that an organization with a large country-wide constituency (the Z.O.C.) has been supplanted by a bureaucracy, by a "roof" without much of a real structure, and since ours is a Zionist-oriented community, there should be only one national coordinating organization — the Canadian Jewish Congress. Nostalgia for the past glory of a separate Zionist organization or Federation would be like the desire of the omelette to become an unbroken egg again.

When the welfare funds came into being in the late thirties, the strongest argument in their favor was that they would eliminate duplication of effort and expenditure. Well, now that we have combined appeals and "efficiency in fund raising" it would be instructive and valuable to undertake a study of the disposition of the vast sums of money that our small Canadian Jewish Community spends annually in and around our efforts for Israel. There is now a proliferation of "co-sponsors." It seems, at times, that to justify their existence, a number of organizations co-sponsor an event that could easily be undertaken by one of them. In some cases, the "co" is fictitious anyway ... The celebration of Israel's Independence Day could serve as a good example. The event is marked by synagogues and various organizations. If there is to be a community-wide celebration, are we so poor in "organizers" that we must maintain a special bureaucracy for this and other such affairs? We harp on the fact that we do not have sufficient financial means for "this" and for "that". Has a serious accounting ever been made of the fat that could be cut from our heavy-laden organizational structure? Somebody recently pointed out to me that a certain high official in the "Zionist family" was receiving as high a salary as the president of the 2.3 million-member Canadian Labour Congress. My query of one of our leaders about this matter was met with a broad smile: "Yes, some of our civil service are among the highest paid in the country."

In discussing this issue with some officials, they tell me that their decisions "are taken by consensus." My definition of such consensus is "an islet of agreement in an ocean of unawareness or indifference ..." To their reference that I am a controversial figure, my response is, "If you and I disagree, I am controversial. What then are you?"

All Dressed Up and Nowhere to Go

When my son Gad was an undergraduate student at the University of Manitoba in the mid fifties, he remarked, "They dress us all up, but there is nowehere to go." He was referring to the fact that university students with a good Hebrew background had "nowhere to go" to give expression to the Jewish knowledge and experience they had acquired. Having come from Calgary, where there was a Hebrew High School and an active Hebrew speaking youth movement, he was disappointed that there was no opportunity at that time for social and cultural activity in Hebrew in Winnipeg's large and vital Jewish community. That was a generation ago, when there were few Hebrew day or afternoon high schools and we had not yet provided our youth with places "to go to," such as Hebrew speaking camps and youth groups.

The Neglect of Hebrew

Hebraists worked hard for many years to gain recognition for Hebrew in Jewish public life. We were always on guard that Hebrew should be heard, even if only symbolically, at Zionist conventions and at public gatherings and celebrations. We used our influence to have some Hebrew included on printed invitations and programmes. And we were looking forward with confidence to the day when Hebrew would come into its own after the fruits of our labour, the graduates of our formal and informal institutions, would take their place in the Jewish community. It is therefore disappointing to witness the present disregard for Hebrew at public functions, when we now have thousands of young people who understand Hebrew. It is all the more regrettable that they are not provided with the opportunity to make use of the Hebrew knowledge they acquired through many years of study and activity. To the best of my knowledge, there is not now even one Hebrew speaking group in the whole of Canada.

During my visit in Montreal in the fall of 1978, I learned that in recent years it has been the Jewish Public Library that has taken the initiative in sponsoring Hebrew lectures. Although there were only three Hebrew lectures during Sept.-Dec. 1977 (only one of the three was co-sponsored by the Canadian Zionist Federation) as compared with fifteen in Yiddish, even these three lectures are to the credit of an institution that has no *special* mission to promote Hebrew. I understand that while the library continues to organize eight Hebrew lectures in Montreal annually, the C.Z.F. defrays half of their cost. It is noteworthy that people imbued with the ideal of preserving the Yiddish language and literature had succeeded in maintaining the library through many difficult years. This unique institution has developed into a centre of Jewish culture, research and adult education, which is now financed largely by the Allied Jewish Services of Montreal. I was fascinated to hear from the present director Mr. C. Treppman and from Chaim Spilberg, a former president, about the progress, the contents, the program and the workings of this magnificent institution.

And speaking of Yiddishists, (the term is used here to denote not doctrinaire Yiddishists, but rather people who are dedicated primarily to Yiddish), it is again to their credit that they are on guard to maintain the hard-won place of Yiddish in the activities of the Canadian Jewish Congress. To me, it seems rather ludicrous that the custodianship of Yiddish has apparently been assigned to the Congress, while the guardianship of Hebrew has been apportioned to the Zionist Organization. Be that as it may, it is unfortunate that the official Zionists are delinquent in the guardianship of the language of our National Renaissance. It was quite painful for me when I attended Israel's thirtieth

Anniversary Celebration at Ontario Place. Hebrew was conspicuous by its absence from the publicity and printed programmes. None of the speakers (not the Israeli Ambassador, nor the representative of the Canadian Zionist Federation) at the main event, at the concert, spoke even one Hebrew word at a celebration of the renewal of Jewish nationhood. The two non-Jewish dignitaries were the only ones to utter the one Hebrew word — *shalom* — that night. When I mentioned this to Mr. Ben Kayfetz of the C.J.C., he said that the C.Z.F. was the chief sponsor and that his organization had merely lent them a helping hand!

My People are Destroyed for Lack of Knowledge (Hosea 4:6)

While knowledge per se is no guarantee that our world will someday become the "best of all God's worlds," ignorance is a certain guarantee that it will not become better. By the same token, Hosea's outcry "My people are destroyed for lack of knowledge" is relevant to the "Jewish condition" in Canada as in other Diaspora countries. Even the greatest of optimists can not look with equanimity on the general increase in Jewish *Am Ha'aratzut* (illiteracy), which is one of the main contributing factors to the disintegration of our Jewish roots. These few examples are symptomatic of this *Am-Ha'aratzut*. The convention Programme of a large national organization carried in Hebrew the name of the organization and a translation of "Plenary Assembly" and of its general theme. All three lines were grossly incorrect! By the way, these few Hebrew words were included in a large four page programme, with equal space in English, French and Yiddish.

In a news item in a Canadian daily newspaper, a Rabbi was quoted as saying, "Jews celebrate New Year in the middle of the year to enable them to look back over and assess the first six months of the year and to prepare and make better the rest of the year."

On the front page of a Jewish magazine there appeared this Hebrew translation of the slogan: "You have come a long way

Jewish woman	יְהוֹדִי אִשָׁה
you have come	לְאתָ
a long way	דֶרֶךְ הֲרִיקָה הָרֵחֵק
baby."	יַלֵד

In Haddassah's monthly magazine, their Hebrew expert translated *"Bein yoshvin u'vein msubin"* (from the Mah Nishtanah) as "between a sitting and reclining position."

And a humorous story about this illiteracy is the one concerning a Yahrzeit. A man told the *shamash* (sexton) that he would be coming to the synagogue on Wednesday to observe his father's Yahrzeit. He would give the sexton twenty five dollars on condition that he should not be given an *Aliyah* (he should not be called up to the Torah). The smart cookie of a *shamash* told him, "If you give me fifty dollars, I will arrange that the Torah should not even be taken out from the Holy Ark that day! (As informed Jews know, on ordinary weekdays, the Torah is read only on Mondays and Thursdays.) I have been appalled in recent years by the large number of people who stumble in reading the Brachot even in transliteration when they are given an Aliyah; most of them don't even know their parents' Hebrew names.

They Influence Jewish Life

With all due regard for their dedication, some of these people are in a position to influence the quality of Jewish life and the future of important institutions. Aside from the lack of real authority and consensus in the Jewish community, people devoid of Jewish background and knowledge sometimes give wrong direction in crucial areas. They appoint Rabbis, principals and educators, often on the basis of the candidate's appearance and sense of humour. In many cases, the candidates "flexibility" or timidity is the determining criterion, in the spirit of the story that following a lengthy discussion, the chairman of a synagogue board summarized it with the statement, "Then, gentlemen, it's agreed that our new Rabbi should be a man with strong opinions, and with the strength not to express them!" That is why a school principal ceases to be excellent when the president or some other influential individual happens to take a dislike to him. That is why individuals who plead poverty when faced with the necessity of important innovations will readily spend many thousands of dollars (of public funds) in severance pay to replace a person of proven ability, effectiveness and devotion. That is why officials and Rabbis can manoeuver relatives, wives and "favourites" into high positions regardless of qualification. That is why in some cases a principal is dismissed because he doesn't have sufficient rapport with some members of the staff, while, in other cases, a principal is considered excellent because he has the teachers "good and frightened." And that is why some of the best Rabbis, principals and teachers abandon the field at the first opportunity.

A glaring illustration of the negative influence of some officials is my experience at one of the largest and most prestigious congregations in the U.S.A. The Rabbi was ready to dispense with an excellent teacher because of $200, but spent thousands of dollars annually on a series of lectures by luminaries. Although a man of strong character, he was so afraid of his president that he sacrificed educational principle for impression and image. An example was his disapproval of my suggestion that we have separate services on the High Holidays for younger and older children, instead of a combined service for all ages, from pre-schoolers to junior high school students. His reason? "The president is always impressed with the large number of children crowded in the chapel." If they are divided into two or three groups, one or two of them would meet on another floor and the president would then be greatly disappointed to see a much smaller attendance when he makes his usual peep into the chapel... To my question, "Why can't you explain to the president the reason for holding separate services for the same large number of children?", his reaction was, "The president is an old man, is set in his ways, and prefers to see a crowded chapel...."

Another case in point is a large community in the U.S.A., where a principal had worked very hard to establish a congregational day school. Some years after it had been in operation with unusual success, the principal returned from his summer vacation to learn that a new president, an opponent of day schools, had engineered a decision to close the day school, without having given the principal any prior intimation whatsoever. He was simply confronted with a fait accompli. He immediately resigned and eventually left the field in disgust. I personally know of no small number of former Rabbis, Hebrew teachers and principals who are now happy working in other fields or teaching in the general public school system.

This situation was summarized caustically by Joe Putter of Winnipeg! "As long as there are no established criteria and authority in Jewish education, and as long as ignoramuses like so and so can determine policy by virtue of their wealth and/or assertiveness, Jewish education will at best continue its ups and downs by mere chance." He told me that in a discussion with Rabbi Avraham Kravetz on this subject, the Rabbi told him a story about the famous *Lubliner Yeshivah*. The *Lubliner Ga'on* (great Rabbi and scholar) was once asked by a *Gabai* (communal leader), "why do we train hundreds of Talmudic scholars in our Yeshivah when Lublin needs only a few Rabbis?" "Aha," answered the Rabbi, "we need hundreds of *Menvinim* (knowledgeable persons) to select, cherish and retain the best Rabbis..."

Experts for the Goyim

Am-Ha'aratzut is manifested also by Jews in the media and in the Public Service, who willy nilly act as experts on Jewish affairs for their gentile colleagues. It is quite irritating (though sometimes amusing) to come across distortions in the pronunciation and meaning of Yiddish and Hebrew words and the interpretation of Jewish sayings and concepts. These are usually attributed by the author or speaker to a "Jewish friend." Apparently, these Jewish friends are either ashamed to admit ignorance or really don't know that they don't know. To paraphrase Hillel's saying "an ignorant person cannot be truly pious," (Avot 2:6), a person devoid of Jewish knowledge cannot be a true Meivin about Jewish education, educators, Rabbis and synagogues; nor can he serve as an expert for the goyim.

On the bright side, there seems to be a trend for more and more people, especially of the younger generation, to join study circles and classes in Judaics that are on the increase in synagogues of all "denominations."

Welcome Back Brother Layton

Although I have never met Irving Layton face to face, I have heard about him from the students we had in common. They were his students in English language and literature at Herzliah High School in Montreal, and mine at camp Massad and the Hebrew Youth Movement. They spoke admiringly of him as an excellent teacher. Although he was known at the time in Jewish circles as an assimilated radical (some even said he was a communist), he apparently did not try to influence his students on political issues. My impression was that he imparted to them a sensitivity for beauty and a sense of justice and human decency. At the same time, it was generally accepted that he was not a Zionist and that he showed no interest in the preservation of Judaism. I personally had a positive attitude to him as a person and a teacher.

Self-Appointed Jewish Spokesmen

When Layotn became a *Ba-al T'shuvah* (a repentant), and embraced Zionism, I — among others — was very pleased to welcome him among those who lend their talents to Jewish creativity. I had heard about his egotism and chutzpah, but one tends to ignore such minor flaws in a fine poet. However, I started to follow Layton's public pronouncements after a non-Jewish acquaintance referred to him as a "Jewish Spokesman." I had already become aware of the mechanism whereby Jews in "high places" among the Goyim wittingly or unwittingly act as if they were Jewish spokesmen. This would perhaps be harmless if some of them did not misrepresent and misinterpret Jewish concepts, values and interests. The danger lies in the fact that many people, including Jews who are detached from Jewish affairs, do not realize that these individuals are self-appointed or self-annointed spokesmen.

I therefore seized the opportunity to tune in one day on a radio conversation with Irving Layton. Although he obviously intended to be entertaining, I was not amused. I had thought of him not merely as a brilliant chiseler of words but as a serious thinker-poet who includes among his functions the sharpening of sensitivity and the refinement of taste. It was painful to listen to bad taste that bordered on sheer vulgarity. Does a poet really have to speak about poetry in terms such as, "people did not talk about poetry; just like masturbation, you do it, you enjoy it, but you don't talk about it." Does a poet like Layton have to get attention by being so crude as to say, "speaking of rich Jews, their lovely wives and daughters are mine for the asking, and I have had some of them!" One wonders why Layton is so obsessed with eros as to bandy about what he seems to consider a veritable gem: "I prefer people in a horizontal rather than in a vertical position. People in a horizontal position are not likely to make war." I rather think that people who are promiscuous horizontally are also likely to be more rapacious vertically...

One may argue that Layton's public-appearance style is his own affair. However, his pose as a Jewish historian or scholar should be of concern in a society where there is little knowledge of what is what and who is who in Jewish life. On the same radio broadcast, he was much too cocksure of himself on some Jewish subjects. In stating that he was born circumcised, he claimed that Rabbis from various countries in Europe "came to see for themselves." As far as he knows, he said, he is "the only Jew who was born circumcised since Moses," and that it was taken to mean that he would be a great man. He even mentioned that this had some Messianic implications. Nonsense! Thousands have been born circumcised, a phenomenon that has no significance whatsoever. Layton also distorted a Talmudic saying (he referred to it as a popular Jewish saying) regarding the fact that "the cow's desire to suckle is greater than the calf's to suck" (P'sachim 112). And he sounded off on one of his favourite subjects — Jesus Christ and Christianity — offering among other gems, "I am known in Quebec better than Jesus Christ!" It is really on this subject that Layton is most irrelevant and disconcerting. Would a serious student of history, no matter what his faith, or lack of faith, write in such an offensive manner about a subject that is sacred to many millions throughout the world? "Nothing so discomfits the pseudo-Christian or so mottles his face with embarassment as having it pointed out to him that the God he is prostrating himself before is a crucified Jewboy; or that the Virgin he gazes at so admiringly is a Jewish mother who quite likely served her son, Jesus, gefilte fish for the Friday's evening meal." Is Layton so well versed in history that he is competent to attribute the Holocaust categorically to Christianity? One of his worst faux pas, in my opinion, was his appearance on television in the film "Who Killed Jesus?" One wonders in what capacity Layton appeared in a film that purported to be a serious historical study of a subject that is charged with so much complexity and emotion.

Did the producer put him there as a historian or as a scholar? Really?! One viewer suggested that the media must always inject some element of entertainment even on serious subjects. Really?! To say the least, Layton's joke that "no Jew will admit that another Jew was a God" may have its place in a bar-room but certainly not in the context in which it was emoted. To me personally and to many others, these words and the manner in which they were said were highly offensive. Be that as it may, I want to make sure, as do many others, that nobody will implicate me or the Jewish community in Layotn's cold war against Christianity.

Yes, Mr. Layton, I welcome you back with open arms as my Jewish brother but not as my spokesman. I am aware of the possibility that you do not claim to be my spokesman, but many have the erroneous impression that you are.

Jewish-Christian Relationships

"If I knew you and you knew me;
If both of us could clearly see,
I'm sure that we should differ less;
And clasp our hands in friendliness."
Author unknown

Some years after my emergence from my Yeshivah in Jerusalem into my new world as I viewed it from my Yeshivah in N.Y., I sensed that if Jews were to strike roots in any total community, while continuing to cultivate their own spiritual and cultural gardens, they would have to be part and parcel of the mainstream of the countries of their abode. Whether it was by Providence or by chance that my efforts were directed mainly to the service of the Jewish community, I was always aware of the necessity to be in tune with our surroundings. I took every opportunity that was open to me to be in touch and to communicate.

In my recent interviews with leading Canadians, I put this question to some of them: Is enough being done to bring about better understanding between Jews and Christians in Canada? For instance, do the Rabbis take an active part in this work? Samuel Freedman's response was one of the most comprehensive: "I think the Rabbis do some of that. I think it depends on the Rabbi himself. A good Rabbi must look in two directions, internally towards his flock and the youth group particularly, and externally as a part of a larger community. It's rare to find the Rabbi who is equally good in both directions. For instance, there was a long period when I think we benefitted from the presence in Winnipeg of Rabbi Solomon Frank, who spoke very well and was highly regarded by the general community. I think the succeeding Rabbis have been less active, but something else has happened: My generation should be credited with something. It made the breakthrough, and here I admit that in these enterprises we stand on the shoulders of those who went before. I take a simple example — the lawyers, my profession. We had Max Steinkopf, S. Hart Green, Mark Shinbane, Marcus Hyman, and E.R. Levenson. These were distinguished lawyers, distinguished people, but no one of them was ever elected to a bench of the Manitoba Bar Association; not one of them, except perhaps Marcus Hyman, was a lecturer at the law school. The situation is different today. We have Jewish benchers; we have Jewish Presidents of the Law Society; we have

Jewish judges, as you know. I think the situation fifty years ago was one of very marked separation between Jew and Gentile. That situation is much improved today, and the relationship does not come to an end at 5:00 p.m. I am not going to say that Jews do not still find their major associations and friends among Jews. I think they do, but coupled with that is a good and natural relationship with non-Jews. In the early thirties we were concerned about Adrian Arcand in Quebec, the leader of an anti-semitic movement. The situation is definietly better today. I know that prejudice is not an easy thing to eradicate. You can't subpoena prejudice. You are working against an invisible enemy, but looking at the picture in its entirety, I think we have made headway. And the relations between Jews and Gentiles are better today than fifty years ago, because I think the Jew tends to be regarded now by his fellow citizens more as a person."

Since I was to address myself particularly to the relationships between the Church and the Synagogue, I spoke on this subject primarily with Rabbis and Ministers. I have always held the view that one of the best lines of communication between Jews and non-Jews would be the continuing dialogue between the Synagogue and the Church because of their important role in influencing the spiritual and social values of our society. At the same time, I knew that comparatively few were the Rabbis who gave due consideration to this work, either because of the reason mentioned by Justice Freedman, or because of their preoccupation within their congregations. As a matter of fact, the Rabbi of one of the largest Conservative Congregations in Montreal shugged off my question on this subject.

During the years I was immersed in Keren Hatarbut work, I nonetheless followed with interest the activities of Rabbi Dr. Joshua Harry Stern in bringing together people of different faiths to know one another, "to see more clearly" and "to clasp hands in friendliness."

There is an expression in Hebrew "*Meshuga Ladavar*", the connotation of which is — a person who is obsessed with some idea. Human understanding and fellowship in the spirit of his book One World Or No World is indeed Rabbi Stern's magnificent obsession. Listening to his discourse on this subject I thought of an interpretation of the verse, "And there was a thick darkness in all the land of Egypt; brother saw not brother," (Exodus 10:22-23). The interpretation of this passage in *Sifrei Chassidim* is: "The darkness is thickest when brother does not see brother." And Rabbi Stern's goal is to dispel this darkness...

Inspired by the ideal of the Unity of God and the Unity of Man, Harry Stern was *the* pioneer in building inter-faith, inter-human, bridges in Canada. As early as forty eight years ago, he initiated an annual Fellowship Dinner which brought together over five hundred people, Jews and non-Jews, in a spirit of fellowship. He instituted the Book Lovers Forum, held six times annually. But by far his most outstanding accomplishment was his creation of the Institute of Judaism for Clergy thirty seven years ago. This institute brought together annually hundreds of clergymen of all faiths who listened to some of the foremost Catholic, Protestant and Jewish scholars discuss subjects relating to the unity and the future of mankind.

When taking leave of Temple Emanuel's Rabbi Emeritus Stern, I inquired about the continuity of the educational institutions he had nurtured with such loving devotion. I detected a note of disappointment and sadness in his response.

During the years of my travels and work in many cities in Canada and the U.S.A., I gained the impression that Canada lags far behind the U.S.A. in associated Synagogue — Church activity for the common good. This is probably due, in part at least, to the more clear-cut separation between church and state in the U.S.A. and to the traditional equality of the three main faiths in that country's public life. Something that is a fact of life in the U.S.A., namely, that Rabbis as well as priests and ministers participate by rotation, and sometimes together, in delivering invocations etc. at official public functions, was recently hailed as a "first" in Toronto. The I.O.I. (Internal Office Information) of the Canadian Jewish Congress of January 21, 1977, reported: "The I.O.I. was informed that at the personal request of Mayor David Crombie of Toronto, Rabbi Dr. J. Immanuel Schochet of the Kelcer Synagogue in Toronto, delivered the invocation at the inaugural meeting of the new City Council of Toronto, on January 5th. It is believed to be the first time that the imaugural prayer has been delivered by a Rabbi.

In the course of my research for this book I have thought that this subject would be a worthwhile thesis for a graduate student of Religion. Some of my recent spotty findings can merely throw some light on the matter. On the whole, I would say that there does not seem to be much communication between Rabbis and the clergy of other faiths in Canada, and that the existing contacts are dominated by Reform Rabbis. One example is the comment by the president of the ministerial association in one of the larger cities. Conceding that there was very little contact in his community, he added, "How can a lasting relationship be developed when there have already been here five Rabbis during my ten years in this city! Furthermore, the Jewish community seems to be preoccupied with fund-raising!"

An experience I had in Toronto may also be symptomatic of this situation. I received an inquiry from Rev. Harold W. Vaughan, Secretary of the Ecumenical Foundation of Canada, as to whether I would be able and willing to attend a dinner to which "all members of the community of Rabbis attached to synagogues are being invited, whether their tradition be Orthodox, Conservative or Reform," and at which "some of the Directors of the Ecumenical Foundation will also be present". The letter stressed "the fact that this interfaith meeting has no ulterior motives in respect of finance. We simply wish to enjoy one another's fellowship and to share information concerning the progress which has been made in several directions in common service across all lines of religious or racial connotation". My answer was affirmative, but I did not hear any further on the matter. When I subsequently discussed Ecumenism with Rev. Vaughan, I was curious to know why the dinner had not taken place. I was surprised by the explanation: Out of the twenty-four Rabbis who were invited, four answered yea and five nay. Fifteen did not respond at all!

Even more instructive was Rev. Vaughan's story about the Toronto School of Theology. This institution is a joint effort of three Roman Catholic, two Anglican, one Presbyterian, and one United Church theological seminaries. Two others, one Baptist and one Lutheran, participate as affiliates. The school's program includes the study of "History of Jewish Culture." Two years ago Rabbis were invited to give this course. I was surprised to learn of Rev. Vaughan's failure to receive an allocation from any Jewish organization for this particular course. He did, however, get some assistance from some of his Jewish friends. In response to my query about the continuity of the course, Rev. Vaughan said that they were now assessing its viability.

My final interview on this subject was with Rev. Dr. Richard D. Jones, O.C., who founded the Canadian Council of Christians and Jews in 1947 and served as its first president until his retirement in 1976. He is an American who had been active in the U.S. in the field of Christian-Jewish relationships and had left his native land to continue his work full-time in Canada. I was therefore interested in his opinion of my impression that there is much more dialogue and joint effort by Church and Synagogue in the U.S.A. He confirmed that this was true, on the whole, for historical reasons.

Rev. Jones exudes warmth and friendship, and seems to be a "natural" for bringing together ideas and people.

The C.C.C.J. is a national civic organization with headquarters in Toronto and regional offices and chapters in key areas across Canada. It raises its funds through a Special Gift Committee consisting of major corporate executives and doctors. Its stated credo is, "that man's inalienable rights must not be violated because of his race, religion or national origin. We believe that community tensions which are based on the existing differences in the human race can be solved by co-operative action of people of good will. We are committed to the radical equality of each human being under the fatherhood of God."

The organization has a wide-range of activities. It initiates projects for the purpose of maintaining an ongoing dialogue between Jews and Christians. It also "participates in and sponsors co-operative programs with existing community organizations and educational institutions." In recent years, it has included Islamic, Hindu, Sikh and other religious communities in its programmes. In 1973, it established the Munk Brotherhood Award of $10,000 which is presented biennually to a man or woman "who has stimulated and encouraged better understanding and co-operation between Jews and non-Jews and has contributed to the world-wide struggle against anti-semitism." In 1977, this award was presented to Mr. Victor Kugler, the heroic Dutchman who hid Anne Frank is his house during the Nazi occupation of Amsterdam.

An Inter-faith Liaison Committee

A recent new development in inter-faith relationships was the establishment in 1974 of a Jewish-Catholic-Protestant Liaison Committee with an Executive comprising three representatives each from the National Religious Department of the Canadian Jewish Congress, the Canadian Conference of Catholic Bishops, and the Canadian Council of Churches. The committee's statement of purpose is "to foster mutual understanding and respect among Canadians, based on common spiritual bonds and justice and the recognition of human rights in Canada; unite against manifestations of hostility and prejudice, especially when based on religion or race; organize dialogues, consultations and seminars at which questions relating to human dignity, human rights and the human community would be studied from a Biblical perspective; identify Canadian issues that require dialogue and action; and establish contact with organizations in Canada and elsewhere, with similar objectives."

Media Pollution

I happened to be living in Northern California when the infamous "Zionism is racism" resolution was pushed through the U.N. General Assembly by some of the most racist countries in the world. I was naturally engaged in the community's (Jewish and general) exposé of this atrocious libel. In that process, I came across some people who were misinformed or ill-informed on the subject, but I do not remember any case of deliberate media bias against Israel. However, such cases have been plentiful in Toronto during the three years since my return to Canada. Some of the media people act as if they were the supreme or "divine" estate rather than the fourth estate.

The distortions, the half-truths, the innuendoes and the outright falsifications could fill a large dossier. A few examples should attest to the need for monitoring the media for the purpose of reacting to and refuting such poisonous statements as follows.

In an article in the Toronto Star of July 7, 1977, Nicholas von Hoffman writes: "By 1974, Israel had found out that the price of conquering territories by war is sometimes more war and the loss of friends who began to use the expression, 'Israeli intransigence'. In its growing isolation it turned to South Africa, another international leper." The uninformed reader will "learn" from this rabid anti-Israeli that Israel set out to "conquer territories" by war. Mr. Hoffman fails to mention that it was the enemies of Israel who went to war in order to destroy it. And notice his "innocent", matter of fact reference to Israel as "another international leper." International indeed, Mr. Hoffman — the international jackals represented by Idi-Amin, Muhammad Quadaffy and the other despots and dictators who have turned the U.N. (at that time, the U.N. membership consisted of only about two dozen Democracies out of a total of a hundred and forty three countries!) into a medium of vilification and hatred of the Jewish people as well as of the American people. By that token, America and other democracies are also international lepers.

An example of falsification is the statement by Peter Mansfield of London, England in his article in the Toronto Star of January 7, 1978: In writing about the Palestinian Arabs, he stated, "... They are unanimous in saying that their national pride has been trampled on so many times since their right to self-determination was recognized by the League of Nations in 1922." Is it possible that Mansfield is so ignorant that he does not know that the League of Nations *never recognized* "the right to self-determination of *the Palestinian Arabs*?" This is a glaring case of a journalist falsifying historical facts with impunity.

In April 1978, a news-story in the Toronto Star referred to the U.N. resolution 242 which, it said, "calls for Israeli withdrawal from all occupied territories." While Mr. Hoffman's diatribes went unchallenged, this story was put right by Mr. Borden Spears, the Star's senior editor, in the issue of April 22, 1978: "That is not what the U.N. resolution says. It calls for withdrawal of Israeli armed forces from Territories of recent conflict. The diplomats who framed it refrained carefully and deliberately from saying "all the territories." George Ignatieff, the Canadian representative, explained the reason in a speech last year:

"We knew perfectly well that we weren't fooling anyone by not putting in withrdawal from all or 'the territories' ... We said that the essence of peace had to be simply this: The Arabs must recognize Israel, and Israel must exist within certain boundaries... which would be recognized and negotiated by its neighbours... We were determined neither to specify those lines nor to sit in New York and draw boundaries. The boundaries had to be negotiated between the parties."

"An error in a news story is not going to confuse the diplomats and statesmen who are working to achieve a basis for peace in the Middle East. But the news story is not published for them, it is for the information of the public to whom the statesmen are ultimately responsible, who want to know accurately what is going on, and who depend on the press to tell them."

Mr. Spears is to be commended for rectifying this wrong, but a news story is likely to be read by many more people than an article. This type of distortion should, in my opinion, be corrected by an "editor's note" right in that very item. Furthermore, many such statements go uncorrected in the Star and in other newspapers.

Speaking of the Toronto Star, while its editorial policy on Israel is fair and balanced on the whole, its news stories and articles are sometimes misleading. Especially specious, and sometimes vicious, are some of its headlines. At times, I get the feeling that the headliner derives special satisfaction from his "creative" gems.

The worst offender is C.B.C. radio! While C.B.C. television and other channels are sometimes subtle, and occasionally not so subtle, in their treatment of the Middle East, the bias of the radio programs "As It Happens" and the "Sunday Morning" program are quite "showing" to anybody who is familiar with the background and the issues of the Arab-Israeli conflict. The trouble is, of course, that the general public is not acquainted with the intricacies of this problem and falls prey to the "pollution" against the Jewish people.

When dealing with the Middle East, the "Sunday Morning" program features Eric Rioou, an avowed anti-Israel journalist, as the foremost Middle-East expert. For the greatest possible impact, he is always introduced as "the dean of Middle East correspondents." To feign impartiality, an Israeli or some other Jewish commentator is sometimes included, but very great care is obviously taken to use people who do not express the true views and interests of Israel, such as Uri Avineri, who represents a very insignificant section of the Israeli public.

The program "As It Happens" often gives me the feeling that it subtly and sometimes not so subtly, represents the P.L.O. A few examples: In 1978, an interviewer on this program began an exchange with a correspondent by saying, "Now that charges of Israeli torture of Arabs have been proven..." For the "cricket" players of "As It Happens" accusations by enemies of Israel are ipso facto "proven". As pointed out in an editorial in the Canadian Jewish News of Sept. 29, 1978, "a commission headed by Prof. André Decocq from the law faculty of the University of Paris has issued a report categorically denying the charges heaped on Israel by two irresponsible organizations. Under the aegis of the Vatican's Pax Romana and the International League for Human Rights, Prof. Decocq surveyed Israeli prisons in January of 1978, met judges and other court officials, interviewed Arab and Israeli lawyers and attended sessions of Israeli military tribunals. The report issued by the Decocq commission not only refuted the baseless allegations made by Amnesty International but praised Israel for its respect towards the Geneva Convention of 1949." To people who know the true nature of Israel, who know that it does not execute even the most brutal murderers of women and children, such a commission of inquiry is just as necessary as a commission to investigate the despicable blood libel — (that Jews use Christian blood in their Passover Matzos). In May, 1979, following the murderous attack on Nahariah, *"As It Happens"* included a program which featured exclusively the "Palestinian" side. It started with a commentary by Eli Zurek, a visiting Arab prof. of Middle-Eastern studies at the University of Toronto. He was followed by a news-story from Beirut, the centre of truth and justice (it would be instructive to check on the number of news-stories emanating from Beirut or other Arab centres as compared with those from Israel!), which was followed by an interview with Mohamud Labadie, spokesman for the P.L.O. This is but another example of the "fair play" of the boys and girls of the C.B.C. But I strongly resent having part of my taxes used for providing a free platform for those who would destroy my people.

What is disconcerting to me and to others with whom I have discussed this matter is the near complete public silence of the Jewish establishment. Except for occasional letters to the editor by individuals, which are not always effective, there have been no official (at least during the past three years that I have been scouring some of the media) reactions to such scurrilous statements as those cited above. More important, we have seen no overt effort to inform the general public of the basic facts relating to Zionism and Reborn Israel. As a matter of fact, my experience is that even many Jews are unaware of these facts. Fortunately, *"As It Happens"* and the others will not determine the future of Israel, but they can and do affect relationships between Jew and non-Jew in Canada. The anti-Israel propagandists are even trying to drive a wedge between Jew and Jew by presuming to separate between Judaism and Zionism. Only people ignorant of Jewish history and creativity fail to realize that these two are inseparable.

To augment my impressions and experiences, I did some research on the subject during my recent travels. Naturally, the work of the Canada-Israel Committee came under discussion. I told Senator Sidney Buckwold of my impressions that, effective as the Committee's work may be among the political elite in Ottawa, I did not see any evidence of their mark on the grass roots. I cited a few cases: I asked the president of the Ministerial Association in Regina, the Canon of the Anglican Church, about his reaction to the U.N. resolution on Zionism. His reaction to me was instructive: "Not all Jews," he said, "are Zionists. We think of Zionists as a bunch of radicals." I then asked him whether he receives materials from the Canada-Israel Committee. He had never heard of this organization! His counterpart in Edmonton showed a positive attitude to Zionism, but he too had never heard of the Canada—Israel Committee. Senator Buckwold questioned whether the "grass roots" were the responsibility of the Committee. That, he thought, "was really the function of the Canadian Zionist Federation." On his part, he gave the Committee good marks at the political level: "From my contact with them, not on a regular basis but fairly often, I think they fulfill a useful purpose. They are feeding me information, and are drawing my attention to things that I might otherwise not have known. They put on an annual dinner for parliamentarians, which is well received. They are maintaining a public relations contact which has paid off. I don't think they have influenced non-Jewish public opinion, other than at the political level, to any great extent. I haven't seen that ... Their bulletins are good, and I look forward to reading them." Gratifying as Senator Buckwold's reassurance is on the political level, there still remains the problem of the grass roots. There must be something lacking in our public education effort if a man like Tom Harpur, Religious Editor of the Toronto Star, can refer to U.N. resolution 242, as calling "for withdrawal from *all* occupied territory." And what prompts a man like Peter Trueman of Global T.V. to confer the title "commandoes" on terrorists who murder women and children in cold blood?!

Some highly placed civil servants told me that nothing or very little can be done about the C.B.C. I and many others question this. Is the C.B.C. licensed for license? How can we have confidence in their reports and programs on other foreign-affairs issues when we know for certain that some of their functionaries are biased on some matters? Is it not their right to be biased that we challenge, but their attempt to "put it over" on an innocent public. Some of the same civil servants suggested that some of this bias may stem, at least in part, from old fashioned, primitive anti-semitism. I personally believe this to be a simplistic conclusion. I am inclined to think that it is due to the smugness and cocksureness of people who put themselves on a high pedestal and who know very little of the background, the history and the contemporary realities of the Middle East in general and of a four-thousand-year-old people in particular. On the question whether it is the lack of knowledge that causes the bias, or the bias that causes the ignorance, I am inclined to opt for the former, at least in most cases.

It seems to me that serious consideration should be given to the creation of a *civic organization consisting of Jews and non-Jews* whose specific function would be the cultivation of mutual understanding and friendship between Canada and Israel by keeping the *general public* informed of the true character of Israel. The destiny of Israel and of the Jewish people should not be left to Jews alone and to the "political level." In the final analysis, it is the people who ultimately determine the "political level" in a democracy.

The Impact of Israel

What has been the greatest force for Jewish cultural and spiritual survival in the Diaspora? My own conclusion is that our National

Renaissance has been in the nature of the "Messiah who was born before the *Churban* (the Destruction)." My own conviction is that were it not for our National Renewal Movement, the disintegration in Jewish life would have been near catastrophic. Even the orthodox, whose religious consciousness is permeated with the faith in the comng of the Messiah, would have been exposed to much greater danger as a minority in a growing desert of disintegration.

Since this belief stems mostly from observation and insight, I have put to many people, in recent years, the direct question: What has been the greatest influence in your life as a Jew? How do your Jewish roots come to expression as a Canadian? In what do you and your children find satisfaction and joy as Jews? Almost invariably, the answer about the "greatest influence" came easily and unhesitatingly — "Israel!" Most stumbled on the question of how their Jewishness comes to expression. Very few mentioned the synagogue. Many said, "by sending our children to day school and/or by involvement in Jewish organizational work."

Here are a few examples. Dr. Fishel Coodin (formerly of Fort-William, studied medicine at Queen's university and in the U.S.A., and now of Winnipeg): He had been alienated in his youth by orthodoxy. What brought him back to Jewish life was mainly the creation of the State of Israel. "For me personally, the birth of Israel was a miraculous and wonderful thing. I'll do everything in my power for the survival of the State of Israel. I am convinced that without Israel, Jewry will not survive another Galut. My roots are really in Winnipeg. My Jewish roots and my Jewish longing are in Yerushalayim." He and his wife Kayla said that their Jewishness is expressed by their involvement in Jewish organizational work and by their children's attending Hebrew school. They both took satisfaction in the fact that their son has saved enough money to take him to Israel if there is a fight for its survival.

Esther Berlind (Gurevitch), a graduate of the Clargary Hebrew School who has been living in Montreal for over two decades, was involved for a long time in work for Israel, especially for the Bond Drive. Her connection with the synagogue is tenuous, as is the case with many of her generation. She tried a closer relationship, but she found it lacking in real content and meaning. She finds satisfaction whenever she has the opportunity to express herself in Hebrew. (We use Hebrew whenever we correspond or meet, as I do with all my former students.) She sent her children to a day school but was disappointed with its program and methods. She is therefore not optimistic about the future. She had been brought up in a home that was more Jewish than hers, and her children's Judaism is much weaker than hers.

Tema Klein, formerly of Fort-William and Montreal, now serving as a social worker in Burlington: Her opinion was of special interest to me because I believe she represents many of the "silent, invisible" young people who are completely disassociated from the Synagogue. She was raised in a "fairly traditional home, which was an island in a sea of a different culture." She looked upon being Jewish as belonging primarily to a religion, and she thought of Jewish in terms of God. At about age fourteen, Voltaire's "The Questions of Zapata" converted her to atheism. Since God ceased to figure in her life, there was no more room for her in a tradition that was based on God. Many years later, as she came to see Judaism as a cultural tradition, she was able to re-approach Judaism without the negativism she felt and still feels about all religion. Modern Israel played a major part in renewing her interest in the history of Judaism, and caused her to identify with it much more closely. She made three visits to Israel, and each of them has "greatly increased her pride in her lineage." Each of them has increased her admiration for the Israelis, and therefore enhanced her own self-esteem.

How does she now give expression to her Jewishness? Although she and her husband did not identify with the Jewish community at the time their son was born, they "went to the trouble of arranging for a traditional *Brit* (circumcision) Ceremony." Although they did not want to have their son involved in the Hebrew School System, his Jewish education was so important to them that they engaged a private teacher at a time when it imposed a great financial burden upon them. In spite of her pride in her heritage and her identification with Jews and with Israel, there is very little outward expression of her Judaism. She writes a cheque annually. To quote her: "I have been a subscriber to the Jerusalem Post for the past eight years, and read the news on Israel with passionate interest. I am deeply concerned about the dangers facing it. In my conversations with people around me, I argue its case with all the emotion that I feel for it ... I am concerned about the future of Jewish life in Canada, and therefore hope my son will marry a person who will be Jewish or will convert to Judaism. My reasons are frankly irrational. They are simply, as Koestler put it, the idea of being a link in a long, long chain. One does not want to take upon oneself the responsibility of being the link that broke that chain, no matter how problematic its cosmic value is. My own belief is that it has a great deal of positive value."

Bernard Klein, (formerly of Winnipeg and Montreal, now an engineer in Burlington), is also representative of a specific background and outlook. Unlike Tema, he grew up in a large Jewish community and received an intensive Hebrew education. As an adolescent, he "out-religioned" even his orthodox parents. After he "lost his religion" somewhere between age fourteen and eighteen when he joined the Airforce, he started to wonder whether he was still Jewish. Nonetheless, he always identified with the Jewish people. "Everybody wants to belong to a group and feel accepted." Although he has no interest in religion and its rituals, he still feels at home when he goes to a synagogue to attend a Bar-Mitzvah, because "all these things still evoke a warm feeling for me." In his case too, it was the restoration of the state of Israel that "gave a terrific boost" to his morale, his ego and identity. "Before that, I'm not sure whether I had any particular pride in being Jewish." Israel restored his interest in the entire history of his people, and he started to read up on it again. How does he give expression to his Jewishness now? "It's difficult to answer this question, because it pre-supposes that there are criteria for expressing Jewishness. I feel Jewish, but I don't give any expression to it. I'm extremely sympathetic with Israelis who are but "one group of Jews, who re-establish the state, but they have no more right to the term Jew than I do. I'm sympathetic with those who go there, but I am far gone from that culture and am too rooted in my present culture to want to immigrate to Israel. I'm sympathetic to Zionists. They are Zionists in the sense that they want to go back to Zion to re-establish the state of Israel, but I have no wish to become one of them." When I pointed out to him that many people say they are not Zionists because they erroneously think that a Zionist is one who settles in Israel, he agreed that he was a Zionist according to my definition (see appendix "The Mission of Zionism"). "By all Arab standards," he added, "I am certainly a Zionist." With all that, he is not "that concerned about the future of Jewish Life in Canada." He would be somewhat saddened if it were to disintegrate but "it's not of cosmic importance."

Some of my Rabbinic colleagues have said to me that the Synagogue has brought back many Jews to Zionism. To whatever degree this may be true, I am convinced that Israel and Zionism have brought back many more to the synagogue, tenuous as their connection with it may be. Another conclusion I have drawn is that sentiment is not sufficient to attract the new breed of Canadian Jews either to the synagogue or Zionism. At least, part of the answer seems to lie in an increasingly closer partnership between the two. Tangible *expression* of Jewishness is hardly conceivable in the Golah without the Synagogue. But it is to become the center of Jewish life for the new breed of Canadian Jews, (including the university graduate, the academic and the intellectual) the Synagogue will have to change (as some have already done to a lesser or greater degree) more and more from a *Beit T'fillah*, a house of prayer and ritual, to a *Beit Midrash*, a house of study and creativity. It will have to become, as Bialik put it, *"Beit Hayotzer Lenishmat Ha'am"*, the house of creativity for the nation's soul. The need of some of the new breed to form their own *minyan*, for their own miniature group within the large Synagogue complex, may be one of the indicators of the necessity for a re-evaluation of its role and content.

A development that augurs well for the future is the increasing number of day-high-school graduates who go for extended visits or periods of study to Israel. As far as I know, the *B'nai Akiva Yeshivah* in Toronto (*Or-Chayim* for boys and *Ulpanat Orot* for girls) is the most outstanding in this program. This institution, the only one of its kind in North America, is unique in more than one way. It is modeled after the

Israeli *Yeshivah Tichonit* (high-school level Yeshivah). Unlike other Yeshivot, its program includes such subjects as modern and contemporary Hebrew literature, and Talmud is studied in Hebrew rather than in English or Yiddish. It has attracted students not only from other Canadian cities, but also from the U.S.A. Upon completion of grades ten-thirteen, almost all the students spend a year or two of studies in Israel, the boys at *Yeshivat Hakotel* or *Kerem B'yavneh*, and the girls at *Machon Gold* or at "Rabbi Cooperman's College" in Jerusalem. This Yeshivah merits special encouragement because it seems to answer more adequately to the needs of our times. There is good reason to hope that its graduates, as well as those of other schools, will eventually fructify "Jewish expression" and contribute to the transformation of the Synagogue in Canada. Those who will ultimately make their home in Israel will bring with them the skills and values they will have acquired in Canada.

The Talmud speaks of a long-short road and a short-long road. The "preachers" of Aliyah would do well to consider the long-short road, education and cultivation, as against the short-long road of *D'chikat Haketz* (forcing the end prematurely), which has brought near-disaster during some periods in Jewish history. Those who "force the end" do not realize that the alternative to "negating Jewish life in the Golah" is not Aliyah, but eventual disintegration.

Canadian Jewry's generosity and devotion to Israel is common knowledge. The "scribes" publicize it fully. They go all the way in fulfilling the human need for appreciation, recognition and plain *Koved* (honor). They go so far as to put "in the company of names such as Albert Einstein" a business person who received the Eleanor Roosevelt Humanities Award for distinguished work for the Israel Bond Drive. Care is taken, of course, to refer to that person as "being a little shy and wondering whether he or she really deserves it". I am reminded of the story about a person who asked a Rabbi: "According to the Midrash (Tanchum, Vayikra), one who pursues *Koved, Koved* escapes him, and one who runs away from honors, honors run after him. Well, I have been running away from honors, but they do not run after me." Answered the Rabbi: "The reason is that you keep on looking back!" Although I do not believe that the end justifies the means, the crucial need for funds does justify the harmless distribution of *Kibudim*, especially if carried out in good taste. The need for recognition may also be explained by the impersonal nature of the giving, which is of necessity by an individual to an organization and by this organization to another organization. These thoughts crossed my mind when I chanced recently upon an individual who, in addition to the customary means of giving, delights in a "person-to-person" approach. Although he is not typical, I believe that Yehudah Mayzel represents the many who have a near mystical attachment to the Land of Israel and its people.

Like many Jews who are not Orthodox or Chassidic, Mr. Mayzel is an admirer of the Liubavicher Rebbe. When he learned of my family relationship to the Rebbe, he practically forced me to go along with him to Brooklyn to attend a celebration of the anniversary of the release from prison of Rabbi Shne'ur Zalman, the founder of the Liubavicher Chassidic Movement. I thus had the opportunity to draw out Mr. Mayzel on his feelings for Israel. It is interesting to record some items of the story I succeeded in wresting from him.

As soon as Mayzel learned about Egypt's sneak attack on Yom Kippur 1973, he told his family of his intention to go to Israel immediately. When his son asked him, "They are fighting a war there; what could you, a seventy year old man, do in a war?" he answered, "I will do whatever I can to lighten the pain of bereaved families." The next day he proceeded to New York where it took quite some pleading with El-Al to make an exception and fly him to Israel together with returning fighting men. Upon arrival, he rushed to Shaarei Tzedek Hospital to ask how he could help. Told that they need urgently a pager, he arranged to have it delivered from the U.S.A. within several days. During his seven weeks stay in Israel, he visited fifty-five bereaved families during their Shivah (mourning period). He believes that the very fact that a seventy year old man came all the way from Toronto for the specific purpose of joining them in their sorrow was of some solace to them. He was stricken with emotion as he told me of the especially poignant tragedy of one of these families. One of their two sons fell on the first day of the war, and the other followed him on the second day. There remained one daughter who was engaged to be married. Told by the Rabbi who accompanied him of the family's extreme poverty, Mayzel made it possible for the young couple to marry by giving them all the money he had in Israel at the time. He promised to come with his wife to the wedding, but she was in an accident a day before their departure. That did not deter him from keeping his promise, and he flew there alone.

He was still in Israel when the Entebbe drama unfolded. As in other cases, Mayzel identified personally with the tragic death of Lieutenant Colonel Jonathan Netanyahu, who commanded the rescue mission. He pledged $136,000 towards the establishment of the Jonathan Institute in Jerusalem, and flies to Israel every year to attend the Jonathan Netanyahu Memorial Service. As a matter of fact, I met Mayzel for the first time when he was told I was the "only person who could prepare for him a proper translation of President Yitzchak Navon's eulogy." I learned later from other sources about many more of Mayzel's "person-to-person" Mitzvot also for individuals (Jewish and non-Jewish) in Canada and the U.S.A.

There is little new about the devotion of Mayzel's generation to the rebuilding of the Land of Israel. Of greater interest and importance is the question of Israel's impact on the new generation and on many of those who have dissociated themselves from the mainstream of Jewish life.

Different Routes to Striking Roots

No matter what the "Aliyah preachers" say or do, the vast majority of Jews in Canada and the U.S.A. will continue to strike deeper and deeper roots in the life of their countries. There are, however, different routes to striking roots. There is the route that leads to the complete disintegration of the ancestral spiritual and cultural roots. It is represented, in the extreme, by a David Lewis Stein, who wrote in the *Toronto Star* of Jan. 7, 1979: "At the family Christmas dinner, my daughter pronounced a Jewish blessing over the wine. No one else at the table could understand it except me, but my wife wanted a sign, however small, that this was both Christmas and the first day of Chanukah." He goes on to say that his daughter's "clear voice struggling over the ancient Hebrew words" in front of the huge Christmas turkey, became for him "an expression of a special kind of faith." (Incidentally, the way he transcribed and transliterated the Hebrew words leads to serious doubt as to whether they were understood even by him...) "My wife", he says, "is an Anglican. I am a Jew, and *we both cling stubbornly to our faith although neither of us practices it very actively.*" (The emphasis is the author's.) They take their children to church and to synagogue, and tell them they "are trying to give them the best of both religions ..." He claims that this is "more than an excuse or a platitude" and that he "has come to believe that such a unity is possible." Simple! Judaism is a mere "faith", which could be unified with Christianity. As simple as that! One wonders how many Jews have already reached this solution....

Then, there are the type of Jews who are "in hiding" without really knowing what they are hiding from. They keep away from both Church and Synagogue. When their identity is somehow "disclosed", they protest that they are really not denying their Jewishness, or their "Jewish origin", but that they are simply not religious, which makes them of course more "full-blooded" Canadians than other Jews. Most riling are those who tell you, "I am not ashamed to be a Jew." There is also the type who declares, "I am proud to be a Jew!" How can one be proud or ashamed of something one doesn't really know or understand?!

With all due respect and regard for everybody's freedom to "strike roots" in whatever way they wish, these people represent an entirely new breed, one which did not exist when Jews started their root-striking process in the U.S.A. and Canada. In the past, we were accustomed to individuals who were not "religious" or "nationalistic" but who nonetheless identified in some way with the Jewish community. They were more or less knowledgeable Jews who, consciously or unconsciously, desired to assimilate. I recall that in a certain city in western Canada there was, in the early forties, one Jew (the only one as far as was known) who did not "show his face" in the Synagogue even on the High Holidays. But he still identified with the Jewish community and was involved in some of its endeavours. I knew him well enough to say that he would have taken great care that his absence from the Synagogue on the High Holidays not be proclaimed on the radio or by any other public means. Today, David Shatsky announces on the radio, almost in the same breath, when Yom Kippur will start and that he will be M.C.ing a show that night in Hamilton. Could the reason for this be that forty years ago even Jews who were heading, consciously or subconsciously, towards assimilation, were still concerned about their Jewishness? Nowadays, such Jews are so assimilated that they are oblivious to Jewish and non-Jewish awareness of their Jewishness. It is also possible that their number has increased to such an extent that they find themselves in large and "good company."

On the other end of the spectrum, a majority of Jews, *whose Canadian roots are just as deep*, continue to cling to their heritage in various forms and degrees. They too have shed their self-consciousness about their Jewishness. They feel as intrinsically Canadian or American as those on the other end of the spectrum. One manifestation of this metamorphosis is the natural manner in which religious and national Jews "do their thing" without awareness of or concern about signs of approval or disapproval from their milieux. Fifty years ago, when I was a Yeshivah student, one could not see even a *Yeshivah Bocher* wearing a *kippah* on the street. I well remember our admiration for one single Yeshivah student who had the courage (or was not bashful) to wear his *kippah* at the university. Surrounded though we were by Jews on the N.Y. East-side, we were somewhat self-conscious about speaking Yiddish, or English with an accent, or reading a Yiddish newspaper on the subway. Until recent years, one could not see people wearing *kippot* even on the streets of Montreal or Toronto, let alone in places with small Jewish communities. Nowadays, the *kippah* is conspicuous throughout the U.S.A. and Canada. Not that the *kippah* is an index of the depth of one's roots in Judaism (to quote Prof. Ernst Simon, "the kippah may be a top value, but it certainly is not a basic value"), but it is one of the outward signs of the numerous Jews who are rooted in both cultures and who are to be found in all areas of Canadian and American life.

Sitting in a hospital waiting-room, I see *kippah*-wearing interns and doctors going to and fro. I meet my gastro-enterology specialist (Dr. Alvin Newman), and find that he is a graduate of a foremost modern Yeshivah in N.Y.; I sit in my dentist-chair (M. Nussbaum) and discover that he is a religious Jew who speaks Hebrew; I make an appointment with an ophthalmologist (Marc Mandelcorn) and recognize him as a graduate of Massad and the Hebrew Youth Movement; and my radiologist (Moshe Miskin) recognizes me from Massad in Toronto, and we converse fluently in Hebrew. Remarkably, I do not seek them out because of their Jewish-Hebraist backgrounds; I just happen upon them....

Towards a Philosophy of Synthesis

If the process of striking roots in both cultures is to hold and progress, there should be serious thought about developing a philosophy of synthesis. To begin with, any such synthesis must begin in the school where there is an unhealthy dichotomy between the Hebrew and the general curricula, where pupils are "Jewish" during certain hours of the day and "Canadian" or "general" during other hours. To the best of my knowledge, the United Synagogue Day School of Toronto pioneered in this area in 1972 by inviting an M.A. student in history with a good Jewish background, Asher Horowitz, to experiment with an integrated history course in grades ten-eleven. According to Dr. Aaron Nussbaum, principal of the school, this course, as well as an integrated course in literature, has continued with some success. He also informed me that the Community Hebrew Academy of Toronto has just now decided to adopt this approach next year. This method is used also by the B'nai Akiva Yeshivah, referred to earlier in this chapter. There may of course be other schools with such sporadic courses, but there does not seem to be even the beginning of a general trend in that direction. Nor does there seem to be any plan to train the qualified teachers who are essential for the institution of such a program.

It seems to me that the situation is what it is because, so far, there has been very little thinking about a general philosophy of synthesis even in the U.S.A., where Jewish scholarship is much more advanced than in Canada. Perhaps this is a question of whether the egg or the chicken comes first. Perhaps there must first be a large number of people who have achieved such a synthesis in their actual lives without developing a formal theory or philosophy of such a way of life. Perhaps there will arise from among the new generation some thinkers and scholars who will formulate such a philosophy on the basis of the actual ways of living that are gradually emerging among the many thousands whose life has been grounded in both cultures. Perhaps they will also bring more democracy into our institutions, and will develop the Canadian Jewish Congress into the one coordinating national organization that will be truly representative of an informed and vital Jewish community. Perhaps one of them will become the Governor General of Canada and Hebrew will be one of the languages he will speak at his inauguration, as Governor General Ed Schreyer used his native tongue at his inauguration!

Are there "many thousands?" Where are they; what are they doing; where are the distinguished ones; how many of them has the "brain drain" attracted to the U.S.A.; and, how many have preferred to be Jewish Jews in Israel? During my tenure at the Keren Hatarbut, I took satisfaction in including in my periodic reports a list of Massad and Hebrew Youth Movement graduates who received some of the highest scholarships, distinctions and positions at universities, etc. Their numbers were always comparatively high — over thirty annually!

In the early sixties, when Hebraists were still classified as "segregationists", I wrote in one of my reports (June 27, 1961):

"In view of the renewed concern of our philanthropic brethren — as evidenced by the rash of alarming articles and letters in newspapers and bulletins — about the bugaboo of segregation, we are glad to point out that all these young people are products of Day Schools and Hebrew Camps! Obviously, it was not necessary for them to crash the gates of Harvard, Yale, Columbia, Chicago U., etc. One of them was even appointed recently to the staff of one of the largest and most important (Non-Jewish) law firms in the British Commonwealth. And lest it be thought that these eggheads excel only in academic studies and Hebrew Culture, let us add that they — and many other products of our so-called ghetto education — have received prizes and scholarships for having distinguished themselves in all phases of life — also *non-Jewish* —on the University campuses, such as Chairmen of Blood Drive, Presidents of University Debating Teams, holders of Golden Keys, members of S.E.C. and athletic teams, and staff members of University papers, in addition to being founders and leaders of Zionist and Jewish societies on the Campus. A whole generation of Ghetto Jews has already been brought up, and their place in American and Canadian society (non-Jewish) is at least as integrated and as prominent as that of the others.... We challenge our would be benefactors to prove to us that their sons and daughters are more successfully integrated in Canadian and American life than ours!"

I hope that some years soon, one or more of these "products" will undertake a comprehensive study that could serve as a pilot of our future course. As a mere indication of what such a study would bring to light, I shall mention here but two examples in each category:

Struck Roots in Canada

Charles (Chaim) Dalfen: Among the positions he held before his appointment as Vice-Chairman of the Canadian Radio-Television and Telecommunications Commission in 1976, were — Associate Prof. of political science at Carleton University, Prof. of law at the University of Toronto and Deputy Minister of Transport and Communications, Government of B.C. He and his wife Susannah are actively involved in Jewish life in Ottawa. Our two recent conversations were entirely in Hebrew, and I was impressed with his knowledge of our Hebrew sources. He apparently has been too preoccupied with his duties to have been able to prepare in writing an answer to my question on his "identity" and "synthesis". In a note he sent me when he thought he could still do it before the publication of this book, he remarked, "It's just as *schever nischt tzu zein a yid* as it is *tzu zein a yid*". (It is just as difficult not to be a Jew as it is to be a Jew.) There perhaps is the kernel for "synthesis."

Cyril (Israel) Kay, a graduate of the Calgary Hebrew School: Prof. of biochemistry at the University of Alta., in Edmonton. He and his wife Fay (Tziporah) are active in Jewish life. When he was invited to the Weizman Institute for a year, he was completely at home in Hebrew. Speaking about the value of Hebrew in his life, he told me, "I did some research at Harvard University on the same subject that former President Ephraim Katzir had done there before me. The Hebrew notes he left there inadvertently were of great help to me in my research work." In Jan. 1978, Prof. Kay was one of two Canadians (the other one was former Canadian Prof. David Sidorsky) who were invited by President Katzir to participate in a symposium on "Israel and the State of World Jewry", Israel is one of the few people who, to my knowledge, have given serious thought to the question of "synthesis"; he delivered a lecture on this subject long before he became "Professor" Kay.

Lost to the American "Brain Drain"

Mair Deshell: a graduate of the Winnipeg Talmud Torah, who was ordained Rabbi at the Jewish Theological Seminary. He served in important positions in the U.S.A., and is now editor of the Jewish Publication Society of America.

Dr. Sidney B. Maerov: distinguished senior research chemist at Corother Research Laboratory in Wilmington, Delaware. He has been very active in Hebrew education. At present, he is President of the Delaware Branch of Gratz College in Philadelphia and Co-chairman of the Education Committee of Temple Bet-Emet in Wilmington. He is also an active member of the local Hebrew Speaking Club.

Serving in Israel

David Roskies: a graduate of Massad and the Hebrew Youth Movement. He received his Ph.D. in English Literature at Sussex University in England, and is at present on the faculty of Ben-Gurion University in Israel.

Dr. Bernard Avishai (Shaikovitch) of Montreal. He is a graduate of McGill and the University of Toronto, and taught political science at the University of Toronto and at York University. At present, he is a fellow of the Van Leer Institute in Jerusalem.

A comprehensive study of the many people with roots in both Hebraic and Canadian cultures, as compared with those who by choice or force of circumstance, have opted to be uni-cultural, will undoubtedly reveal that the former have enriched not only their own lives but also the lives of the countries wherein they live.

"Oy, Noch A Yiddishe Neshome"?

The outcry of my Rosh Yeshivah, *"Oy, noch a yiddishe neshome"*, (woe, another lost Jewish soul) which accompanied my departure from the Holy Land more than a half a century ago, re-echoed in my mind as I traversed the events since that fateful moment in my life. Obviously, my own view is that I certainly did not lose my Jewish soul, but what would my Rosh Yeshivah in Yerushalayim say about the metamorphosis of my Yiddish Neshome? The answer was perhaps given by a Rosh Yeshivah in whose presence I reminisced recently about those days in Jerusalem. "Well," he said, "you have contributed to the creation of new forms of Jewish life and thereby helped in holding the dikes against the flood of assimilation." This sagacious observation may assuage the *"Neshome"* — pangs of the individual, but what of the large question about the health and permanence of the *Yiddishe Neshome* outside its natural soil? Although there seems to be no definitive answer, I went to search for some clues.

In the mid twenties, there was not even one Yeshivah in Canada. I and another few Canadians (two Drazin brothers, Stitsky and Cooper from Toronto, and three sons of Rabbi Vachtfogel of Montreal) had to go to study in New York. Today, there are Yeshivot with many hundreds of students in Toronto and Montreal.

In 1941, twenty Yeshivah students, of the few Jews who were snatched from the claws of the Nazi beast, arrived in Montreal. Nine of them were Liubavitcher Chassidim, and they formed the nucleus of the Liubavitcher Yeshivah. The others formed the basis for the Mercaz Latorah Yeshivah. In 1969, the Yeshivah Gedolah was established, and amalgamated with Mercaz Latorah in 1972. These Yeshivot accommodate hundreds of students at the elementary, secondary and higher levels. Although their purpose is "Torah Lishmah", to educate Jews who are to be steeped in the learning and practicing of Torah, many of their graduates serves as Rabbis, principals, teachers, shochatim and sofrim in the U.S.A. and Canada. The head of the Liubavitcher Yeshivah is Rabbi Leib Kramer, a Talmudic scholar from Poland. Significantly, the other Yeshivah is headed by two American-trained Talmudic scholars: Rabbi Moshe Glustein, born in Montreal, and Rabbi Mordecai Weinberg, a native of the U.S.A.

Because of my Chassidic background, I lingered more at the Liubavitcher Yeshivah. Here there was also an emotional touch because of Rabbi Kramer's and the other Rabbis' special regard for my father. As I was chatting with them and observing students engrossed in the Talmud, I was transported, as if on a cloud, to my Yeshivah "Etz-Chaim" in Jerusalem. There was no difference whatsoever! The only difference was on the "Outside". I pondered on the strength of the "inside" to cope successfully with the "outside"....

An Inspiring Experience

In the brief process of re-living my Yeshivah days, I had one of my most profound spiritual experiences, when I found myself at a celebration at the center of Liubavitch in Brooklyn. The scene is truly indescribable. I watched with wonderment as throngs of old and young people poured into the large hall where the Rebbe was to deliver his discourse. There was a sort of serene "heavenly" atmosphere in the hall and in the demeanour of the people who had been awaiting quietly (some of them for hours) the appearance of the Rebbe. At exactly 9:30 p.m., the mass of thousands rose to their feet in a complete hush as he entered and proceeded to the center of the huge platform, which, I was told, is always reserved for the eldest and the youngest (some of them barely of Bar-Mitzvah age). The Rebbe's discourse always lasts for five hours. Every half hour is punctuated with rapturous song and clapping of hands. At each of these intervals, many of those who are seated at the tables fill their tiny glasses with wine as they turn their eyes to the Rebbe for his acknowledgement of their "Lechayim" greetings. The very narrow tables (to allow for maximum seating) are reserved for the older people. The thousands of Yeshivah Bachurim (youths) stand throughout the five hours on tiers of benches pressed against the walls. As I looked on the faces of these thousands of students, some of them swaying rhythmically to and fro, and others with closed yes, to achieve maximum concentration on the Rebbe's Toireh, I thought: "Would that Rabbi Isser Zalman Meltzer, who had been concerned about the fate of my Yiddishe Neshome in America, could feast his eyes on these American born Yiddishe Neshomes!

On my way to the airport at three a.m., I reflected on the controversy between the believers and non-believers in the future of Jewish life in the Diaspora. I thought of all the evidence in favour of the believers. But I recalled a conversation on this problem with my father many years earlier. He was not ready at that time, as I am not ready today, to state categorically "yea" or "nay", but, he did suggest that I bear in mind his interpretation of a Talmudic statement on this subject.

Living Inside or Outside of the Holy Land

The Talmud states (K'tubot 110:2), "He who lives in the land of Israel is like unto one who has a God; he who lives outside of the land of Israel is like one who has no God". The question arises: Why is it written "is like unto" one who has or does not have a God when the implication is apparently that only he who lives in Eretz Israel has a God? Explained my father: "One who lives in the Land of Israel, even if he "has no God", i.e. even if he is not religious, it is as if he has a God, because he and his descendents will not be lost to the Jewish people, and they may some day return to God. But he who lives outside of the Land of Israel, even if he *has a god* i.e. even if he is *very* religious, it is *as if* he has no God, because his children or his children's children may be lost entirely to the Jewish people...."

The End of the Matter

As for myself, only for myself, "the end of the matter, all having been heard", (Ecclesiastes 12-14), all having been said, I sometimes wish I had never left the simple, beautiful world I was part of in the land of my ancestors....

A Laughing Pessimist or a Crying Optimist

I once told my son Asher, when he was fifteen, that I had seen somewhere a definition of a pessimist as a reformed optimist. He at once came forth with his own definition — that a pessimist is an informed optimist. According to Albert Camus, man in our times has but one alternative — to be a laughing pessimist or a crying optimist. It is very difficult to be an optimist these days, but I think I would classify myself as a crying optimist. I try to think of optimist versus pessimist in this way. The optimist tells the pessimist: "I think I see a light in the distance." The pessimist looks in that direction and quickly pronounces, "I see no light!" The optimist reacts by enlarging his vision of the light into a "burning bush," and proceeds slowly and painfully in its direction. Whether or not he reaches his destination, or when he reaches it, even if there *was* no light there, he brings with him the light he has created on his journey....

Appendix A
Familial Roots

"Look unto the rocks whence you were hewn" (Isaiah 51: 1-2)

The importance of knowing one's roots is already implied in the Bible (Numbers 1:2), when "God spoke unto Moses—take ye the sum of all the congregation of the children of Israel, by their families, by their fathers' houses..." The purpose of knowing one's roots is indicated by the prophet Isaiah (51: 1-2): "Harken to Me, ye that follow after righteousness, Ye that seek the Lord; look unto the rock whence you were hewn; And to the hole of the pit whence you were digged; Look unto Abraham your father and unto Sarah before you..."

It was in that spirit that my parents would refer to our lineage when I grew up in Tsfat. They never told us in a direct manner of our "distinguished geneaology". Without a speck of pride, they would tell us when we misbehaved (quarreled with one another or spent too much time at play, at the expense of learning Torah): "Such behaviour does not become the descendants of so and so". In scolding us, they would often invoke the great scholar or tzadik after whom we were named. To me, for instance, they would say: "Don't forget that you bear the name of your ancestor the great Rabbi Aharon of Karlin". I do not think that I or any of my brothers and sisters took notice of the fact that we were a distinguished family. I do not remember that I ever mentioned this to any of my peers. Why would I have mentioned my remote *yichus,* [distinguished lineage] when it never occurred to me to refer to the immediate fact that my father, Isaiah, was the chief Rabbi of the city? Later, when I went out into the "big world", I was so firm in my conviction of the complete equality of human beings (in the egalitarian spirit of the times) that if I were at all conscious of *yichus, it would have been a taboo to give it any credence. In later years, Rabbis and scholars sometimes referred to my distinguished heritage, but I never took the trouble to delineate it.*

In the early sixties, I received my father's latest book, "Eden Zion—The Holy Places in the Land of Israel". As I was turning its pages at the dinner table, I came upon a hitherto unknown "fact" about my family and I exclaimed, "Listen, listen, according to this, we are descendants of the prophet Samuel and of King David." My eldest son, Gad, reached for the book, saying, "let me see, let me see"; the middle one, Yigal, exclaimed, "Huh-ha!", and the youngest, Asher, said quietly, "so what?"

These three different reactions (not Haley's "Roots") have prompted me to record here our roots, primarily for those of my descendants who will say "let's see, let's see" and for the interested members of our very large far-flung family.

The Shelah—Rabbi Isaiah Horowitz

My father's book deals with the holy places and the tombs of the prophets and Talmudic and post-Talmudic scholars. There is a description and history of each holy place. In the case of the tombs, there are short biographies of the people buried therein.

My father—Isaiah—is a direct eleventh-generation descendant of Rabbi Isaiah Horowitz, known as the Shelah Hakadosh [the Saintly Shelah, c1565-1630, so called after the initials of his main work "*Shnei Luchot Habrit*" (The Two Tablets of the Covenant")]. In connection with the item on the Shelah, my father writes about his and my mother's paternal and maternal *yichus*.

It is not my purpose to include here a translation of the twenty large, compact pages about their lineage. I shall rather refer very briefly to the main line of their ancestry.

Instead of giving an outline of the Shelah's biography as it appears in Encyclopedias, I shall summarize the biographical sketch in my father's book: "He was a great scholar, Cabalist, and saintly person. He had thousands of students and disciples . He and they spread Torah throughout the Jewish world. His moral teachings and devotional and ascetic guidance exerted great influence. He was sought after and served as Rosh-Yeshivah and Av-Bet-Din (literally, head of the yeshivah and of the Rabbinic Court) in many large communities in Europe. Later, he became the chief Rabbi of the Land of Israel, where he lived first in Jerusalem and then in Tsfat. He was not only the dedicated shepherd of Israel, but he also supported many scholars. His table always abounded with guests, often as many as eighty, not only on Sabbaths and holidays but also on weekdays."

My father then lists the heads of the families who preceded the Shelah up to the beginning of the twelfth century. They, like those who succeeded the Shelah, were all great Rabbis and scholars. One of them, Rabbi Avraham Mordechai, wrote that they were descendants of the prophet Samuel. The twenty pages dealing with the family *yichus* include a long charming letter by the Shelah to "his children and children's children until the end of days". It tells of his life work in the Holy Land, and enjoins his descendants to "keep away from sin": "Therefore, hear, my children, the instruction of your father. May God give you a pure heart to live morally and ethically, and be sure to follow in the righteous ways expounded in my writings." It is not clear from my father's involved Rabbinic Hebrew whether it was the Shelah or his son who stated in his will that he had not written about his family *yichus* as a matter of pride, but "so that you should know who you are and who your ancestors are and transmit it to your children and they to their children forever and ever."

The name Horowitz started with Rabbi Isaiah Halevi Ish Horowitz (died in 1517) who was the "Sar" (the meaning probably is the greatest Jewish leader and authority) in the city of Harovice in Bohemia (the name Von Horovice was probably conferred upon him by the Emperor). People who bear the name Horowitz and are of the Levite Tribe are usually paternal descendants of the Shelah, unless the name was adopted by them or their forebears. There have been many Talmudic scholars and distinguished Rabbis in the Horowitz family up to the present. Of those in the family who are known to me, there are but few who now carry on this tradition. In my immediate family, only descendants of my eldest brother, Rabbi Shmuel, whose deep roots are in Israel, continue to be Talmudic students and scholars. Most of my family and those known to me have turned to science and academia. From time to time, I come across a distinguished Horowitz, such as Lord Weindenfeld of Weindenfeld and Nicholson Publishers, who wrote me: "My mother has in her possession a chart of a geneological tree which traces from father to son the lineal descent from the Shelah down to my maternal great grandfather". According to my father, he had it on good authority that the pianist Vladimir Horowitz is a descendant of the Shelah. So is David Horowitz, world renowned economist and former Governor of the Bank of Israel. My father had three brothers, Moshe, Menachem Mendel, and Dov Berl (He died at a young age during the First World War). His only sister, D'vorah, also died during that war, which took a great toll by famine and disease.

A characteristic of the Horowitz family is the striking resemblance not only among siblings, cousins, etc., but also among descendants of the Shelah whose particular kinship is difficult or impossible to identify. This can be exemplified by a recent incident. I chanced to meet a person who looked like a Horowitz. A short conversation between us disclosed that his name was indeed Horowitz and that he was a descendant of the Shelah. We could not, however, establish how we were related. He then told me this amusing story. He was having dinner with his family in a restaurant. Somebody tapped him on his shoulder and greeted him with "Hello Horowitz." Taken by surprise, he said "How do you know my name? I don't think I've ever seen you before." "Oh, come on Horowitz, don't jest; I know you are a son of Rabbi Horowitz of Winnipeg." "I never heard of Rabbi Horowitz of Winnipeg, and where is Winnipeg anyway?" It took some effort to persuade the Winnipeger that it was a mistaken identity. Dr. Horowitz, who teaches Hebrew language and literature at a N.Y. University, gave me a photograph of himself to show to my family. I asked my brothers and sisters whose picture that was. Some said it was my brother Isaac's, and others said it was my brother Israel's. When Israel's wife saw it, she exclaimed, "This is a picture of Israel!" The unusual similarity may be due to the widespread practice of intermarriage that prevailed among Rabbinic families. My father's description of our intertwined yichus is a maze I could not completely unravel. As a matter of fact, both of my parents are descendants of many of the same savants.

As to my father's maternal yichus, his grandmother was a descendant of Sheneur Zalman of Lyady (1747-1813), founder of the Liubavicher Chassidic movement, and of the great Rabbi Aharon of Karlin (d. 1772) who traced his ancestry to King David. My father passed away at age 96, on the twenty-second of Tevet, 5738, January 1, 1978.

My Maternal Geneology

My mother's father Yitzchak Lorberbaum was an Iluy [child prodigy] and a great Talmudic scholar. He was the Rosh Yeshivah of Tsfat, but preferred to make a living by importing sugar from neighbouring countries. He was greatly revered for his modesty and generosity. He was a descendant of Jacob Ben Jacob Moses of Lissa (c. 1762-1832), an East European Rabbinic authority and the author of Derech Hachyim ("The Way of Life"), among many other books. He in turn traced his ancestry to Judah Low ben Betzal'el [known as the Maharal of Prague (c. 1525-1609)], who was widely recognized as one of the leading Rabbinical authorities of his time and as a great Kabballist. The creation of the legendary Golem (a dummy which according to legend came to life) is attributed to him. Rabbi Lorberbaum was also a descendant of the Chacham Zwi [Zwi Hirsch Ashkenazi (c. 1660-1718)], Rabbi and great Talmudic scholar who traced his lineage as far as Aharon Hacochen, brother of Moses.

My mother's mother was the daughter of Shmuel Heller, the highly revered and beloved Rosh Yeshivah, Chief Rabbi, and Physician of Tzfat. He died in 1884 at the age of ninety eight. He was a descendant of Yom-Tov Lipmann Heller (1573-1654), outstanding Rabbinic scholar who was appointed Rabbi in Prague at the age of eighteen, and subsequently served as Chief Rabbi in Prague, Vienna and other cities. His most famous work is Tosafot Yom-Tov ("Supplements of Yom-Tov"), a logical and concise commentary printed in the margin of the Mishnah. According to my father, my mother too traces her geneology to King David. The "conspiracy" between Samuel the Prophet and King David has apparently continued down to the present.....

It is noteworthy that the Rabbinic-Talmudic tradition in my mother's family is also continued only by those children of one of her sisters (Sheindel) whose roots have remained in Israel. Sheindel's husband was Avraham Leib Zilberman, who was Chief Rabbi of Tsfat for many years and who was succeeded in this position by his son-in-law Rabbi Simchah Kaplan. On the other hand, two *grand children* of one of my mother's brothers, Rabbi Avner, are Talmudic scholars. One of them, Rabbi Yaakov Weinberg, is Rosh Yeshivat Ner Israel in Baltimore, Md.; the other, Noah, is now Rosh Yeshivat Esh Hatorah in Israel. One of their sisters, Chavah, is maried to an American born Rabbi, but they immigrated to Israel many years ago.

My mother had another brother, David, who was also a Talmudic scholar, and two more sisters, Malkah and Channah.

My mother Zipporah (Feige) passed away at age 90 — on the eighth day of Sivan, 5737, May 25, 1977.

Appendix B
The Mission of Zionism

(Address delivered by Rabbi Aron Horowitz at the National convention of the Zionist Organization of Canada, held in Montreal during January 19, 20, 1941.)

I know I am repaeting what has become a platitude when I say that Zionism in America—and to a certain extent, in all other parts of the Galuth—has been based on charity and crises. It is true that this is a generalization, and—like many other generalizations, it is not entirely correct. For one thing, it does not account for the historical forces and circumstances that are responsible for this situation. Nevertheless, if we are to be honest with ourselves, we must admit that there is very much truth in this statement. We cannot deny that Zionism is one of the most confused and abused concepts. To some people Zionism means the transportation of all Jews to Palestine, while to others it signifies the giving of succour to our "unfortunate brethern" by settling them in Palestine, where they will be safe from persecution and slaughter. The quip thus originated that "a Zionist is a person who approaches a second person for a donation in order to settle a third person in Palestine."

What is the mission of Zionism? Does Zionism imply the mere raising of funds for the rebuilding of Palestine? Does it confine itself to the physical rebuilding of our Homeland for those of our people who are expelled from their countries of birth or adoption? In other words, does the mission of Zionism begin and end with the rebuilding of Palestine, or does Zionism have a mission also for the Jews of those parts of the Dispersion who never intend to go to Palestine?

Again, if we want to be honest, we must admit that Zionism on this continent has considered its mission to be essentially one of fund-raising for the rebuilding of Eretz Israel. Whatever the cause or causes of this situation may be: whether it is to be attributed to the fact that the past years have been wrought with so many difficulties, so many tragedies, that we have perforce had to concentrate on the alleviation of the sufferings of our people: or whether the cause of this situation is to be found in the fact that the past generationhas been steeped in the fool's paradise of assimilation and has simply not been prepared to respond to our Movement's call for cultural and spiritual revival, the fact is that the Zionist Movement has, in the main, followed almost the same methods that have been employed by the ideological philanthropists, against whose entire program and philosophy—or lack of program and philosophy—the Zionist Movement revolted. In other words, instead of propagating Zionism, instead of bringing it to the fore as a movement of national, cultural and spiritual revival, or as the renewed expression of the indomitable will of our people for renewed national life, as against assimilation, the movement for self-negation and for the gradual destruction of our national will-to-live, Zionism concentrated, or—if you will—has had to concentrate on proving that it is the best form of philanthropy.

In order to illustrate the fact that Zionism has concentrated on fund-raising and has neglected to cultivate its own soul, Mr. Bistritzky, the staunchest fighter for what he calls the fourth sphere of our national politics, the political policy of national education, tells the following little story: At a certain school, where the children were trained to deposit a coin every day in the J.N.F. Box, above which hung the photograph of Dr. Herzl, one of the children exclaimed one day while depositing the coin, "This gentleman likes a lot of money." I have actually experimented and asked young people to tell me the first association of ideas that the word Zionism brings to their minds. The immediate and sharp reply was: "fund raising."

Herein lies at least part of the secret of our Movement's failure to lay hold on the imagination, the heart, the soul of our people, especially of our youth. It is because we have not made the word "Zionism" evoke thoughts of national regeneration, cultural and spiritual renaissance, the renewal of national life and dignity, that Zionism has gradually become another form, albeit the best and most constructive form of philanthropy.

If Zionism is to fulfill its real and true mission, we must return to its real meaning; we must return to its soul. We must make it clear that Zionism is the antithesis to assimilation, that Zionism is the return to ourselves, to our cultural and spiritual heritage as well as to our corporeal national existence. We must renew the declaration of our relentless war against the disease of assimilation which has eaten into our national organism. The rebuilding of Palestine then becomes a need that arises out of our will to live. Eretz Israel then becomes translated into an imperative need for national premises to continue to develop our national life and history. This imperative need does not then arise only from the fact that millions of our people are homeless and are in dire need of a haven of refuge; it finds its roots also in the reawakening of our people from their national lethargy, in their regaining their unconquerable desire for cultural and spiritual rejuvenation. American Jewry is then just as much in need of Palestine as Palestine is in need of American Jewry. In other words, Zionism is at one and the same time the rebuilding of our Homeland for the physical and cultural preservation of our people and the rebuilding of our people to make possible the rebuilding of our Homeland and the continuity of our national life in the Golah.

This brings us to the old question of what comes first, the rebuilding of the land or the rebuilding of the people. To this question we must give the old answer, namely, that neither of these comes first, but that they both come together, that one is impossible without the other. Zionism in the Golah must therefore be not only a means to an end, a means for rising funds for the rebuilding of a National Home, but also an end in itself, a way of life, our philosphy of our national and cultural continuity. The various spheres of Jewish life in the Golah, therefore, cannot and may not be separated into those in which Zionism has a stake and those in which Zionism has no stake. Zionism must be conceived not as one corner in our life, but as a complete approach to every aspect of Jewish life. It must permeate all our existence as Jews. In a word, it must become synonymous with Judaism.

It therefore follows that the Zionist problem in the Diaspora is essentially one of education. For we must first infuse a Ruach Chaim, a breath of life, into our "Atzamoth Yveishoth", into the dry bones of our national organism so that our people should will redemption and revival. If we do not want Zionism to be based on the fluctuation of the political market; if we do not want Zionists "al'tnai," people who are Zionists on condition; if we want Zionists "shel af al pi chen", people who are Zionists in spite of all difficulties and in the teeth of all obstacles; if we want to give vitality to our movement; if we want to bring forth our inherent positive forces, we must re-shape and re-mould the cultural and spiritual life of our people in the Galuth. As our great teacher Achad Haam expresses it so well: Only by learning to understand to value the ideas for which we have stood in the past can we become capable of desiring to stand for something in the present and the future.

It then becomes evident that if we are not floundering and if we really want to achieve the revolution of Zionism, we must educate and prepare the young generation to make possible the realization of that revolution.

I know that some practical people, who see only the moment and who deal only in figures, will maintain that at a time when the entire foundation of Jewish life is shaking and millions of our people are being uprooted, we have no time for the cultivation of the spirit and that we must therefore concentrate on the raising of more funds. I should like to call the attention of these people to the fact that without education, it will become increasingly difficult to raise funds. I shall now tell you one of my many experiences. We were discussing the difficulties of fund raising at the home of one of the most active Zionists in Western Canada, when his young daughter exclaimed: "Daddy, if you find it so difficult to raise money for Palestine, you can imagine how difficult it will be for me." Let the practical people remember that if we will not give earnest attention to the problem of bringing back our youth to us, the time will not be far when it will be almost impossible even to raise funds. Let those people remember that it was not charity that has preserved our people to this day, that it was not charity that gave us courage to suffer all the agony, all the humiliations, persecutions and slaughters. It was the spirit of our people, the readiness for Kidush Hashem that has given them courage to defy our mortal enemies and to continue to live in spite of their tremendous blows. Let us not forget that it is not charity that begot this spirit, but that this spirit begot also charity.

We should therefore make it clear that Eretz Israel and Golath Israel, Palestine and Diaspora, are, at this stage of our struggle, like the Siamese twins— one is dependent upon the other. We must make it clear that just as there can be no healthy national existence in the Golah without Shivath Zion in the true sense of the word, the rebuilding of Zion is impossible without a healthy and conscious Jewry in at least parts of the Golah. If our Movement is therefore not one of the moment or the hour, we must give the utmost attention to what constitutes the roots of the tree. It is true that most people see only the tree. But it is the roots that enable the tree to live and grow. Every national movement, good or bad, understands this simple truism. Even the totalitarian states, which have all the means of brutal force, must employ propaganda and education for the preservation of their life. Certainly we who have no other force but education must not neglect this mightiest of all forces.

And let no one say that this is not the task of the Zionist Organization. If our Movement will not assume this duty, the products of the educational process will be entirely different from what we want them to be. And let us not forget that any movement that depends on other organizations to fulfill its functions, especially the functions of cultivating the soldiery that is to continue its struggle and life, that such a movement will not live for long.

We are now in an age of transition, when Jewish life on this continent is assuming shape and form. If our Movement wants this life to develop in accordance with its living principles, Zionism will have to consider its mission in the Golah to be the reorganization and revitalization of our national life. It lies within the power of our Movement in this country to greatly influence the shape of our life. The question is whether it will understand its mission and whether it will not, in the welter of fund-raising, forget and neglect what is the most important thing, the cultivation of the soul of our great Movement.

I know the need, the tremendous need, the desparate need for funds, for far greater funds than we have been obtaining. As a Palestinian I know the value of funds. I maintain, however, that the best and surest way of raising the funds we need is through education, through the reawakening of our will-to-live.

We can begin a new era for our Movement by reviving one of the ancient principles of Israel, namely, the cardinal principle that puts Torah, education, above everything else. Let us therefore adopt, along with our other three spheres of national politics—our foreign policy, our settlement policy and our financial policy—let us also adopt an educational policy.

I am reminded of a story I heard from one of our leaders. A pious Christian lady, who was in charge of the charitable work in her village, wrote to the priest and requested him to tell her some of the new methods of fund-raising. The good lady had tried all known methods and still found it impossible to raise the necessary funds. Whereupon the priest answered her that the best method of fund-raising is by practising Christianity. The best a surest way of fund-raising for the needs of Zionism is to practice Zionism, real and full-blooded Zionism. Let us therefore cultivate the soul of our Movement; let us cultivate Zionists who will practice Zionism. This will be the best and surest way of receiving the outmost our people can give for the continuation of our struggle for liberation and revival.

APPENDIX B

Appendix C

Memorandum

To Mr. A.J. Frieman, President, Zionist Organization of Canada, on the Policy of the Zionist Organization With Ragard to Jewish education.

By Rabbi Aron Horowitz

March 27, 1941.

(Copied from "Zionism—A Way of Life", by Aron Horowitz, Issued by Federation of Young Judaea of Canada—Western Divsion, and the Calgary Sharon Zionist Club.)

On August 20, 1939, three months after I assumed my present office, I submitted a memorandum to the Zionist Organization on "Zionist activities in Western Canada". In that memorandum, I made the following observations on Jewish Education:

"To me Jewish education is the foundation of our movement. If our youth movement (granting that such a movement is in existence) is based on a very shaky foundation, it is, to a large extent, due to the fact that our youth did not receive a Jewish eduaction at all, or, if they did receive some kind of Jewish education, its basis was not our national or cultural renaissance. We have. for example, some good schools in Western Canada, but they are 'good' schools only from the point of view that they succeed in imparting to their pupils some knowledge of Hebrew, Bible and Ancient Jewish History. From the point of view of national and cultural rebirth, and the education of our children to participate in the rebuilding of Eretz Israel, the eduaction they receive is very much the same as it was before the appearance of Practical Zionism. Our childrens' ignorance of the most elementary knowledge of Zionism and modern Eretz Israel is appalling. That is why the graduates of even our 'good' schools do not constitute the sources from which our youth movement should and could draw its forces.

"It is, therefore, obvious that if we are to strengthen the structure of our movement. we must first make sure that its foundation be sound and firm. I propose the following program for our schools:

"1. The creation of an Educators' Council whose primary functions will be:

(a) To find ways and means of teaching our children "Be-ur-ach Ha-mo-le-deth" (in the spirit of our Homeland).

(b) To educate our children to participate in the rebuilding of Eretz Israel through active work for our national funds.

"I have no doubt that if we succeed in creating a good Educators' Council it will not only fulfill these functions, but will also succeed in the systematization and revitalization of Jewish education in Western Canada.

"I should like to stress the fact that an active program for the Hebrew schools will serve also as a means of penetration into the Jewish home".

On December 27, 1940, I submitted a report of the activities of the Western Division, in which I referred as follows to the work of the Educators' Council:

"A conference of Hebrew Educators and communal-workers was held in October, 1939. As a result of this conference, the Council for Jewish Education was set up, with a view to centralizing and revitalizing Jewish education and making it an integral part of Zionist activities. The Council has made a good beginning, and it is to be hoped that, with greater assiatance of the Zionist organization, Jewish Education in Western Canada will gradually be brought under the direct influence and supevision of the Zionist Movement. To date, the Council has to its credit the following accomplishments:

(1) Two Conferences took place, one in Winnipeg in October, 1939, and the other in Calgary in July, 1940.

(2) The Western Executive Director of the Z.O.C. was elected Educational Supervisor of the Hebrew Schools. His function is to inspect all schools and to cooperate with the local educational committees, in the solution of their eduactional problems.

(3) A uniform curriculum, including the subject "Palestine and Zionism", has been adopted as the basis of our educational system.

(4) Uniform examinations will be given this year for the first time in the schools of the larger centres.

(5) An annual scholarship of $100.00 has been established to enable one student each year to attend the Hebrew Teachers' Seminary. A number of prizes will also be distributed annually in order to stimulate competition and scholrship.

(6) A Seminary has been established for the training of teachers for the smaller centres.

(7) It was recognized that the National and Cultural Renaissance of our people is the foundation of our educational system.

"I should like to emphasize that if the Council for Jewish Education is to strike permanent roots and continue its activities, the Zionist Organization will have to give it much greater moral and financial support than it has received until now."

Before I proceed to make concrete suggestions, I should like to emphasize the following:

(a) In my opinion, the greatest need of Zionism in this country is to identify it with Jewish life. If Zionism is to become a vital force in our national life, we must assume the responsibility of influencing and shaping the cultural and spiritual life of Canadian Jewry. If the Zionist Organization of Canada agrees to what seems to me to be an axiom, then we must certainly assume certain oblgations in the field of Jewish Education.

(b) During the two years that I have been in Western Canada it has become increasingly clear to me that the improvement and centralization of Jewish Education is one of the most difficult problems that Canadian Jewry is faced with. This problem is especially acute in the smaller centres. It is clear that individual communities cannot possibly undertake to even attempt to solve this difficult problem, which could and should be tackled only by a National Organization. I am convinced that Canadian Jewry will look for guidance and leadership to that national organization which will assume this important task.

(c) While in other countries it may be difficult for the Zionist Organization to bring the Jewish educational system under its direct supervision, there is no doubt in my mind that we can do it in Canada. It is true that we will have to overcome certain obstacles, but I am convinced that if the Zionist Organization declares Jewish Education to be an integral part of its national policy, the various communities will abide by the decision of our Movement. (In connection with the points I have mentioned, I would suggest that you read the address on "Zionism and Jewish Education", which I delivered at the Zionist Convention in Montreal. A copy is enclosed herewith.)

Now to come to the concrete suggestions:

(1) I consider it of the utmost importance that our Organization should establish a Department of Education and Culture, the functions of which will be:

(a) To organiza a national council of Jewish Education under the auspices of our Organization. The work of this Council will be to carry out the program I have outlined in my above mentioned article, or any other program that will be prepared by our Organization.

(b) To prepare educational programs and material for the various communities. The lack of such material forms one of the major problems in our Zionist work. To give you one example, I have organized Educational Committees in every one of the larger centres in Western Canada. It is clear, however, that those committees must be provided with suggestions and suitable material. Under our present set-up, it is impossible for any one of the Directors to attend to his work properly.

(c) To co-operate with and offer guidance to our Youth Movement.

(d) To consider ways and means of training leaders for our Youth.

(e) To co-ordinate as much as possible the educational and cultural activities of the various branches of our Movement.

With regard to the budget of this department, I am confident that if the Zionist Organization will undertake to work towards the improvement and centralization of Jewish Education, every school that will be affiliated with our Council will be glad to contribute a nominal fee annually towards its budget. We have found in Western Canada that most of our affiliated schools are ready to make such a contribution. This will bring in an income of several thousand dollars a year. The balance should be met by our Organization.

In closing, I wish to say that I realize that I am suggesting that our Organization should undertake a very difficult and great responsibility. Nevertheless, I, for one, feel certain that the future of our Movement in this country depends on what we are going to do in this most important field.

Appendix D

Excerpts from Interview with Mr. Justice Samuel Freedman Relating to the Hebrew University of Jerusalem

Question: When did you first become interested in the Hebrew University, and what activities did you undertake on its behalf prior to 1940?

Answer: I have been interested in the Hebrew University of Jerusalem ever since it was formally opened on April 1st, 1925. In preparation for that opening, the authorities of the Hebrew University did what universities customarily do in that situation: they extend invitations to various universities around the world. Most universities would reply with a message of greeting and good will. The University of Manitoba, however, did more. Some of the leaders of the Menorah Society of the University of Manitoba felt that this was an event which merited more than formal and perfunctory notice. They persuaded the University to send an official representative to the opening. They suggested that the representative be Rev. Dr. E. Guthrey Perry who was then professor of Hebrew at the University of Manitoba. The Menorah Society undertook to supply the funds, which were obtained on the strength of a bank note endorsed by Mr. Max Steinkopf. The university cooperated by allowing Professor Perry to accelerate his teaching course so that he could leave in late February, and he travelled to the opening along with Max Steinkopf who went on his own. I understand that at the opening, Professor Perry brought the greetings of the University of Manitoba in English and in Hebrew. Well, there is something dramatic and romantic in that kind of occurrence. I was active in the work of the Menorah Society and continued to be active in succeeding years, when our activities were directed in part to payment of what came to be known as the Perry debt. But it was paid off.

Ten years later, in 1935, Mr. Max Steinkopf was requested by the American Friends of the Hebrew University to help arrange an event to commemorate the University's tenth anniversary. I was a young lawyer at that time in his office. Since Mr. Steinkopf was not well (indeed this was his last illness; he died in May 1935), he turned over to me the request to arrange for an appropriate commemoration. We did that with the cooperation of the University of Manitoba and that gave me a link with the Hebrew University, tenuous, let it be admitted, but still one that helped to keep alive in me my interest in that institution. I lead ahead to 1944 when, as you indicated, Allan Bronfman became the National Chairman of the Canadian Friends, and the organization was launched on a national basis. Allan Bronfman and Mark Shinbane came to see me in this courthouse shortly after I was appointed a judge of the Court of Queen's Bench. I was appointed in April 1952. My chief Justice, the Hon. E.K. Williams, had told me that for a year it would be advisable for me to drop extra-judicial activities. I was invited to become chairman of the Winnipeg Chapter of the Canadian Friends. At that time, they had a chapter, not a large one, but it was in existence under the leadership of the late Louis Matlin. I told the Committee, Allan Bronfman and Mark Shinbane, that if they came to see me a year hence I would say yes, and I did. So from 1935 to the present day, not only my interest but my active participation in the work of the University has been a solid and substantial fact. In 1955 I was invited to attend with Allan Bronfman a meeting of the International Board of Governors of the Hebrew University in Jerusalem. I did so attend and I was elected a member of the Board at the end of that meeting. I have continued to be a member of that Board for the last twenty three years.

Question: Were there any activities on behalf of the University between 1935 and 1940, when I started to include the celebration of the University's anniversaries among the annual events of the Z.O.C.?

Answer: Let me refer back to the tenth anniversray celebration in 1935 which was held in the form of a dinner. Following the dinner, we sent the press reports to the New York office of the American Friends. We got splendid coverage because of the participation of the Chancellor and the President of the University of Manitoba and Professor Perry. The press reports were so enthusiastic that they led to a request from Mr. Finkel that we try to capitalize on this by fund raising. Unfortunately, I am not a fund raiser. I got people likle Montague Israels, H.E. Wilder and Gerti Rosen, who appreciated the role of the Hebrew University, to help me arrange a meeting. They too were not fund raisers, but since the request was made, we tried to do something. In January 1936, we brought Ludwig Lewison to deliver a lecture, the proceeds to go to the Hebrew University. We had a wonderful cultural event. We showed a profit but not a large one. Apart from the dinner to which I've referred and to the meeting with Ludwig Lewison, both of these being temporary ad-hoc activities, there was no continual group or work in respect to the Hebrew University till after 1944.

Question: The founders of the Hebrew University had a vision that "from Zion will go forth knowledge" and that there would be a mutual exchange of ideas, of values, of influences with the Diaspora. My impression is that the work of the Canadian Friends is limited to fund raising and that little if anything is done in the cultural area.

Answer: I don't think I would accept that in its entirety. There is no doubt that the major energies of the Canadian Friends were directed towards the raising of money for the University. But that didn't exhaust it. There was on the part of many workers a sensitive appreciation of the special role of a university and its cultural and moral effect in building a better Israel. It was always kept before some of these workers as an objective, as a goal. I would just like to refer to something that I heard from the second President of the State of Israel, Yitzchak Ben-Zwi. A few members of the Board of Governors in Jerusalem and from abroad were invited to the President's home for tea. I remember him telling us that he had been present at a conversation between Achad Haam and Ussishkin, two giants in Zionism. The question that was being sought was what kind of a state do we want to create in Palestine? Achad Haam said if it was to be another Montenegro, the effort would not be worthwhile. (Montenegro, almost forgotten, now swallowed up as part of Yugoslavia.) It seemed to me that the point of the observation was that not only must we have a State, a Homeland, not only must it survive but it must survive significantly and creatively. And it's in that area that an institution like the Hebrew University can play an honourable role.

Question: But has the Hebrew University had any influence on Canadian Jewish life?

Answer: Oh, I think so. First of all, there are Canadian students attending the Hebrew University. It started off with small numbers, followed by more and more. And the fact of life surely is that there is a strong link, a strong bond between the communities of Israel and the communities of the Diaspora. They are part of the same circle; Israel at the centre, the other communities fanning out towards the circimference. And I think that the interesting thing is that each gives the other validity and signifigance.

The Forgotten Cause

*The Functions of the Jewish Congress and
the Zionist Organization in the Sphere
of Jewish Education*

by Rabbi A. Horowitz

(Published in The Canadian Zionist 1954)

Jewish education has been the step-child, the forgotten cause, in the scheme of things of Canadian Jewry. Now and then a voice is heard on behalf of this forgotten cause, but it is always a voice in the wilderness, which is drowned in the welter of campaigns and conventions.

Of late, with the comparative reawakening of Jewish consciousness among the masses as a result of both negative and positive forces, there has been evidence of a greater and more genuine interest in the sphere to which educators fondly refer as "the very foundation of Jewish life." Unfortunately, this interest is still in the nature of groping in the dark. There is no indication of any endeavors to evolve a plan of systematic action based on a comprehensive study of the situation. This is evidenced by the fact that some people are ready to assign the task of education to different organizations at one and the same time. The same individuals who jump on the bandwagon at the convention of one national organization to refer to it the authority in the field of education appear at the convention of another national organization and assign to it the very same task. Generally speaking, many people feel that "something must be done," but are not at all clear as to who should do it.

In considering this problem, one naturally thinks of our two main national organizations, namely, the Canadian Jewish Congress and the Zionist Organization. Most people who give some thought to this subject seem to feel that both these organizations have some duties and prerogatives in the sphere of Jewish education. However, there appears to be a lack of clarity and unanimity as to the respective spheres of both these organizations. It therefore seems to us that before any national plan can be adopted and implemented, there must be clarification and a certain measure of agreement as to the duties of both these organizations in the sphere of education. In a word, there must first be a definition of functions of the C.J.C. and the Z.O.C. in this important field.

It seems to us that the Congress, by its very nature, should engage in activities which tend to unify whenever unification is desirable and possible. In order to maintain its integrity and national leadership, the Congress must not enter controversial fields, which might defeat the very purpose for which Congress came into being. It must avoid certain spheres that would become a source of friction, which in turn would lead to disharmony and disunity.

Few people who are *directly connected* with Jewish education will deny that in this sphere less unification is possible than in any other field of Jewish endeavor. For in education one sees the *sine qua non* for the realization of his "Weltanschung"; in education one sees the possibility of cultivating his philosophy of life, so that it touches the very heart and soul of his being.

We therfore cannot understand how the Congress can be urged to assume the authority and responsibility in the field of education, which is divided at the present into several distinct systems. For example, the resolution which was adopted at the last Congress convention calls for the appointment of three regional directors. (We have already stated that similar resolutions could be carried through at the conventions of other organizations!)

The question thus arises: "What will be the functions of these directors?" Speaking generally and broadly, one would say that they would have to supervise, guide, and promote Jewish education throughout the Dominion. One therefore has the right to ask, "What system of education will they promote?" To say that they will promote all systems of education suggests that there can be neutrality in this most controversial sphere. From the point of view of some laymen who are not vitally interested or directly involved in this field, all systems of education should and could be encouraged. From the point of view of the educator, however, one must have definite ideals and ideas in a sphere that will determine the nature and character of the future Jewish community. It is thus difficult for us to imagine that educators of the different educational systems will accept the authority of one who would claim to be an *expert* and an idealist in all the different educational systems. (We believe that no one will argue the point that in order to achieve anything in this field, one must be an expert and an idealist.) We cannot conceive of a man of convictions and intellectual integrity who would undertake to be neutral in matters about which he must have definite ideas, if, of course, he is a real educator. Moreover, if we assume, only for the sake of argument, that such a person could be found, there would always be room for complaints on the part of one educational sytem or another about the partiality or bias of the director, which would serve as a powder-keg to cause disharmony and friction in the ranks of Congress.

Let us now be more specific with regard to the activities of the regional directors. Since we are aquainted with the situation in Western Canada, we shall deal only with this region.

It seems to us that the main problem at present is the lack of qualified modern teachers and able principals who would be in a position to organize and *maintain* a sound educational system and an active cultural program. Frankly, we do not see how a Western educational director will solve this problem. And it is superfluous to dwell on the fact that an educational director will be able to do practically nothing in communities where there are no qualified modern educators who are possessed of initiative and resourcefulness, no matter how often the director will visit those communities. (There seems to be a general tendency to attempt to solve all problems by the appointment of an ever-increasing number of arm-chair strategists in the large centres, while smaller communities must continue to workwith their limited facilities and personnel.)

Another possible function of the director would be to prepare material for the schools. First of all, we do not think that this activity warrants the maintenance of a director in each region. Secondly, we think that the communities that have qualified eduactors have recourse to the same material that the directors would have. Most important of all, the material that will be suitable for one system will be unsuitable for others, and vice versa. This point can be proved by us not in theory, but in actual practice. For several years we have been receiving material from the Education Committee of the C.J.C., which is most definitely unsuitable for modern Hebrew schools. (We would suggest that it would be far less expensive in the long run if the Congress were to present each school with a number of standard books, from which much richer material could be drawn.) This fact also proves our point that it is neither desirable nor practicable to have the same director for the different systems of education.

Another function of any director would be the inspection and supervision of schools. We submit most respectfully that educators worthy of the name will not accept a supervisor who would claim to be an expert in all systems of Jewish education.

It therefore seems to us that the co-ordination of each system should be undertaken by separate national organizations which identify or should identify themselves with the philosophy of the respective educational systems. The modern Hebrew schools, for instance, should, in our opinion, come within the sphere of the Z.O.C. If the latter continues to maintain its adamant attitude towards an activity which will determine the future of Zionism in this country, then it is our opinion that the leading Hebrew educators should take the initiative in this field. It would then be necessary to engage one director for all the Hebrew schools, whose functions would be to co-ordinate as much as possible the programs of the various Hebrew schools, and to offer guidance and assistance wherever and whenever it will be necessary. The other system or systems could organize a similar set-up. We would thus have two national directors who would be experts in their respective systems and who would be accepted by their various colleagues of similar convictions and ideology.

From what has been said so far, one may have formed the impression that we ignore the role of Congress in the field of education. This is definitely not the case. In our opinion, the Congress has or should have the following functions in the educational field:

1. It should engage itself in a field hat is common to all educational systems, such as general propaganda among our people re the importance of education, the compilation of statistics, etc.

2. It seems to us that the Congress has some very important tasks also in the external sphere, namely in matters such as the teaching of religion in the public schools, the organization of interfaith activities within schools, etc.

3. We believe that the Congress could render a great service to the cause of goodwill by launching a movement to introduce the study of Hebrew as a foreign language in the high schools of at least the larger centres in the Dominion. Needless to say, this would be a difficult but very significant undertaking, which, if crowned with success, would serve to bring about better public relations than many other projects.

These activities would not require the appointment of special directors, as they could be carried on by the present personnel of the Congress.

We know from the past that certain people who always demand tolerance from others and are ready to brand as intolerant anyone who happens to disagree with them, that these people may cry "disunity upon you Israel." We therefore wish to emphasize a point that to us appears to be a maxim, namely that to be tolerant and respectful of other peoples' views and activities does not mean that one should, nay, that one could with a clear conscience help cultivate and promote these views.

In conclusion, we wish to stress the point that before any national plan is adopted, there should take place a conference of Congress representatives, Z.O.C. representatives, and of leading educators who are *directly* connected with the field of education, in order to fully discuss all these important problems, so that an agreement could be reached. This, in our opinion, is the only way of ensuring the successful implemtation of any plan that will be adopted in the field of Jewish education.

Appendix F
Hebrew Education in Canada
Suggestions for Reform

(Translated from Hebrew)

(Lecture delivered in Toronto at National Convention on Jewish Education in 1948, and published later in "Shivilei Hachinuch", Educational-Pedagogical Quarterly)

The problems of Hebrew edcation in Canada, which — in the main — are similar to those in the U.S.A., have their origin in both internal and external factors. Some problems are due to the special characteristics of our time or of a particular locale, and others are due to the personalities and educational methods of those who are involved in Hebrew education.

We must therefore classify the communities with which we are concerned into three main categories: a) small centres, which, because of their very small Jewish population, cannot afford to employ either a teacher or a "Sochet"; (Translator's note: a "Sochet" is in charge of ritual animal slaughter.) b) Small communities that are capable of maintaining either a "Sochet" *or* a teacher; c) Middle-size and large communities.

The situation in communities of the first category is very bad. There, Jewish children grow up without Hebrew education whatsover, and thus are completely illiterate as far as Judaism is concerned. Restricted to their narrow milieux, they know nothing of their Jewishness and have no understanding of their place as Jews in Canadian society. Even though the number of these choldren is not large, we must not abandon them to their fate. Before suggesting some steps that can be taken to correct the situation in those places, I would like to deal with the second category, for some of my proposals are applicable to both of these categories.

The situation in the communities of the second category is somewhat similar to that in the first, although they employ a "Shochet" who functions also as a teacher. In such centres, the children do learn to *read* Hebrew, and — in some places — they also learn a bit of Bible and history, but the over all results of this education are almost nil and sometimes even negative. Children who live in an atmosphere that is completely devoid of religious and cultural Jewish activity often perceive the "shochet" (teacher), who is invariably an old person from the old country, as a queer alien character. For, the shochet-teacher lacks the professional and psychological training to understand and empathize with his pupils. He is therefore unable to provide them with meaningful and enjoyable Jewish experiences which would give them a *positive* identification with the Jewish people. The negative effects of this kind of education often nullify its small benefits, for the sochet-teacher may come to personify — in the eyes of these children — the totality of Judaism, as they seldom — if ever — come in contact with any vital expressions of Jewish religious, social and cultiural life, thereby intensifying their estrangement from their heritage.

It will be extremely difficult to correct the situation in these communities, for it is a direct result of the disappearance of the *positive* aspects of the Jewish ghetto experience, but we are not entirely helpless. These are my suggestions: a) Among the small towns, there are a number that are located within easy travelling distance from one another — such as Kamsack, Yorkton and Melleville — in Western Canada. Instead of having a sochet in each of the three, they could cooperate for the purpose of having one teacher and one sochet to serve the three communities simultaneously. The teacher could serve also as a cultural leader and cordinator for the whole area, including those communities that cannot afford a teacher or a sochet. The teacher could then serve all the children and youth in the area, promoting the reading of books on Jewish subjects, organizing youth groups, and creating links with the youth in the larger centres through the organization of regional conferences, and so on.
b) Many children from the small centres already attend summer camps run by "Young Judea" in various parts of Canada. The programs of these camps could be expanded, and special classes could be held in them for children from small communities.
c) There is a need for a national office to maintain contact with all the small communities, and supply them with such services as assistance in setting up curricula, supervision, general guidance, and — perhaps — correspondence courses. Such an office could be of great value to the teachers in these communities.

Many of you may already be wondering: "Where will we find the teachers to take on these difficult tasks at a time when there is a great shortage of teachers even in the large cities"? My answer is that we must make a special effort to train new teachers and inspire them to dedicate themselves to this great project. At this point, none of us can say: "We have tried and have not succeeded."! I am convinced that if we could summon up the necessary faith and enthusiasm, the problem of the shortage of teachers could be ameliorated. As substantiation of this proposition, I can point to an effort that was undertaken in Western Canada *in 1940*, when I was regional director of the Zionist Organization and consultant-supervisor of all the Hebrew schools in the area. At that time, we were able to persuade about twenty young people to prepare themselves for the task of serving the small communities. They volunteered for the project with a sense of understanding, with the enthusiasm of youth, and even with a feeling of religious dedication. The teacher's seminary which we set up for them functioned well for over a year; but we eventually had to close it down because we could not find a single Jewish organization that was ready to understand the importance of the project and assume responsibility for its very minimal budget. It should be pointed out that the idealism of the young people influenced some of the faculty members to volunteer their services for no pay at all, and some for a very modest honorarium.

While the problems of Hebrew education in small cities are due primarily to external circumstances, in the middle-sized and large communities they are largely caused by internal factors, such as the communal leaders, the educational philosophies — or lack of clear philosophies — and the teaching methods and programs. Progress in these communities will depend on action in two important areas: a) The creation of a strong national organization composed of recognized leading educators, together with those community leaders who are willing to accept their guidance in such matters as educational content and method, in contrast to leaders who believe that their involvement in the educational sphere automatically endows them with the right to determine *educational* policies and programs. b) The undertaking of a basic study of our entire educational system, of its present role and the role it ought to play in our lives as Canadian Jews.

Obviously, it is impossible to spell out in this presentation the details of these two proposals, each of which requires much careful study and deliberation. At this time, I can only point to a few general considerations:

a) *The Role of Education in the Life of the Jewish Community:* Hebrew education in Canada is far from enjoying its rightful place in our society. The blame cannot be fixed solely on communal leaders. We ourselves have done little to educate the Jewish public to the understanding of the crucial importance of Hebrew education to the survival and cultural renaissance of our people. So long as we fail to place Hebrew education at the centre of our Jewish community life, whatever measures we take for its improvement will remain mere palliatives. Hebrew education must not be restricted to the confines of the school house. It should pervade all spheres of Jewish life, acting as an essential catalyst for the cultural renaissance of the emerging Jewish community on this continent. The Hebrew school must be at the centre of our Jewish life especially in the middle-sized centres, for in them the quality of Jewish living will be determined by an educational system that could serve as the focus of Jewish religious, social and cultural life and would thereby gain the support of the community and involve it in the life and activities of the school.

b) *Curriculum:* In my opinion, our curriculum and educational methods suffer from an excess of verbalism and a lack of vitality and dynamism. Our schools do teach; they do impart knowledge, but they do not educate, and they do not involve the students in the contemporary cultural life of our people. If our aim is to raise a generation that will participate actively in the life of the community and achieve a synthesis between their Judaism and Canadianism, we shall not achieve this aim so long as our curriculum is restricted to the study of prayer, Bible, Rashi and Talmud. I do not question the value of these studies, but they should be taught at the appropriate stage of the intellectual development and the linguistic capacity of the students as well as in the context of a wider and more vital educational program. They should not overshadow essential subjects such as the spoken modern language, Hebrew literature, modern Jewish history, Zionism, the Land of Israel and its relationships with Canada, and contemporary jewish life. At present, many of our schools teach Bible to small children who have not yet learned basic Hebrew language skills, and Talmud to youngsters who have not yet so much as tasted of our literature. Also, they concentrate on the past and more than minmize the present. To me it is obvious that a poem like Yitzchak Lamdan's "Chain of Dances" is more effective in relating our children to the life of our people than a chapter of the tractate Bava Metziah of the Talmud.

Some teachers argue that the expertise of the teacher is more important than the material he uses. I disagree. For even if we grant — for the sake of argument — that the material is not of prime importance, we must bear in mind that many of our teachers lack the necessary expertise to adapt the material to the capacity of the children. In my opinion, even the excellence of a teacher cannot make up for the inappropriateness of the materials he uses. I believe it is high time for a thorough reform of the established curriculum and for the revitalization of our educational program through the introduction of current and relevant subjects, modern Hebrew pronunciation, progressive methods, and the creation of positive experiences of involvement in Jewish thought and creativity. In short, our curriculum should be based on the principle that learning should lead to living.

c) *Discipline:* Much has been said and written about this important problem in our schools. In my opinion, our approach must consist in education for self-discipline rather than the use of coercion. The problem of discipline will be partly solved by a relevant curriculum, but the essential goal is to cultivate understanding between teachers and students through the cultivation of the teacher-student relationship into one of effective communication, cooperation and respect. Most teachers deal with the problem of discipline by taking what seems to them the short and easy way of coercion, but this path is ineffective and destructive. The seemingly longer path of understanding the personalities and individual needs of the students, of involvement in their lives and problems, may appear circuitous and impracticle, but it is in effect the shortest and most effective path. Both education for self-discipline and preparation for active participation in Jewish community life can be greatly enhanced by the development of an independent youth organization within the framework of the educational institution. Such an organization would not merely grant "self-government" to the student body; it would also provide them with the essential means of creativity. It would give them the opportunity to develop their own social-cultural activities, such as dramatics, art and crafts, journalism, music and dance, communal meals planned and prepared by the students, holiday celebrations, sports and trips. In all these activities, the teacher should act as an older comrade who is ready to assist, guide and counsel — not as an authoritarian ruler. The children should be convinced of their teacher's confidence in them and in their capacities. The students must be given the opportunity to take the initiative in the development of their own social and creative powers. All of this can obviously not be achieved if the teacher is available only during the hours of work in the classroom. He must be a willing participant in the creative life of the students, and serve as a model for them in everything he does.

d) *The Teacher:* Clearly, we will never have such idealistic master-teachers if we do not succeed in extricating the Hebrew-teaching profession from its present low social and economic status. I am aware of the recent improvements in the situation, but I think they are a direct result of the acute shortage of teachers, rather than of any fundamental change in the attitudes of the parents and community leaders. I suspect that if the situation should change either in the supply of teachers or in the economic conditions, Hebrew education and Hebrew teachers will become the first victims. This is the main reason that very few — if any — of our talented youth are attracted to careers in Hebrew education. The situation has deteriorated to the point that anyone with a smattering of Hebrew can wrap himself in the mantle of a "Teacher in Israel", and any young person who has attended a Hebrew school for a few years can be admitted into a teaching seminary, even if his attainments are so slight that he could not qualify as a student in any Hebrew High School worthy of the name. The teaching profession is in decline, and is in danger of becoming the occupation of "Failures". The crucial element in education is the teacher; so long as there is no powerful national organization capable of defending his interests and raising his status in the community, Hebrew education will continue to decline and deteriorate. The "Igud" (Translator's note: a loose and weak association of Hebrew schools) must therefore assume this important and difficult task.

e) *Hebrew Camps:* Great possibilities for the improvement of the educational process have been opened up by the recent establishment of Hebrew summer camps in the U.S.A. and Canada. The Hebrew camp can be a partial solution to the problem of the abscence of vital Jewish community life, especially for the smaller centres. In the Hebrew camp, the educator can realistically aspire to educational wholeness — to a fusion of home life, street life and general community life. The camp affords us a powerful tool for the education — not the mere teaching, but the *education,* properly so called — of the Jewish child. If Hebrew camps were established throughout Canada, they could bring about a veritable revolution in our educational system. I can foresee the day when every school worthy of the name will establish a special camp which will enable its participants to enjoy its benefits.

The most sacred and difficult task that confronts us today is the organization, improvement and revitalization of Hebrew education in this country. We will realize this great objective only if we can rise to the challenge of the fateful times in which we live and find the way to unite our forces in raising the banner of an effective and meaningful Hebrew educational system. The time has come, in my view, to merge the Igud (Association of Hebrew Schools) and the Keren Hatarbut (Association for Hebrew Culture) into a single movement dedicated to the advancement of Hebrew education and culture in Canada. Our path will not be strewn with roses, but with our united forces and with faith in our objectives and capabilities we can succeed in overcoming the many obstacles and in making our contribution to the spiritual and cultural renaissance of the Jewish People.

Appendix G

The Place of the Hebrew Language in the Education of the Adolescent in America

(Translated from Hebrew)

(Published in the Year Book of the Jewish Education Commission of the United Synagogue of America in 1967)

At first sight, it seems strange that such a question should be raised at all, for we are not dealing with the teaching of a foreign language, but with the instruction of the student in the language of his own people. Would it occur to any other people to question the importance of imparting its national language to a particular age group? The very idea that the place of language in the education of a people may be called into question should itself be called into question and categorically rejected.

But we are forced to face this question by the reality of American Jewish life, a reality which flies in the face of logic; in the "diaspora" (America may not be "exile", but everyone will agree that it is a "diaspora") logic and action definitely do not always coincide. It is possible for us to change our reality, but we must study this reality in order to understand and change it.

The very *formulation* of the question contains the core of the problem in all its gravity. We are confronting a problem which, in my opinion, basically affects our national survival in the diaspora. This problem is rooted in the prevailing attitude and approach toward our national language, an approach which is itself one of the causes of the unnatural state of affairs that necessitates discussing a question which members of another people would consider absurd, just as absurd as questioning the place of speech as such in the education of the adolescent. I know that this analogy will be regarded as an exaggeration even by those who affirm the importance of Hebrew in education, but in my opinion this problem is a matter of "to be or not to be" for the future of Hebrew education in America.

Our subject is the adolescent, but we cannot discuss the place of the Hebrew language in the education of the teenager without touching upon the question of the place of Hebrew in our life in the diaspora — just as one cannot consider the cultivation of a tree without giving attention to the health of the roots.

It is an open secret that the prevailing attitude toward Hebrew is one which regards it as a foreign language. And for this reason the approach to teaching Hebrew, e.g. *when* Hebrew is to be taught, *how much* is to be taught, and *how* it is to be taught, is almost like an approach to teaching a foreign language. (And if Hebrew is "almost" a foreign language, why should Jewish students study Hebrew instead of French or Spanish in the high schools of New York? The fact of the matter is that the number of high school students taking Hebrew in that city — which has been called a "second Jewish Kingdom" — is paltry indeed.) It is also well known that many educators are convinced that "we must teach ideas, not language". Teachers with such an outlook have gone so far as to despair altogether of the possibility — and therefore also of the necessity — of teaching Hebrew in America. I shall cite here only one case in point among the many which I have encountered. In a debate between myself and a high school principal about the need for preparing Hebrew materials suitable for high school students, the man wrote to me in a categorical mode that in America we should not devote time to teaching a language but to teaching subjects such as history, philosophy, and sociology.

We know the attitude of the *sh'lichim* from Israel toward our national language. I will confine myself to only a few examples:

(1) Attending a farewell gathering for a *shaliach* who had been working with young people in Canada, I did not hear so much as one word of Hebrew, not even from the Consul General of the State of Israel, who saw fit to end his speech with "au revoir" rather than "shalom".

(2) The Jewish community of Montreal was found worthy of receiving a visit from David Ben-Gurion, but the Hebrew language was not found worthy of being used in the invitation to the reception which was held in his honour at the Israeli consulate.

(3) Montreal was the first Jewish community in Canada to hold a Hebrew Book Week. The celebration held to honour the Hebrew book was splendid and well attended, but the address which the Israeli Consul delivered on that occasion did not include a single word of Hebrew.

It is well known how little Hebrew is spoken even in institutions which exist expressly for the sake of providing a Hebrew education.

What is at the root of this atttitude? Some say snobbery. Some say just plain lack of respect. In my opinion it is neither the one nor the other. This attitude derives primarily from a general failure to appreciate the tremendous power of language and from a disregard for the crucial value of the national language particularly in national education.

The educators who have decided in favour of "ideas" over "language" have cited in their support the saying of the Rabbis that the *Shema* may be recited "in any language you can understand" — as if the Rabbis had meant this to be taken as legislation regarding the value of the Hebrew language for Jewish survival! Actually, this Rabbinic ruling applies solely to the recitation of the *Shema*, not to the question of the place of Hebrew in the life of the Jewish people. The Rabbis never intended to minimize the value of the Hebrew language, but sensed instinctively that the language is the very soul of the people. That is why we have so many statements in Rabbinic literature like "the day the Bible was translated into Greek was as sad for Israel as the day the Golden Calf was made", and sadder "even than the day the Temple was destroyed". Surely there is no need for interpretation of the trenchant words, which clearly refer to the value of Hebrew for the survival of the nation, for the "eternity of Israel", and not, like the ruling on the recitation of the *Shema*, to a particular obligation of the individual in his daily life.

What our Rabbis felt intuitively and knew from the depth of their life experience about the power and function of language has been corroborated by modern scientists in research covering various areas of knowledge. It is, of course, impossible within the limits of this article to delve into all the aspects of this subject, namely, the place of language in human culture. We will touch upon it only insofar as it is necessary to point out the fallacious character of the widespread misconception that language is nothing but a garment, an external form for the content, the idea, and that, since the garment is a secondary consideration only, any garment may be used for the dissemination of the idea, which is the main thing. I will confine myself here to quoting only one scientist whose brief words leave little to be added. According to this scientist, Julian Huxley, "the words which a man utters not only express his thoughts but also shape them. Language is more than an instrument; it is an environment. The power of language in the shaping of philosophy and politics is like that of geography or climate in the shaping of a society." Realizing this truth, scientists and philosophers are now devoting attention to the role of translation from one language into another as a factor in the creation and solution of human problems. As one example I will mention the comment of the well-known semanticist Stuart Chase on the congratulatory telegram which Pope Paul VI sent to Alexei Kosygin when the latter was named prime minister of the Soviet Union. The Pope expressed the hope that the historic aspirations of the Russian people would be advanced under Kosygin's leadership. The translation of the Pope's message, as prepared by the official translator in the Vatican, created the impression that the Pope had given his endorsement to the new regime. The ambiguity of the Pope's message created confusion and displeasure among all those concerned. And while we are on the subject of translations, we might mention two seemingly trivial examples from an absurd experiment in translation. In a translation from English into Russian by computer, the saying "the spirit is willing but the flesh is weak" was rendered as "the whiskey is good but the meat is rotten"; and "out of sight, out of mind" emerged as "blind idiot". In summary, we maintain that it is a gross error to believe that *any* idea lends itself simply to a proper translation into another language, and that a neat distinction can be made between language and idea, form and content.

Returning to our central theme — Hebrew in adolescent education — I must emphasize my considered conviction that this problem will only be solved if there is a change in our attitude toward the Hebrew language. Accordingly, this means that we will succeed in the education of adolescents in the diaspora only when the leaders and shapers in this field realize that our goal and our task is not to teach a foreign language, or an "extra" language, but to educate our children in a Jewish milieu; and that the character of any culture is created not only by its language *per se* but also by the distinctive shaping power of that national language. (Obviously "culture" includes religion, especially in the case of Jewish culture in which religion and peoplehood cleave together like wick and flame on a lit candle. This much should have been clear from the start. Why then make it explicit? Only in order to avoid becoming entangled in debate on a subject where there is nothing to debate.)

This brings us to the question of what we are to do about those adolescents who enter high school without knowing any Hebrew at all. Do we devote the few hours we have with them to the teaching of *ideas*, or should we perhaps revive the effort to instruct the youth in the Hebrew *language*? In order to answer this question we must first define the principal aim of Hebrew education in the diaspora. Simply stated, in my opinion, that aim should be to get the student to identify with the contemporary life of his people. (The subconscious identification dating from his childhood should evolve into conscious identification during adolescence.) If this is our principal aim, then it is our task to teach the language even under the present difficult circumstances. As for the widespread argument that we should not "squander the short time during which we have these young people to ourselves simply on language and never get to the philosophy of Judaism", we shall be able to refute it categorically if we keep in mind that: (1) the Hebrew language will not be devoid of ideas if it is taught in a Jewish setting by a competent teacher; (2) our principal aim, if there is to be lasting or further success, is not merely to inculcate abstract knowledge but to bring about the student's identification with his people by educating his emotions, so that he may be motivated to continue his Hebrew studies and to conduct himself in accordance with what he has been taught, even after he has passed out of our hands. If we remember the profound pedagogical teaching of Plutarch that "the mind of the child is not a vessel to be filled but a flame to be fanned", we shall be able to awaken in young people the desire to study, to know, to understand and to act, so that the continuation of their studies will not be determined by "the short time that we still have them to ourselves".

If we continue to be cowed by the pressure of the "short time", we will not succeed in filling them up with knowledge in any case, and the knowledge which we do instill will remain at best an ephemeral knowledge ("for the short time that we have the student to ourselves"). (3) Hebrew education in the diaspora today must be linked with the struggle of our people for redemption and rebirth in its own land. Have we any better or more effective means for bringing the youth of our generation to identify with its people than the State of Israel, which blends within itself the values of the religion, the life and the future of the people of Israel? (4) If we set our sights on national education (and need we stress again that our religion is rooted in our national culture?), we cannot conceive of national education in our generation without the national language. In my opninion there is a great deal of truth in the words of Vladimir Jabotinsky, who said that in national education the content is the form and the form is content, and that the school therefore implants in the hearts of its students not the language it teaches but the language *in which* it teaches. Support for Jabotinsky's views may be found in the words of many of our Sages, including Rabbi Judah Loew ben Bezalel of Prague. I do not remember Rabbi Judah's exact words, but as far as I can recall, the idea is as follows: Every nation has its own idea and form. The idea is a matter of pure cognition; the form is both cognitive and also the concrete, sensuous mode through which the idea finds expression. According to Judah Loew ben Bezalel, language is the distinctive form of the nation just as speech is the distinctive form of the individual, and if the language of the nation is lost, so too will be its form.

If we are not going to teach Hebrew as a forcign language, or as an "extra" language, but instead educate the young *in* the language of their people, there must be a basic change in our approach to the teaching of Hebrew. Instead of concerning ourselves with grammar, translation drills and mechanical reading, with the illusion that we will in this way enable our children to understand the Torah in the original and to read Hebrew literature, let us use a scientific approach (which never becomes petrified, but keeps on researching, experimenting and creating), and let us create a climate of spoken Hebrew and of Hebrew culture. In this way we shall link the student with the life of his people that is rebuilding its land and its culture. This link, this identification with the Jewish people, is the basis for instruction in the Hebrew language, in Jewish culture and in Jewish religious values. Let me make it clear that I am not setting "spoken Hebrew" against "the reading of books". Rather, I believe that speaking Hebrew must come before the reading of books — from the points of view of both pedagogy and psychological development. I believe that the experiments and experiences that are now on the record and the results which have already been achieved in various parts of the diaspora, bear out this view. I will cite only one out of many cases in point which typify the profound disappointment of many in our generation with the approach which was used on them in our schools, an approach which renounced the value of the living Hebrew word.

One of my friends, who received an intensive Hebrew education, studied the Bible, the Talmud and so forth, was appointed to an important position with the United Nations and escorted Ralph Bunche and Count Folke Bernadotte when they visited Palestine during the UN debate on the founding of the State of Israel. He told me about the pain and humiliation he felt when he found that all his studies of so many years had not been sufficient to enable him to converse in Hebrew with the Jews he met in Palestine.

We are led to the conclusion that the first year of high school should be devoted to two things (naturally, we are thinking of students who enter high school without an adequate background in the Hebrew language): (1) Instruction in the living Hebrew language. This must be done through conversation, song (song, too, can be effective in teaching a language if the teaching is done by competent individuals), dramatics, celebrations and other activities. This means that we should concentrate on the sort of learning which leads to action and on learning in and through doing. This approach should aim at laying the linguistic foundations during the first year to prepare the student for studying the sources in subsequent years. (2) Preparing the student in the psychological sense, so that he *wants* to continue his studies. All this must be done by competent teachers who know the spirit of the present generation and the psyche of the student.

I can already hear the question, "How can such a thing be done?" "Hasn't experience taught us we have not succeeded and cannot succeed in teaching the Hebrew language under the difficult conditions at Talmud Torahs? How can we succeed in awakening, inspiring identification with the Jewish people by means of language alone?" My answer is: the key to understanding why we have failed is in the formulation "mere language", that is to say in our assumption that language is not important. From this attitude spring many of the sins which we have committed against language in general and against our own language in particular. Let us address ourselves to just one sin, the original sin in our attitude towards Hebrew. In our belief that "language is not the main thing", we have hired teachers whose main strength lies in the teaching of English texts and who teach Hebrew also, because it's part of their job, whether or not they know how to do it. Let me mention only two examples. In one high school class I saw a teacher who did not even know the rudiments of Hebrew and was therefore, figuratively speaking, climbing the walls in his effort to teach the language. When I asked the principal, "How did this fellow ever get into a Hebrew class?", he whispered into my ear, "He relates well with the children". In other words, the aim was that there should be a good relationship with the students, not success in teaching the language. In another class I happened into the midst of a debate between the teacher and his students about a textbook which they found boring and about the teacher's unsystematic methods. Let it be said to the credit of the teacher and of the students that this debate was simultaneously to the point and courteous. It was clear that the students wanted to learn and that the teacher wanted to teach, but that he was unable to teach them (and he knew it) because he simply hadn't been trained to teach Hebrew. He had been trained to teach physical education in the public schools! One must assume that he would not have been permitted to teach physical education in the public schools without the appropriate training. These examples are not exceptional cases. In short, it is not the fault of the Hebrew language but of the approach and the attitude of those who in belittling its merits as an aim of Jewish education merely betray their unwillingness to acquire the necessary and sufficient means for its proper and effective instruction.

And this brings us to the question of where we shall find teachers. I will dare to repeat my constant refrain, "attitude and approach"! Is it conceivable that so rich and powerful a Jewish community as that of America will be unable to find the solution once it comes to the realization that this is vital to the very survival of the Jewish people? A solution will be found when there is a change in the attitude and approach toward the Hebrew language.

In conclusion, I wish to present several suggestions which seem to me to be practical in the solution of this problem: (1) The subject of "language study" must be introduced into the curricula of the teachers' training schools. Every teacher, regardless of his specialty, should be acquainted with the nature of the Hebrew language, its roots, its development, its value and its shaping power. (2) The curricula of the teachers' training schools should include more and more instruction in "how to teach". (This subject has been completely absent from the curricula of certain institutions!) We must introduce into the classes those textbooks which are, relatively speaking, good ones; we must explain what is good in a textbook and what is not, how to make use of teaching materials and how to connect the present with the past and one subject with another. (3) I have noticed in many high schools that teachers trained to teach Hebrew are teaching all the subjects, even those taught in English, in one or two classes. In my opinion, such teachers should be entrusted with the teaching of Hebrew in the largest possible number of classes. (4) We must train special teachers for the high schools, and particularly for teaching Hebrew language and literature. There is an urgent need to train teachers able to concentrate on the teaching of Hebrew. Instead of making a teacher with a special and relatively rare competence teach all the subjects in one class, or in several classes at one high school, we should assign him the largest possible number of Hebrew classes (especially in the beginning classes), so that the fundamentals of the language are taught properly. The chances will then be good that the students will not be disappointed and will not despair of these studies while still in the first year of high school.

In passing, I will mention here that after indicating that only a few teachers were succeeding in teaching Hebrew in a certain area of New York, I suggested that these teachers should not teach both Hebrew and other subjects in one school only, but should concentrate on teaching Hebrew at all the high schools in the area. I know, I said, that there will be technical problems in implementing this suggestion, but in my opinion it is possible and necessary to overcome them. (5) This leads to another suggestion. Despite all the negative things I have heard and read about Israeli teachers, I have found that many of them have been exceptionally successful in teaching Hebrew; some of them do their work like veritable artists, like orchestra conductors. I would therefore take the liberty of suggesting to the Jewish Agency's Department of Education and Culture that its contribution to the advancement of Hebrew education in America should take the form of supplying expert teachers, who will really teach the Hebrew language, instead of (if it isn't possible to combine the two) sending us celebrities who deliver a lecture here and a lecture there and devote most of their time to tasks which could be carried out by members of the local communities. If, for instance, the department were to assign one or two teachers to teach Hebrew at all the high schools in the area for a year or two, their success would persuade the regional Board of Education to continue this project, with the schools in the area now perhaps footing the bill. I know that it will at once be asked why the region should not do this under its own power. My answer is that my recommendation concerns a pioneering effort which has yet to demonstrate its effectiveness. Since it is the duty of the Agency's Department of Education to direct its efforts to pioneering projects, this recommendation points the way to a more efficient utilization of the Agency's resources for the advancement of Hebrew education in America. I can testify that the teachers sent by the Department at its expense to Canada while I served there as director of the Hebrew movement, and who did real teaching in pioneering projects (similar to the one I am suggesting here) in various parts of the country, helped bring about a change in attitude both to the Israeli teacher and to the question of the place of Hebrew in education in general. (6) Touching only briefly on another basic question: the painful problem of the need for preparing suitable teaching materials, suitable textbooks for Hebrew schools in the diaspora. It is time that the leaders in Hebrew education in America, and the educators in Israel who have been entrusted with the task of advancing Hebrew education in the diaspora, devote themselves seriously, systematically and persistently to the solution of this crucial problem. It should be emphasized that the authors of such textbooks must be educators with firsthand knowledge of the situation, and that they should do this work in consultation with other educators and in collaboration with those who are actually working in the field. I take the liberty of returning to my old refrain: if there will be a change in the attitude regarding the role of language and a change in the approach to the instruction of the Hebrew language in the education of the present generation, the ways and the means will be found to fill this vital need.

In closing, I would like to quote the words of Professor Solomon Schechter which, in my opinion, ought to serve as a warning to our generation: "The Hebrew language is a treasure vault in which there is stored the best of the spiritual life of k'lal yisrael. Were it not for the Hebrew language, we would be cut off from the great tree of life. Hellenistic Jewry was historically unique in daring to try to detach itself from the Hebrew language, and it ended by disappearing. It withered away and became cut off completely from Judaism." In my view, these words express a stern warning: There can be no Judaism which is not Judaism in Hebrew.

Appendix H to Chapter 27

In the absence of a Rabbi or a principal, the Chairman of the Board of Education, Marcia Machol — a knowledgeable and dedicated person and the first female education chairman I had ever worked with — would rush from the public school where she taught, to serve as a surrogate principal-supervisor. Originally, one person — untrained as a teacher and with little knowledge of modern Hebrew — was in charge of the weekday classes. The children were divided into two groups, one of which studied from 4 to 5 and the other from 5 to 6. Since children were admitted at any and every age, there existed the abnormal situation — characteristic of most afternoon or "supplementary" schools — of a mixture of ages, ranging from 7 to 11 in one group and from 9 to 13 in the other. There were thus no homogenous levels, and the teachers rotated from one individual or group to another. To remedy the situation, the teacher's wife volunteered her services, so that the pupils could be divided into 2 groups for each session. When the occasion arose for me to commend the volunteering wife — who was a trained teacher but not for Hebrew schools — I was told that she had had no alternative, because her husband "could not cope with the situation and might have been replaced". (It should be remembered that the "congregation" was very low in funds because many in the "community" were not members, using the familiar argument that they had no children in the school and were therefore not obligated to support it.) Furthermore, some of the pupils arrived late, so that very little could be accomplished.

The Sunday School staff consisted of the two weekday teachers, a nursery teacher, a kindergarten teacher, and an additional staff member — all untrained and inexperienced. The 2 groups who attended twice on weekdays had an additional hour of Hebrew at 9 a.m. before the Sunday classes started.

The two-hour Sunday program consisted of the usual hodge-podge of materials — all under the heading of "HISTORY" — without any activities such as arts and crafts, drama and singing. Strange to say, even the Sunday classes were not grouped in accordance with ages, but rather on the basis of the weekday classification, with those who attended only on Sundays (an entirely optional matter as in many afternoon Hebrew Schools) assigned — according to their respective ages — to the weekday groupings. In other words, the older pupils who attended also on weekdays did not study on Sundays together with their peers but with the younger children who were their classmates on weekdays, although the Sunday school program was conducted entirely in English. Obviously, this type of learning was "boring" and ineffective not only because of the differences in the mental capacities of the children, but also because of the aggravated disciplinary problems it created. As is the case in most Sunday schools, lateness and absenteeism were rampant.

To begin with, I realized that we could not institute any basic changes without at least one more teacher, in addition to myself, so that we would be able to classify the pupils with greater regard to age differences and to levels of knowledge of Hebrew. Since it was impossible to increase the school budget in the middle of the year, my wife — an experienced and effective teacher — volunteered her services, and I taught almost full time.

We then reorganized the pupils into two categories, one based on age, and the other on levels of Hebrew knowledge. Students thus studied in two different classes: 1) Hebrew — with children of a similar level in their knowledge of the language, and 2) subjects taught in English — together with their age peers.

The reorganization of the school resolved also the transportation difficulties for parents whose children attended different grades and had to drive back and forth twice on each school day. The enlarged staff enabled us to reschedule all the classes from 4:30 p.m. to 6:00 p.m. (a change from 1 to 1 and-a-half hours per school day), so that all the pupils attended at the same time. The added one hour of Hebrew on weekdays made it possible to eliminate the additional hour on Sundays (for those who studied also on weekdays) so that on Sundays too, parents did not have to drive their children twice. This change also solved — almost entirely — the problems caused by the latecomers, and undoubtedly contributed to the parents' confidence in the competence and efficiency of the school and elicited their cooperation in other matters.

There was still the problem of pupils varying sharply in ages and studying Hebrew in the same class. Little could be done to normalize this situation, except to encourage parents that their children be prepared individually for higher levels, which the children themselves always welcomed. We did, however, rectify the situation for the future by enforcing the rule that new pupils must begin to attend at age 6. We made it clear that those who would not do so would be admitted only after having been prepared individually — at their parents' expense — for their proper Hebrew language level. The same regulation applied to new residents' children who would move to the area in the beginning or middle of the year.

Obviously, we were still faced with the larger problem that children had been free to attend on Sundays only. I realized that it would not be easy to change a tradition that was recognized almost as a "democratic right" throughout the U.S.A. and Canada. I therefore set about cautiously to prepare the ground for this "revolution" to take place the following year. The reaction of the Education Board Chairman was enthusiastic and immediate. When the matter was first broached at a meeting of the Educational Committee, there was a mixed response. Those who took seriously the Hebrew education of their own children readily agreed that an educational program based on Sunday attendance only was — to say the least — inadequate. Others were convinced that our proposal was tantamount to abolishing the "sacred" Sunday School, that it was impractical and unacceptable to the general Board, and could lead to a new rift in the community. Sensing that more time and ground-work were essential for avoiding such a rift, I suggested that we give the matter further consideration, that we first consult with the leaders of the Congregation, and that — for the time being — we treat the matter confidentially (how naive!), in order to prevent an organized opposition even before we could convince the powers that be of the soundness of our proposal. As happens often in Jewish communities, it took one member to inform her husband of our "plot", who in turn brought up the matter the very next day at a meeting of a committee which had no function or jurisdiction in the school. Sides were soon taken for and — mostly — against, and a few — among them the first vice-president of the Board — were indignant at the notion that we could or should "dictate" to parents about the number of days a week their children should attend Hebrew School.

To make a long story short, I invited all the parents to "A BREAKFAST WITH THE RABBI", and used all my persuasive powers to convice them that we could not possibly give their children even a smattering of knowledge of our rich culture, let alone a sense of identification with our people, with a MERE Sunday School program. With the exception of one parent, who said the decision would be up to her seven year old daughter, all agreed to the following attendance schedule:

1. Six year olds: Sundays only;
2. Seven year olds: Sundays and once on a week-day;
3. Eight year olds and over: Sundays plus twice on week-days.

It is noteworthy that I invited the parents as my personal guests, in order to avoid any problems that might arise were I to apply to the Board to cover the cost of the breakfast, as it could not be met by the skimpy school budget. More important, I wanted to prepare the ground before bringing this "revolutionary" idea out in the open. I have considered it necessary to mention these facts for the benefit of some Rabbis who told me time and again, "It can't be done", and who hide behind the screen of REALITIES, REALITIES...

The educational "revolution" we engineered in Petaluma was so firmly established that the Board of Education Chairman was surprised when I suggested — before my departure from the community — that further implementation of the three-day-a-week plan for the eight year olds be postponed (because of the shortage of full time teaching staff), until a full-time Rabbi could replace me. She was determined to proceed with the full program. Furthermore, she was strongly opposed to even considering the engagement of a certain candidate for the position of Rabbi because of his response — "It is better they attend only on Sundays than not at all" — to her question: "What do we do, Rabbi, if some parents want their children to attend only on Sundays?" The candidate, who "strongly desired to live in Northern California", did not even know the reason for his failure...

In addtition to transforming the school structure, we introduced the Sunday-Activities Program, the Credit System, and the Student Council as an integral and effective part of the school, as described in the chapter on Hamilton, Canada. The only difference was that while the annual visit by the Hamilton students was to New York, in Petaluma we divided the pupils into two age-groups: the seven to ten age-group spent a weekend at a camp made available to us by the above-mentioned Mr. Irving Newman, and the eleven and up age-group spent three days as guests of Congregation Temple Sinai in Los Angeles. Both groups were elated by their experiences, constantly talked about them, and are sure to remember them for many years to come.

The general pattern of the educational program was based on the same principles as the one in Hamilton. (See Chapter 25)